Praise for *Mi*

'An amazing read! I galloped through it'
Lady Antonia Fraser

'My pick for gardening book of the year is this page-turning life story of Ellen Willmott, a wealthy lady with a passion for plants but a reputation as a mean-spirited eccentric. With access to the family's archives, the author, Sandra Lawrence, tells the riches-to-rags tale of this trailblazing plantswoman'
The Sunday Times

'Lawrence has done an excellent job of recreating this eccentric gardening guru's life'
The Times

'A fascinating read. It contextualises the burgeoning horticultural developments, personalities and enthusiasms of the era, and there is no doubt Lawrences access to the newly discovered archive material illuminates the remarkable like of one of our lesser-known female horticultural pioneers'
The Horticulturist

'Sandra Lawrence tells [Miss Willmott's] story with brio and affection'
Daily Mail

'Packed with detail'
The Spectator

Sandra Lawrence has written for all the broadsheets and over 60 magazines and websites, usually focusing on history, heritage, folklore and gardens. Her books include *Anthology of Amazing Women, Atlas of Monsters* and *The Witch's Garden*. She has been fascinated with the ruined gardens at Warley Place since her very early teenage years, and with the ruins' owner, Ellen Willmott, for not much less than that. Five years spent recovering Willmott's physical – and digital – world have taken that fascination to an obsession that will stretch long beyond the publication of *Miss Willmott's Ghosts*, which is her first biography. She lives in London.

Miss Willmott's Ghosts

The extraordinary life and gardens of a forgotten genius

SANDRA LAWRENCE

BLINK
bringing you closer

First published in the UK by Blink Publishing
An imprint of Bonnier Books UK
4th Floor, Victoria House,
Bloomsbury Square, London,
WC1B 4DA

Owned by Bonnier Books
Sveavägen 56, Stockholm, Sweden

Hardback – 978-178658-131-0
Paperback – 978-178658-155-6
Ebook – 978-178658-132-7
Audio – 978-178658-165-5

All rights reserved. No part of the publication may be reproduced, stored in a retrieval system, transmitted or circulated in any form or by any means, electronic, mechanical, photocopying, recording or otherwise, without prior permission in writing of the publisher.

A CIP catalogue of this book is available from the British Library.

Designed by Envy Design Ltd
Internal illustrations © Jitesh Patel
Printed and bound in Great Britain by Clays Ltd, Elcograf S.p.A

1 3 5 7 9 10 8 6 4 2

Copyright © Sandra Lawrence, 2022

First published in hardback by Blink Publishing in 2022
This edition published in paperback by Blink Publishing in 2023

The right of Sandra Lawrence to be identified as the author of this work has been asserted by her in accordance with the Copyright, Designs and Patents Act 1988

Every reasonable effort has been made to trace copyright holders of material reproduced in this book, but if any have been inadvertently overlooked the publishers would be glad to hear from them.

Blink Publishing is an imprint of Bonnier Books UK
www.bonnierbooks.co.uk

*For Pat, Charles, and Mary, who discovered
Warley Place with me so many years ago*

Contents

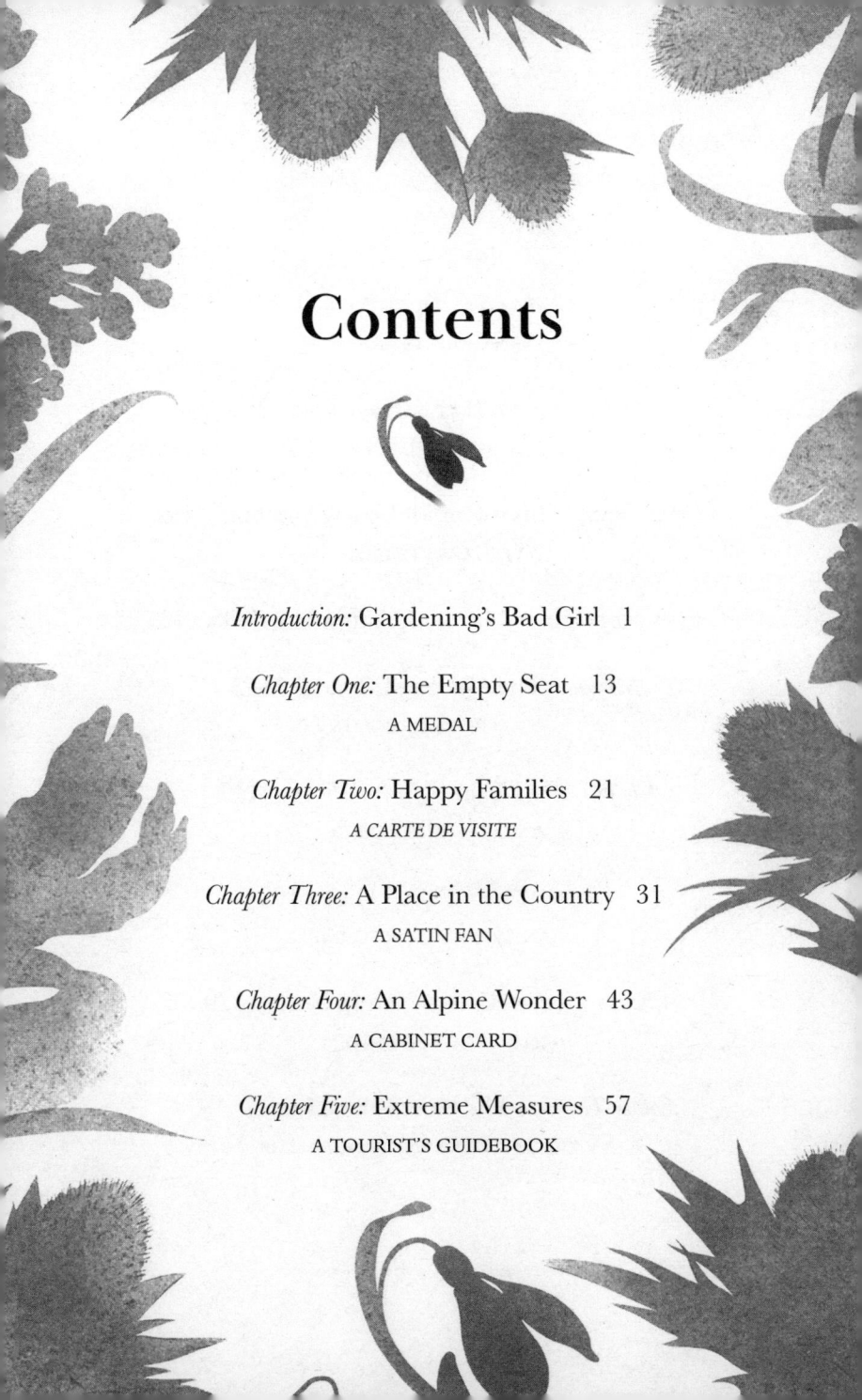

Introduction: Gardening's Bad Girl   1

Chapter One: The Empty Seat   13
  A MEDAL

Chapter Two: Happy Families   21
  A CARTE DE VISITE

Chapter Three: A Place in the Country   31
  A SATIN FAN

Chapter Four: An Alpine Wonder   43
  A CABINET CARD

Chapter Five: Extreme Measures   57
  A TOURIST'S GUIDEBOOK

Chapter Six: Tresserve   71
AN ORANGE TREE

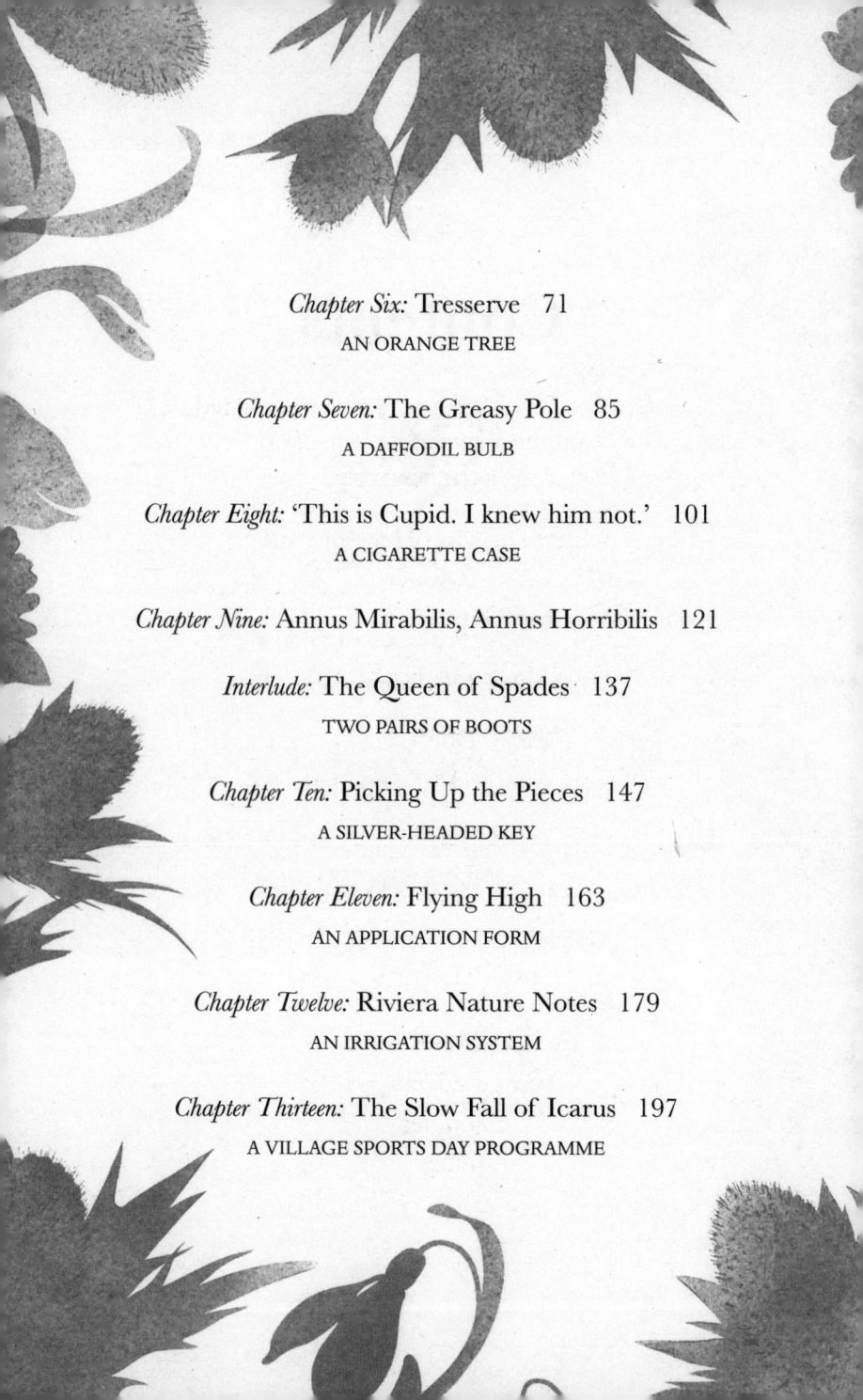

Chapter Seven: The Greasy Pole   85
A DAFFODIL BULB

Chapter Eight: 'This is Cupid. I knew him not.'   101
A CIGARETTE CASE

Chapter Nine: Annus Mirabilis, Annus Horribilis   121

Interlude: The Queen of Spades   137
TWO PAIRS OF BOOTS

Chapter Ten: Picking Up the Pieces   147
A SILVER-HEADED KEY

Chapter Eleven: Flying High   163
AN APPLICATION FORM

Chapter Twelve: Riviera Nature Notes   179
AN IRRIGATION SYSTEM

Chapter Thirteen: The Slow Fall of Icarus   197
A VILLAGE SPORTS DAY PROGRAMME

Chapter Fourteen: Digging Holes 215
GENUS ROSA

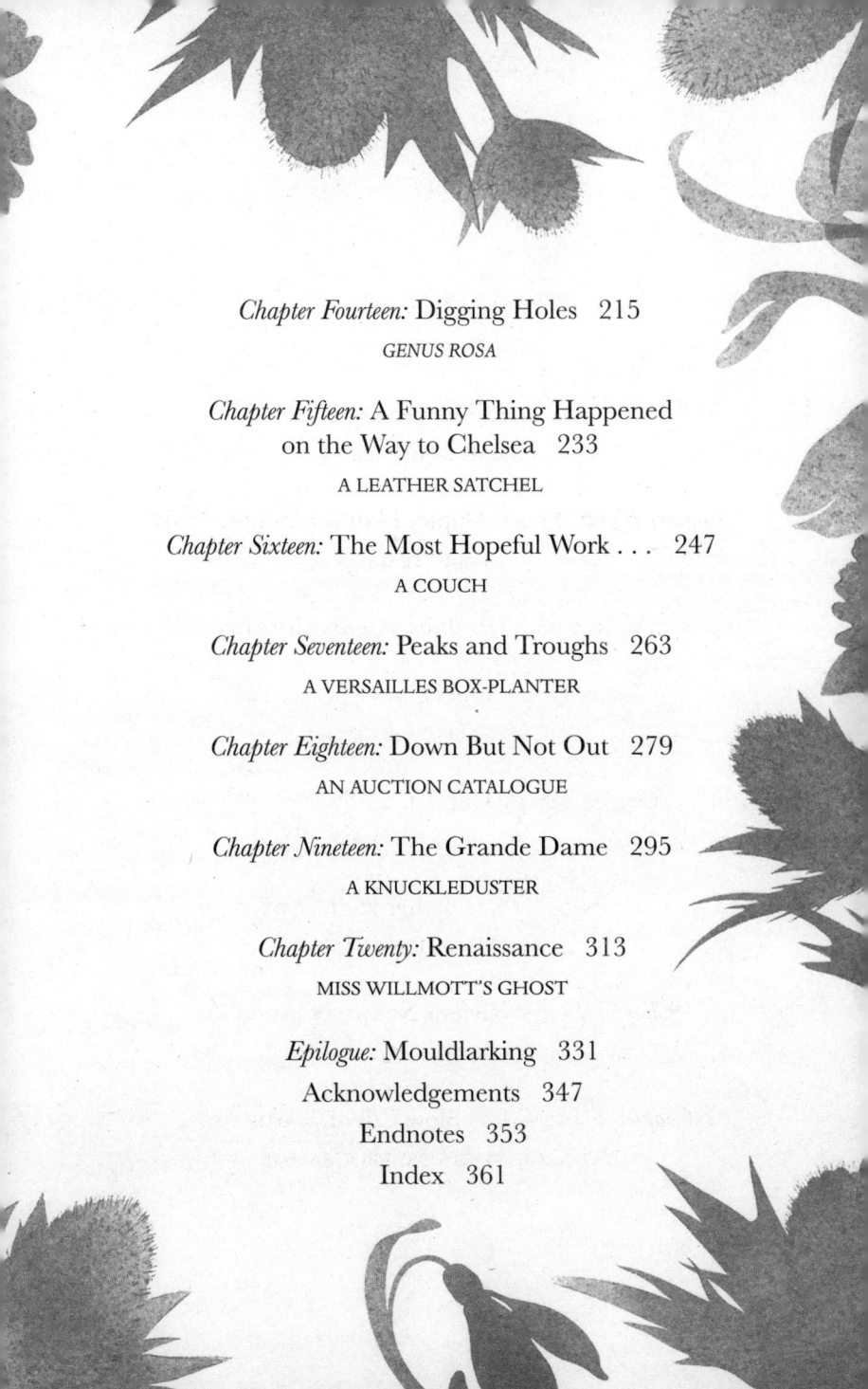

Chapter Fifteen: A Funny Thing Happened
on the Way to Chelsea 233
A LEATHER SATCHEL

Chapter Sixteen: The Most Hopeful Work . . . 247
A COUCH

Chapter Seventeen: Peaks and Troughs 263
A VERSAILLES BOX-PLANTER

Chapter Eighteen: Down But Not Out 279
AN AUCTION CATALOGUE

Chapter Nineteen: The Grande Dame 295
A KNUCKLEDUSTER

Chapter Twenty: Renaissance 313
MISS WILLMOTT'S GHOST

Epilogue: Mouldlarking 331
Acknowledgements 347
Endnotes 353
Index 361

Introduction:

Gardening's Bad Girl

THE ROOFLESS, BROKEN walls seem to crumble even as a breeze whispers through glassless windows. The visitor pauses, faintly aware of . . . something . . . a fleeting presence nudging the corner of an eye; a sensation. Perfumed roses. Chinking glasses. Distant voices. Beyond the ruined conservatory's empty doorframe shadows flit through dense woodland. A bird flutters into the undergrowth, causes a small commotion then skitters off into the silence. The winter garden settles back to solitude. It is hard to imagine this shattered carcass was once a lodestone for royalty, both horticultural and regal.

Warley Place near Brentwood, Essex, is just eighteen miles from London but it might be a world away for all it has in common with the capital. Already old when Miss Ellen Willmott arrived here with her family in 1876, its rural hillsides would be transformed under her guardianship, as she rose from horticultural maverick to one of gardening's greats.

Our traveller moves on, past a mass of naturalised yellow daffodils tumbling down Warley's steep slopes, honed to heady perfection in times past. Today's golden mongrels may no longer be prize-winners, sought out by the great, the good and the gawping, but they still dazzle in the sharp spring sunshine.

The atmosphere changes as brightness returns to shadow. Brambles part, vague outlines form and strange apparitions manifest in the tangle. Moss-covered phantoms morph into broken cold frames. Heaps of brick become crumbled steps; hollows turn into underground chambers. For a brief, intoxicating moment in the late nineteenth and early twentieth centuries, Warley played host to one of the most important gardens in the country. Then it descended into darkness, taking Miss Willmott with it.

Shallow dips and half-buried boulders conjure more spectres: of Willmott's fabled three-acre 'alpine ravine' of gushing streams, dramatic valleys and sheltered pools. One poor ghost, the filmy fern cave, is buried so deep in leaf mould it's hard to see how anyone managed to get inside at all. That's probably a good thing; it's a deathtrap now.

The old walled garden shelters more visions: an incongruously exotic Chusan palm, an ancient camellia, the remains of tightly clipped box hedging, now blousy shrubs rapidly succumbing to the modern horrors of box-tree caterpillar. Black and red terracotta tiles peep through fallen leaves; the crumbling remains of a fountain just about cling to existence. A raised pond in the labyrinth of ruined hothouses miraculously still holds water. Underground boiler rooms and mushroom houses play host to owls and bats and heaven knows what other spirits.

Even Miss Willmott's home is a phantasm. Jumbled foundations and mosaic floors hint at a music room, a library, a chapel. White-tiled, fern-fronded walls of a basement kitchen merge into the curved brick arches of a long-dead wine cellar. Victims of landslides, rockfalls and even a Second World War bomb, they whisper: of champagne, of cigars and dancing 'til three. It all seems a long time ago.

The only part of Warley Place still standing is that crumbling conservatory. It's said an elderly, embittered Ellen Willmott spent her final days seething here, watching her garden descend into chaos in a red mist of fury.

I don't buy that. In fact, the deeper I delve the more I don't believe she had time for sitting around at all. Ellen Willmott was a woman of decided eccentricities but languishing in self-pity was not one of them.

I grew up not three miles from Warley Place, not that I knew it at the time. In those days it was sleeping so heavily few locals knew it was there. By the early 1980s a small group of wildlife enthusiasts had hacked back enough of the undergrowth to hold occasional public open days. I was just a kid, visiting with my family, but for me it was a *coup de foudre*. Warley was Cair Paravel, Satis House, Misselthwaite Manor; my very own *Secret Garden*. I knew the drill: there was buried treasure here. All I had to do was find it.

It was only as I grew older that I began to wonder who made this shattered fantasy. Volunteers shrugged: a grumpy old woman, apparently, who had been quite famous in her day but, they were sorry to relate, 'wasn't very nice'.

Ellen Ann Willmott (1858–1934) is still quite famous – in gardening circles, at least. She is also still 'not very nice'. Unlike her contemporary, Gertrude Jekyll, Willmott acquired a reputation as a prickly, difficult eccentric in her lifetime that no one bothered to argue with after her death. Prefaced with words like 'seminal' and 'genius' in practically every garden history book, her name has remained saddled with the same repeated 'facts', mainly derogatory, often told as a joke: 'What an eccentric, mean old woman. You'll never guess what she said/did . . .'

I became a journalist, even wrote a few features about Warley for newspapers and magazines. Miss Willmott never went away. I obtained a second-hand copy of the only biography of her and devoured the (very) few articles available, mainly from the 1980s. She didn't come off well.[i] 'I think that Ellen Willmott's is the only unhappy story in this collection,' wrote Dawn MacLeod in her 1982 compilation *Down to Earth Women*.[ii] 'She afflicts me with gloom.'

The sheer number of unpleasant anecdotes intrigued me: of spectacular miserliness, of gardeners refused time off for their own weddings, then being sacked for taking it anyway. Of random rages, booby-trapped daffodils, and the revolver this pugilistic old battleaxe allegedly carried in her handbag. One tale even had a gardener dying at his post. 'Poor Miss Willmott,' MacLeod sighed, 'it is so hard to find anybody who has said nice things about her.' The evidence available at the time seemed to tell the same story. A set of letters at Harvard's

Arnold Arboretum Library, publicly available for over forty years, came to represent what Ellen Willmott thought of fellow members of her sex. They did neither her nor her subjects any favours, and there seemed little to counteract them.

Around this time surfaced the best-known tale of all: that Willmott carried seeds from a particularly invasive sea holly in her pocket to scatter in other people's gardens as an act of unfocused spite.

After a short burst of late twentieth-century interest, Willmott sank back into the undergrowth as the difficult Latin part of nigh-on 200 plant names (basically, anything with '*Willmottiae*' or '*Warleyensis*' in it will be something to do with her). She popped up occasionally in garden history books, an entertaining but minor 'character' whose bright beginnings ended in bitter malice radiating out of that old conservatory.

How does someone get that way? What could have happened to a happy, bright young girl to turn her into a Halloween bugaboo? Come to think of it, how much of this was true anyway? Few seemed to know.

I met John Cannell while researching a feature for the *Daily Telegraph*. John is one of the Warley Place Volunteers, a group that began looking after the site in the 1970s. After clearing giant hogweed, sycamore and an invasion of bamboo that could have supported the world's panda population, the work party had embraced a new role: archaeology. This sturdy band still meets every Monday, come rain, come shine. Barely a week goes by where they do not find something: a York stone path, a wrought-iron gate, an underground chamber; the base of some long-lost sundial. John took me around the garden with an historian's eye, showed me photographs of what once was there, and discussed Miss Willmott's reputation: veritable genius as a plantswoman; veritable nightmare as an individual.

The more I found out, the more I wanted to know. Her biographer had done a sterling job – with what she had. The 1970s would have seen Royal Mail and shoe leather as Audrey Le Lièvre's best weapons of research but the most difficult part would have been working out where to start. Le Lièvre tracked Miss Willmott to Spetchley Park estate in Worcestershire, home of her beloved sister Rose. On Ellen's death in 1934, her papers had been bundled up and shoved into trunks in Spetchley's basement.

Dr Le Lièvre was granted access to *some* of those trunks. I have been through *Miss Willmott of Warley Place* line by line, trying to figure out her sources, and she was thorough. Audrey le Lièvre was not a woman of fancy. If she says something, I tend to believe her . . .

. . . except where I don't. This is nothing to do with scholarly rigour. Reading obituaries, journals, the material she was given access to and interviews with contemporary experts, she painted the picture she saw. She just didn't see the whole thing. In the absence of evidence, she made some assumptions that, frankly, I would have made, too.

She did have one resource I don't: a small group of elderly witnesses. Their parents would once have been employed by the wealthy Willmott family; by the time they were growing up, this was no longer the case. Many of their childhood memories are somewhat sour images of an eccentric old woman that lived in the Big House and told them off. They are vibrant descriptions of the lives of Warley estate workers and what village kids got up to in the 1920s – but they are a warped vision of Miss Willmott.

I started my research where le Lièvre left off. There must be *something* she had missed? I had been warned that access to her papers, held by the Berkeley family, the descendants of Ellen's sister, was notoriously difficult. Some Willmott fans even told me not to bother asking. I was astonished to get a reply at all, let alone the one I did. Karen Davidson, the recently appointed Berkeley Estate Archivist, was happy for me to see the documents but . . . was I aware that a whole bunch of new material had recently been discovered, deep in a damp basement?

What on earth might fetch up in hundreds of 'new' letters, notebooks, lists and receipts? In thousands of photographs, all taken, processed and printed by Miss Willmott herself from around 1880 onwards? Friendly as she seemed, however, Karen wasn't about to let someone she had never met poke around uncatalogued material. If I cared to wait eighteen months, while two volunteers finished a very long job of listing it all, I would be welcome to peruse it then.

Eighteen months? *Really?* But this was good, I told myself. There was a whole internet out there; who knew what else there might be? I made it my business to track down Miss Ellen Ann Willmott in every archive I could think of. It took me – metaphorically, at least – around the world: America, Australia, New Zealand, China, Japan, Russia, the Netherlands, France, Hungary, Germany, Italy . . . if Miss Willmott hadn't physically visited all these places, she corresponded with people, often important people, from them.

She consumed me. I read everything I could find, in any format. I made new friends and intriguing acquaintances. Willmott aficionados are a small but passionate band, many of whom research very specific aspects of her horticultural prowess. For me, looking at 'the whole story', a new Ellen was beginning to emerge. Yes, there was shocking stuff, but also huge intellect, endless curiosity and profound fascination. Yes, there was eccentricity, but it was not *always* inexplicable. Yes, hers was a riches-to-rags descent, but that didn't make the bitterness all-consuming. Yes, there was anger, but this was a woman making her own way, alone, in a gentleman's world. In the same position, I like to think I'd have fought as hard as she did.

In June 2019 I was finally granted access to Willmott's papers, temporarily housed at Berkeley Castle, Gloucestershire. Karen Davidson was as interested in the new material as I was, and the pair of us worked together, joined by John Cannell whenever possible. Remotely, he and other 'Friends in Willmott' helped with the seemingly endless job of transcription. This is as much their graft as mine.

Mr Frederick Willmott was particularly helpful, 130 years after his death. Ellen didn't keep a journal but her father wrote a nice, hundred-odd words a day for around ten years. Of course, his diaries too were incomplete but what we had was good. Less useful was the seeming incapacity of any of Ellen's friends to date their letters. If we were lucky, we'd find a couple of missives from the same batch marked, 'Tuesday 1st June' or 'Friday 9th October' that we could triangulate to work out which year it was, but more often it was '1st Feb' or even 'Thurs aft'. We weren't too worried; we were finding incredible material practically every visit.

In August 2019, the last person that remembered Miss Willmott passed away. I had planned to formally interview Miss Juliet Berkeley, our sole surviving link; alas, I was too late. Her passing, however, did allow for something entirely unexpected.

I met Karen at the castle gate one morning, full of new material I'd been digging up in other archives. I was quite proud of my sleuthery and suspect I may have been babbling. I didn't notice Karen was uncharacteristically quiet. When I finally took a breath, she said, 'I have something to show you too.'

Upstairs, in our 'turret', she sat me down with a packet of letters. It took seconds to work out what they were. It would take twenty-four hours and a sleepless night to work out what they meant. Could they possibly solve a mystery that had surrounded an incident in Ellen Willmott's life since the very day it had happened? If so, could this throw light on the direction her life would later take?

We had little time to dwell on specifics. Mr Henry Berkeley, who had inherited Spetchley two years earlier, had realised that renovation on the crumbling, Palladian mansion could wait no longer. As part of the conservation, the entire house must be emptied, attic to cellar. A projected sale of important items at Sotheby's, slated for December 2019, was already attracting international interest. Time was of the essence.

During a routine once-over, Karen checked a suspicious bunch of rotting trunks in the darkest, dampest part of the cellar. Some bore faded chalk markings: 'not worth saving', and at first glance, they weren't. They looked as though, nine decades ago, someone had put the open travelling boxes at one end of a very long room then hurled the remains of Miss Willmott's life at them from the other, steeped the contents in cold tea, drained it, then allowed the brew to stand for ninety years.

We had four days to clear the lot. Kitted-up in boiler suits, head torches, industrial masks and latex gloves, we 'mined' those trunks. Mice had shredded the top layers, leaving desiccated carcases and, occasionally, skeletons. Squirling silverfish damage bored through damp-fused bricks of correspondence; the perpetrators scuttled over the remains. Black beetles staggered, dazed, across our hands. Clouds of rainbow spores puffed into our faces. In each trunk a thin stratum of salvageable stuff was followed by a heartbreaking base of perfect loam. There were other casualties: I could have sobbed as, soaked, one of Fred Willmott's lost diaries fell to pieces in my hands like a dunked biscuit.

We had to concentrate on what could be saved. We had letters and artefacts, birthday cards and calling cards, deeds and diaries. A leather satchel, a thumb-o-graph (an autograph book for thumb-prints, who knew?), Christmas decorations, books, receipts, bills, catalogues, newspaper clippings, mourning cards. A feather boa disintegrated into a cloud of salmon-pink fluff even as I opened the box. Upstairs, the finds were in better condition, including certificates hidden behind books in the library and even a few colour photographic plates. We had no time to inspect anything; all we could do was scoop it, wholesale, into battered, third-hand bankers' boxes. We ended each day looking like coal miners and not much less exhausted, but scrubbing around in that filthy, spore-ridden basement with someone who shared my passion for discovering the real Ellen Willmott was the most heart-pounding, mind-racing time I have known.

Many biographers find themselves scratching around for new information. At first I thought I would be too. Now I had the opposite 'problem': such an embarrassment of high-quality new evidence, I didn't know where to start. We began recovering the barely dry material in early 2020, teasing disintegrating letters open with razorblades.

Then COVID happened.

Months of mind-numbing thumb twiddling passed in a kind of liminal dream. Pandemic lockdown brought two good things: enforced 'leisure' led to lateral thinking – and the opportunity to jump down rabbit holes. I re-read letters I thought I'd squeezed everything from. I called in favours from friends and brazenly contacted strangers across the world. They were locked down too, and often had more time to talk than they might otherwise have had.

Ever since, it has been a game of catch-up; archive visiting, expert consulting, letter transcribing and lucky dipping into a truly surreal bran tub. Every time we sank a latex-gloved hand into the Willmott tombola we genuinely had no idea what might come out. A childhood portrait? A hundred-year-old chocolate bar? Botanical watercolours from a female illustrator in Africa? A paper screw of desiccated seeds? A 1771 letter from the Empress Maria Theresa? Or just another bloomin' silverfish . . .

With the sincerest hat-doff to Audrey le Lièvre, forty years on, Ellen Willmott's story needs retelling. Hers is a shadowy world of phantoms that, like Ellen herself, were once famous, once infamous, once rich, once poor, once powerful, once powerless, once complacent, once angry, but that is not the whole story. If the bitter old woman in the conservatory even existed, she is by far the least interesting part of an extraordinary life.

This book is not a traditional 'garden history' or even 'garden biography'. Details of Ellen Willmott's staggering horticultural heritage – including her plants, photography and gardens – will justify separate volumes of their own. I have the notes but not the space; at least not for this outing. Because so very much is new, I must focus first on Ellen Willmott's *life*; try to fathom out what made this uncommon woman so very special before exploring her manifold legacies.

I have no intention of reinventing Audrey le Lièvre's wheel. Her detailed work on the Willmott and Fell families, for example, needs no further elaboration. I want to fill the gaps, to focus on aspects of Willmott's life le Lièvre could not have known. I have had the privilege of delving more deeply than she was able to; not just because I have been granted access to material she never saw, or can luxuriate in the information lagoon that is the internet, but because the world has moved on.

In 1982 Dawn MacLeod, lamenting Miss Willmott's 'sad' life, asked, 'Did she experience a great sorrow or disappointment of which we know nothing?' Forty years later, I think I can answer her question.

Chapter One:
The Empty Seat

A MEDAL

Cast in solid gold and 'the size of a shilling',[1] this brand-new award, in the fashionable art nouveau style, has been struck in recognition of Her Majesty Queen Victoria's Diamond Jubilee year, 1897.

Its superscription 'Royal Horticultural Society' is bookended by two tree roots, lending an impression not dissimilar to the circled band of the Most Noble Order of the Garter. As with those loyal knights of old, this is an exclusive honour, to be held only by a certain number of living individuals at any one moment in time.

---

[1] Approx. the same as a 10p piece.

L UNCHTIME, 26 OCTOBER 1897. For the last ten months, Queen Victoria's loyal subjects have been celebrating sixty glorious years of unparalleled reign. A street-dressing here, a thanksgiving service there; exhibitions, galas, publications, parades and general jubilation pervade her British Empire. Now, at the Hotel Windsor in London's Westminster, it is the turn of her gardeners. The great and the good of the Royal Horticultural Society gather for one of the most important luncheons in their history: the inauguration of the highest honour known to gardening: the Victoria Medal of Honour.

It has been a rocky few years. Financial difficulties and political infighting have seen the RHS crash from towering monolith, boasting none other than Prince Albert as president, to a homeless, debt-ridden club. The extraordinary, twenty-two-and-a-half-acre RHS garden that once ornamented Albertopolis[2] is exterminated, its graceful Italianate balconies, fountains, statues and flower beds razed for grand residential mansions. The gigantic, glass-walled winter garden remains only as ghostly shadows in the brickwork of the Royal Albert Hall. The humiliation still rankles.

Those were the bad times.

Since the dark days of the 1880s, the RHS has dragged itself up by its thick leather bootstraps and is, at last, a viable concern once more. Membership is up and interest piquing among the all-important aristocracy. Members may no longer have a 'home' but they're working

---

2 The area of museums and institutions around Exhibition Road, named for Prince Albert.

THE EMPTY SEAT

on it; a new Horticultural Halls built to the highest art nouveau specifications in nearby Vincent Square. In the meanwhile, in memory of Dearest Albert, Her Majesty has remained patroness and, today, the Fellows are gathered to celebrate her jubilee by honouring horticulture's sixty finest living representatives in front of their peers. The formal, white tablecloth, silver service luncheon at one of Westminster's most glamorous hotels is only the beginning. Later, the party will decamp to the lofty, cast-iron galleried London Scottish Royal Volunteers' Drill Hall for the award ceremony itself.

There will eventually be sixty-three Victoria Medal of Honour holders, one for each year of Her Majesty's reign. The title VMH will remain gardening's highest award into the twenty-first century.

The horticultural world being what it is – a tangled web of intrigue, public disagreements, private backbiting and personal vendettas – means the choice of recipients has not been without controversy. Many excellent gardeners have been left out, and salt was rubbed further into smarting egos when an ill-judged press release proclaimed the wrong list of recipients the previous month. The individual responsible has been dismissed but it is hardly surprising that one or two gentlemen have stayed away today. They are acknowledged as 'having their reasons' and tacitly excused.

One absence is not so easily forgiven.

Miss Ellen Willmott has not been mentioned by name. She doesn't have to be; she is the only female medallist who has not turned up and, given there are only two women among the sixty recipients, this puts the Committee in a spot, as many a horticultural newspaper, journal and magazine of the day will highlight in their next edition.

President Sir Trevor Lawrence, Bart., makes no secret that he is now forced to address the '*lady* and gentlemen'.[3] He feels, he admits, 'a sort of embarrassment' having to utter the phrase. On saying, 'I wish they were

---

3   There are many accounts of the event in the horticultural press and the Society's own records. *The Journal of Horticulture and Cottage Gardener* relates Sir Trevor's speech verbatim, including pauses for applause.

both present', he receives a pointed round of applause. He continues: 'One is so accustomed to say *"ladies* and gentlemen" that when you deal with the more commanding sex in the singular it becomes, to a certain extent, embarrassing.' After spending a few words on the selection methods for the award, Sir Trevor returns to his embarrassment: 'I am extremely grateful to the *lady*, and to the gentlemen here present for their being so kind as to be here today.' It does not seem to have occurred to anyone that, had more than two women been bestowed with the honour, Sir Trevor might not have had to blush at constantly using the singular form.

The chorus of disapproval rumbles on as the Society gets down to business. Renowned horticulturist Dean Reynolds Hole, responding to the president's speech, once again notes that just one lady is present, but purrs that 'no other could have represented the fair sex so appropriately, so royally, at this Jubilee meeting'. Miss Gertrude Jekyll, who *has* honoured the luncheon with her presence, is acknowledged by all as 'the Queen of Spades'.

And so it happens. The company adjourns to the Drill Hall. The Jubilee medals are bestowed to much applause – and the character of Miss Ellen Ann Willmott is, without even being named, tarnished. She will receive her medal by post and everything will, seemingly, go back to normal, but gardeners never forget. Failing to turn up to the RHS's finest moment on a dull afternoon in October will not be forgiven lightly. She has been allowed a window into this overwhelmingly male world, granted one of two prizes allocated to the 'fairer sex' when there were only sixty to be had in the first place. Many excellent male candidates, who would have been glad of the honour, have been overlooked; and yet she has thrown that generosity back in their faces. Missing male medallists, of course, have their own, private reasons for absence, but what possible excuse could a woman have for such rudeness, other than pride and ingratitude?

Miss Jekyll is now horticulture's brightest star. Ellen Willmott, the second most famous woman in Victorian gardening, has just become her Miss Hyde.

❧

It is not surprising that Miss Willmott's failure to turn up irritated the gardening establishment. In their eyes she was lucky to be allowed to join at all. Most institutions, especially those with a scientific bent, had strict, no-women policies. It wasn't so very long ago that extraordinary fossil hunter Mary Anning (1799–1847) could only reveal some of the greatest paleontological discoveries made in Britain to the Royal Society and the Geological Society via the mouths of men, who habitually neglected to mention their source. Anning was finally recognised by the Geological Society of London – even eulogised by the president – but no woman would be allowed to actually join the club until 1904. The Royal Society barred women Fellows until 1945.

The Horticultural Society was founded in 1804, at Hatchards bookshop, Piccadilly, by seven men, but one thing that can be said in its favour is that, from 1824, women were allowed. Admittedly, all they could do was attend anniversary dinners but, in 1827, a committee of well-connected lady patronesses were allowed to organise tickets for fêtes. The first female Fellows were admitted in 1830, after someone pointed out there had never actually been a rule debarring women; it had just never occurred to the founders they would ever be considered.

The financial difficulties and scandals the Society would find itself in over the next half-century would be entirely mismanaged by men.[i] From the misappropriation of funds to the blatant awarding of prizes to influential members threatening 'consequences' if they didn't win, the RHS lurched from one embarrassment to the next. Eventually, in the 1880s, it emerged from the brink of bankruptcy battered, bruised, but solvent and even optimistic, looking towards a day when members might not have to meet in hotels and the local Drill Hall. A new century beckoned. A new start.

By announcing two female winners of a prestigious prize, the new-look RHS was presenting itself as modern and progressive for the forthcoming century. One of those two women turning out to be a no-show made them look bad all over again. The slight would not be forgotten, and the nineteenth-century stain continues to spread today, in twenty-first century tittle-tattle and gardening folklore. Even people not particularly interested in gardening have heard of Gertrude Jekyll, the kindly little old lady that designed pretty borders with that handsome young architect Mr Lutyens. Virtually no one has come across her 'evil twin', a woman just as brilliant, but who, somewhere along the line, reached too far, then fell from grace.

Ellen Ann Willmott was active around the late nineteenth and early twentieth centuries. Her family wasn't super-wealthy but she had the next best thing: an almost fairy godmother, the phenomenally wealthy Countess Helen Tasker, whose fortune she would eventually inherit.

Ellen Willmott met, discussed and formed serious (platonic) relationships with the great men of her day. They were always astounded at her knowledge and enthusiasm, intelligence and vigour. They admired her youth but, at first, missed the chip on her shoulder. She was only too aware that, being female, her education was flawed, her Latin self-taught, her knowledge acquired through hard graft. Today we would call this 'Imposter syndrome'. She preferred not to call it anything. She just got on with it.

The 'bad girl' image didn't surface immediately after the Victoria Medal of Honour incident – or at least not among those who hadn't been present. It would take years for her reputation to percolate, and Miss Willmott did her best to make up for any offence caused that day, serving on endless committees and enthusiastically taking part in shows and events.

But mud sticks. That lunchtime in October 1897, when Ellen Willmott

THE EMPTY SEAT

publicly snubbed the RHS committee and, by implication, its members and possibly the whole horticultural community, was the beginning of an end her reputation still pays for today. It wasn't even the specific absence that shifted her peers' attitudes to her, however subconsciously; surely one no-show would not be that calamitous. Ellen herself had changed and afterwards would never be the same again.

Where was she that day? What was she doing? Why did this horticultural doyenne spurn the gardening shindig of the century, where she was, at last, to be granted the recognition she had craved for so long? We know *where* she was: at Tresserve, her French villa near Aix-les-Bains. But why? Tresserve was a spring garden – a riot of alpine blooms, freshly freed from their snowy blanket in April and May. They were followed by an elegant mass of *Iris germanica* then, in June, the garden would hit summer with pergolas draped with Miss Willmott's signature passion: roses, scenting the mountain air.

By October, Tresserve would have been readying itself for winter. Miss Willmott *did* visit Tresserve in autumn, to enjoy the spectacular colours and witness the grape harvest, but there was nothing so very exceptional there to keep a plantswoman who had a date with horticultural destiny. It wasn't as though this was a last-minute engagement. The press had been trumpeting the award since January, and Ellen had always been in the running. She had received the official invitation on 26 June and, young and ambitious, loved nothing better than to be seen hobnobbing with the great and good. She could have easily made it back in time. For 120 years her absence has been a mystery. Miss Willmott's previous biographer suggests indifference: 'While the award must surely have flattered her self-esteem, it is very odd that she apparently made no effort to attend the ceremony.' Others shrug: 'For some reason Miss Willmott did not attend the ceremony and so Miss Jekyll was the only woman present.'[ii] I don't think that 'for some reason' is good enough. This was Ellen Willmott's big moment – and she missed it.

In youth 'Ellie' Willmott was popular, intelligent, light-souled and the possessor of a dry sense of humour that surfaces in the photographs she took with an almost fanatical frequency. Before 1897, there is little record of discord in her life. After that date her image becomes 'difficult'. She seems hardened, more determined to show her mettle, keener than ever to stand up for her place in the world, even picking the odd horticultural fight, sometimes justified, others less-so. Light-hearted 'Ellie' was rapidly disappearing, replaced by a more decisive, battling 'Ellen'.

There is a long list of faults some people – even purporting to be fans – have lain at Miss Willmott's doorstep. She was proud, reckless, eccentric; spendthrift *and* miser. She treated her staff badly and 'expected perfection', but even her enemies admired her enthusiasm, energy, courage and the way she fought every last indignity. Her behaviour is, by today's standards, hard to stomach on occasion, but often no worse than that of horticultural 'gentlemen'. The Victorian/Edwardian gardening community could be a veritable cauldron of boiling acid. Had she been a man – or even a married woman – her behaviour would have been shrugged at, even admired. But unmarried . . .

I have spent years trying to fathom what happened to Ellen Willmott on 26 October 1897, and now, at last, I think I have an answer. This book attempts to put it – and her life – into perspective.

Chapter Two:

Happy Families

A CARTE DE VISITE

At just four inches by two and a half, this studio portrait depicts a little girl dressed in her Sunday best, clutching a small basket of flowers. The photo will have been taken very late 1871, just after the December publication of Lewis Carroll's Through the Looking Glass, as our seven-year-old is wearing the Victorian equivalent of cosplay: a puff-sleeved dress with a deeply frilled, white pinafore. An 'Alice band' holds back her shoulder-length hair. She perches on a wooden, cloth-covered table with a cheeky, dimpled grin, her boot-clad feet swinging freely.

ELLEN'S FATHER, FREDERICK Willmott, was a canny man. He also lived in an age where being middle class was beginning to be a very good thing. But things could always be better.

Born in 1825, Fred did not follow his father and three brothers into the family business, a dispensing pharmacy in Southwark, South London. He wanted to be a solicitor. In 1848, a year or two after qualifying, Fred set up his own practice next door to the family chemist shop, directly down the road from London Bridge. A four-storey, eighteenth-century warren of offices and warehousing, like many premises in Old Borough, it was deep and rambling, mainly rented by seed and hop merchants. Frederick Willmott would eventually own the whole property and, naturally, occupy the best room, at the front, with large, graceful windows, afternoon sun and a fine view of the street below.

He had one foot on the ladder, but caution was required. Sound investments needed to be made, the right people needed to be met and, above all, he needed to marry well. As Charles Dickens so often relates, Victorian solicitors were only ever on the cusp of respectability and, for the rest of his life, Frederick Willmott would be conscious of his status. While his brothers were happy enough to describe themselves as 'chemists', Fred always signed himself 'Frederick Willmott, gentleman'.

There are a couple of ways Frederick Willmott, respectable gentleman, may have met Ellen Fell, nice young lady. He may have known her stepfather, wealthy coal merchant Thomas Fell, or another relation who was also a solicitor. It's unlikely he'd have met her by accident. Nice young ladies from Aylesbury didn't habitually visit The

Borough, the thriving but grubby engine room for the City of London, on the seedy, 'wrong' side of the bridge.

However they met, it was a good match. He was young, handsome and ambitious; she was young, handsome and wealthy. There was just one problem: the Fell family were Roman Catholics. Fred bit the religious bullet and converted. The wedding took place on 15 May 1856. The witnesses were Frederick Willmott's mother, Ellen Fell's uncle, the extremely wealthy Joseph Tasker, and his equally wealthy daughter, Helen Ann. The Taskers were an old Catholic family, famous for their philanthropy, contributing the equivalent of multi-millions to – and even paying for outright – the construction of chapels, convents, shrines and churches.

If nice young ladies didn't visit Borough High Street, they certainly couldn't be expected to live there. Fred and Ellen Willmott did what many affluent young couples were doing in the mid-nineteenth century: they looked to the suburbs.

By the time the Willmotts were viewing the new-build Spring Grove housing development at Isleworth in 1855, it was part of London's rapidly expanding commuter belt. Adverts in the *Illustrated London News* boasted an estate of 'Villas and commodious and handsome Detached Residences' that included lawns, private enclosures, gas and water. Best of all was the promised 'short walk' to the local South Western railway station that would take Mr Willmott back to Borough via Waterloo each day.

Vernon House was a double-fronted, three-storied declaration of intent, with lozenge-shaped flower beds and a built-in coach house. Despite the elegant carriage drive and smart corner gates that sound like something out of the Disney version of *Mary Poppins*, chez Willmott was 'not one of the most imposing houses in The Grove'.[i] While none of the self-consciously executive homes would have been *un*imposing (when it was demolished in 1975 Vernon House's footprint was used for an entire block of flats), given his ambitions, Frederick Willmott would not have considered it his family's forever home. For a start, it was rented, and Fred harboured a dream of his own property empire. Still, it would do for now, not least because not long after they finally settled in, a daughter arrived.

Born 19 August 1858, she was named Ellen Ann, jointly for her mother Ellen and godmother Helen Ann Tasker, but throughout her childhood, she would be known as Poppy. Poppy was followed by Rose, 29 September 1861, and Ada Mary, 2 June 1864. The family employed a cook, housemaid and nurse, and would gradually add to the staff as Fred's investments grew. His firm, which had just expanded to include two new partners, was doing brisk conveyancing trade, and he used the profits to buy railway stock across the globe: Argentine Railways, New York Central Railway and, closer to home, the Metropolitan Railway. He also quietly acquired parcels of land in Southwark, along with warehousing in Great Guildford and Newcomen Streets.

The money was rolling in, especially when Mrs Willmott's mother died, leaving her considerably more than the substantial wealth she'd acquired as part of her marriage settlement.

What little remains of Poppy's early years is a happy blur: of tender letters from Fred Willmott to 'his girls' and laboriously scribed missives to both parents. Now spattered with mould and eaten through by silverfish, they convey a most un-Victorian closeness, far from the traditional impression of austere, arms-length, nineteenth-century parenthood. Poppy and 'Rosey' exchanged new-fangled, commercial greetings cards – in stamped paper lace with gaudily printed flowers, birds and religious scenes.

Not that Fred would have overdone the familiarity; the parenting of girls was still a female job. Father's study would have been sacrosanct, an oasis where he could sit in his leather armchair, tot up accounts, smoke and enjoy the newspaper. The girls would have crowded into Mother's parlour to write letters, do embroidery, a little watercolour painting or light mending work. Ellen and her sisters did no housework but they would have been expected to prepare themselves for their own parlours and their own husbands with leather armchairs, cigars and newspapers.

Mid-nineteenth-century girls' education was patchy at best, a case of covering the skills a woman needed to be a wife and mother plus a few flourishes. Nothing that might encourage earning a living. Working was for poor people; a woman even receiving pin money would bring shame on a husband who, by inference, could not afford to look after his family. Some women even avoided being seen on 'commuter-hour' trains when going up to London to shop or socialise in case it looked like they were going to work.

Most upper-class girls had governesses. Education wasn't compulsory for working-class girls, and those that did go to a charity-funded school learned the 3Rs – reading 'riting and 'rithmetic – and little else. The comfortably middle-class Willmott sisters were lucky: they went to school.

Today, the Charlotte Brontë-sounding Gumley House, Isleworth, a convent school run by the Sisters of the Faithful Companions of Jesus, teaches a full curriculum. Its Victorian incarnation, however, remained far behind any equivalent for boys. An advertisement in the back pages of the *Catholic Directory*, 1858, describes the seventeen-year-old establishment as combining the advantages of a 'continental' education (anything European and particularly French was seen as highly sophisticated) in an agreeably situated location 'just eight miles from Hyde Park Corner'. The ad goes on to describe the school's gardens and pleasure grounds as 'truly beautiful, spacious' and, more ominously, 'walled-in'. This may have bothered the mainly resident boarders; the Willmott girls were, happily, day girls. Classes comprised English, French, Italian, German, geography, botany, natural philosophy,[4] history, writing, arithmetic, and both useful and ornamental needlework.

At first glance this seems to be a reasonably comprehensive

---

[4] The early, Aristotelian vision of science through studying nature.

education. But all these subjects are specifically aimed at young ladies being rendered suitable as a husband's helpmeet, rather than developing an independent mind. Missing here are the 'masculine' subjects being taught in contemporary boys' schools across the land: the classics, Greek, Latin, mathematics, rhetoric, sciences,[5] politics, commerce and current affairs. Newspapers were banned from many girls' schools as 'unsavoury', as were 'modern' French novels, which everyone knew had questionable morals. Zola, Gautier, Flaubert and Balzac, for example, probed some very dark intimacies indeed, and the less said about *that* the better. Financial education was unnecessary. Husbands managed that kind of thing.

One of the best-known stories about Ellen Willmott is that from the age of seven she came downstairs to breakfast on her birthday every year to find a cheque for £1,000 from her godmother, Helen Tasker. A welcome gift today; in 1865, given to a seven-year-old, a thousand pounds was an almost unimaginable fortune. A single birthday cheque would today be worth £126,588.[6] Ellen was never taught the value of that money. It arrived both regularly and mysteriously, handed to her, literally, on a plate.[7] There seemed no end to the supply; she didn't need to think about where it came from. For most of her life, if she wanted something, she bought it, without thought to the cost.

For now, the most important thing was acquiring those accomplishments. At Gumley House, music, drawing and dancing were recommended extras. Fred Willmott invested in them all and Ellen, in particular, excelled. She was a good artist and painter but music became an obsession. From a very young age she seems to have been one of those sickening people who can get a tune out of any instrument they lay their hands on. She developed a passion for Bach, medieval and early

---

[5] Botany is the exception. It was considered perfectly feminine to study and, particularly, press flowers.

[6] Throughout this book I will be using two sources for money conversion. The Bank of England Inflation Calculator for large sums of money, which gives equivalents for the year 2020, and the National Archives Currency Converter for small amounts.

[7] Rose would later also receive a similar cheque.

modern music, especially madrigals. On her sixteenth birthday, Ellen's musical diligence was rewarded by her father with a magnificent 1766 Jacob Kirkman harpsichord once owned by Princess Amelia, daughter of George II. One of just twelve ever made, its burr-walnut casing was embellished with exquisite floral marquetry, its two-manual, five-octave range picked out with ivory naturals and ebony accidentals. The inset rose on the soundboard depicted King David playing the harp. The instrument was worthy of a museum. Fred Willmott deemed his daughter worthy of it.

Ellen and her sisters did not live in the rarefied, upper-class realm that would see them officially 'come out' as debutantes but the middle classes had just as many codes. Dinners, meetings, outings, even dancing had its own etiquette, cards, and rules regarding rank. 'Paying calls' on neighbours was a complicated process which involved printed calling cards and strict rules about who could call on whom at which hour of the day. Woe betide anyone confusing the 'dinner call' (to be undertaken around a week after a dinner party) with afternoon 'at homes', where even the order of 'who rose to their feet first' was highly ritualised. Calling-card size, colour, edgings (different thicknesses of black lines told the recipient how far into the equally codified mourning process someone might be) and even which corner of the card was turned down would speak volumes about the visitor. These calling cards are not to be confused, by the way, with the *carte de visite* at the top of this chapter, which is so named for its size. No one would be vulgar enough to leave photos of themselves on the silver salver of a neighbour's hall table; photographic cards were special mementoes. Sometimes *cartes de visite* of famous people were bought and swapped like collector-cards today.

Being able to play the piano, converse in French, German and Italian or embroider a handkerchief was a sign of having enough leisure time to learn such things and was never to be 'shown off' in the public sphere. Carol Dyhouse talks about femininity – so prized in Victorian life – as representing economic and intellectual dependency. She discusses its 'prescribed service and self-sacrifice as quintessential forms of "womanly behaviour". From early childhood girls were encouraged to suppress (or conceal) ambition, intellectual courage or initiative – any desire for independence.'[ii] Given such prospects, it's hardly surprising that many women who could afford to remain single, chose to do so, preferring a life of celibacy to one of submission. After all, sex was something to endure, to 'get over and done with' – giving up '*that*' must have seemed more of a blessing than a loss.

Ellen Willmott would be part of the first generation of women to begin to challenge the notion of the ideal Victorian lady as submissive wife and mother, to reject the idea of sacrificing her own life and intellect to minister to her family. She would, throughout her life and of her own volition, supplement her 'girls' education' with extended learning – at first via 'acceptable' channels; later encroaching on male institutions to gain the knowledge she craved. She took extra lessons in painting and astronomy, attended lectures, visited museums, concerts and shows, taught herself new skills and even indulged in a little-known craze among late-Victorian ladies for wood and ivory turning.

In some ways she was too early. We don't know exactly when her formal education ended, but there was never any thought towards continuing onto one of the new-fangled ladies' colleges or even finishing school. University was out of the question. Girton College, Cambridge was founded in 1869, Lady Margaret Hall, Oxford in 1878, but the first female undergraduates would have been the children of 'radicals' and 'free-thinkers'. Frederick Willmott was fiercely conventional. His position as 'gentleman' was too hard-won to risk veering even slightly from the rigid Victorian path.

For the moment Ellen was compliant enough. She didn't have any brothers to whom she would have needed to show deference (or be jealous of), and the idea of learning Latin or how to write academically (both of which she would later do off her own bat) would not have occurred to her. She was happy and popular at school, testified by the sheer amount of letters from nuns and former school chums from Gumley House. Ellen's teachers and classmates follow her progress up the horticultural ladder, rejoicing with her successes, comforting her distresses, and though we don't have any of *her* letters to *them*, it is clear the relationship was long, fulfilling and two-sided. She was, at this point, an average, wealthy young girl who loved sport, music and pretty dresses but she had another fascination, too. Mrs Willmott had passed on her love for gardening to all her daughters, but nine-year-old Poppy showed particular precocity. 'I had a passion for sowing seeds and was very proud when I found out the difference between beads and seeds and gave up sowing the former,' she would later write in an undated letter to her friend Charles Sprague Sargent.

An endearing vision of the four female Willmotts drifted to the top of Ellen's rotting correspondence in March 2020. It came in different parts and, had it not been for the love of an elderly woman for her young friends, we might not have known to put them together.

I was wading through a bunch of sympathy notes written to Ellen Willmott on the death of her sister Rose in 1922. Heartbreaking letter after heartbreaking letter, the outpouring of grief made desperately depressing reading. My spirits sank when I opened the predictable missive, in familiar, doddery-old-lady writing, from 'Old Moll'.

Despite a promising musical career, Anna Molique (daughter of composer Wilhelm Bernhard Molique) had ultimately done the 'right' thing. Giving up everything to lead a virtuous life of 'good deeds', however, did not make 'Old Moll' happy. Pious, full of compassion and dedication, there is a desperate sadness in her letters that must have made her young friend determined not to become caught in the same snare. Her 'Poppy' would have seen only too clearly what happened to spinsters who conformed.

Opening Old Moll's letter – for once dated, 4 September 1922 – I dreaded the contents. This was not, however, her usual meandering, melancholic missive.

MISS WILLMOTT'S GHOSTS

Dearest Poppy, I send you the enclosed, which your dear mother gave me, and now I should like some of her own to have it, as when I shut my eyes, no one will care for it here.

My heart thumped as I checked to see if 'the enclosed' still was.

I was in luck. It was a photograph, fashionably calling card sized, and for once clearly labelled on the back: 'Adie W'.

Little Ada Willmott is a gap in Ellen Willmott's early life. We knew virtually nothing about her and had certainly never seen a picture of her. Yet here she was. A cheeky, dimpled moppet with ringlets sitting on the studio photographer's table, wearing an *Alice in Wonderland* costume, swinging little booted feet and hugging a basket of flowers.

Across the table from me, my fellow researcher John Cannell had, by complete coincidence, and from an entirely different box of mouldy grot, fetched up more photos from the same session. Eleven-year-old Rosey, pictured in black, her hair in bunches. Thirteen-year-old Poppy, looking coolly, perhaps even warily at the camera. Two other photos show a young Mrs Willmott with and without her coat. A Willmott women family day out. Two months later, seven-year-old Ada was dead.

Death was omnipresent in the Victorian world but that doesn't mean the loss of a child was any less keenly felt. For a family as close as the Willmotts, Ada's sudden illness was devastating. The bright, cheeky little girl in those photographs is no weakling. It would take six weeks of horror for diphtheria to break her. When she finally passed, from kidney failure, on 15 February 1872, the family was so exhausted and distraught that the nursemaid had to officially register the death.

West London was no longer a haven of joy. Rented and beginning to go down in the world, Vernon House now held too many memories. It was time to move on.

Chapter Three:

A Place in the Country

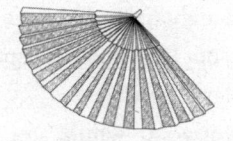

A SATIN FAN

Sixteen inches long, thirty inches across, in plain cream satin and with ivory sticks, this lady's fan is almost entirely without ornament. No tassels, no lace, no images adorn its leaf; it was designed to keep the user cool, without frivolous nonsense. Its only addition is an engraving on the guard:

E.A.W & E.T.C

Lawn Tennis Tournament

Warley Place July 29th 1882

MOVING UP THE housing ladder, Frederick Willmott applied the same criteria as he had when first stepping onto it. He wanted somewhere as swanky as possible, near the 'right kind' of people and within commuting distance from his offices at London Bridge. While the final decision would have rested with the man of the family, Fred's wife and two remaining daughters would have had a long shopping list of features to add to that – not least plenty of space in which to entertain and, most importantly, a large garden.

First time round, Brentwood would not have even made it to Fred and Ellen's longlist. London's eastward sprawl hadn't made it much past the East End, and Essex, a charming county of sleepy market towns and sleepier villages, was inaccessible to city commuters. All this changed in October 1874. The opening of London's Liverpool Street station brought speedy links to the Essex countryside, as yet unspoiled by ever-blackening city smog, which meant that a whole set of previously hard-to-sell country houses were suddenly very attractive indeed.

Great Warley, just outside Brentwood, was a typical English village, dating back to the Domesday Book and boasting a smithy, pub and picturesque jumble of variously ancient large houses and tiny cottages. It still is. Take away the constant stream of traffic and the war memorial on the village green and Warley today could be the one Ellen Willmott would later capture with her ever-present camera.

Countess Helen Tasker probably alerted the Willmotts to the sale. Still very close to the whole family, she lived a mile or so to the other side of Brentwood.

A fine Queen Anne mansion, if Warley Place was not quite grand

A PLACE IN THE COUNTRY

enough yet for *all* of Fred Willmott's ambitions, it had gravitas. The estate had once been owned by Barking Abbey, had great views, plenty of land and the potential for acquiring more. Two miles from Brentwood station it was also commutable in the family brougham, a light, four-wheeled, horse-drawn carriage.

Socially, the village looked promising, too. The local area was studded with country piles, inhabited by notable gentry, several of whom were prominent Catholic families. It would also not have escaped Fred Willmott's notice that Warley Garrison was just down the road. His girls were approaching marriageable age, and officers from nearby Warley Barracks enjoyed an active programme of dances and soirées. Yes, Warley Place would do nicely, after a few alterations.

The auction took place on 4 November 1875. Frederick Willmott won. We don't know how much he paid for the house, cottages and about thirty-three acres, but he and his daughter would spend considerably more over the next forty-odd years, adding to the estate, adopting a coat of arms that may or may not have had something to do with the family, having maps and prints made in the style of eighteenth-century nobility and perpetuating various romantic 'gardeners' tales', including one old chestnut that persists today. Alas, while I would love nothing better than to know that diarist John Evelyn created Warley's garden, the facts just don't bear out the fantasy.[8]

Fred Willmott's grand makeover involved serious building work, including a new wing, library, winter garden, two extra main bedrooms, five servants' bedrooms, a storeroom, linen cupboard, second WC and a small first-floor chamber his daughter would later turn into a darkroom. In deference to his adopted faith, Frederick included a small oratory. He also converted the billiard room into a music room to house Ellen's growing collection of musical instruments.

Work must have been speedy, or perhaps the family didn't mind living on a building site, because they seem to have moved in by Ellen's

---

[8] George Harper demolishes the John Evelyn chestnut in *Warley Magna to Great Warley* (Dickens, 1984).

eighteenth birthday, 19 August 1876. Both she and Rose, fifteen, would have left school much earlier, and been itching to get their hands on that garden. So would their mother.

Mrs Ellen Willmott fascinates me. When I first came across her, it was in photographs from the late 1880s as a hunched old lady with a twinkle in her eye, but not much else to make me want to know her better. As more material turned up, however, she became an individual. Ellen Fell had clearly once been strong enough to have three girls, run a household and still have time to be an active, hands-on gardener, as plant-curious as her namesake daughter.

The photos from the studio photo-shoot (the ones including little Ada) were a wakeup. Frustratingly, Mrs W's 1871 diary, which we fell upon with huge excitement, turned out to be the record of a punishingly dull-sounding holiday to York, where she spent most of her time having tea with clergymen. What a transformation, though. In less than twenty years this upright, commanding, capable matron shrank to an elderly granny who had to be wheeled around in a Bath chair. Yet, in the search for *Miss* Ellen Willmott's horticultural inspiration, we need look no further than her mother.

Born far too early for any kind of female emancipation, in her younger days Ellen Willmott Snr still clearly had a mind of her own. From her many botanical watercolour paintings we know she was a skilled artist, but she was also an avid and active plant-completist. One of the Willmott women's first Warley tasks was hunting down 'Essex plants' not already in the garden, beginning an obsession with plant collecting that would reach the furthest corners of the world. When Uncle Charles Willmott emigrated to New Zealand, it was Mrs, not Miss Willmott to whom he addressed parcels of seed from the rare antipodean ferns that would grace Warley's glasshouses long before most of Europe had heard of them.[9]

---

9   Poor Uncle Charles's own garden disappeared under Lake Rotorua after Mount Tarawera erupted in 1886.

A PLACE IN THE COUNTRY

Mrs W's heart must have sunk as her husband proudly oversaw 'respectable' flower beds cut near the house to impress the neighbours. She loathed the Victorian obsession with mass planting and gaudy annuals, instead finding inspiration in the controversial writings of Irish maverick William Robinson.

Born in 1838, Robinson had come to London as a foreman at the Botanical Gardens in Regent's Park, but was destined for greater things. His book, *The Wild Garden*,[10] controversially advocated the 'natural' look over nineteenth-century Britain's rigid public park formality and carpet bedding. Mrs Willmott and her girls would have pored over his cutting-edge, alternative magazine *The Garden* and, later, *Gardening Illustrated*, which put those principles into practice. All three became obsessed. Ellen's 1884 birthday present to her mother was *The Wild Garden*'s follow-up, *The English Flower Garden*, hot off the press.

Warley was by no means all gardening, however. The newly extended house needed furnishing, and the 1870s' zenith in Victorian knick-knack collecting and general household clutter struck home with the Willmott girls. While Mrs Willmott acquired a suitably impressive household staff, Ellen and Rose acquired the art of acquisition. Visiting country-house sales with Helen Tasker, they accumulated furniture by Hepplewhite and Chippendale and dinner services by *Famille Verte*, Royal Worcester and Delft. Even Ming porcelain found its way into Warley's newly enlarged, newly decorated salons. Poppy and Rosey learned to sniff out only the very best and, since the countess often paid for their trophies, money was no object. Indeed, money wasn't a problem anyway, since both girls were still getting that £1,000 cheque every birthday.

The cash was going to keep on coming, too, if Frederick Willmott had anything to do with it. His Grand Plan was going nicely. He had a splendid house in the country, a loving family and a growing collection

---

10 Published 1870.

of servants and coaches: on 3 September 1883, Mr and Mrs W spent the entire afternoon spuriously visiting every neighbour in the area 'in our new Victoria', an elegant, convertible carriage. He was also making serious investments. In addition to more railway stocks and property in London, whenever land turned up for sale in the neighbourhood, he quietly added that, too, to an ever-burgeoning portfolio. In 1882 he purchased twenty-two acres on the eastern side of the Brentwood Road, earmarked for a new home farm. Overseeing Warley's current agricultural activity in minute detail was now a personal passion. Fred's dream was coming true. He'd make country squire yet.

The daily commute had turned out to be less convenient than first hoped but the solicitors' practice had matured to a point where Fred could semi-retire, aged fifty-four. In 1877, after handing the day-to-day business to his deputy, he was able to spend a leisurely few days a month in town dealing with major clients, visiting wine merchants, tailors and cigar shops and hobnobbing with city friends and acquaintants. He – and occasionally the family – enjoyed dozens of theatre visits: from pantomime to Shakespeare, Mr Henry Irving's latest production to Mr Barnum's 'Greatest Show in the World', often two or even three times a week.

Most of this detail comes from a series of fat, 'rough' Letts diaries, which Fred began in 1877, writing on an almost-daily basis, right up to his death. They include dizzying minutiae, from the day's weather and the number of eggs his chickens laid to who his daughters had taken tea with, but we will never be able to read them all. One crumbled in my hands. Another had rotted to the point where we only know what Fred was doing on Mondays and Thursdays. More are missing entirely, probably forever; we are finally running out of places such material can hide. What we have, however, provides a tantalising window into Frederick Willmott's world, a curious mixture of hard-nosed business and sugar-sweet sentimentality. Among lists of stocks and shares he's planning on purchasing, including the elevated railroad at New York (now the High Line) Fred gives his cows names like Strawberry and Snowball, calls Mrs Willmott 'wifey' and makes extended visits to Battersea Dogs' Home, seemingly just to say hello to the strays. The whole family was dog crazy, sometimes having as many as seven pooches in the household at once. Not that these were mutts from the Dogs' Home. The Willmotts' own animals were pure breeds, including Rose's Newfoundland, Czar (who may or may not have bitten the postman, kicking off a court case), Germano, a sandy Pomeranian shaved to look like a lion, a St Bernard who suffered the indignity of wearing a barrel of brandy round his neck, plus any number of old English sheepdogs, corgis, collies, dachshunds and small, unidentifiable yappy things.

Frederick Willmott's diaries also reveal his plans for his daughters, something that would have begun almost as soon as they moved in. He had chosen Warley with its neighbours in mind and he was going to make the most of those new connections.

Fred threw himself into the Warley social scene. It was important to be seen holding parties and soirées for the local gentry but he also needed to hit that sweet spot in the marriage stakes. Life in the early 1880s became a social carousel as the family attended – and hosted – a giddy, Jane-Austen whirl of officers and flirting; soirées, concerts, balls and afternoon tea. A lot of afternoon tea. In their various seasons, garden parties and balls could take place anything up to three or four times a week, but 'paying calls' and afternoon tea was constant and repetitive, the same rounds of the same people, day after day. What seems like a glamorous lifestyle must have quickly become a chore. Young Ellen Willmott sought relief in vigorous walks, hunting and sport, something Fred was in favour of, especially when it meant mixed doubles.

Lawn tennis had only been codified in 1873, but in a few short years it had become a craze. Ellen was mad for it. Local newspapers reported middle-class tournaments, usually at the Barracks, recording, blow-by-blow, who beat who, in which round. Ellen does not seem to have been particularly brilliant; most of the press reports show her being defeated, but on 29 July 1882 her proud father was finally able to report:

> *Miss Ind and Patrick O'Byrne won the 1st prizes and Ellie and Mr Clayton the 2nd. Wife gave the 1st ladies prize, a silver scarf holder & I gave the 2nd. The Cup to O'Byrne . . . a walking stick mounted in silver, Ellie 2nd ladies prize, a white satin fan, the second gentleman's prize a cigarette case.*

Back in 2000, Mr Gerald Gurney, a racquet-sports collector, found the very same satin fan presented to Ellen by her father at an antiques fair in Suffolk. After reading an article by him in *The Tennis Collector*, I gambled a stamp writing to an address stapled to the clipping and was delighted to receive a phone call from Gerald's widow Joan, who still treasures it. It sums up quite beautifully Ellen Willmott's joyous, carefree early twenties: feminine, flirty and fashioned of the finest materials, but with a streak of practicality that suggests a joyful sense of independence.

The girls also played badminton, golf and croquet, and Rosey took daily constitutionals around the village with her father. Ellie sometimes joined them but found the same views boring and usually opted for longer, harder, more varied rambles.

Europe was only just emerging from the Little Ice Age.[11] Snow arrived, and lingered, most years. Close inspection of one of Ellen's photos – of Fred, Rose and a friend walking through the snow – reveals all three carrying skates. During the exceptionally hard winter of 1879–80 the girls were on Warley's frozen lake all day, every day, until their parents pointed out the ice was melting.

Ellie's favourite activity, however, would have pleased Fred no

---

11 A period of regional cooling, roughly between 1300 and 1850. Weather extremes continued afterwards, however, seriously impacting Victorian gardening.

A PLACE IN THE COUNTRY

end. Dancing with gallants from the 56th Regiment, aka 'the Saucy Pompeys'[12] and the 44th (the 'Fighting Fours') in the Officers' Mess up the road until 3 a.m. was normal. Ellie always went (escorted by her father, no funny business); Rose doesn't seem to have been so keen. Fred Willmott encouraged the officers to return the visits, breaking out the champagne, port and cigars with an optimistic eye.

Parties at Warley Place grew in number, both of the garden fête and soirée variety. On 21 July 1880, Fred proudly recorded: 'About 70 came to our ball. I had ordered for 80, the floral decorations were very beautiful and all went off well. Wine consumed: 36 champagne *Heidsieck*, 7 *de Venoge*, 7 claret, 6 sherry, 1 port, 2 brandy'. At a garden party on 17 July 1882, for which Fred had specially gone into town to spend a fortune ordering ice cream, he notes: 'about 100 were present', relating with some satisfaction, 'It was a great success. Macdonald left quite drunk.'[13]

The Willmott household was once again filled with laughter and joy. Little Ada would never be forgotten – appearing in newly registered Latin plant names, graveside visits and painful memories on birthdays for the rest of Ellen's life and beyond – but the family was healing and the future was bright.

Lydia Bennett herself could not have been sadder than Fred Willmott when the Warley officers were transferred during the mighty Childers Reforms[14] of the early 1880s. He held a farewell party for 'a great many officers' 'to drink a glass of champagne, about fifty altogether. In the evening I went to hear the band at the barracks for the last time.'

The Willmotts did visit their old friends in their new quarters at Chatham – once – but had a carriage upset on the way home, breaking

---

12 It is said the Pompadours' coat linings were the exact purple of Louis XV's mistress's underwear. Oddly, Fred Willmott always refers to the regiment as the 6th.

13 Macdonald is either a footman who had been caught and dismissed for drunkenness two months earlier, or Father Macdonald, the local priest. Neither seems quite right, neither seems quite wrong.

14 A wholesale reorganisation of the British Army Infantry. This must have particularly upset the 56th, who not only became the 'junior' battalion, but had their saucy uniform facings turned white. Purple was reinstated in 1936.

Fred's wrist and leaving Ellie and Rosey cut and bruised. An amalgamated Essex Regiment remained at Warley Barracks and the family would stay friendly enough, but it would never again be like old times. That didn't mean the end of young gentlemen. They came and went; some even accompanied the family on holiday. Names flit through Fred's diaries, and, for a while, one, George Ainslie Hight, on leave from the Indian Forestry Commission, seems to have got Fred's hopes up. George and Ellie saw each other a few times in 1882, but with no obvious budding relationship, and the connection didn't last beyond his return to the subcontinent.[15]

Fred wasn't too bothered that romance had failed to blossom for either of his daughters. There was time. While never seeming to blame any lack of knowledge on their formal education, the girls – and especially Ellie – were still dissatisfied enough with embroidery, etiquette and comportment to want more. Now was the time to build on any learning they'd missed out on. There aren't too many young people who would use their birthday money to go up to London to hire a live-in German teacher, but that's exactly what Ellie and Rosey did in 1880. They went to concerts, lectures and exhibitions and read avidly, widely and open-mindedly. Ellie bought a telescope. Rosey, and almost certainly Ellie, was an early member of the fledgling Society for Psychical Research.

We don't know exactly when Ellen began experimenting with photography but my money is on the late 1870s, with the invention of the dry plate method. Until then, the 'wet collodion' process meant practitioners needed to expose an image and process it within minutes, in a cumbersome darkroom with lots of chemicals and awkward equipment. For this reason it was best suited to studio photography, as with the exquisite shots made by Julia Margaret Cameron. It is

---

[15] George Ainslie Hight would become a distinguished scholar of Norse mythology, Viking history and Wagnerian philosophy, translating the saga of *Grettir the Strong* from Icelandic. He and Ellen reconnected – platonically – in 1918.

A PLACE IN THE COUNTRY

possible Ellen used wet collodion to start with, but the sheer volume of photographs she was taking by the 1880s – she was getting through glass plates like a modern teenager snapping with a smartphone – would preclude her being able to process them, even in one of the new-fangled 'portable' darkrooms. The dry process enabled users to pre-coat plates with a gelatine-based concoction stable enough to expose then store for processing later.

Early photography was more democratic than we might at first expect. Women were not particularly discouraged from working in the medium, though it was a rich person's pastime. Few women became household names – even Julia Margaret Cameron would face misogynistic opposition from mainly male photographic circles claiming her nuanced work was 'out of focus' – and even fewer would become professionals. Photography as a hobby, however, was perfectly acceptable and pretty snapshots of friends or pets were considered charming. Ellen Willmott wanted more. Landscapes, gardens, still life, botanical portraits, reportage, travelogue, low-light, even comedy and trick photography, she was determined to master her craft.

Some of Ellen's prints initially look like duplicates, but it soon becomes clear that she has been having fun in the darkroom, experimenting with effects, light and shade. Cloudy skies in the 'same' photograph range from dark and ominous to entirely bleached out; images are differently cropped or printed on unusual types of paper. Her photos were often collected in gift-albums for family and friends. Others were kept in specially commissioned leather cases, embossed with her initials and the collection: *Rome, Calais, Warley,* etc. Few are labelled with a date, place or name, though most have mysterious codes pencilled on the back, presumably relating to a catalogue that hasn't survived. Frederick Willmott's diaries allow us to date some. Exposure times were drearily long but Ellen Willmott appears not to have expected her subjects to keep straight faces. Many are laughing or joking around – we have a fun series of shots depicting a group of fashionable young women having tea on a terrace in France. It takes a moment to realise Rose is doing sundry silly things with a fork.

Carrying around glass plates was heavy, awkward labour. I haven't yet figured out whether, just out of every shot, there is small army of pack-servants lugging tripods and crates. From my own experience picking up glass plates from a basement floor, transporting even a few would be backbreaking stuff.

A snapshot, probably from around 1894, shows Ellen at a pavement café in Aix-les-Bains, with (probably) Helen Green, her painting tutor. Helen is making a watercolour sketch; Ellen is nursing a large, wooden box camera. Clearly considered portable in its day, it takes up most of her lap, and that is in its closed position. Opened out, it would have had its own set of bellows to increase the distance between the lens and plate.

In all this talk of country rambles, glamorous balls and photographic profligacy, Mrs Willmott seems to have gone a bit quiet. Indeed, even her husband was beginning to slow down. Fred's constant colds, lumbago and gout, however, were nothing to the rheumatism Mrs W was dealing with. As the 1880s progressed, she went from rude health to chronic, crippling pain, sometimes unable to walk or even stand. While never losing interest in plants (on such days she'd content herself with riding Warley's hills in a donkey chaise), Ellen Willmott Senior was beginning to be ruled by her rheumatism. Finding relief from pain, both physical and emotional – the loss of little Ada still omnipresent – was now a matter of family concern.

Chapter Four:

An Alpine Wonder

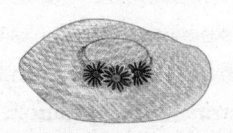

A CABINET CARD

A professional souvenir photograph taken at Atelier Muegle, a studio in the lakeside town of Thoune. Three women in Swiss national costume sit in a fake 'alpine meadow' in front of a 'mountain chalet' backdrop, wearing linen blouses, peasant skirts, embroidered bodices and lacy headpieces. Each woman clutches a studio prop: a basket of flowers, a shepherd's crook, a milkmaid's hat. The image is badly damaged; indeed one of the women's faces has been completely eaten away. Of Rose Willmott, standing in the centre, only the eyes remain. Her sister Ellen, however, sits virtually unscathed, directly challenging her viewer with a secret, Mona Lisa smile.

TRAVEL HAD ALWAYS been part of the Willmott family's world but after Ada's death it seemed even more important to get away. The first written account we have of European holidays is by a seventeen-year-old Ellie, writing in her nightgown in the early hours because she is so excited she can't sleep. She has been to dinner in Paris – but what a dinner! A giant sole was paraded in, ornamented with crayfish and mushrooms studded with shrimps, with patterns of olives and truffles![i]

Soon the Willmotts were making a sortie abroad at least once a year. In 1880 it was Belgium, Antwerp and Paris, where the family went to the Jardin de Luxembourg and the Bois de Bolougne; Ellie and Rosey went shopping in *Bon Marché*. In the evening Fred took the girls to the *Opera Garnier* to see *Les Huguenots*. In 1882 the family went to Marseille, Cannes, Nice and Monte Carlo before travelling back up via Paris again. Intriguingly, this time the usually strait-laced Fred deposited his wife and daughters back at the hotel and quietly disappeared to the *Folies Bergère* with a Captain Scott.

Ellie's camera snapped away, capturing major cities and famous tourist attractions: great lakes, picturesque towns, bucolic countryside, hearty peasants, sunshaded cattle, mountain streams and rugged coasts. All was thoroughly explored. Sometimes she includes the means of travel in her photos, reminding the viewer what a palaver it would have been just to get around. Even a regular road can't have made for a comfortable ride and the family travelled mainly by rail, catching the boat from Folkestone or Dover. One set, of around 250 shots of life

AN ALPINE WONDER

around the Calais docks in June 1889, was clearly taken by a bored Ellie waiting for the ferry home.

More and more, the family was drawn to the Alps, not least for the famous, health-giving waters. The two older Willmotts were developing more aches and pains by the day. Fred's gout and Ellen Snr's rheumatism had seen them sampling the great spa towns of England in search of cures but now they needed something stronger. Mrs Willmott, in particular, was suffering badly. Fred's journal often laments 'wife would not go out'.

Rose and Ellen, sometimes accompanied by girlfriends, were more interested in sightseeing, hitting the shops and dressing up. Our cabinet card – the next size up from a *carte de visite* – is the result of such an expedition. Back home in Warley's conservatory, Rose and her (unidentified) friend wore their costumes once again, this time for Ellen's own camera.

The studio portrait sums up a carefree world of young women with their lives ahead of them, established enough not to have to work, wealthy enough to buy anything that took their fancy. Clothes weren't the only souvenirs that found their way back to Essex. Ellen was a big fan of Napoleon Bonaparte and collected anything about or once owned by the French emperor. When she heard about a wooden cabin he was rumoured to have stayed in during his almost mythical crossing of the Alps in 1800, she just had to have it. Fred mentions its arrival in his journal, 5 February 1880: 'Ellie began the erection of her Gipsy Hut near the Pond.' The chalet lived out its dog days at the edge of Warley's lake, partially suspended over the water to form a boathouse. Bonaparte's 'mule' from the famous Delaroche painting would have been represented by the donkey that pulled Mrs Willmott's little cart, by now the only way she could get around. The fancy dress outfits were kept inside the chalet, along with 'herdsman's gear', whatever that consisted of. Alas, no trace remains of hut, shepherds' kit, dressing-up clothes or, indeed, the donkey.

Ellen the tourist had been thoroughly bitten by the alpine bug. Ellen the gardener was only just beginning. Up to this point she had dug alongside her mother and sister, working various areas of the garden as they were built, but not, as far as we know, striking out on her own in any major way. As the family visited the wild places of Europe, however, something stirred in Ellen's soul.

The Victorian craze for all things 'natural' had, for some time, seen doughty, tweed-clad individuals clambering up hills and through woods, denuding the British countryside of anything that looked like a fern. For a growing group of wealthier tourists, however, the lure of the dainty alpine bloom was impossible to resist.

The word 'alpine' is given to plants growing wild at high altitudes, wherever they come from in the world. Thriving in the bitterest conditions, their roots delve into crevices, anchoring themselves against harsh winters and high winds. Many have evolved into low-lying, compact bursts of greenery with miniature, fluorescent-hued flowers that punch their way through the snow to dazzle in bright mountain sunshine. Others dance through lush alpine meadows in the heat-baked summer months.

These miniature gems have fascinated plantsfolk for centuries and travellers have brought specimens back for their gardens from the earliest times. Sadly, the British climate is diametrically opposed to the conditions these fussy little divas demand. They can survive plunging temperatures, nutrient-free gravel and any amount of snow, but rich British soil makes their growth weak and sappy and our waterlogged winters rot their toes. It was a badge of honour to be able to cultivate a true, full-fledged rock garden. It still is. One of the reasons so few of the great nineteenth-century rockeries remain in their original state is the sheer amount of work that has to go into keeping these exquisite little tyrants alive.

Few Victorian gardeners could resist having a go, though. Wealthy gentlemen (yes, usually men) constructed faux cliff faces, often covering

AN ALPINE WONDER

several acres. Middle-class imitators dabbled with more modest back-garden affairs; the rest made do with an old sink by the back door. Some, keeping in mind William Robinson's ideals of wild gardening, tried to make their heaps of boulders as natural-looking as possible. Others revelled in high kitsch, especially after Sir Charles Isham introduced the garden gnome to Britain in 1847.

Ellen Willmott was smitten. She had seen these tiny, stage-bright jewels in the wild and determined to have an alpine ravine all of her very own.

Willmott folklore holds that on 19 August 1879 – Ellen's twenty-first birthday – she asked permission to spend some of her money building an alpine garden. Her father agreed, as long as it was out of sight of his study window. Warley was still a building site, with a peach house, palm house, orchid house and vinery under construction. Fred's study was in the northeast corner of the house, right next to where the old Georgian stable block was being entirely rebuilt in Victorian faux-Tudor, and the back of the house was being remodelled (again), moving the kitchens downstairs to the basements. It's hardly surprising he dictated that any extra construction must be well out of sight and, ideally, earshot.

We can't be sure of the twenty-first birthday story, though given how long it would take to build a three-acre alpine ravine with vast slabs of rock cut from the Derbyshire peaks, shipped down country by rail and dragged uphill by horse and cart, it doesn't seem impossible. The first definite mention of the project: 'Ellie began her new Alpine Garden' in Fred's diary, 1 April 1882, when she was actually twenty-three, may refer to her starting to plant up her wonder rather than building it. However, 1882 also saw the family's first visit to the spa town of Aix-les-Bains, in the Haute-Savoie region of France; perhaps that inspired her.

Everything about the new rock garden had to be of the best possible quality. Not for her the upstart artificial stone invented by James Pulham & Son of Broxbourne, Hertfordshire, however convincing (and, it would transpire, durable) it might be. Miss Willmott wanted the genuine article.

Based in York, James Backhouse & Son doesn't, at first sight, seem the obvious choice of builder for a project in south Essex. Images in the University of York's digital library of the company's 'showroom', however, reveal good reasons for Ellie's decision: forty glasshouses and a staggering alpine garden showcasing the species available in the company's catalogues. Photos depict densely planted 'mountain peaks', mysterious 'caves' and hummocks of alpines cascading into fern-fronded pools.

The construction team was led by Richard Potter, Backhouse's top alpine expert, who had an extensive knowledge of the mountain regions, and his pet mongoose, who had an extensive knowledge of Warley's rodent population.[16] Under Potter's expert eye gigantic slabs of granite were installed to look as natural as possible, creating ravines and valleys, crags and mountain paths.

Keeping the promise to her father, Ellen chose a place away from the formal lawns and bowling green. Here the hill was not as steep as elsewhere in the garden, allowing her to do something most rockery builders didn't bother with. Rather than suddenly confront her visitors with a pile of stones plonked in the middle of the lawn, she slowly introduced the idea of moving from one world to another via an undulating 'alpine meadow' planted with thousands of miniature bulbs. As her friends left the familiar, blousy comforts of herbaceous borders and shady, moss-lined world of 'Evelyn's' chestnut trees, they encountered oddly placed limestone boulders and tempting stone pathways before them. Slowly, the rocks increased in number; bigger, more imposing, until the visitors found themselves transported to an alpine mountainside in the middle of Essex, surrounded by such a profusion of plants it was hard to see where the path ended and the stone began.

---

16 I am not 100 per cent satisfied that the Mr Potter with the mongoose is the same Mr Potter that was sent to Warley by Backhouse for three years, though I have no reason to believe there was a second.

AN ALPINE WONDER

Reviewers were stunned. *Lyon-Horticole* magazine wrote:

> *Constructed entirely in hollows, you don't see it while you are in the meadow; then, suddenly, you find yourself in a sort of narrow valley winding between layers of rock all covered in flowers. At the back runs a stream, sometimes cascading down, sometimes forming a little lake. An undulating path, hardly visible, follows the edges of the water where the sides of the rocks rise up. Sometimes you have to get over on stones lying on the bed of the stream itself, while you are confined between blocks three times your own height.*[ii]

Standing today, in light, largely barren woodland, it can be difficult for a modern visitor to figure out that they're looking at a rock garden at all, let alone determine where any of those 'undulating paths' were. For years I couldn't work out why there were no photographs of the 'climax' of Willmott's showstopper-within-a-showstopper: a single-slab, stone bridge across a massive ravine, under which cascaded a waterfall. Indeed, *all* the pictures of Ellen Willmott's most famous achievement, including magazine etchings and hundreds of prints are a bit of a puzzle. The images we have – of three exotic pools, complete with 'disporting' goldfish, thrice-human-height cliffs and several densely planted limestone islets – are definitely *of* Warley's alpine wonder; they just don't *look* like it. The mystery is only surpassed by the photos we *don't* have. Views of the bridge as it spans the gorge, for one, but also the famous filmy fern grotto (installed in 1894), now a roofless archway studded with lethal iron shafts. This major feature warranted ecstatic description in several journals of the day, yet to my knowledge not a single photograph of it exists.

I am now beginning to believe our *Lyon-Horticole* reviewer, who tells us Willmott's 'rustic bridge [was] entirely hidden under the greenery'. The only way to fathom out the pictures is to acknowledge that today's 'big hitters' were not considered worth spending a glass plate on; there was simply better stuff to snap.

I am convinced that much of Ellen Willmott's alpine garden remains *in situ*, slumbering under a good couple of metres of leaf mould. Some has been lost only very recently, when a troop of badgers moved in and began remodelling. Perhaps one day, tougher volunteers than me may take it into their heads to excavate Warley's lost mountain paths, ravines and rock pools. They will have to be burly; the whole thing ranges over three acres and the gorge alone is sixty-five metres long but, oh, what a project.

♣

Having built her mountain marvel, Ellen needed to populate it. We recently discovered pictures of the newly completed rockwork, which show just how many specimens she'd have needed to buy to make it look even half-decent, let alone the riot of colour visitors would travel from the other side of the world to see. She had been digging up the odd root on trips to the Swiss countryside for years, but her entire haul wouldn't fill one crevice with the kind of luxury she envisaged. Plant purchase was required, and on an epic scale.

The Victorian alpine collecting craze attracted some truly seamy practices. Unscrupulous chancers would strip the best specimens from a mountainside or alpine pasture then torch the rest to make their loot more valuable. Swiss horticultural titan Henry Correvon was appalled at the wholesale destruction of his native meadows and determined to do something about it. His answer was a garden, *Floraire*, just outside Geneva, where he grew sturdy stock at such cheap prices that the plant pirates might, just, be put out of business.

Ellen Willmott was a moth to Henry Correvon's flame. For his part,

AN ALPINE WONDER

Correvon was impressed with the budding young alpinist and the two began a friendship that would last to his death. He admired the taste with which she planted the treasures she purchased from him and, in years to come, he would trust no one else with newly collected seed brought back by plant hunters from across the world. That trust intensified, even after Ellen poached one of his best journeymen, nineteen-year-old Jacob Maurer, to lead the alpine team at Warley.

By this point, however, it wasn't just rocks, plants and labour she was buying at an alarming rate. Ellen Willmott's spending was becoming more lavish by the day. If she saw something she wanted, she bought it. She bore in mind the countess's lessons in good taste, and only bought the best, exemplified by hundreds of receipts for jewellery, clothes, hats and accessories from the finest purveyors in London, Paris, and beyond. She collected curious objects (often decidedly strange *memento-mori*) and built an enviable library of medieval manuscripts, ancient herbals and rare tomes. Antique dealers, booksellers, musical instrument salesmen, auction rooms and friends wrote regularly, alerting her to juicy new items. Her father occasionally upbraided her for her extravagance but his admonitions largely fell on stony ground. Money just 'arrived'; it never occurred to her that it would ever stop arriving, and I do not entirely blame her for thinking so. For his part, Frederick Willmott was still working on the 'it will all be fine when she gets a husband' wheeze. He actively excluded Ellen – now in her twenties – from making financial decisions by travelling up to town alone to invest his daughter's money on her behalf, instead of introducing her to even basic budgeting.

However reckless her spending, even Henry Correvon couldn't fault the way Ellen Willmott was handling her purchases. Warley's ravine, he declared, was 'constructed on a very original plan, exhibiting an exquisite taste . . . I was in fancy transported to the delightful scenery of our Swiss Alps.'[iii]

Ellie's alpine garden was growing ever more magnificent, but other, more energetic activities were beginning to decline. The two older

Willmotts were not the only family members in pain. Ellen herself, still in her twenties, was also increasingly troubled by rheumatism. Most of the time she blasted through it. She had no intentions of missing out on anything just for the sake of tedious agony.

Mr and Mrs W continued their quest for cures, trawling the British seaside towns of Ramsgate and Hastings, continuing to Bath in spring 1888, where Ellen clearly pulled some strings to get into the newly discovered but not yet open to the public Roman thermal baths. The supporting timbers from the archaeological excavation are visible in her photos.

Visiting Prior Park with Philip Herbert, one of several hopeful young men who hung around from time to time, the sisters bumped into a friend, Canon Williams. The Canon introduced the group to a 'Major and Mrs' Robert Berkeley,[17] from one of the oldest aristocratic families in England. Ellen and Rose soon became thick with the couple's daughter, Maud, who took the girls to visit her relatives at Berkeley Castle near Gloucester.

A few weeks later, on 4 June 1888, Frederick Willmott wrote with immense glee: 'the girls are to spend a short time with the Berkeleys at Spetchley Park at Worcester'. Over 140 years later, it's still almost possible to hear Fred's hands rubbing together. Could this be the moment one of his daughters would finally find a wealthy, well-connected suitor?

In May 2021, Karen and I found a damp-wrecked photograph album in the basement at Spetchley: a souvenir of the visit, between 7 and 14 June 1888, that would change so many lives. Ellen's images of olde-worlde Spetchley estate cottages, their inhabitants standing stiffly in doorways with babes in arms or tools in hand, contrast with the Palladian splendour of the Big House and its incumbents. Mr Robert Martin Berkeley, Lady Catherine and various Berkeley

---

17 Fred erroneously describes Mr Berkeley as 'Major' and Lady Catherine as 'Mrs'.

sons and daughters enjoy a picnic in the woods and formal tea on the mansion steps. The young people take a daytrip to Redstone Rock, a local tourist attraction. Indoors, they mess around with musical instruments. One very boring photograph of Spetchley's rear wall was a complete puzzle – until Karen zoomed in on a window, revealing two Berkeley brothers horsing around with shaving foam. My personal favourite from the visit is a 'ghost' shot, taken in Spetchley parish church. Ellen's previous attempts had depicted her 'ghost' (woman in a sheet) pointing at a scared-looking chap in a blazer, but had accidentally reversed the trick to show the 'phantom' as a solid figure and the 'human' as a transparent apparition. This time she gets it right. No fewer than three, sheet-clad 'spectres' 'haunt' an ornately carved memorial as a blurred, wild-haired Rose 'wails' on her knees before disporting stone cherubs, which, somewhat disturbingly, are the only things in focus. The book is the earliest example we know of Ellen's 'thank-you' photo albums. She continued to send gifts of photographs after visiting people's homes right up to her death.

The sisters were amused by the attentions of several Berkeley sons, who followed them around Spetchley's ornamental gardens like lap dogs: Robert Valentine, the oldest, serious and already beginning to shoulder the family responsibilities; Mowbray, the fun-loving soldier; Hubert, another military son. Eighteen-year-old Wolstan, and Oswald, the traditional one-Berkeley-child-destined-for-the-priesthood, probably didn't do much chasing, but Maurice, a handsome army captain with a twinkle in his eye, even in snapshots, was particularly attentive. In Ellie's photographs, the chaps stand solicitously in tweed and boaters or exaggeratedly 'pour tea' for the tightly corseted, bustle-skirted ladies.

Later that summer, Maud and Maurice arrived for a return visit to Warley. After that, the sisters 'happened to meet' sister and brother several times in town. Maurice began to appear at Warley on his own. For a man who was looking out for a husband for his daughters, Frederick

Willmott seems to have been oddly oblivious to what was going on. On 16 August he was enlightened. Fred came home to discover that Maurice Berkeley had proposed to Rosey.

This was awkward.

Socially, the Berkeleys, as aristocratic landed gentry, were high above the lowly station of a London Bridge solicitor. But Maurice was a younger son, unlikely to inherit, and as such, actually less wealthy than the aforementioned London Bridge solicitor. Rose's family were not at all convinced by Maurice. It might have been the money thing or, could it possibly be, the dashing, worldly glint that 'man about town' Maurice seems to exude from photographs?

Rosey told Maurice she would 'write to him'. Four days later the entire family packed up and disappeared to the continent. They would not return for ten months.

Frederick Willmott records in detail the family's Grand Tour, majoring on train times, hotels, restaurants, entertainments and attractions. He never reveals his own thoughts or opinions but he appears to have been equally oblivious to his youngest daughter's emotional state. Fred lists his spa trips and gout treatments and describes with gusto various daytrips and luncheons, remarking only that 'Rosey had a headache'.

Rose had refused Maurice's proposal. A letter to her sister insists that while she knows that neither Ellie nor her parents like her suitor, she has made the decision not to marry him of her own free will. She seems to have convinced Ellie of her indifference. She definitely convinced her parents. She even convinced me – until August 2021. Working through a seam of Rose's most personal papers in the never-ending boxes of mouldy correspondence, we found an envelope containing two photographs. We recognised them immediately; they had been somewhat inexpertly cut out of one of Ellie's photo albums from the Spetchley visit the previous June. Inside that envelope, kept secretly for 130-odd years, Maurice and Rosey are together, in a life that was never to be. We don't know how Maurice took the rejection, but he remained single for the rest of his life.

❧

The Willmott's Big Vacation ranged across France, Italy, Switzerland, Germany and Belgium. Ellen's camera snapped busily. The Boboli Gardens. The Leaning Tower. The Sistine Chapel. Hadrian's Villa. The Uffizi Gallery. Wiesbaden. In Naples, Vesuvius rewarded Ellen's curiosity by erupting the day after she climbed to the top. In Rome, Fred, struck by an unknown illness, was bed-bound for six weeks. His wife couldn't go out either, though they both managed to stagger to their feet for an audience with the Pope.

Parental inactivity wasn't going to stop the two daughters stepping out. Rosey eventually rallied to join her sister exploring catacombs, churches, the Vatican library and, of course, the shops. They especially enjoyed the city's annual Carnival and watched, fascinated, as Roman 'roughs' rioted in the streets.[18] Back at Spetchley Park, Ellen's thank-you gift, filled with carefree moments and silly, innocent fun from the previous June, ended up in the basement – the only photograph album from that period not carefully preserved in the library.

There was one blot on the landscape. In January 1888, Ellen's beloved godmother Helen Tasker had died. The young spinster with roses and Spanish mantilla in her hair, gazing wistfully from a disintegrating, anonymous pastel drawing we found in the cellar had, in later years, reinvented herself into a tough old lady, twinkling with mischief in Willmott family photos. The countess's passing hit hard. The fortune she left to Ellen and Rose was neither here nor there. They had plenty of money already; they wanted – and would deeply miss – *her*. The harp and jewellery she left to Ellen would have been much more poignant than the cash. But cash is cash. Even after properties entailed to distant

---

[18] Rioting seems to have been such a regular occurrence I have been unable to work out which this was.

cousins, bequests to sundry relatives and vast sums left to the Catholic Church, earmarked for yet more good works (including a fanciful notion to build a neo-Byzantine cathedral at Westminster), the money was impressive. The sisters, as residuary legatees, each received around £143,000 – well over £19m today.

A young woman could do a lot with such a sum, and just at the moment, she probably needed to. As Ellie's back troubles grew, the great spa towns of her beloved Alps called to her. Some of these places were becoming very fashionable. Pick the right one and you might bump into anyone, from gentry and celebrities to full-blown royalty.

Chapter Five:
Extreme Measures

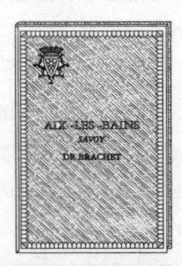

A TOURIST'S GUIDEBOOK

A scarlet, clothbound manual, with gilded lettering and embossed golden crest. Written in English with eight engravings: 'Aix-les-Bains in Savoy: the medical treatment and general indications' steers the would-be medical tourist through Docteur Léon Brachet's unique system of high-pressure mineral water cure. A one-stop-shop approach reassures the reader of guaranteed medical efficacy <u>and</u> a spectacular social life.

THE ANCIENT SPA resort of Aix-les-Bains nestles between the still, grey waters of the Lac du Bourget and Mont Revard, stalwart of many a *Tour de France* mountain time-trial. The town's sulphurous hot springs were harnessed by the Romans at least a century before Christ. Archaeologists have discovered the remains of a large thermal bath complex, and there are scattered ancient remains throughout the area.

Aix became fashionable again at the beginning of the nineteenth century, thanks largely to the 'Bonaparte women'. In 1808, Napoleon's favourite sister, Pauline Borghèse, fought the desperate ennui of salon life in the town; Empress Josephine wrote to her ex-husband of her fright at being caught in a storm on the Bourget. Napoleon replied drily that it would be a shame for an island girl to die on a lake. His stepdaughter/stepsister, Hortense de Beauharnais, adored Aix's *vie de cure*[19] despite the horrors of witnessing her best friend, Adèle de Broc, dragged beneath rapids on a sightseeing trip. Later, Hortense's son Napoleon III made the place fashionable all over again.

For a Napoleon nut like Ellen Willmott, Aix-les-Bains was catnip. Not only was the town set in stunning alpine scenery and patronised by royalty, those thermal springs sang to her throbbing spine. The most recent edifice of the *Thermes Nationaux*, begun in 1857, was a solid, neo-classical affair, but Aix had greater ambitions. A fresh vogue for 'taking the waters' in the second half of the nineteenth century saw a gold rush of ever more glamorous art nouveau hotels jostling to service the whims of its aristocratic clientele.

---
19 Literally 'cure-life'.

The Willmott family first visited Aix in 1882, on their way home from a trip to Nice, and it wasn't long before the town became an annual fixture. Monsieur Bernascon, at the Hôtel de l'Europe, saved the same rooms for them each time, presumably to prevent their eyes wandering to other alluring hostelries springing up across town. Ellen photographed the Temple of Diana, the grand Arch of Campanus and the treacherous waterfall that had done for poor Adèle de Broc. She snapped Rosey meeting the inhabitants of mountainside convents, inspecting wayside shrines and lonely alpine churchyards. In town, she captured her sister investigating, with some curiosity, moustachioed chaps in caps lugging what can only be described as the love child of a sedan chair and a Punch & Judy booth. These were the notorious *porteurs,* the grease that kept Aix-les-Bains' healthcare conveyor belt rolling. Without these grim-faced, trudging 'taxis', the town's famous panacea, the *douche-massage,* may have caused more invalids than it cured. Watching these strange, seaside-striped litters silently transporting mummy-wrapped invalids between great stone buildings must have been like witnessing some arcane ritual, and in many ways it was. It was far too weird for an out-of-towner to grasp. Luckily, someone had written a guidebook.

The volume described at the top of this chapter is in Glasgow University Library, freely available online for anyone fancying a peek. Ellie would have pored over her own copy, not least because the very same doctor that wrote it became *her* doctor, and Ellen Willmott always did her homework.

The son of a former mayor of Aix, Brachet was one of the town's first 'celebrity doctors', with strong opinions about women's health. He placed great emphasis on hysteria, a popular concept based on a melange of vaguely 'nervous' pathological conditions, to which women in particular were thought liable. Symptoms of hysteria included impatience, anxiety, insomnia, vague floating pains, feelings of suffocation, convulsive outbreaks of crying – or laughter – hiccoughs, temporary weakness of limb, tacit resistance to exercise and loss of appetite. Because their reproductive system was the cause of many basic diseases, Brachet believed women should also avoid activities that would put their uteruses under any form of stress. Sport was out, and as a founder member of the Alpine Club of Savoy, he was convinced it was 'absurd and dangerous' for women to attempt altitudes of 2,300 or 2,500 metres.[i]

By late 1889, Ellen Willmott could ignore her pain no longer. Sports – and dancing – were a distant memory. Mrs W had refused to allow her daughter to attend the Bachelors' Ball in Chelmsford the previous November because she was in serious danger of putting her back out. Ellie had been trying to ignore the growing back pains that would haunt her for the rest of her life, but even her stoicism was beginning to fail.

If she bought it in 1884 when it first came out, Ellen may have merely purchased Brachet's guide for its general introduction to the locality. He warms up the reader with romantic local history and charming legends, alpine meadows and distant mountains, ancient ruins and afternoons by the sun-kissed lake. He then risks losing them again as he goes into a probably-overdoing-it-for-a-tourist-guide scientific breakdown of the mineral content of the region's various natural springs. Finally, he gets down to business. For some people, he admits, the fresh mountain air is enough to clear their lungs. Others need to purge themselves by drinking the local water. Most, however, will end up at the enormous municipal thermal baths where a number of treatments are available.

Ellen would have scanned through the various ailments catered for – gout, neuralgia, sciatica, rhinitis, pharyngitis, bronchitis, syphilis, scrofula, psoriasis, eczema, herpes, acne, vaginitis, uterine diseases, irritable bladders, hysteria, anaemia, paralysis and 'disturbances at the Epoch of the Change of Life' – but her eye would have alighted on the most common of all: rheumatism.

Brachet had been exercised by the idea of women and rheumatic pain ever since he had translated a pamphlet by a Dr Ord entitled 'Hysterical Rheumatism of Women at a Critical period or in connection with certain Uterine derangements'. He considered the subject a particular speciality. Suffering from rheumatoid arthritis in one's twenties was unusual but not unheard of, and once under Brachet's care Ellen would have been constantly monitored through 'frequent analysis of the urine'. He was pretty certain rheumatoid arthritis was caused by 'uterine derangement', though neither of the two main culprits he suggests – difficult labour and 'time of life' – would have applied to her.

The two older Willmotts were no longer in any shape to go gallivanting around the French Alps, but Rose, still getting over the Maurice Berkeley unpleasantness, was keen to accompany her sister. The pair set out for Aix in 1889, on their own for the first time.[20] Young, excited and armed with chequebooks against newly vast reserves, they were ready to party, even if this time Ellen herself was going to venture inside one of those peculiar Punch & Judy booths. Letters tell us they followed Dr Brachet's advice: a first-class overnight 'rapid train', leaving Paris at 7 p.m. and arriving at Aix at 5.33 a.m., costing 71.65 francs.

We get something of the treatment itself through long, chatty missives sent to their parents by both girls. For those who could afford the tariff, the *douche-massage* was most efficacious undertaken in the mornings, leaving the rest of the day for fun, or at least to recover from the trauma. If some of the more intense treatments seem a bit 'out there' today, their mother's replies suggest it was pretty radical then, too. Admittedly, her husband had once consulted Dr Brachet, but he had never made it past the basic *douche-massage*.

The *douche-massage* was an Aix staple. A typical treatment would begin around 6 a.m. when the *curistes* started to arrive, swathed in hooded flannel robes and followed by servants loaded with sheets and towels from their hotels. The *Thermes* were owned by the government, who did not supply such fripperies. The 200-odd *doucheurs/doucheuses*[21] and other establishment staff were also employed by the French state.

---

20 Save for one servant, Clapton, whose services do not seem to have been up to scratch.

21 Professional washers.

In season,[22] the *Place des Thermes* first thing in the morning sounds like the Pump Rooms of Georgian Bath. The entrance halls were 'full of patients on their way to their bath or waiting to have a few words with their own particular medical adviser . . . friends of the bathers and numerous idlers swell the crowd and walking up and down or sitting on seats either within or without the entrance, reading, sketching or conversing is the order of the day; a pleasant hour many make of this general meeting time at Aix.'[ii] These were the highest-paying *curistes* and this would have been an excellent opportunity for two wealthy young women to make the 'right kind' of connections. Once inside, however, there was no escaping what the fashionably sick had really travelled here for. Docteur Brachet describes the douche itself:

> *The patient sits down on a wooden chair, with his feet in hot water, and one or two* doucheurs *or* doucheurs *propel jets of water all over the body, hottest of all on the feet and legs. Simultaneously, for several minutes, the* doucheurs *shampoo, rub and knead every part of the body, thus stimulating the capillary and general circulation; the temperature, strength and duration of the douches and shampooing are previously indicated by the doctor. Baths and douches are frequently 96 degrees.*

We don't have accounts of everything that Ellen underwent. Her letters back home unsurprisingly focus on nicer subjects such as the flowers she's seen or asking after the plants she's left behind. Of her treatment, both girls usually stick to the seemingly endless *douche-massages*. Ellie would eventually hire her own masseuse, for the more painful-sounding

---

22 Mid-spring to mid-autumn.

'dry' massages. Christine worked directly in Ellen's hotel room and was posh enough to take tea with the sisters afterwards. Rose would write to her mother while waiting for Christine to finish 'rubbing' Ellie. The postal system was fast enough[23] to send flowers home, including 'wild lilies of the valley, so sweet',[iii] presumably gathered early one morning while her sister was inside the *Thermes*.

Picture postcards from the time depict the *douche-massage* in full swing. Jolly 'patients' smile bravely at the camera, their heads sticking out of *Berthollet*[24] vapour baths that look like something out of Professor Branestawm's lab, against a backdrop of pristine, art nouveau-tiled, pipe-lined rooms. 'Come on in,' they seem to say, 'the water's fine. Honest.'

On top of the *douche-massage*, Ellen ingested sulphurous vapours, taken twice daily with two glasses of local *Challes* water, tinged with iodide of potassium, which she mentions several times as 'too horrid'.

Back in 1884, Léon Brachet had been experimenting with electricity. He had discovered that 'continuous currents are successfully employed in cases of chronic rheumatism', but it seems that by 1889 galvanic therapy wasn't the only weapon in his arsenal. Ellen underwent what would become the doctor's signature 'firing' treatment:

'Brachet heats over a spirit lamp an iron thicker than a lead pencil with a rounded end & when red hot he touches my back for 2 or 3 seconds each place. The object is to make a sore place which blisters & sticks . . . I have already 37 places & am to have many more. He does it over the sinews to loosen them eventually.'[iv]

Her mother was not convinced. As time wore on, Ellen began to weary of the constant douches, asking the doctor repeatedly when they might end. Both daughters relate an incident where she rebelled against having any more. Brachet, in full paternalistic mode, threatened to

---

23 When it worked. It was very irregular and letters often went astray.

24 Named for local chemist Claude Louis Berthollet who, by complete coincidence, accompanied Napoleon to Egypt.

telegraph her English doctor telling him he could no longer treat her.[v] Presumably he blamed her resistance on a deranged uterus rather than the multiplying lesions on her back.

Despite the scars and seemingly endless pummelling, the sisters' letters remain cheerful, and this is probably due to the rest of the *curistes'* day. Having been boiled, pounded, pumped full of purgative, fired to scarring, heated to 'an artificial fever' in an iron steam cabinet and prodded with electric probes, the patient was swaddled in sheets and blankets and discreetly deposited into a stripy sedan chair for transportation back to their hotel. There, the *curiste* would be swathed in even more blankets, then a quilt, and left to sweat out whatever was left of their will to live. After a prescribed amount of time they were unwrapped, rubbed down by an attendant and were finally free to enjoy the lunch of 'invalid' food directed by their physician.

Ellen eventually got used to the routine, and although her letters constantly talk of wanting to finish the course (Dr Brachet 'would not hear a word'),[vi] her protestations increasingly feel more like a case of impatience to get on with the Aix social life than misery over the pounding waters.

❃

The centre of Aix was compact and easily walkable. The sisters spent freely in milliners, dress shops, drapers, lace-makers, jewellers, florists, patisseries, bookstores, *many* antique and curiosity shops and photographic suppliers. When they ran out of money, they just went to the bank for more, though even then Rose found herself short and had to ask her father to send £20[25] to tide her over. There were parks to stroll, shady avenues for shelter in the 'sultry season', bandstands to pause by and cafés for refreshment with newly encountered acquaintances, or just to sit and write postcards.

---

25 Approx. £2,600.

The sisters had already 'done' Aix's tourist attractions with their parents years ago. Far more important now would have been learning about the town's movers and shakers. They could have a stab at socialising by attending the races, playing golf or trying their hand at pigeon shooting, but Brachet is clear: the best way for a *curiste* to establish themselves for the season is to visit a casino.

One needed to be personally introduced to join the *Casino Ancien Cercle*, built by subscription and non-profit making. All takings were ploughed directly back into the coffers by a terrifying-sounding committee, making the club even more glamorous and the season even more sparkling. A brand new, 700-seater theatre, 'elegant and commodious' had just been built. The *salle de jeux* (baccarat only; none of that vulgar roulette nonsense) was decorated with golden mosaics by Murano glassmaker Salviati, so extraordinary that Queen Victoria came specially to view them. Many of the great art nouveau buildings of Aix are lost, but that jewelled gaming hall glows in the afternoon sun like a Byzantine cathedral.

Once properly introduced, membership was forty francs per person, per season – a wise investment. For this the sisters could enjoy the reading room (with British and French daily newspapers), pavilions, terraces, talks in a dedicated lecture hall, a 'gallery' of ice cream, a world-class restaurant, a band playing twice a day in the gardens, and alternate performances of opera and classical concerts by the orchestra of the Châtelet, Paris, always very crowded. Sunday balls in the magnificent *salle des fêtes* always concluded with Rose's favourite, fireworks.

The *Cercle's* rival casino, *La Villa des Fleurs*, also 40f a season, provided similar amusements and spacious grounds, albeit a very little more downmarket, offering operettas, music hall and open-air theatre. The sisters took a belt and braces approach and joined both institutions. After all, not everyone was here to relieve their aches and pains or even to enjoy the spectacular views, and variety was the spice of Aix life.

Aix was a magnet for royalty. Queen Victoria visited three times, posing as 'the Countess of Balmoral' and fooling no one. The Emperor of Brazil, the King of Greece, the Prince of Monaco and hundreds of aristocrats descended so densely that, in season, the town became overrun with posh foreigners and French celebrities. Victor Hugo, Guy de Maupassant, Alexandre Dumas and Honoré de Balzac all spread the word; soon Americans were arriving too.

The Casino opened from 15 May to 1 October. Full dress balls were held on Thursdays and Sundays and there was music every other evening. Everybody went. Gentlemen of the medical profession and their wives enjoyed free admission, which was a good thing for Dr Brachet as the *Cercle* was otherwise strictly 'strangers only, no locals'. He may have introduced the Willmott sisters to the Aix ex-pat community; more likely, all he needed to do was introduce them to one person.

Lady Harriet Whalley was such a character she even merits an entry in Brachet's guidebook. Not-very-subtly anonymised as the 'Hon. Lady W—' she had, for many years, been the gracious hostess of some of Aix's finest hospitality, and although less active since being widowed in 1883, was still a force to be reckoned with. The only description I can find of this elderly Irish *salonnière* is in Queen Victoria's diaries. Their first meeting, Thursday, 9 April 1885, was rather less than sparkling: Victoria was taken aback to find her would-be hostess had only just got out of bed. This is hardly surprising given the Queen seems to have arrived exceptionally early and without notice, walked straight into the *Maison du Diable*[26] and taken herself upstairs to enjoy the view of the *Dent du Chat* mountain. Lady Whalley, 'a nice looking, lively old lady of past 70', wandered in and 'nearly dropped' at the sight of Queen Victoria standing in her drawing room. Gamely, Lady W rallied, and invited the Queen to her boudoir, where there was an even better vista. Her Majesty did some sketching then left, leaving the old lady wondering what had just happened. It's possible that, once again, Dr Brachet was

---

26 There are at least three legends as to how Lady Whalley's house got its name. They involve a forsaken shepherdess, a cunning pilgrim and lazy housebuilder prepared to exchange his soul for a day's work by the devil.

responsible for the incident, since he orchestrated the Queen's itinerary ('he is the leading doctor here, and has been most civil and obliging in arranging everything for me').[vii] Perhaps he said something like, 'Oh, you must drop in on Lady Whalley, she'd love to meet you', and the Queen took him at his word. To be fair, his instinct would have been correct; the women became firm friends.

Ellen and Rose Willmott hit it off with this indefatigable *grande dame* too. She clearly enjoyed having young folk to show around; for the sisters, missing their mother on a daily basis and still mourning the Countess Tasker, she was a comforting figure who could guide them through Aix's giddy social calendar. Ellie and Rosey saw her on an almost-daily basis, visiting all the best people and seeing the finest shows. She made a useful chaperone; unmarried women 'on their own' at formal events was hardly a savoury state of affairs. With Lady Whalley as their guide the sisters could go to concerts, balls and soirées, secure in the knowledge that they could be introduced to anyone: prince or . . . painter.

For Ellen Willmott, meeting Alfred Parsons would have been as thrilling as encountering any monarch. The young artist, no stranger to Aix, had just won both gold and silver at the 1889 Paris Exhibition, but Ellie and Rosey would know him better for his exquisite woodcuts in the ground-breaking 1883 illustrated edition of William Robinson's classic, *The Wild Garden*. Garden books had carried the odd illustration before, but the sheer quality, accuracy – and relevance – of Parsons' engravings marked a step change in publishing. He had continued to work with Robinson on a regular basis in *The Garden* and *Gardens Illustrated*; for the Willmott sisters, Parsons *was* royalty.

And then there were the afternoon outings. Gentle, open-air exercise was considered essential for recovery, and Léon Brachet's guidebook includes a wide overview of the local countryside and tourist outings including mountain ascents, grottoes, picturesque villages and alpine valleys. He includes maps and travel options: carriages, horses and donkeys that could be hired by the day, month or just the hour, and though he mentions omnibuses and charabanc outings, it seems unlikely any of his patients would stoop to such plebeian activities. For his best guests, the doctor went one better. He and his wife Nelly invited crowned heads of Europe to their home; Ellen and Rose he personally escorted on daytrips. This was no one-time, keep-the-punters-happy courtesy, either. Brachet took the sisters out on a regular basis, sometimes on social calls but, just as often, knowing their love for horticulture, deep into the mountains and valleys to go plant hunting.

However much Ellie and Rose were enjoying Aix's social carousel, gardening was never far from either of their minds. Their letters constantly ask after the Warley garden, rejoicing (a little insensitively) when it rains at home, and making suggestions for improvements. The girls froth with the plants they have seen in the hedgerows: 'the woodruff is in blossom, so lovely with the wild alliums'[viii] and, when they might survive at Warley, the roots they have collected.

'Today I sent home a large box by post of firm roots of that tiny white water-lily with small leaves,' writes Ellen. 'I thought Preece could put a nice packet tied up in a fish basket or bit of canvas with some stones in it & sink it in the pond where our rose walk leads to.' She is confident enough of her horticultural expertise to send no-nonsense instructions for the family's new head gardener,[27] insisting that the roots be contained rather than just chucking the lot in the pond. 'It is a horrid way I hate & seldom works in spite of what they say.'[ix] The sisters sent industrial quantities of purchased plants home, too: 'I am sending boxes of that lovely verbena home. I hope enough for a bed by the Rosary.'[x][28]

It is clear from their letters, however, that a great number of plants the sisters were finding would not do well at home. As they fell deeper in love with the French Alps – to the point where their father was teasing

---

27 Hired in 1890, James Preece arrived from the Wernher family estate at Luton Hoo.

28 The rosary was a rose-covered pergola at Warley. The area next to it was 'for carpet bedding' – a tiny area kept formal for their father's benefit.

them for an overuse of superlatives – hotel life was beginning to cramp their style, and Ellie's long-term prognosis was not encouraging.

Dr Brachet is refreshingly honest about what his methods are capable of achieving. 'We must not lose sight of the fact that rheumatoid arthritis is essentially a slow but progressive disease,' he writes. 'A few weeks' treatment cannot be relied on to produce a permanent cure.' Ellen's condition *was* improving, but it would only ever be a temporary fix. As soon as she stopped taking those *douche-massages* her limbs would stiffen again, and the rheumatism she had watched cripple her mother's body would return to her own. Aix was going to be part of her life, and the idea of finding somewhere permanent was beginning to germinate in both sisters' minds. Perhaps it is uncharitable to suggest that Léon Brachet had the long-term patronage of one of his best-paying patients in mind when he first took the sisters to further inspect the picturesque village of Tresserve. There is no denying, however, that this most fashionable of suburbs was stunningly beautiful. Perfect, in fact, for anyone who might be interested in creating a spectacular new garden on its sun-drenched slopes.

Chapter Six:

Tresserve

AN ORANGE TREE

Alone, but proud, in a galvanised, creeper-strewn pot on a sun-kissed alpine terrace, this miniature citrus plant has been grown with obvious care. Its dense, tiny leaves are speckled with fragrant, star-shaped blossoms; it also bears several tiny fruit.

DURING THE SECOND part of her reign, Queen Victoria was not quite as popular as we might imagine today. Her subjects hardly saw her. Constantly in mourning and unwilling to take part in official events, she was a shadow; rarely glimpsed and, some began to whisper, poor value as a monarch. She would have been even less visible had her grand plan to move to France materialised.

Perhaps she first fell in love with Tresserve that awkward morning in 1885 when she barged into Lady Whalley's house without a by-your-leave. By 1887, however, she was so enamoured of the picturesque alpine village that she started acquiring land there like it was going out of fashion. Of course, the more she purchased the more fashionable it became. Gentry fell over themselves to buy there too and the suburb became something of a housing bubble. Even the proposed building site was a tourist attraction; the Willmott family went for a gawp in 1888, Fred noting even then, 'Ellie is rather sweet upon it.'[i]

There was an obstacle facing Queen Victoria's plans, however. An elderly local woman living in between the patchwork parcels of the Queen's land refused to sell, however much cash she was offered. Victoria, unused to being denied anything, was furious. The project faltered; the situation stagnated.

By autumn 1889, Ellie and Rosey, aged thirty-one and twenty-eight respectively, were visiting Tresserve every day. Each time they reached the brow of the hill, the *coup de foudre* struck again. High above Aix, the sleepy suburb looked out at the sparkling lake below. Grey-shaded, misty mountains slumbered in the distance. Golden leaves and brimming garden potagers turned the hillside to a shimmering rainbow. Ellie's photographs reveal a bucolic world of smiling French peasants, brim-hatted padres and cute children posing by thatched barns, chatting in lanes, spinning tough mountain wool in the shade of rock-lined cave entrances and gathering water from natural springs. Log piles, shuttered windows, vine-covered eaves and rickety outdoor stairways were standard features of Tresserve's solid, winter-proof dwellings, clinging to the late-season mountainside.

Thanks to a nudge from Dr Brachet, the sisters' eyes alighted on an unoccupied, single-storey 'cottage' currently owned by Parisian restaurateurs Jacques and Marie-Françoise Daudens. Perhaps Ellie and Rosey even sighed a little over it – after all, the views of the *Dent du Chat* would be even more spectacular from the 'Daudens villa' – and look at all that land, rolling gently down towards the lake! What kind of a garden could be fashioned there? What rare plants could be grown? What vineyards? What borders? What if they followed in the footsteps of Josephine Bonaparte herself and created a rose garden, like the world-famous *rosaraie* the empress built at Malmaison?

We don't know when Ellen Willmott acquired her copy of the ultra-rare *Les Roses* by Belgian artist Pierre-Joseph Redouté but she would certainly have known the work by 1889.[29] Redouté spent years painting botanically accurate watercolours of Empress Josephine's rose collection. The three resulting volumes, published between 1817 and 1824, are exquisite: one variety per page spread, with descriptions by C.A. Thory. Could a spark have fired in Ellen Willmott's imagination even as she met Alfred Parsons at the *Cercle*? Like Redouté, Parsons painted exquisite botanical portraits; perhaps she could be the C.A. Thory to his P-J Redouté? It was a nice dream.

In early 1890 the dream – of Tresserve at least – seemed within the sisters' grasp. Brachet gave them what was probably a confidential letter

---

29 She also owned at least two Redouté originals.

from Mme Daudens, telling the Doctor her villa was for sale. A couple of years beforehand it would have realised an astronomical price, but with Queen Victoria thwarted in her bid to build her palace, there were now few aristocratic takers.

Ellie and Rosey's letters from May 1890 fizz with excitement. Perhaps surprisingly, given his former zeal for land purchase, Fred Willmott was less keen. It seems strange today that two mature women should require permission to spend their own money, but Ellen and Rose are clear: they will not buy their perfect, fantasy villa if their father disapproves. Of course, they have no plans of allowing him to do any such thing. The pair of them wage a subtle war of attrition, triangulating attacks, isolating their enemy and finally crushing all-comers in a devastating pincer-movement.

The initiating letter is lost, but of the extant material, they begin by making sure their parents know their hotel this year is very substandard. M. Bernascon has been forced to let 'awful' people have their regular rooms ('the father has a nose like Fr. Mac's,[30] multiplied by 12', writes Rosey),[ii] and although the hotelier has tried to make up for it by giving them the royal apartments, *they* are upstairs – and they *must* bear in mind poor Ellie's back. The multiple staircases at Warley are quietly forgotten. Rose solicitously informs their worried parents: 'I fancy Dr Brachet means to keep her [Ellen] longer, though he is being very careful not to say so exactly.'[iii] For a couple of days, the sisters make subtle references to 'the Daudens Villa', just happening to mention all the influential, titled people who have seen it and think it's a great bargain. Rose throws in a reassuring 'father figure' endorsement: 'Ellie & I went up to Tresserve yesterday & inspected the Villa with Dr Brachet who was charmed with it, he thinks it a good investment.'[iv]

Ellie chimes in with her two penn'orth: 'He went all over the

---

[30] Perhaps Father Macdonald, the maybe-drunken priest from the Warley Place garden party.

TRESSERVE

Daudens Villa & was delighted with it all. He says that at the very least it would pay us 2½ per cent, that is after paying the taxes etc.'[v]

Rosey finishes the day's onslaught. 'We certainly should very much like to have it, if Papa does not think it too stupid, but I really think if he were here & went into the details as Dr Brachet is doing, he would not think it unwise,' adding, 'but of course if he does object very much we will not do anything about it.'[vi]

The letters continue in a similar vein for several days: 'If only you could have been there this afternoon you would have been so charmed with it . . . You cannot imagine how heavenly and exquisite the garden is . . . Lady Charleville was enchanted with it . . . and is thinking of buying or renting at Tresserve . . . People up there yesterday again who said they were going to buy it . . . I am sure there would not be the least difficulty in selling it again . . . We are so anxious about our answer from Papa.'

Disaster.

'Of course, we were awfully disappointed at Papa's answer, although we do see he is quite right under the circumstances,' wrote Ellen on 8 May. The 'circumstances' are lost, though it looks as though Fred Willmott thought there would be too many repairs needed on the ageing, long-empty property. The sisters are not downhearted, however, because they have a new wheeze. Monsieur Bernascon the hotelier will buy the place and rent it to Ellie and Rosey with the option to buy. Obviously, if this happens, they'll have to pay tax twice which *surely* isn't efficient . . .

No, even this won't work. Ellie writes again: 'There is not nearly so much to do as you seem to think & now M. Daudens has come down in price, Dr Brachet thinks it cheap & he thinks it is the very best view over Aix . . . we shall be so sorry if we cannot have it. We would be so careful & not spend anything until the money was sent.'

Eventually the sisters let poor Fred have it with both barrels. Ellen writes to her mother 'a little private word' to warn her they will both be writing to their father the next day, and to ask for her connivance in buttering him up for when the letters arrive. Ellie knows her mother's Achilles' heel: 'you would like it so to go in a Bath chair about the garden'.[vii]

Resistance was futile. On Thursday, 15 May 1890, Ellen was finally able to write to her mother: 'We both do not know what to do for joy, how we should hug you if only we were together.' A few days later she and Rosey walked to Tresserve, which 'has never seemed so lovely as it does now & our garden too'.[viii]

They had done it. Together, as they always had been. Rose's letters are just as plant-mad, just as crazy for Tresserve as Ellen's. Neither ever actually articulates, in as many words, the desire to remain single together and become spinster-sister gardeners at Tresserve, but the implication is there. Young men, from their letters, at least, are a distant memory; at Aix the sisters are socialising with older people anyway: religious folk, celebrities and nobility. They are completely content in each other's company, each with as profound a passion for horticulture as the other. Every garden book will tell you that Ellen Willmott bought Tresserve. She didn't. I have never seen the deeds, if they even still exist, but it is clear from these (and later) letters, invoices and newspaper articles that both sisters bought the villa at Tresserve together. It cost 50,000 francs. All that fuss over what was essentially one year's worth of birthday money each.

Fred Willmott was right in one respect: the place needed a makeover. Given how 'perfect' the sisters had considered the villa before they bought it, it's surprising just how much work was essential to make it 'habitable'. After rejecting every stick of furniture that came with the pile, the sisters brought in Jules Pin, Aix's town architect, to remodel the place. Pin added a covered, colonnaded veranda to frame the best views across the Lac du Bourget, knocked together two already-large rooms to create a gigantic salon, built a whole new storey, then put extra rooms in the roof, turning the Daudens' holiday cottage into a ten-bedroom palace.[31] Oh, and he added a fake sixteenth-century tower, based on one Ellen had admired in Aix.

Extensive shopping was necessary for the interior. Ellie, a big fan of William Morris's Arts & Crafts movement, wanted a romantic look. She gave the whole thing a 'rustic' whitewash and bought alpine furniture from various Swiss antiques dealers found by Henry Correvon, mixing it with Louis XV and XVI suites for a fantasy 'French' melange. Everything, rugs to guest towels, was of the finest possible quality, keeping merchants happy far and wide. She installed a second music room to house the overflow from her ever-burgeoning Warley collection of priceless instruments, and a library dedicated to Napoleon-related volumes. The villa's regular library included a 28-volume dictionary. The remodel took three years, during which work began on the main event: Tresserve's new garden.

While still actively collecting plants for her alpine ravine in Essex, Ellen had something unique in mind for Tresserve: her own personal interpretation of a French *jardin*, filtered through William Robinson-style wild gardening, punctuated with moments of sharp formality and odd quirky things she'd been unable to resist along the way. There was, seemingly, no overall grand design. Certainly none survives. The garden developed organically; in that respect, it fits the Ellen Willmott 'brand' perfectly. Notebooks turn up on a regular basis, their undated pages hastily scribbled in pencil, along with dozens of plant lists, some labelled 'desiderata', some typed, some just scrawled on the backs of envelopes. Which garden the jottings relate to, where the plants went or how they were grown is usually a mystery.

Much like Warley, Tresserve was on a steep hill. A true gardener's gardener, one of Ellen's first improvements was installing an irrigation system, unglamorous but essential, as was a heated greenhouse against the region's frozen winters. The Daudens' elderly fruit trees had to go,

---

31 The history of this extraordinary building is recounted in Geneviève Frieh-Giraud, *La Marie de Tresserve: demeure et jardin d'Ellen Willmott* (Association pour la Sauvegarde du Patrimoine de Tresserve, 2012).

but Ellen kept the grapevine-draped pergola. More vines were installed in traditional rows, in gleeful anticipation of evenings at Warley uncorking Willmott own-brand estate wine. A gentle, winding pathway led down the hill to a broad avenue of fifty-seven plane trees, 'terracing' the garden as it meandered. The estate wall was rebuilt, including an immense roofed gateway, with a small wicket door for secret escapes to the lake.

Part of the estate became an arboretum for trees Ellen had been unable to grow at Warley while three further pergolas gave Tresserve its unmistakable 'look'. A small, rustic 'tunnel' at the bottom of the hill frothed with climbing roses and more vines; at the top, nestling into a retaining wall, another walkway groaned with extraordinary, ornamental squashes. The largest of all, deep, shady and edged with high-built beds of trailing treasures, boasted thirty-three arches covered with roses, wisteria and clematis. At various points Ellen installed pausing points: a rustic log bench; an eye-catcher at the end of an avenue; a circular seat girdling one of the larger trees. Two wells were given a wrought-iron makeover and a colonnaded surround, while a little thatched hut of trelliswork, clothed in clematis, provided shade and refreshment for visitors. Ellen couldn't resist another log cabin, and while this time there were no claims to Napoleonic fame, she did surround it with Swiss rarities supplied by M. Correvon.

The Tresserve garden was Ellie Willmott 'at play'. Warley was tranquil, silent, studious, serious. In France she could delight in candid shots of Head Gardener Claude Meunier working with his team, watched by his children. Meunier would stay for thirty years, marshalling his men as they pruned trees, picked apples and preened Tresserve's gravel-lined paths, unencumbered by the rigid uniform Warley's gardeners had to wear.

In one respect the two gardens were the same. They were both crammed fuller with plants than any sane gardener would have attempted. If Ellen Willmott was overspending in Essex, it was nothing to the bonanza the nurseries of France now enjoyed. Letters, catalogues and receipts show her purchasing from over fifty French suppliers, and that's not counting the many vendors from Germany, Italy, Switzerland, Netherlands and even further afield.

For all its avenues, pergolas, potagers, shady walks and secluded rest-points, Tresserve was, first and foremost, an experiment: Ellen Willmott's chance to build collections of her favourite plants. Many she couldn't hope to grow in the chilly climes of Essex; others she wanted to observe on a scientific basis, comparing and contrasting their progress in two different situations. These were mainly plants that did particularly well in one short window of the alpine year, May and June, so she could visit at the garden's zenith. She began seriously collecting irises, tulips, clematis – and roses, inspired by Her Imperial Highness's aforementioned legendary garden at Malmaison.

Ah, Josephine. The first non-scientific horticulturist to dedicate an entire garden to one kind of plant – the rose – yet all we remember her for today is an apocryphal tale of bedroom rebuffal. The empress was obsessed with roses. Even during the Napoleonic Wars, merchants were issued special passports and safe passage through blockades so they could continue supplying Malmaison with novelties.[ix] Not that we have much idea of what it looked like. Pierre Redouté, for all his pitch-perfect renderings of individual varieties in the empress's *rosaraie*, failed to come up with one sketch of the site itself.[32] Josephine wanted an example of every known rose in the world and became patron to several international plant-hunting expeditions. As well as collecting she was at the forefront of breeding programmes and experiments to perfect the art of grafting. By 1813, she held nearly 200 varieties, starting a craze that continued long after her death. In 1830, Paris nurseries could supply more than 2,500 types of rose.

After Josephine's death in 1814, her beloved *rosaraie* fell into

---

32 There is one rough sketch, by someone else, of a cross-formation.

disrepair, was looted of its rare plants by all and sundry and left to descend into ruin. Ellen must have shuddered at the thought. What a horrible end. There was still Redouté's book, however, and Miss Willmott had money to burn.

At Tresserve, she concentrated solely on French roses; unlike her heroine, she had a garden in England for the British equivalent. Begun in 1893, and honed with the advice and approval of legendary rosarian Jules Gravereaux,[33] it was Ellen's *rosaraie* most visitors came to experience. By 1904, her friend J. V. Viviand-Morel would write that her French garden held more than 12,000 roses of over 900 varieties, including thirty-three very non-William-Robinson-friendly nursery rows of works-in-progress for scientific observation.

But among all these roses, where is the real Rose? The sisters' letters are clear: Tresserve was 'ours', and receipts for the initial alterations were sent to *Mesdemoiselles Willmott*. But after that the bills – from furniture and decorations to antiques and plants – always seem to be addressed to Ellen. In truth, Rose had already taken her eye off the ball.

If relations had been a bit delicate with the Berkeley family immediately after the 'Maurice incident', Ellie and Rosey at least remained friends with Maud. The three women would meet up in London and, gradually, the circle widened, including Maud's other brothers. Once again Rose's sweet demeanour attracted attention – and a proposal. This time her suitor was no younger son, but the heir himself. Three years earlier, Robert Valentine Berkeley's[34] solemn charms were probably overshadowed by the younger lads' boisterous fun – he is not the one covered in shaving foam in Ellen's photographs – but now his quiet ways seem to have mirrored those of the more serious Willmott sister. For Rose the proposal was a major social step up, but this was no

---

[33] Gravereaux would later recreate the Empress Josephine's rose collection at Malmaison.

[34] To avoid confusion with two other Robert Berkeleys that crop up in this book, I'll usually refer to Rose's husband as Robert Valentine.

angling trip; the relationship was a straight, mature, and ultimately, an enduring, love match.

This time Frederick Willmott couldn't have been more excited. He made as big a splash as possible in announcing the engagement. The *Tablet*, 27 June 1891, told the entire Roman Catholic universe that the marriage of Mr R. V. Berkeley and Miss R. Willmott would take place on 20 August that year. It did not mention that that date would be one day after the chief bridesmaid turned a very spinsterish thirty-three.

The *Tablet* also describes Rose's grand society wedding, held in the new, palm leaf-filled Catholic church at Warley. The report takes up almost one and a half of the journal's broadsheet-sized pages and, on the surface, everything looks very glamorous. The bride, glowing in rich ivory brocade and rare old Venetian lace, was unadorned by jewellery but carried 'an exquisite posy of white flowers with real orange blossom'. Her eight bridesmaids, in cream bengaline and gold trim, each sported badges of the Berkeley family fashioned in gold, with the bride and groom's initials in diamonds. As second son, poor Maurice Berkeley was obliged to perform the unenviable role of Best Man for his brother. His gift – a mustard pot – shows little enthusiasm for the union. It wasn't even the only one. Among the dozens of duplicate salt cellars, sugar dredgers, muffin trays, grape scissors and elephant tusks, the couple received three such vessels.

The gushing description in the *Tablet* would not have dared to mention any tension there might have been at the match. Indeed, there is nothing written down anywhere that could imply things might not be completely wonderful. Like so much non-traditional history, we have to look at what's *not* there to uncover a possible alternative story.

Several prints show the happy couple returning to Spetchley Park from honeymoon, the mansion's great portico decked out with flowers and swags and banners. Afterwards, however, there is a 'strangeness' in the air. Rose is never again listed as attending family celebrations, weddings, christenings or funerals; neither does she appear in any group photos. Her husband and children attend only rarely. Her letters are also odd. 'Something' is going on, leaving "poor Rosey" tired, ill and strained, but it is hard to know exactly what. Ellen already knows the situation and does not need it spelled out. Only with the chance discovery of a letter held by the Roman Catholic Archdiocese of Birmingham does the story finally begin to emerge.

Writing to his bishop in 1893, Monsignor Francis J. Weld is keen to explain the truth behind some very unpleasant local gossip: that Mr Robert Valentine Berkeley has thrown his parents out of Spetchley Park. Weld explains that for the past eighteen years Mr Berkeley Snr and Lady Catherine have been spending wildly beyond their means, to the tune of £25,000 (£2, 476,000 today). Their son bailed them out but they continued to run up new debts. Mr B offered to leave Spetchley, on condition Robert Valentine paid off these bills, too, and give his parents £2,000 (£198,000) a year. He agreed, but they then refused to go.

By 1891 Frederick Willmott was also helping pay the Berkeleys' creditors, a situation that "no doubt hastened the death of Mr Willmott". Eventually Mr B realised he would indeed have to go. He asked his son to pay his new debts, continue the £2,000 a year and make annuities for the rest of his nine children. The only way Robert Valentine could do this was by using Rose's money. "He and his wife will be for a long time in very straightened circumstances," sighs the monsignor. To add insult to injury, Rose and Robert's names are by now the proverbial mud across the county - "he has received most disagreeable communications" - meaning they cannot even live at Spetchley themselves.

What does all this mean for Ellen? In the short term, it was rather good. While one thing was certain: there would be no spinster-sister gardening team now, her beloved sister was at least going to stay in Essex for the foreseeable future. Fred Willmott bought Warley Lea, the estate across the road from Warley Place, and commissioned young up-and-coming architect Edwin Lutyens to gussy it up for the young couple.

In a poignant, single glass-plate positive, Ellen captures the little wooden gate through which the sisters could visit each other in under five minutes, via a handy 'secret' path between their homes. It is an unusual shot, in that there would normally be no reason to take a picture of a simple picket gate in a hedge, yet the tenderness with which the camera captures this unassuming corner of the estate is touching. The place conjures a sweet melancholy, even today. Once a fragrant meander through the old orchard garden to a charming country lane, it is now a forgotten bit of broken perimeter fencing that spews intruders back out onto a busy road after ripping them to shreds on hidden barbed wire.

Mrs Berkeley had her own life now. She had a house to manage, servants to instruct, a garden to keep and, in time perhaps, children to take the place of a beloved sister. Miss Willmott was an 'old maid', still living with her parents. Audrey le Lièvre tells us that at the end of the wedding reception Ellen realised she was still holding some orange blossom from Rosey's bouquet, and set about finding a vessel to pot it up into, perhaps as something to do. She also tells us the cutting took. I hope both statements are true. There do seem to be a lot of photographs of one particular container-grown, miniature orange tree, growing alone on the terrace at Tresserve . . .

As her sister disappeared off to a Continental honeymoon in a dress of fawn cloth and hat trimmed with pink roses, Ellen did what any young woman might do on being left by her best friend: she bought a lathe.

Chapter Seven:
The Greasy Pole

A DAFFODIL BULB

Smooth, fat, firm, round, and of a deep, rich, chestnut brown, this fine narcissus hybrid is already the result of years of hard graft. With overlapping white petals and a golden, lightly frilled trumpet it has the makings of a potentially perfect specimen. It is already earmarked for the RHS exhibition bench – perhaps as early as 1897. Any winner of that all-important First Class Certificate can be worth a fortune. It may even – eventually – be brought within the pocket of horticulture's latest amateur: the daffodil enthusiast.

TODAY, THE MOST popular time of year to visit Warley Place is the same as it was in its prime: March and April, when hundreds of thousands of daffodils cloak its valleys, banks and meadows with a haze of yellow. Daffodils, narcissi – the words are more or less synonymous – disappear back into the soil once they've flowered, which accounts for fewer of them having been looted after 1935, when so many of Warley's horticultural treasures found their way into light-fingered gardeners' wheelbarrows.

We delight in this vista of massed golden glory, but the Victorians would have still been gape-mouthed at the novelty of narcissi in a garden at all. In the mid-nineteenth century the humble 'Lent lily' had been just that – humble. It was delightful enough encountered while wandering the countryside, lonely as a cloud but, pale and unassuming, hardly something fashionable gardeners wanted alongside the gaudy exotics in their formal beds. It never completely went away – there would always be the odd daffodil-fancying enthusiast – but narcissi hybridisation is not for the impatient. Even now it still takes around twelve years to coax a new variety from promising seedling to commercially viable specimen. There is something uniquely joyful about anything so beautiful, so early in the year, though, and when daffodils were 'rediscovered' in the 1880s with crisp new strains, clean colours – and eye-watering prices – they were a sensation. For Ellen Willmott they would become an obsession.

It wasn't her first of course. She still adored her alpine ravine, and spent hours practising her various musical instruments. She'd bought an Amati violin from W. H. Hill & Sons in 1885, only thinking to actually take a lesson ten days later. In 1890 she bought a viola, then a cello, then another violin, completing her own Amati quartet.[35] Ellie's softly atmospheric photos of candlelit musical soirées depict Rose and friends playing the various viols, pianos and, most often, Princess Amelia's harpsichord.

Then there was the lathe. Okay, I'll own up. Ellen didn't buy it immediately after the wedding – she'd actually acquired it in March that year – but her reason for purchase would have been the same. Robert Berkeley encroached on more and more of her sister's time, and there was nothing that took one's mind off unwelcome change like an expensive new hobby to be equipped, mastered and added to the roster. As usual, she bought only the best, a Holtzapffel, costing £425 (more than £55,000 today).

Ellen Willmott was no hobby-butterfly, alighting on one craze, buying all the kit, attaining a certain competence then moving on. She kept and used that lathe for years. It's more useful to imagine her as an insatiable snowball of curiosity, sweeping up and enveloping skills, interests, memberships, friendships and collections as she rolled through life. One passion layered into the next, sparking a whole new avenue of enquiry, fascination and, on occasion, obsession. Thanks to her turning, for example, she started collecting antique carpentry and farriers' tools. Why not, she collected everything else.

What Ellen really did after her sister's wedding was rather more predictable: she launched herself back into gardening. At Warley, yes, but also in France, where she determined to make Tresserve the paradise she and Rosey had dreamed of. She worked alongside her staff, getting to know every inch of the terrain, fathoming which situations and which soils were best for which plants, laying groundwork for the future collections she was already beginning to dream of. She was not always alone; the new Mr and Mrs Berkeley turned up on more than

---

35 I have not found proof that Ellen ever owned her rumoured Stradivarius – indeed, she appears to have chosen her first Amati over an offered Strad because it sounded better.

one occasion. Her parents also made the bumpy journey to see what was going on at the villa. Mr Willmott in particular would have been eager to know if his daughters had bought a turkey.

He can't have been too horrified. Fred Willmott's collector instincts had always involved land. His bid to turn Warley Place into a proper 'estate' had continued with the sizeable Headley Garden, close to Rose and Robert's new 'cottage' and liberating Warley's walled garden from kitchen-supply duties. Well Mead, near his projected Home Farm, would be perfect for growing-on collections of rare and expensive plants. He also acquired cottages, gardens and other buildings in the village as they came onto the market, useful for housing Warley's ever-growing staff. Not bad for a lad who'd grown up over a shop in the Borough.

He would not enjoy his purchases for long. On 22 August 1892, missing his first grandchild by four days, Frederick Willmott died. Although he hadn't been well for some time, his death was unexpected and threw the family badly out of kilter. Amid the chaos of a new baby (named Eleanor so as not to have three Ellens in the family), Fred's obituary took considerably less space in the *Tablet* than Rose's wedding the previous year, yet in many ways he was the embodiment of the Victorian ideal: the man who had pulled himself out of the Borough, moved out to the country, provided wealth for his family and ensured a daughter married into the aristocracy. Frederick Willmott was buried at Brentwood Cathedral, a mark of his rise to respectability. Right by the house, where every visitor, however scathing of 'the old ways' would see it, Ellen always kept the formal carpet bedding her father loved, in his memory.

Henry Correvon visited often – her mentor, advisor and friend; even, perhaps, a replacement father figure. One of the reasons he and Ellen got on so well was that while he respected and admired his protégée, he could also stand up to her without being patronising. He wrote his honest, not always complimentary opinions of her planting decisions, knowing she would make her own choices, and that was okay.

In many ways, though, Willmott was Correvon's confidante, too, as one of the few people who knew about his money problems. He introduced her to (usually all-male) specialist alpine and botanical societies. *She* introduced *him* to wealthy potential customers and became a high-rolling client herself. It's often related how Correvon admonished her for recklessly ordering some of the more common plants from him rather than more easily (and much more cheaply) obtaining them from British suppliers. I don't think she was that naïve. While she had money, Ellen Willmott was generous, both with charitable donations[36] and to her friends. Purchasing plants by the 10,000 was both advantageous to her grand ambitions and a discreet way to help the nurserymen she relied on to make her gardens true centres of excellence.

One of the things Correvon loved so much about Ellen's alpine ravine was that, unlike most British rock gardens, the visitor wasn't just dumped into it from out of nowhere, but introduced to the concept through a meadow bursting with thousands of bulbs which, little by little, were joined by horticulture's latest sensation.

In a miniature version of seventeenth-century tulip fever, narcissus bulbs had started changing hands for ridiculous sums. By the 1890s a single bulb might easily fetch £30 (around £4,000); some went for far more. A daffodil bulb was an investment. It was not just an object of reverence in itself, or even a promise of immense, rare beauty, the horticultural equivalent of an Old Master. Bulked-up, it had commercial potential, especially in the bull market of the 1890s, but it was also a risk. Bulbs could desiccate, rot, become battered by storms, eaten by pests or, on occasion, turn out not to be the prized variety at all, substituted for a regular, run-of-the-mill daff, either by accident or downright chicanery. Sharp practices sprang up, from innocent-sounding 'amateur lady gardeners' advertising 'rarities' in the back pages of newspapers and

---

36 In 1892, in true Countess Tasker style, she and Rose dedicated a side-chapel in Prior Park College, Bath.

dispatching bog-standard rubbish, to breeders pretending to 'exclusively' sell someone their entire stock of a particular variety only for it to turn up in someone else's garden and instantly plummet in value. It wasn't just dodgy nurseries, either. Irish plantswoman Frances Currey, one of the few female professionals, complained to her friend Ellen Willmott of head gardeners demanding commission for placing orders with certain nurseries. These chaps might find themselves 'unable to grow' bulbs purchased by their employers from places that hadn't supplied the necessary kickback. Against such odds, narcissists (not the official term but too delicious to resist and sometimes only too apposite) would sometimes form syndicates to spread the risk between both their pockets and their often variable growing conditions.

For all its hazards this horticultural Wild West was exciting. Daffodils had everything: big money, big stakes, big rewards and big characters: passionate, dedicated and bitchy. A disproportionate number of the biggest names were clergymen, but this does not seem to have stopped them from falling out with each other at the drop of a wide-brimmed hat. Sometimes disagreements spilled over into the gardening magazines, more often it was kept to snippy comments and 'private words' in letters between 'friends'.

❀

Every spring, the entire population of Tresserve would gather for a free show as the Willmott villa opened for the season. The housekeeper, Claude Meunier's sister, Gasparine, would meet the Willmott family butler, who travelled ahead by train with vast amounts of baggage. James Riches Robinson was fresh from Alnwick Castle. He'd been seeking a post where he could marry his sweetheart of three years – when he could afford to, which he estimated would be in about four years' time – and hoped for a position that might eventually include a cottage. Mrs Willmott had taken pity on his plight and, in what would turn out to be an inspired move, hired this capable, humane man in

1891. Robinson's was a skilled job that ranged from overseeing a liveried household staff of around fourteen in Essex to fitting in with a largely French team at Tresserve.

The 1890s gossip magazine *The Gentlewoman* kept close pegs on what was happening at the fashionable 'foreign' resorts, noting any rising stars. On 2 June 1894, 'The Gentlewoman Abroad' section lists around thirty gentry of note newly arrived at Aix-les-Bains. Of all the lords, ladies and dukes, only 'Mrs Berkeley and her sister Miss Willmott' get a paragraph to themselves. The columnist confides:

'The two last-named ladies, with whom Lady Henry Grosvenor is at present staying, do a great deal of entertaining at their villa on the hill overlooking Cape Bourget, and they had a large afternoon party there on Thursday, to celebrate the birthday of the Queen.'

The article goes on to whisper about the present state of Victoria's stalled construction plans. 'A notice, *"Terrain à vendre"*, indicates that the Queen is prepared to sell it, and one hardly knows whether to be amused or disgusted at the stupid greed of the local people which has defeated itself by preventing the Queen from building.'

Fascinating though any royal gossip may be, *The Gentlewoman* is more revealing in its casual recognition of the sisters' new relative positions: 'Mrs Berkeley and her sister, Miss Willmott.' Rose, despite being the younger sister, now takes precedence for being married.[37] Back in 1889, Lady Whalley had had to ease her charges into the British clique. Now Rose had married a Berkeley, though Ellen kept up in another way, in creating a garden everyone was talking about. Down at the Casino, the *Cercle*, in all its snobbery, was theirs for the taking. Once acquired, however, the bauble of popularity seemed less sparkling. Ellen happily met with the ever-changing social whirl, and kept up good relations with M. Bernascon, the hotelier, who was also coming up in the world. She still went to the opera, theatre, concerts and balls, but more and

---

37 It's also the only instance I have ever seen the sisters' villa at Tresserve named: 'Maisonette'.

more she was only seen in town on rainy days, when the gardening was less good. Society could come to her.

Ellen now lived the rhythm of the countryside, often getting up at 5 a.m. and working until she conked out, mid-evening. It was said she knew the whereabouts and current condition of every plant. While she was away from one of her gardens, the other was expected to send a daily update of what was happening on the ground. Eventually she bought a printing press[38] and supplied her gardeners with pre-addressed postcards. Many of these survive, each inadvertently revealing a little of the writer's personality. James Preece, Head Gardener at Warley: professional and to the point. Thomas Candler, Herbaceous Foreman: a man who knew his own mind and ventured opinions that some might consider mildly insubordinate. Jacob Maurer, Willmott's Swiss Alpine Foreman: still mastering the English language but steady, methodical and comprehensive, labouring at the Essex rock face even as his employer built a second *alpinum*, this time actually in the Alps.

Ever more impressive gentry started booking their slot to visit the garden at Tresserve before they even left London. As noted by *The Gentlewoman* in 1894, it was the turn of Lord and Lady Henry Grosvenor. Lady Dora Mina 'Minnie' Grosvenor was a carnation nut, but also a very good friend of George Engleheart, a noted daffodil enthusiast. It seems she introduced Ellen to Engleheart just before they went; perhaps when Ellen finally took the plunge and joined the Royal Horticultural Society. A key moment in her career, joining doesn't seem to have been much of a deal at the time. The moment was right, that was all.

The Society was on a recruitment drive after the unpleasantness of the 1870s and '80s; they needed members to swell the coffers but they still didn't just let 'anyone' in. Ellen was elected as a Fellow on 8 May

---

[38] Holtzappfel, naturally.

1894. Almost immediately afterwards she disappeared to Tresserve, but something must have gelled in her mind because soon after-wards her gardening letters turn sunshine yellow. Ellen didn't always hurry home from Tresserve, sometimes staying at Lady Whalley's holiday villa in Nice or spending a few days shopping in Paris. This year, however, she went straight back, full of plans for her new daffodil garden.

Ellen's relationship with George Engleheart, one of the true nineteenth-century daffodil superstars, typifies a pattern she had begun with Henry Correvon and, to some extent, Léon Brachet. An expert in his field, highly educated, highly motivated and highly ambitious, Engleheart would take Ellen under his wing. In him she does seem to have found a genuine friend, though of course we don't have his letters to anyone else. Or, indeed, hers. She would become his client, collaborator, benefactor and muse. As with all her 'conquests', however, the relationship would also become a strange, see-sawing power-struggle – of pride, rivalry and, almost certainly, unstated sexual tension.

It's usually suggested that Miss Willmott never married for one of two reasons. Either that she wanted to keep her own property or she was too 'fierce' to attract a man. Certainly she would not have cared to have a husband dictate how to spend her money, but to me the 'financial control' theory seems unlikely if she'd really wanted to spend her life with a man. The Married Women's Property Acts of 1870 and 1882 would have prevented a husband automatically subsuming her wealth into his. As for the 'too scary' argument, from her extensive correspondence, Ellen was clearly very attractive to men. Dr Brachet, Henry Correvon and the Revd. Engleheart were just the first of several (usually, but not always, married) men with whom she would enjoy a very close friendship. Crucially, this was not sexualised, at least not on her part. I'm less convinced of the platonic nature the other way around. While Engleheart's letters are formal, their sheer number – sometimes twice a day, and up to twelve pages long – over many years, reveal a pair of kindred spirits, and a closeness that would not go unmarked by his wife.

It must have been quite a shock to Ellen not to have been able to just buy whatever she wanted, in bulk and instantly. Engleheart was not ready to release any of his precious seedlings. He did have, however, a fair amount of stock acquired from other people that he was prepared to part with. In fact, he had to. The Reverend was not a rich man and, gardening out of a tiny cottage near Andover in Hampshire, he would struggle all his life to keep up with the big boys. He needed the cash. He was happy enough to come over and advise on siting and preparing her new garden, however,[39] and in August 1894 he visited Warley, full of recommendations, from leaf mould to bulb varieties. It would have been on this trip that they solidified their friendship. And friendship it almost certainly was. His letters (we don't have hers) are never anything less than formal: 'Dear Miss Willmott'. A good 99 per cent of their content consists of technical narcissus minutiae – and Engleheart blowing off steam about his rivals.

A compassionate, thoughtful soul in many respects, and one of the era's most talented hybridisers, the moment George Engleheart got onto the subject of daffodils, any notions of Christian charity deserted him. In his letters to Ellen, Engleheart got onto the subject of daffodils a lot. He was generous about some growers, including fellow man-of-the-cloth Charles Wolley-Dod, but was far more likely to warn his daffodil newbie against individuals he didn't care for, not least superstar grower Peter Barr, the 'Daffodil King', with whom Engleheart enjoyed a long-running jealous feud, even falling out over which one of them first named a daffodil 'Mars'. This behaviour was not untypical of Victorian gardening bigwigs. Passions ran high, whatever the plant, be it hothouse exotic, dainty fern or vegetable marrow, and the smaller the interest group, the narrower the classification, the more there was

---

39 He was sometimes cash-strapped enough to ask for the train fare.

riding on it. Specialists, especially when a twelve-year gestation period was involved, lived and breathed their horticultural babies, often to the detriment of human relationships. These intense rivals both needed their fellow enthusiasts and feared them. Friendships were made and broken over the tiniest incident.

Perhaps that's why Ellen initially bought into a syndicate to purchase the Reverend's wares, spreading the cost of acquisition across several individuals. She could easily afford to purchase outright any bulbs that took her fancy but there was safety in numbers. She joined fellow enthusiasts including, predictably, her own sister, which would have also given them some collective leverage. Growers' letters from the time constantly talk of refusing to sell things to individuals they just plain don't like, however much money is offered.

Her purchases made and planted up, all Ellen could do was wait for spring. There was plenty to do, however, not least of which involved taking photographs of all her best plants. Her first published image appeared in *The Garden* in 1893. From 1895 onwards, her work featured on a regular basis. William Robinson was the only horticultural publisher making prolific use of photography, mainly because it was a pricey process. The investment paid dividends, though. *The Garden* and sister publication *Gardening Illustrated* became two of the biggest horticultural magazines in Britain, and it was the photographs, often by Ellen Willmott, that made them stand out.

Engleheart was unconvinced by William Robinson, though for non-narcissus and even non-journalistic reasons, and it's somehow refreshing to hear a lone voice of dissent against this gardening deity. Engleheart felt Robinson was too dogmatic in his approach to wild gardening, throwing out the historical baby with the horticultural bathwater. 'What grieves me,' he wrote, 'is to see people following him blindly and ruining beautiful old gardens that were laid out by people who loved their houses and knew how to surround them with perfectly appropriate gardens.'

By this point Engleheart could air his thoughts freely. Ellen's replies may well have been similarly fruity. Like family, they fell out with each other, forgave each other, badmouthed each other, lauded each other then fell out again.

Engleheart's garden at Appleshaw was not only small; it had poor soil for daffodils. He envied Miss Willmott's space, her growing conditions and, of course, her help. Warley hadn't yet reached 'peak staff' but there were still plenty of gardening hands to go round. In October 1894, he asked if she might be able to grow-on some specimens for him; a 'plant sanatorium', as he described it, also mentioning Tresserve as a possible venue. Over several years theirs would prove to be a mutually beneficial partnership. He created new crosses; she took his 'teenage' seedlings, bulked them up at Warley and showed them, both to admiring potential customers, and on the exhibition bench. Her many extant notebooks – and a giant outsize packet of prize certificates – show just how seriously she took the task. Every time she won gold with one of Engleheart's daffodils, his reputation as registered breeder was enhanced. For her part, Ellen was beginning to hold one of the finest collections in the country. Soon Warley's entire garden was covered in them, and not just with varieties bred by the reverend. If there was something new out there, she wanted it, whoever had bred it. Even beds officially dedicated to a different kind of plant enjoyed a flash of yellow each spring before the real incumbents poked through the ground.

Willmott and Engeleheart's unofficial partnership was successful but their friendship was a strange one, filled with an unspoken, underlying tension; one that is hard to tease out today with less than half of the information and a 125-year gap. At Christmas 1894, Engleheart plucked up courage to ask something, disguised as a throwaway, by the by:

'Another reason for this note is to ask you whether I may have your kind leave to name one of my new seedling Daffodils after you. The one

I have my eye upon is a fine red cupped flower of the *incomparabilis* class . . .'[i] Engleheart goes on to praise the seedling's vigour and beauty, but humbly adds that Ellen can pick out another if she chooses.

Narcissus 'Ellen Willmott' becomes, in Engleheart's letters, almost like a surrogate child; a shared 'something' between them, referred to constantly: 'The foliage is still growing and looks mightily healthy . . . I believe the plant is not yet full-sized & that the flower next year will be enormous . . . It must certainly live at Warley for a season with many others of my best things . . . EW quite ready, and is a lovely bulb . . . I have dug up "Ellen Willmott" – bulb not very big but very heavy and healthy . . .'

Gearing up to reveal his baby to the world at the Birmingham Narcissus Show, 5 May 1895, Engleheart was a cauldron of nerves:

'Wednesday 8am. Several of the best judges said to me perfectly spontaneously that "Ellen Willmott" is undoubtedly quite at the top of all Daffs and a long way ahead of anything yet raised. Mr Poe said that Weardale[40] was nothing beside it! The papers all agree that it is quite the finest Daffodil in the world . . .

'Wednesday Night. Show here a great success – your namesake got the medal for the finest flower in the show. Barr senior was there and helped to judge & was quite humble in the presence of the big flowers. It made quite a small excitement. I got the medal for "you".'

They had done it. A couple more years and *Narcissus* 'Ellen Willmott' would be ready for her ultimate challenge: the RHS exhibition bench. The coveted First Class Certificate was within touching distance.

This was all very well, but there were actually three living humans in this relationship and one of them was rather less delighted.

When they first met, Ellen Willmott and Mrs Engleheart had got on well enough. Mary was a lonely soul who brought up the couple's son among few friends and had committed the heinous crime of not being

---

40 *Weardale Perfection*, one of Peter Barr's best offerings.

particularly interested in daffodils. Even folk who only have a passing interest in daffs, however, would be flattered to have one named after them, especially when their husband is boasting of 'several beauties waiting for worthy appellations'.[ii] Of the more than 700 plants named by George Engleheart, not one of them is called 'Mary'.

He did bring his wife and son to stay at Warley, which went off very well. The visit was even returned; just the once, probably because there was no room for Ellen at the vicarage and she had to stay at the local inn. After that, George often met with Ellen in town, stayed at Warley and even visited Tresserve. Mary did not. It wasn't long before his daffodil obsession became a fixation in itself for poor Mary Engleheart, focusing on one particular irritant: Miss Willmott. Every time George wrote a letter to Ellen, met her in town or tended her namesake flower, a little part of Mary wilted.

Heaven knows what she made of Ellen's suggestion that George take up a living[41] at the Holy Cross and All Saints church, Warley. He was clearly tempted. The living at Appleshaw was a poor one and he would have welcomed the opportunity to be close to 'Ellen Willmott'. George's eventual reply is long, difficult and awkward. His excuse is reasonable – he is unsure about converting to Catholicism – but the letter is heavy with unspoken alternative reasons for refusal.

Narcissus 'Ellen Willmott' is, currently, lost, but that doesn't necessarily mean it's gone forever. Thousands of unidentified daffodils bloom at Warley, with only a very short window each year in which to identify varieties. 'We collect as many descriptions as we can and play snap,' says Anne Tweddle, one of the holders of the Engleheart National Plant Collection. Top of her wish-list are two of Engleheart's all-time-finest achievements, 'Golden Bell' and 'White Queen'. Paid-up members of Team Ellen, however, hold out for her controversial namesake: *Narcissus* 'Ellen Willmott'.

---

41 The retainer allowing a clergyman to live while providing pastoral duties. The position was usually arranged by the landowner.

Human Ellen Willmott was on her way up the ladder now, in part thanks to yet another horticultural spat. Engleheart's beloved Narcissus Committee was in trouble; abolished by the RHS Council 'without one word of notice or consultation with its members'.[iii] His rival Peter Barr was fuming too. Putting their differences temporarily aside, he invited Engleheart to speak at a protest conference the following April. Engleheart accepted the olive branch but suspected the RHS was already beginning to reconsider its rashness in underestimating daffodil men scorned. The committee would return, and, when it did, Ellen Willmott must be part of it. But, he warned, 'we shall very probably see a debacle at the General Meeting of 1896.'

Chapter Eight:

'This is Cupid. I knew him not.'

A CIGARETTE CASE

Discreet, elegant, barely three inches in height, this silver cigarette case has seen a lot of action. While its front has tarnished to a dull grey, the back, gently curved for tucking inside a breast pocket, has worn to a deep shine that still gleams after nearly ninety years. On clicking open the clasp, no time at all seems to have elapsed. The elastic is still good and there are even a few flakes of tobacco caught in the hinges. The hallmark reveals it was made in 1896 by Harrison Brothers & Howson, holders of a Royal Warrant to Queen Victoria.

THE 'NAUGHTY' NINETIES were good times for those who could afford it. Britannia ruled the waves, British industry was booming and Victorian society had matured enough to allow just the tiniest loosening of the cultural stays. While demure wives shopped for trinkets in magnificent art nouveau department stores, louche gentlemen with roving eyes enjoyed saucy songs in smoke-filled music halls. Across the channel, the daring 'new art' was sweeping Europe, including music, architecture, painting and general *joie de vivre*. The outrageous cancan may not have polluted the refined concert halls of Aix-les-Bains but the avant-garde hotels, casinos and pleasure grounds springing up around town were beginning to rival anything offered by the 1889 Paris Exposition.

That's the thing about corsets. You can't just allow some breathing room in one place. A little easing in the ribs and the rest of society's underpinnings begin to strain. Seams start to pop and eventually the body wants out altogether.

In some cases this was literal. Perhaps surprisingly, I can't find that Ellen Willmott enjoyed the latest 'rational dress', where women rebelled against tight lacing by throwing out stays altogether.[42] Most images show her in highly restrictive formality, well into her late forties. She did, however, enthusiastically adopt the gigantic puffed sleeves and masculine-style 'armour' of the New Woman.

The New Woman of the early 1890s, in equal parts revered

---

42 There is one painting of her dressed in a loose, flowing, rational-style gown. The whereabouts of the original is unknown and the only image I know of is a monochrome photograph.

'THIS IS CUPID. I KNEW HIM NOT.'

and reviled, was an attitude rather than an organised movement. Throwing off the shackles of submission, young, mainly middle-class women began to ask if there was more to life than procreation. Although never a homogenous group, New Women adopted masculine styling, took vigorous physical exercise and asserted their independence by travelling without chaperones, challenging every cherished ideal of the Victorian universe. Worse, they began to want to develop intellectually and even discuss science and politics. This did not endear them to the establishment. Between 1883 and 1900, over 100 novels were written starring the New Woman. Between 1885 and 1900, *Punch* magazine carried no fewer than 200 cartoons[i] lampooning the 'Manly Maiden': a fearsome Amazon with gigantic feet (from all that walking) and massive hands (from all that 'doing things that aren't embroidery'), leaving a flotsam of terrified men in her wake. *Punch*'s other favourite single woman was the sour-faced, ugly spinster/bluestocking who pretended she didn't want a man because she couldn't get one.

Scholar Tracy Collins has assembled a checklist of *Punch*'s New Woman:

- Young
- Middle class
- Single on principle
- Financially independent
- Athletic
- Cycles
- Rides trains and buses unescorted
- Belongs to all-female clubs and societies where the talk is of ideas
- Seeks freedom and equality with men
- Smokes

Ellen Willmott ticks every single box. She may not have actively championed women's rights (though she was a member of the Primrose League, pretty much the only way women could officially be involved in any kind of politics at the time) but she did one better: she *lived* the very earliest first-wave feminism. Her athleticism alone embraced tennis, golf, shooting, skating, cycling, fishing, bowling, croquet and vast amounts of walking. Chaperones could whistle. Her horticultural prowess was built on William Robinson's principles of 'Wild Gardening', but *she* was pure 'Wild Woman', a term originally coined as an insult by fanatical anti-feminist campaigner Mrs Eliza Linn-Lynton.[ii] New Women of the 1890s wore such slights as badges of honour. The establishment's venom had backfired; parody had become an ideal. Even *Punch*'s harridans were fit, active, intellectual and free. Men were horrified; young women found the notion alluring. More began to attend university or college. They became doctors, lawyers, journalists – horticulturists – and they weren't turning back now.

When gossiping about 'Mrs Berkeley and her sister Miss Willmott' partying at Tresserve in early June 1894, *The Gentlewoman* could not have known that, underneath the elegant hospitality, things were not quite as they seemed. The family had kept very quiet that Rose's second child had died not six weeks earlier.[43] At seven months, baby Rosamond would have already been a 'person' when meningitis snatched her away, bringing back memories of another much-missed person: little Ada.

The Willmott sisters' answer to profound grief was escape, to Tresserve, where they felt safe, and it was easier to put up a glossy front for society. Their houseguest, however, would have been only too aware of the sisters' profound heartbreak. Indeed, she would have been dealing with grief herself. Minnie Grosvenor had very recently attended the funeral of her close friend Lady Wolverton, and I am convinced she was not the only person staying at Tresserve that spring.

---

43 Rosamond Berkeley, 24 September 1893–20 March 1894.

'THIS IS CUPID. I KNEW HIM NOT.'

Miss Georgiana 'Gian' Tufnell had lived with her aunt, Lady Wolverton, since her mother's death.[44] Over a few years, both aunt and niece had become great friends with their neighbour, the larger-than-life Princess Mary Adelaide, Duchess of Teck, dubbed by the British press 'the People's Princess'. Always jolly, always scheming – and always broke – the duchess was a notorious sponger, but was such good company it had taken a long time for Lady W to lose her patience. By the time she did, the duchess had moved on. She had finally managed to snare the Queen's grandson, handsome Prince George, as a husband for her daughter, Princess May, and was still rubbing her hands at becoming mother-in-law to the future King George V.

Gian Tufnell was less sure. She was close to Princess May; indeed, she had been on the very holiday in Cannes where the duchess had thrown her shy young daughter at George. Gian had lost her best friend, now she had lost her aunt, too. Worse, Lady Wolverton's estate was entailed away to a distant relative; all Gian would inherit was a small bequest and a painting of her aunt by G. F. Watts. She was twenty-nine years old, but thanks to Victorian patriarchy, had been sheltered to the point of helplessness. In deep grief, she now must also leave her beloved home at Coombe Wood, near Kingston, so it could be sold. She stopped eating, shut herself away. Her friends worried about her mental state.

I am convinced Minnie Grosvenor suggested Gian accompany her to visit Rose Berkeley and Ellen Willmott at Tresserve in spring 1894. Photographs of her there – a slight, young-looking woman in deep mourning, often lying in a steamer chair with a rug over her – almost certainly date from this time.

Partying hard is one way of dealing with loss, and the Tresserve party certainly didn't shut itself off from Aix's social whirl. On 24 May, M. Bernascon, the hotelier, threw a swanky dinner to celebrate Queen Victoria's birthday, the menu carefully preserved by Ellen: *Consommé*

---

44 Why her twin sister didn't live there too is unclear. Gertrude Tufnell is rarely mentioned and only as 'my twin', who Gian apparently sees once in three years.

'Victoria' – *Truites 'Windsor'* – *Filets de boeuf 'Prince de Galles'*. A set of studio photographs taken in the town, of Rose, Ellen and Gian, were probably taken at this time, and we know from *The Gentlewoman* that Rose and Ellen were doing a lot of entertaining themselves. Ellen's snapshots of Rose messing around with the fork are almost certainly also from this trip.

Ellen and Gian became very close, perhaps because Rose and Minnie would have had to spend at least some time with their respective husbands. All in all, the visit appears to have been the tonic everyone needed. By the time Ellen returned to Warley to begin her daffodil garden, resigned stiff upper lips were the order of the day.

Until Karen presented me with that packet of letters in October 2019, this chance meeting and pleasant holiday wouldn't have seemed worth noting, particularly given the contrast in letter volume between Gian and some of Ellen's other correspondents. I now think it may have had a profound influence on Ellen's life; even, perhaps, her later reputation.

Not that, even reading Karen's stack of letters, anything immediately seems to have happened. *The Gentlewoman* could be forgiven for not picking up on Rose's lost baby but sometimes Victorian Britain's premier gossip mag was just plain behind the times. Take its 'Overheard by the Little Bird' column, 31 August 1895, telling us that Miss Tufnell is – *whisper* – the Duchess of Teck's new lady-in-waiting. This is old news by over a year. Gian was actually given the role in 1894, just after she would have first met Ellen Willmott, probably as soon as she returned to England. Attending to the People's Princess was a full-on job. If she wasn't traipsing round after the duchess as the ageing party animal reviewed fire brigades, distributed medals, attended state balls and opened hospitals 'for the dying', Gian was chained to her desk replying to hundreds of letters from well-wishers. Over in Essex, Ellen was busy with daffodils, photography and overseeing construction on a new garden feature: that subterranean filmy fern cave. Instead, we must

'THIS IS CUPID. I KNEW HIM NOT.'

fast-forward to December 1894, to the wedding of Gian's friend – and her employer's son – Prince Adolphus, to Minnie Grosvenor's sister-in-law. Gian really should have been present. She wasn't.

Virtually none of Gian's correspondence is dated; we have had to cross-reference each letter with incidents mentioned within it to work out what comes in what order. From the content and black edging on the notepaper, however, we know the following letter was written in very early spring 1895. It is the earliest surviving letter from her to Ellen. I quote what is left of it in full. It becomes pretty clear where Gian probably was in December 1894:

Coombe Wood
Kingston-on-Thames
Monday evening

Darling,
I don't know what time you get back tomorrow but anyhow this will be at home before you are. It was so lovely here across the lawn this afternoon, the bare trees are beginning to thicken & they have got that red look in the twigs, which means that they are soon going to live again & your birch trees on the lawn here had their trunks dyed pink by the setting sun. I wished you were looking out of the window <u>with</u> me for I know exactly that you wouldn't have said anything, nor should I, but it's just possible that you might have kissed me & I should have known that you liked it too.

I love a sunset, it's one of the things that makes me most still. I have been reading dear [illegible book title] again in its new coat, I think I love it more every time I read it & now it always reminds me of Xmas night, *when you let me into your heart. I wonder if you ever knew how I had longed that you would let me share in ever so small a degree with you that heavy sorrow which had fallen on us both but for you so much more heavily. I think Minnie knew all about it, for it was not <u>only</u> just the sympathy that one would feel for another whose heart one knew was heavy, but it was such an intense longing, to rest you & to give you the only thing which I had got to give you, love, however unworthy, but love which has suffered somewhat & lost much is sometimes made more peaceful for others who are left. It makes one's soul very quiet when so much is taken away, doesn't it! I know it is so with you, dear heart. I wish so I could tell you often what Xmas night was to me when you were given to me, to love, dear heart.*

However great or however small your sorrow or anxiety, you will let me share it, darling, as I will do with—

The rest of the letter is missing but, from this moment on, Gian's letters become truly intense. Before rushing to conclusions, though, it's worth taking a breath.

Many Victorian women enjoyed deep friendships that, on paper, can come across to today's eyes, searching for sexual connotations, as more than they are. This is further complicated by the fact that modern ideas of homosexuality are exactly that – modern constructs. History has seen many degrees of love, some of which, though occasionally physical, may still have been somewhere in between what we now call heterosexuality and homosexuality, and the 1890s was a time of sexual flux.

Only a few remain of what were obviously many, *many* letters

'THIS IS CUPID. I KNEW HIM NOT.'

between these two women. They are often incomplete and, like so much of Ellen Willmott's correspondence, we have only one side of the conversation. Gian had her letters burned, so nothing from her Ellie survives. We are forced to do what fashionable historians call 'reading against the grain'. What follows has been put together from cross-referencing memoires, newspaper articles, official lists, society reports, receipts, obituaries, photographs and fleeting mentions in other people's correspondence. There isn't room to reproduce verbatim all that remains of Gian's letters, but I have tried hard not to skew her intentions by selective quotation.[45]

We also need to be aware that people often used different ways of expression in the nineteenth century, which can look over-effusive to us today. For me, these particular letters seem to go beyond the usual emotive Victorian style, largely thanks to their content – the events within, rather than the words used to describe them. Not a single one of Gian's (few) remaining letters to other people smoulders with the kind of fire with which she addresses Ellen.[46]

Victorian society had only itself to blame for the way things were changing. It had created a fiction in which women's relationships with other women were the purest forms of love, perhaps even 'practice' for when they eventually gave themselves to a man. They were also an excellent way of preventing the ultimate Victorian horror: fornication. Everything was above board because women were asexual, only undergoing intercourse to please husbands and make babies. Male homosexuality had always been illegal, and the notorious 1885 Labouchere Amendment enabled the prosecution of all forms of male homosexuality. Women's sexual activities were not criminalised for the simple reason that they didn't exist, either in law or medical textbooks. Anything else lived in the filthy fantasies of 'certain' scientists and pornographers.

---

[45] I take the liberty of adding some punctuation. Gian rarely does.

[46] These include letters to her 'best friend' Princess May and May's brother, 'Prince Alge', to whom she signs herself 'Gian Tuffy'. The letters are chatty, friendly and affectionate; nothing more.

One of the most all-pervading outlets for the 1890s New Woman was fiction, by women for women, which often depicted female 'romantic friendships'. Prominent same-sex relationships were now openly talked about in intellectual circles, but while Oscar Wilde was being thrown into jail, his female counterparts generally managed to stay within the bounds of 'just regular spinsters, living together'. For most this was, indeed, merely a pragmatic 'marriage' of convenience – two financially strapped single women society had left on the shelf sharing the bills. For some, it was a barely disguised full-blown love match.

Reading between what lines remain it looks to me that theirs was a serious, possibly sexual, definitely romantic relationship filled with passion, laughter, flirtation, jealousy, tenderness – and not a few tiffs. Like anyone else, both parties had different interpretations of love, intensity and, crucially, longevity, but for three intoxicating years Ellen Willmott flourished on two levels: as an up-and-coming horticulturist climbing the ladder of fame, and as an individual with a fulfilling, happy personal life. As a theory it holds reasonable water. But I preface this entire chapter with a caveat: this is *all* theory. It is based on evidence, none of which (so far) contradicts itself, but it's likely we'll never know the truth of what really happened between Ellen Willmott and Gian Tufnell.

From the start, however, it was stained with loss. On 27 December 1894, George Engleheart wrote to Warley with terrible news. Ellen already knew, however, that ten minutes before midnight on Christmas Eve Minnie Grosvenor had died, giving birth to a son.[47] News travelled fast; postal deliveries arrived even on Christmas Day. Was this new grief the final horror that brought Gian and Ellie together that very night?

The loss was keenly felt. The Reverend sent Ellen one of his two precious carnation seedlings, 'Lady Henry Grosvenor',[iii] and advised on the Latin engraving for a christening cup. Ellen was to be the child's

---

47 William Grosvenor, future 3rd Duke of Westminster.

'THIS IS CUPID. I KNEW HIM NOT.'

godmother and, yet again, her non-classical education was letting her down. For Gian, Ellen was the only comfort in her 'shock in Minnie's death which I cannot shake off, though I feel so much better for coming to you both in body & mind dear, dear heart'. The pair took solace in that, perhaps, Minnie had known all along exactly what she was doing, throwing the two women together: 'it was so dear of you to tell me what Minnie had said to you'.

Slowly, the world rebalanced and the couple – yes, I will, for now, call them that – were able to get back to normal. Crucially, they didn't hide the relationship. At the start, Gian's friends had written to Ellen thanking her for taking her on, as though she were a 'project'. Gertrude Eleanor Molyneux ('Gem') was delighted Ellen had 'taken little Gian in hand'; Gem's mother, Lady Sefton, was just 'thankful she is with you and eating'. As the relationship progressed, however, there does seem to have been a little raising of eyebrows: 'Darling, I was stupid about Gem,' Gian writes, talking of an apparent lapse of confidences. 'I only wanted her to know how _safe_ I was with you.'

In general, Gian and Ellie seem to have become an accepted 'couple'; as pointed out earlier, close female friendships were not necessarily seen as threatening. Reverend Engleheart even refers to Gian as Ellie's 'partner', though naturally this would have carried different connotations too.

Gian's letters are tender, passionate and charming, and it would seem she received much the same in return: 'Your blessed letter this morning was indeed a real surprise & what you say in it is a real joy to me, but darling you do spoil me so . . . you couldn't love me as much as you do & not know something of what I feel. I keep thinking of Tresserve & how delightful it was when you used to come in & sit on my bed, in bed & then all the day, & every day.' Later, she writes: 'Darling, I do feel the sympathy which you feel when you hold me & it is perfect. I know nothing more resting or more peaceful to me & I would love if I could have you oftener.' There is clearly passion on both sides: 'You will tell me that I am imitating what you say but I can't let <u>you</u> only say the things, darling.'

Both women were big fans of John Ruskin: 'Now I am going to make you delightfully angry. Will you read in your *Frondes Agrestes* passage 11, it is page 13, it so exactly describes what I think & feel about you but which is so difficult for me to express, besides you would never allow me to say it!'[48] The chosen passage is intriguing:

> *I believe the first test of a truly great man is his humility. I do not mean, by humility, doubt of his own power, or hesitation of speaking his opinions; but a right understanding of the relation between what he can do and say, and the rest of the world's sayings and doings.*

This does not sound like the later, battling Ellen Willmott we have been sold down the decades, though it does tie in with Henry Correvon, referring to her in 1895 as 'retiring'. Gian quotes Ruskin again in another missive: 'It clasps all that it loves so hard that it crushes it if it be hollow,' she writes, adding: 'I am not afraid to clasp you "so hard" for the harder I clasp you the more I shall find & do find.'

The letters bubble with life, of days out – 'promise to come to the Arts & Crafts with me'[49] and nights in: 'I would like you to be playing the Harpsichord to me' – but the pair were often parted, either through Gian's duties to 'the Missus' or Ellen's horticultural commitments. At Warley, the newly installed filmy fern grotto needed populating. Ellie's new daffodil garden was just about to bloom, and she was becoming ever more deeply embroiled in work with the RHS, joining committees and working alongside heroes she had only previously nodded to at

---

48 *Frondes Agrestes* (Rustic Leaves), John Ruskin, 1884.

49 The 5th Arts & Crafts Exhibition took place in October 1896, at the New Gallery, Regent Street.

'THIS IS CUPID. I KNEW HIM NOT.'

shows and finding them interested in her work too. It must have been heady stuff when she was also getting letters like this:

> *Darling,*
> *I do miss you so quite dreadfully & I have no words to thank you for all you have done for me & all you have been to me all those heavenly weeks we have been together. I would so like that you could realise all the difference you have made in my life, & the fresh interest you have given me in everything dear, dear heart. I love you so & you must know it in the same way that I know you love me. No time to tell you more, my dear heart, except that I want you very badly. I feel so lost without you.*

In other words, theirs seems to have been like any other human relationship, trying to balance independent lives with emotional dependency and the needs of other people; embracing equal amounts of the divine: 'I wonder what time you will go to bed tonight. Goodnight, your loving Gian', with the mundane: 'P.S. I will bring the macaroons.'

While Gian was abroad with HRH, she left Ellie with a go-between: Chang, a cheeky black Pomeranian dog who appears in many of Ellen's photographs. 'Don't forget to kiss Chang for me'; 'Chang takes you many thoughts which I whispered in his ear & will doubtless want to kiss you, my dear, dear heart'; 'I wish I was Chang . . . to meet you at the station.' Occasionally objects take Chang's metaphorical place: 'Oh, darling, I forgot my weather glass. I haven't set it but you know all about it & it winds up like a clock, & its name is "Juliana" & it's so amusing to watch it wriggling up & down. I enclose your pencil case. They have both lived in my pocket.'

The couple spent time together whenever possible. Sometimes at

Warley Place, but just as often at Gian's soon-to-be-sold home. Ellen almost certainly would have already known the house. To be more precise, she would have known its grounds: England's first 'Japanese' garden. A magnificent fantasy of cascading waters, leafy majesty and timeless rockwork had been built by the famous Veitch nursery, which had leased Coombe Wood's gently tumbling valley as a show garden.[50]

Spring 1895 wore on; Gian knew she must leave. 'My pens are as dilapidated as the house,' she wrote, 'there is an all-pervading smell of damp straw, dust & packers', but there was still a little time left to entertain friends in Veitch's water gardens. My favourite-ever Willmott photograph was taken there in summer 1895. Gian stands on the arched Japanese bridge across middle pond, deep in conversation with another woman, whose identity we don't know. I sometimes wonder if she could be the militant suffragist and feminist composer Ethel Smyth. Famous for her opera *The Wreckers*, the suffragette anthem *March of the Women* and her famously unconventional sex life, including several alleged, long-term affairs with women, Smyth was a good friend of Ellen Willmott's. Both were well known for their forthright opinions, love of music and passion for dogs. The pair would play Warley's gas-organ very loudly together, to the horror of Robinson the butler, who was in charge of firing the thing up. Since he was dealing with a noxious mix of company-supplied and home-made acetylene gas, and had to use a Bunsen burner to light it every time Miss Smyth arrived, Robinson risked fulfilling his task in the most literal sense.[iv]

Whoever the other woman is, the picture is remarkable. Not just for its sublime composition, using the lily-filled lake to mirror the gentle arc of the bridge, but for the casual intimacy of its subjects. The women stand close, wearing masculine-style suits with sharp tailoring and giant leg o'mutton sleeves. Gian has a bow tie, the other lady a regular

---

50 The story of this extraordinary estate is related in *Warren House Tales* by V. K. Good (Third Millennium, 2014).

'THIS IS CUPID. I KNEW HIM NOT.'

necktie; both sport straw boaters. By summer 1894, the New Woman look was a common declaration of intent – women would soon be demanding their rightful place in society – but I'm more intrigued by their jackets. Many styles of the day were deliberately designed not to meet at the front, but if something in Victorian fashion was meant to be buttoned up – as these jackets clearly are – polite society expected it to stay that way, whatever the weather or occasion. These women are relaxed enough in the depths of Coombe's shady, acer-draped pools – and each other's company – to allow their garments to hang loose, definitely against received decorum.

I get the feeling that those last few weeks at Coombe were probably the happiest the couple knew together, but Gian's uncle's will was clear: she must leave. Much of their time was now snatched between Ellen's increasing committee obligations at the RHS and the Duchess of Teck's social life. The obvious solution was to rent somewhere round the corner from the RHS's temporary headquarters.

'How I wish I was going to the Drill Hall tomorrow to meet you,' wrote Gian, putting a brave face on her new prospective home. 'I hope you will look at 16 James Street as you go by & think how nice & close it is, & that it won't take Mr Engleheart any time to run in for tea or anything on his way to a train.'

Later, she admitted: 'Darling, I'm afraid you would scold me for I can't settle myself to read & try to forget that this is the last evening I am ever likely to spend in this house . . . I have been supremely happy here, & for a very short time supremely miserable, but I think that little passing cloud only made the rest more precious to me.' She continues: 'I am so glad to have begun to know you here because I love you to be connected with the associations which are dearest to me, dear heart.'

Number 16 James Street is still there.[51] Smart, Queen Anne red-brick,

---

51 Now 16 Buckingham Gate.

genteel, yes, but the term 'Drill Hall' gives away what mainly went on in the area. 'I slept very well,' Gian writes, the day after she moved in, 'but very dull & couldn't think where I was this morning, till I heard the drums in the barrack yard.' Even today, the house still looks out onto British Army property.

After daily troop drills outside Gian's front window, holidays at Tresserve were a blessed relief. Ellen's photographs capture her sitting reflectively in a rose-covered arbour and almost certainly her on a daytrip into the alps, sitting, somewhat incongruously, next to a roadside cross, two cows' backsides and a couple of puzzled locals. She holds three freshly picked daffodils; Ellen's spare camera lies on the grass beside her.

It seems Gian was called back early from the visit. 'Dear heart, here I am safe, we didn't get in till 8 o'clock last night.' The duchess set her straight to work, 'writing 38 letters to these tiresome Guild people of H.R.H's. How I do miss you.' She continues, 'I do not like London after Tresserve. When I woke this morning . . . I heard the soldiers fussing about & I knew I wasn't with you anymore.' The loneliness hit hard. 'I feel so lost without you & my house doesn't look "lived in" yet. Dear heart, I do want to hear from you so badly . . . tell me all you are thinking about.'

Ellen sent gifts from the villa. Gian writes: 'your flowers always seem like a bit of you . . . I think of the dear garden at Tresserve & wonder what you are doing & I long to be helping you take photographs', but it was a strain. 'You don't know what a horrid feeling it was to wake up in the morning here & realise I left you. You know how sleepy I am when I wake, dear heart.'

They couldn't catch a break. Just as Ellen came back to England, Gian was whisked off to the Continent by the duchess.[v] 'My dear, dear heart, we are going round Paris . . . My darling, I do miss you so badly. I long to be back with you. Will you ever believe that I love you, perhaps someday you will.'

'THIS IS CUPID. I KNEW HIM NOT.'

Like all couples, they were not beyond teasing each other. On 14 March 1896, George Engleheart wrote to Ellen, 'It is quite too wicked of you – here is a most serious note from Miss Tufnell, thanking me for wishing to give her name to a Daffodil and saying she prefers a <u>pink-eyed</u> one. If I get a note, as is quite probable, from the Duchess of Wellington or someone else thanking me for arranging a blue-eyed Daffodil to her portion, I shall refer her to you to provide it, and shall decline all participation in your evil deeds of this kind.' Trying to think of a diplomatic way to tell Gian that pink-eyed daffodils don't exist, he continues, 'you will have to paint the eye of a common one for Miss Tufnell, just as the bird dealers in Seven Dials paint sparrows and sell them for gold finches'.

It's at points like this that having so much of the conversation missing is particularly frustrating. 'Darling, believe me, you did <u>not</u> hurt me by teasing me but I hurt you by being cross & it is for me to be sorry,' writes Gian. Does this letter refer to the pink-daff tiff, or some other incident? Who knows, but the making-up was nice. 'Darling Heart, my telegram was indeed explicit. I do badly want to hear from you always & I love to wake up & find a letter from you . . . Nothing that you have ever done has altered what I think about you, except to make me love you more.'

Gian's 'moods' are something of a theme: 'I'll try & not be moody but it's unfortunately natural & sometimes I don't struggle hard enough against it . . . I am quite miserable about yesterday at Melchior's, for you were full of dear, kind, blessed thought to give me pleasure & I was too horribly tiresome & I don't know how to thank you or show you how sorry I am . . . I will try & remember that you are not like Gem who pays no heed as to whether I am "peevish" or not.'

In these moods, Gian also seems to have found a way of poking at a small, jealous knot of insecurity within Ellen. 'I love being with you more than anyone – except Gem,' she taunts. 'It wouldn't be nice of me not to think of my other friends.' She then protests with wide-eyed innocence when she gets a reaction. Lady Sefton tells Ellen to ignore her. 'Gian is acting like a "naughty spoilt child".'

Gian's childlike naivety is, occasionally, surprising. Take the incident in which she inexplicably acquired a lamb, then was called away by the duchess. The animal arrived at Warley with instructions: 'His diet is that he has one Spratt's cod liver oil biscuit dry, broken up, at breakfast time, 2 ditto, soaked with 2oz of meat in the middle of the day & the same in the evening about 7 & if he won't eat his dinner in the middle of the day it doesn't matter.'

Unfortunately, Ellen was at Tresserve. Left to administer this frankly odd diet to a baby herbivore, Mrs Willmott was soon forced to ask Ellen to break the news of the creature's death, but how did a thirty-year-old woman have so little idea of what sheep eat?

In other ways, though, Gian *was* a modern woman, in a modern world. A photo in the Royal Collection shows Princess May and her brother Prince Adolphus of Teck – the chap whose wedding Gian missed – perched in a window at the Villa Clementine on that fateful holiday in Cannes where the Duchess of Teck chased poor Prince George to ground. Gian, in the centre of the picture, is very clearly enjoying a cigarette.

Smoking was one of the New Woman's most outrageous habits, even worse than her prolific use of the safety bicycle. The establishment was horrified. Was nothing sacred? Tobacco was the ultimate statement of masculinity – after all, 'a woman is a woman but a good cigar is a smoke', Rudyard Kipling had declared in 1886.[vi] Some cited medical grounds for condemning female smokers, and not just that their uteruses couldn't take it – they actually risked developing moustaches from all that extra lip-movement.[vii] Yet Gian was clearly a pretty heavy smoker: 'Such a delightful surprise. I got your letter at 3.30, darling, this afternoon, & when my Uncle had gone I went off to the birch trees with the dogs, 2 cigarettes & your letter & there I was very peaceful indeed, only I wanted you there so much

'THIS IS CUPID. I KNEW HIM NOT.'

too, but not having you I had your most blessed letter & that was a bit of your heart.'

Whatever the establishment thought of women smoking, tobacco companies just saw the cash. Advertisements appeared in the better magazines for dainty boxes of mild, lady-sized, gold-tipped smokes with names like *Pour la Dame*, *Two Roses* and *Miranda's Dream*. Major artists such as Alphonse Mucha were recruited to create gorgeous posters for cigarettes, specifically designed to appeal to the female market. Cigarette holders, lighters and, especially, cases became discreet, highly acceptable gifts between New Women.

Sometime in 1896, Gian gave Ellie the silver cigarette case described at the top of this chapter. It appears to have been one of the best gifts she ever received. Certainly, given the state of it, it was one of the most used. In 1935 it ended up at the back of a top shelf in Spetchley's strongroom. In 1949 it was mis-catalogued in the house inventory: *Ellie from Gran*, and forgotten. Karen found the entry in February 2020 while looking for something else. She read it out loud to me; we both froze as we realised what the engraving must really say. An agonising hour and a half's wait for the person with the key to finish a meeting was followed by heart-stopping silence as I reached into the darkness.

It wanted to be found. Smooth, rounded, achingly simple, the tiny case nestled into my palm, crying out to be picked up. I teetered back down the ladder, physically shaking. By now we knew only too well the scruffy, looping handwriting and those squiggly Es and Gs. Any correspondence concerning the gift bearing the legend *Ellie from Gian* is long lost, but I have never seen a piece of metal so well and truly cherished before or since.

Many years later, while showing some young friends around Warley, an elderly Miss Willmott passed a single pink rose, halted abruptly, and announced, 'That is Cupid. I knew him not.'[viii]

This statement is not strictly – or indeed at all – true. Even the Russell sisters, authors of the recollection, tell us Ellen was well known for random, dramatic statements, but I think that at that point, in that particular moment, she believed it. Ellen Willmott in love must have been something to behold. Ellen Willmott betrayed in love – well, I'm beginning to wonder if that is what the world has been experiencing for the past 120-odd years.

Chapter Nine:

Annus Mirabilis, Annus Horribilis

Nothing to see here, move along, please.

THE YEAR 1897 was a curious one. The Empire was very nearly at its zenith, but even as the map turned an ever-deeper shade of pink, a feeling was beginning to nag that things couldn't stay like this forever. Tiny cracks were appearing, not least in South Africa. An astonished Britain was still reeling from the previous year's botched Jameson Raid and was now defiantly – but no longer quite so confidently – facing down the Boers. Technology, once exciting and malleable, now seemed to be going 'too fast'. From the discovery of the electron to the first wireless message across open seas, the world was shrinking, and, for the first time, Britain was not completely convinced she was in control.

The Empire was hurtling towards the twentieth century, but the nineteenth wasn't ready to let go yet. Oscar Wilde was released from prison only to be forced into exile. Physician, sociologist and eugenicist Havelock Ellis published *Sexual Inversion*, in which love between women was either 'inverted' or 'perverted'. Society's stays had loosened too much, too fast; the puritans were pushing back. Fashion plates reflected this new sobriety as the New Woman's giant sleeves, crisp fabrics and masculine outlines shrank within a single season to regular size, restrictive lines, soft lace and unthreatening, girly *frou-frou*. What society dictates in public is often reflected in the personal, as Ellen Willmott was about to find out.

The year started out well enough for her. She was gaining more attention in the horticultural universe than ever and, as far as can be told, things were fine personally, even if Gian's employer was beginning to show signs of overdoing the 'hardworking royal' cliché. So what

ANNUS MIRABILIS, ANNUS HORRIBILIS

happened that October, when Ellen would go AWOL for her big moment in the horticultural sun?

If there were bits missing from the story in the last section, they are nothing in comparison to the gaping maw left by 1897. My 'object' for this chapter, therefore, is a space – a blank, where history runs out. As usual, Ellen's own voice is largely absent. The only way to tackle what I believe was the most tumultuous year of her life is to take it month by month, day by day; to piece together the most likely story from journals, letters, diaries, photographs, visitors' books, memoires, maps, itineraries, newspaper reports, gossip columns and a very large, extremely nerdy spreadsheet on my computer.

Nowhere was the national withdrawal back into a comfortable Victorian past more obvious than the year-long celebrations of the Queen's Diamond Jubilee, a re-declaration of power desperately needed by the Empire. Sixty glorious years! How on earth to mark something so unprecedented? Obviously there would be the official celebrations – parades, state balls, thanksgiving services, garden parties, receptions – but what about the rest of the country? Town halls buzzed with children's parties, bandstand concerts, electric light shows and souvenir spoons. Clubs and societies held events, published books and built 'Jubilee Halls'. At the annual meeting of Fellows at the Royal Horticultural Society on 9 February, President Sir Trevor Lawrence announced the inauguration of what would become the highest award in gardening: the Victoria Medal of Honour. Sixty solid-gold medallions, to be designed by – shock! – a lady[52] would be awarded to sixty luminaries from all areas of horticulture, including professional growers, botanists and amateurs. It was to be an ongoing decoration but, to prevent dilution, there would only ever be sixty living VMH holders at any one time. The inaugural ceremony was to take place in October, before an audience of the gentlemen's most distinguished peers.

---

52 Margaret Giles, FRIBA.

The buzz even reached the non-gardening press. Who would be chosen? Names flew, diaries emptied. Ellen Willmott must have been quietly confident. By now she was featured in garden journals on a regular basis, both as subject and contributor. On 20 February, William Robinson's *The Garden* had highlighted Miss Willmott's 'Hardy Bulbs among the Shrubs', featuring a photograph of Turk's head lilies that would become one of her best-known. March 6th saw a long article, 'Narcissus in the Grass at Warley Place', accompanied by Ellen's photographs and cultivation tips.

There was *one* issue in those early months: Reverend Engleheart's wife had finally seen red. Things seem to have come to a head back in 1896 when Mary sent a telegram announcing she would be accompanying George to stay at Warley. Ellen had taken at his word the reverend's insistence that she should 'always meet a frank self-invitation by an equally frank negative if inconvenient',[i] and told her that it *was* inconvenient at such short notice.

In late April 1896, Mary Engleheart had let rip, in public, at an RHS event in the Drill Hall. As ever, we only have one side of the story (his), but even as he tries to pour oil on his wife's very troubled waters, George reveals himself. 'For her to behave in such a way to you, it is in great part, entirely beyond my power to comprehend or explain,' he writes. Many women, both then and now, might invite the reverend to 'take a wild guess'. George tells Ellen that Mary had 'not had the least intention of <u>deliberately</u> affronting you'. Indeed, he says, she had wanted to go to Warley immediately afterwards to apologise. 'My wife is really the best and truest of women,' he continues, 'but she has times when she gets thoroughly "hipped" and out of sorts, and then takes quite unreasonable notions and likes and dislikes into her head.' He explains that Mary had been lonely when he'd visited Aix and 'formed the notion that I was away from her too much and making friends apart from her'. Who'd have thought it? George blames himself for not 'trying to overcome this feeling' or 'making allowances for it' given Mary's lonely life. She has, he says, 'extremely little recreation or holiday'. He admits the telegram incident was his fault, that he'd suddenly become ill and asked her to accompany him without thinking that it was a bit late in the day to change arrangements. Ultimately, however, he continues, 'when a woman's mind is pent up for want of change & variety and feeds upon itself, it exaggerates everything and makes a great grievance & wrong out of something quite innocent'.

Now, Ellen could have been more accommodating in welcoming Mrs E so late in the day. Would one extra really have made much difference to arrangements? But the reverend's blindness to – or failure to do anything about – his wife's distress over a period of many years has to hold at least equal culpability. The man really can't help himself – in the *very same letter* he is *still* crowing about *Narcissus* 'Ellen Willmott': 'Did you see the note about "the finest trumpet Daffodil" in the last *Garden*?' There is no doubting that George Engleheart was a horticultural genius, and his letters *are*, nearly always, about gardening minutiae. When it came to women, however, he really didn't get it. 'She has been in all things a dear, good wife to me,' he writes, 'but at times she has had extraordinary and unintelligible moods of morbid and absolutely unreasonable feeling.'[ii]

The upshot was that Ellen Willmott's name became the proverbial mud in the Engleheart household. George got her to write to him via various go-betweens, under various aliases, and saw her only at RHS meetings or Gian's place. Did Mary benefit from this subterfuge? I suspect not. On 5 February 1897, Mary Engleheart gave birth to a daughter, sixteen years after her last pregnancy. George remained disingenuous. Seeing Ellen's name at the top of a letter he was about to write 'about some simple gardening transaction', he was baffled that 'she went into such a terrible state as to cause me extreme alarm', but hastened to add that 'nothing on her part has been done deliberately or with real <u>responsibility</u>'.[iii]

All in all, it was an awkward time for Engleheart's *other* baby to come of age. *Narcissus* 'Ellen Willmott' finally won that coveted RHS First Class Certificate. Like all 'FCC' winners it was awarded a portrait in *The Garden*. Resident artist Henry George Moon's delicate, glowing watercolour is a poignant memorial to what might have been. 'Ellen Willmott' would remain in cultivation, in small, highly expensive numbers, for some years, but thanks to Engleheart's domestic difficulties, the daffodil would never know the commercial success everyone had assumed it would enjoy.

It didn't help that Gian seemed to be in another of her moods. Lady Sefton's 'naughty spoilt child' letter dates from 20 February 1897, though Lady S herself would not be able to referee much longer. The following month, her son Charles took a fall at steeplechase, suffering life-changing injuries. Ellen did what she could, sending flowers on a continuing and regular basis, but as far as lovers' tiffs were concerned, she was on her own. Things blew over. Gian brought her 'Missus' to visit Warley on 8 April. Unsurprisingly, the duchess was enchanted.

There was another intriguing visitor at Warley that month. On 20 April, Canadian railroad magnate 1st Baron Mount Stephen came for lunch. George Stephen was an interesting chap but recently bereaved and one of the wealthiest men in Britain; most of his invitations were currently from single ladies. Mount Stephen knew Miss Willmott through his adopted daughter, and presumably it would have been a nice change for the ageing millionaire to talk about regular stuff with Ellen, but fellow guest Lady Wolseley wasted no time jumping to conclusions. 'Can he be thinking of Miss Willmott?' she asked her husband. 'He was in high spirits,' she continued, allowing that Ellen herself 'seemed distraite'.[iv] Nothing came from the speculation; perhaps it was assumed that the difference in their ages – her thirty-eight years to his sixty-seven – was the barrier.

By May, Victoria's jubilee celebrations were beginning in earnest. One of the biggest social events of the London season was the opening of the brand-new Empress Club, founded by women for women.

ANNUS MIRABILIS, ANNUS HORRIBILIS

Coverage of the inaugural event, in publications such as the *Telegraph* and *The Lady,* ooh-ed and aah-ed over the sumptuous, refined Dover Street premises – *so* much more elegant than those uncomfortable 'suites of the "shrieking sisterhood"'[v] of just a few years ago. 'There is beauty everywhere,' breathed *The Boudoir* gossip mag. Facilities included a Sèvres-blue club room, red and gold drawing rooms, spacious dining areas, a winter garden, seventy bedrooms, a tickertape machine for stock market news, an office for interviewing prospective servants and an oriental-style smoking gallery. The passport to membership was 'good social standing' and if there was still a little way to go in the equality stakes ('the wines have been chosen by gentlemen experts'), *The Boudoir* was, at least, happy to reassure 'some of the alarmist writers on the daily Press' who 'will be glad to learn that bridge is not played at the Club'.

It's possible both Ellen and Gian were present in the Empress's opening crush. Ellen joined,[53] and since the club was founded by the 'Ladies of England' – basically a group of royal ladies-in-waiting – it's likely Gian would have too, though she may not have had her mind completely on the fun. The Duchess of Teck had been overdoing things again and, on 29 April, was taken ill. Physicians were called, and on 3 May, the public held its breath as the People's Princess underwent a 'serious' operation. The newspapers were vague about details, reporting only that she had 'passed a good night' and was 'progressing favourably',[vi] but warned it would be several months before things would be back to normal.

Gian would have been needed at White Lodge more than ever as the carpets of flowers, piles of gifts and support-filled letters poured in. She would not have been human, however, if she hadn't quietly started to think about what might happen if her employer *didn't* get well again.

❦

---

[53] We're not exactly sure when but we live in hope of finding a personalised, golden 'founder member' medal.

This year, there would be no joint visit to Tresserve. Ellen went alone (or possibly with her sister) and it was a quieter season all round. Even so there was much to do in the garden, and she found herself writing to George Engleheart: 'We have stayed on here rather longer than intended,' adding 'but if there is an RHS meeting on the 23rd I should certainly make it.'[vii] Her comment is important – if Ellen Willmott was coming back for a regular RHS meeting, surely she would have moved heaven and earth to be present at the shindig of the century later in the year? Not that she could officially write to Engleheart at all; by now he was employing red ink in the bits of his letters that warned her to absolutely *not* contact him at home.

June saw the beginnings of Her Majesty's official celebrations. A thanksgiving service on the 20th was followed by the much-publicised Diamond Jubilee procession on the 22nd. There had been some concern in the papers as to just how popular this was going to be – after all, Victoria had not been seen for years and, for regular folk, times were tough. Would they really want to celebrate a phantom? Columnists conjured visions of Victoria's coach dragging through London, flanked by cohorts of the Empire's military might, eyed by a few stragglers and the odd dog. A big splash was made by the authorities about how brilliant it was going to be. Souvenir maps of the route were produced, including handy royal-spotting glossaries and what to look out for in the various battalions' uniforms.

They needn't have worried. All London turned out for the free show. Crowds lined the streets, people hung from top windows, rooftops and lampposts. Bunting fluttered from every shop, every bridge, every church and every monument. Crucially, the sun shone. Her Majesty's open carriage wound through the streets of Westminster into the City, where a brief service was held on the steps of St Paul's Cathedral, then crossed a swag-strewn London Bridge into the Borough. Everywhere she went, Victoria was hailed, and hopefully she was far enough ahead not to hear the much-louder cheering

ANNUS MIRABILIS, ANNUS HORRIBILIS

behind her, directed at the Duchess of Teck, who had rallied enough to steal the show.

Gian was not in the duchess's carriage; she would have had to wait at the palace. There was no way Ellen was missing the spectacle though. We know exactly where she was: in her father's old office in Borough High Street, hanging out of a first-floor window, then wandering the streets, taking candid shots of procession-goers with her box camera.

An even better thrill came two days later when Ellen was formally offered the Victoria Medal of Honour. The only other woman to receive 'the letter' was Gertrude Jekyll. It arrived with an official invitation to the presentation ceremony: Tuesday 26 October 1897.

Gian's life was a whirl. The 28th of June saw a garden party at Buckingham Palace, the 30th was a full state banquet; the state concert came a few days later. July the 2nd took a step up even from that: the greatest fancy dress party of the nineteenth century. No fewer than two books have been written about the Duchess of Devonshire's 1897 *bal costumé*, where 700 guests vied to outdo each other in priceless and outrageous outfits, emptying the country houses of England of every last jewel. Princess Mary Adelaide went as her ancestor, Sophia, Electress of Hanover, dripping with pearls and diamonds. Gian was 'the Electress's attendant', 'very pretty' in ivory satin with sable and gold embroidery.[viii] It was intoxicating stuff. Gian had always mingled with the upper classes, but now she was in the epicentre of the social melee. On the 9th, she and the duchess were forced to rush between a garden party at Holly Lodge in Hampstead (home of the Burdett-Coutts, friends of Ellen's; perhaps she was present) and yet another state ball. Eventually, though, even the duchess had enough. She gathered up her family, Gian and thirteen servants and went up north to recuperate.

Ellen would have been cool about this. She had things to do and people to entertain, not least her old friend, artist and astronomer Nathaniel Everett Green, who painted some stunning watercolours of Warley that summer. They turned up in Spetchley's basement during the writing of this book. Horticulture pals Charles Wolley-Dod, Alicia Amherst, John Bennett Poë, Alfred Parsons and William Robinson all dropped in too that August. If Ellen was receiving letters from Gian, however, they haven't survived.

Then came September.

Ellen had never been particularly close to the Berkeleys at Spetchley. They lived the other side of the country, and if she was going to the area, she was more likely to look up one of her gardening chums. Indeed, Spetchley Park itself carried an uncomfortable portent, of a disturbing future in which Rose was Spetchley's mistress, no longer a five-minute stroll away, no longer part of Ellen's daily life.

On 9 September 1897, the future happened. Robert Berkeley Snr died, leaving Robert Valentine to inherit Spetchley Park. This time it was real, instead of a debt and the name on a deed. The funeral was a large affair. Ellen wasn't there and given what we now know about local gossip condemning the 'new' Mr and Mrs Berkeley for throwing their poor parents out of their home, I cannot blame Rose for not going either. It was by no means certain the estate's new mistress would receive a sparkling welcome; the move wasn't to happen immediately, but the wheels of change were now in motion. For Ellen, the thought of 'losing' her beloved sister would have been devastating.

Up north, the Duchess of Teck continued her jolly progress around the country houses of England. She'd been told to rest, but continued to meet her public and entertain friends, and her diary back home was filling up too. In early October, she and her entourage started zigzagging south.

Of Ellen Willmott at this time we know nothing. I have no reason to think she was not at Warley. She would also have been caring for her mother (who was, by now, quite ill), presumably looking forward to her RHS shindig – and the return of Gian.

It was all getting closer by the day. The duchess's retinue left Appleby Castle in Cumbria on the 9th. On the 10th or 11th they stopped off to visit

Lord Mount Stephen at his country pile, Brocket Hall in Hertfordshire. Then, on 13 October, the *Times* Court Circular caught society off guard.

To the surprise of pretty much everyone, it announced an engagement: of Miss Gian Tufnell to Lord George Mount Stephen.

Jaws dropped. It wasn't just that Mount Stephen was thirty-five years older than his prospective bride (though the papers didn't hesitate to point out the fact),[54] it was that no one had seen it coming. Miss Tufnell was the ball everyone had taken their eye off. 'A withered up old maid, married to a man of seventy!' gasped one 'friend', Garnet Wolseley. 'Plain, somewhat awkward-mannered, clad always in tailor-made English coats and skirts,' sniffed his daughter Frances, 'her boots were the thickest of the thick.'[ix] No one that I can find was aware of any attachment between the couple or that Gian even particularly knew Mount Stephen. His adopted daughter Alice Northcote had known nothing; the news came to her as an unpleasant shock.[55] Mount Stephen is not listed as present at any of the official celebrations over the summer and generally seems to have kept himself to himself. Princess May wrote to Gian the same day as the *Times* article, congratulating her, of course, but in complete astonishment – she'd only seen her friend a couple of days beforehand. When did all this happen?

If anyone had actually thought about it – or the situation – from the bride's perspective, it might have made better sense. Gian had been watching her employer burn the candle at both ends for years. The duchess had had more than one health scare and was *still* partying. If she died, Gian would be left with a rented house and whatever remained of the money her aunt had been allowed to leave her. Women didn't marry women; besides, I can't help wondering whether by now, in the new puritanism of 1897, in her mind Gian hadn't already begun to drift away from Ellen. Perhaps she had always thought of their

---

54 As late as 1906, the *Lincolnshire Chronicle* ran an article about 'ancient bridegrooms'.

55 She and her husband disappeared off to India soon afterwards.

relationship in the 'Victorian' sense: a lovely, intimate friendship that would turn to something more 'normal' when she found a husband – and now was the time.

Mount Stephen's motives for remarriage would have been simpler. He and his first wife had not produced biological children and he needed a sturdy young woman who could give him the 2nd Baron Mount Stephen. There *is*, however, one intriguing entry in the Warley visitors' book for August 1897: none other than George Stephen himself and his adopted daughter Alice, who dropped in on the 20th. Had Mount Stephen been considering Ellen Willmott as a potential bride after all? I can't see that he called in to break the news to her about Gian. It was a good two months before the announcement and Ellen wouldn't have been considered a close enough friend for special treatment. Could my theory be entirely wrong, and Ellen be thinking of marrying him herself? She didn't need to financially, so if she had, it would have been for love, and I can't see any attachment there at all. There are certainly no letters of any kind from him at the time or beforehand. I briefly considered the notion of Ellen as matchmaker between George and her friend but, having lived with her as long as I have, much as I love her, this seems an altruism too far, even for the young Miss Willmott. Besides, if she *had* played Dolly Levi to the couple, relations would surely not have been quite so categorically – or immediately – cut off.

I suspect the first Ellen probably knew of the engagement was friends' gossip, which would have been swift arriving, though no correspondence survives from the time, certainly not from Gian herself. Maybe she sent an explanatory letter only to be shredded into Warley's fire.

The wedding date was set. It was soon. Very soon: 27 October, in fact, less than two weeks away and one day after Ellen's own Big Event.

ANNUS MIRABILIS, ANNUS HORRIBILIS

The morning of 26 October was overcast as the gentlemen – and lady – of the Royal Horticultural Society arrived at the Hotel Windsor for their grand jubilee luncheon. Ellen Willmott's place was empty.

I've already described, in Chapter One, the reaction at Ellen's no-show. Most people then – and since – have assumed that she just plain couldn't be bothered to turn up and receive her award. I don't think so. For me, this is a case of good old-fashioned heartbreak. The woman Ellen loved was to marry a man. For money. Without telling her. I think she did what many people would do in such a situation: she ran away, to lick her wounds in private.

Before 1897, Ellie Willmott was a different person to the image we're usually sold. Light, fun, generous, retiring, kind, rarely in her first thirty-nine years does she display eccentricity, meanness, rudeness or 'difficult woman'. *After* October 1897, laughing, delighted Ellie became the much more serious 'Ellen' – determined, sharp-tongued and, on occasion, yes, 'difficult'. Still funny, right up to her death she could turn a phrase on a sixpence, often using herself as the butt of the gag – but no one would ever get to her heart again.

Around her, attitudes changed too. How abominably rude could you get? She had been given a place at the men's table and had thrown it back in their faces. I can't see that an apology was sent for her absence; there is none mentioned in the minutes. No longer horticulture's golden girl, no one could deny Willmott's genius at growing things (often seeds they couldn't get to germinate themselves), but these men had now seen a different side of that 'girl': a woman, who was clearly getting above herself. It was glossed over on the day. Gertrude Jekyll, who had turned up, was declared Queen of Spades[56] and the medals were distributed, but, subtly, the world turned; things would never be quite

---

56 I once read a modern article suggesting that, at the same time as calling Miss Jekyll the 'Queen of Spades', Dean Hole named Miss Willmott 'Queen of Hearts'. After many hours in the Lindley Library searching for this reference, I think I've found the confusion. The Queen of Hearts is not mentioned but Dean Hole *does* talk of two other queens in his speech: Victoria, Queen of England, and the rose, Queen of Flowers.

the same again. It was all a horrible mess, and things were just about to get a whole lot messier.

That night, the Duchess of Teck took a turn for the worse, needing an immediate, emergency operation. She never woke up.

Next morning, White Lodge was in uproar. On 27 October – Gian's planned wedding day – Ellen received a telegram at Tresserve: PRINCESS MARY DIED SUDDENLY YESTERDAY MORNING. It had been forwarded from Warley; Gian was clearly unaware her former friend was not at home.

Shaken to the core, Gian followed up with a letter the next day, black-edged, also addressed to Warley, the only letter of hers we can definitely date to 1897. 'Darling, it is difficult to write – this awful shock has simply stunned one.' At the end, she hints she still needs Ellen, ending, 'I am here certainly till next week.' Did she get a reply? We'll never know.

The Gentlewoman was adamant the duchess would not have wanted the wedding to be postponed too long and the magazine got its wish. The nuptials were postponed by exactly one month, to 27 November. Princess Mary Adelaide was buried in St George's Chapel, Windsor. Gian performed one final duty for her Missus, walking ahead of the coffin with Lady Katherine Coke, the duchess's other lady-in-waiting.

Warley's visitors' book records a curious visit for 14 November that year, scrawled in familiar, looping handwriting. The obvious reason for Gian Tufnell turning up a few days before her wedding would be to set things straight with Ellen, but was her former intimate even there? Did she arrive only to find Ellie still at Tresserve, and just spend time with the by-now-extremely-poorly Mrs Willmott? There is a photo in the archives of 'something alpine', dated 18 November 1897, that implies Ellen was still in France, but there are also two other signatures from the day after Gian's visit: gardening pals John Bennett Poë and William Gumbleton, maybe visiting to find out what had happened to their friend a couple of weeks earlier. Perhaps she was there to receive them, perhaps not.

Late in 1871 the four 'Willmott women' visited professional photographer Byrne & Co in Hill St, Richmond. Top left to bottom right: Ada, aged 7, Rose, aged 11, Ellen, aged 13, and Mrs Ellen Willmott. Ellen and her mother are dressed identically.

© *Berkeley Family and Spetchley Gardens Charitable Trust.*

Top left: Mr Frederick Willmott.

Top right: Countess Helen Tasker.

Bottom: Warley Place, 1890, by painter and astronomer Nathaniel Everett Green FRAS.

© *Berkeley Family and Spetchley Gardens Charitable Trust*

Top left: Family holidays seeded Ellen's lifelong passion for everything alpine as shown here by a badly-damaged cabinet card photographed by Atelier Muegle, Thun, Switzerland. Left to right: unknown lady, Rose Willmott, Ellen Willmott.

Top right: Back home, the girls dressed up in the costumes again. Here Rose poses for Ellen's camera in Warley's conservatory.

Bottom left: The rock garden at Warley, Ellen's ultimate expression of alpine joy.

© *Berkeley Family and Spetchley Gardens Charitable Trust*

Top: Warley Place, Essex, the Willmott family home.

Bottom: Taking tea at Warley. Left to right: Frederick Willmott, Rose Willmott, Mrs Willmott, Countess Tasker.

© *Berkeley Family and Spetchley Gardens Charitable Trust*

Top: Spetchley Park, the Berkeley family seat.

Bottom: Taking tea in the portico. Left to right: Mowbray Berkeley, Constance Berkeley, Lady Catherine Berkeley (seated at table), Etheldreda Berkeley (seated on rug), Maurice Berkeley, Maud Berkeley, Wolstan Berkeley (pouring tea), Rose Willmott.

© *Berkeley Family and Spetchley Gardens Charitable Trust*

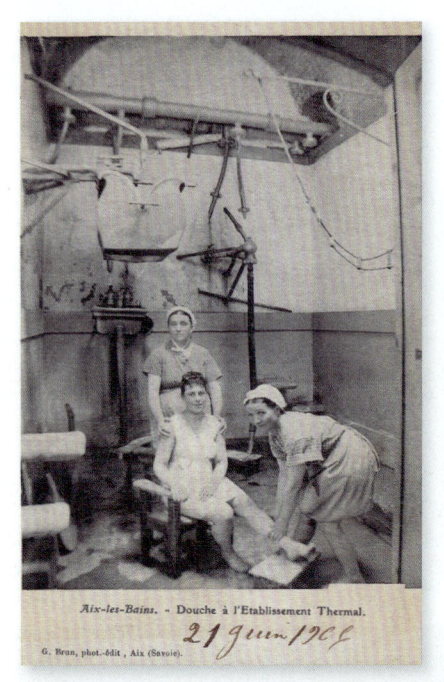

Aix les Bains catered for the health tourist's every need. From their douche-massages in the baths patients were transported home by porteurs to spend the rest of the day – and night – socialising.

Top: The villa and gardens at Tresserve.

Bottom: Mr Henry Correvon (probably) inspects early layouts at Tresserve.

© *Berkeley Family and Spetchley Gardens Charitable Trust*

Top: Taking tea at the Hotel Savoy, Aix les Bains. Left to right: unknown lady (standing); possibly Gian Tufnell (seated); possibly Lady Henry Grosvenor (pouring tea); Mrs Rose Berkeley (standing with cup).

Bottom: Mrs Rose and Mr Robert Valentine Berkeley.

© Berkeley Family and Spetchley Gardens Charitable Trust

ANNUS MIRABILIS, ANNUS HORRIBILIS

If Ellen had returned to Warley, and if she did, indeed, see Gian, she wasn't mollified. On 27 November, Gian Tufnell and Lord George Mount Stephen were married at St Margaret's Church, Westminster, reported by many papers, not least for the ghoulish 'wedding-halted-by-royal-death' angle. *The Gentlewoman* mentions the event in both its 'Overheard by the Little Bird' and 'Social Peepshow' columns. The bride 'looked radiantly happy'[x] in ivory satin; young Eleanor Berkeley was one of four bridesmaids. Out of respect for the duchess it was a simple affair, attended only by 'intimate friends'. Gian's *most* intimate friend of the previous three years was not present.

Ellen was back in England by December. Her mother was dying. Rose was expecting another child and unable to care for Mrs Willmott; there was no one else. In obvious distress Ellen called on the services of a physician.

Doctor Norman Moore was a brilliant man who could not only keep up with her intellectually, but stretch her, and Ellen Willmott's mind liked nothing better than to be stretched. Over the next twenty-odd years the pair would write to each other on a very regular basis and, for once, we have much of both sides of the conversation.[57] Moore was initially brought in to tend her mother, but Ellen confided that she herself was suffering, both from her old back trouble and new, persistent headaches. He prescribed for both.

I've spent a lot of time battling with the events of 1897. I'm now pretty sure that as someone who once told Norman Moore she never discussed her troubles with anyone,[58] there had been only one option for Ellen Willmott that October: to get out of town. To have been in Britain and *not* gone to the wedding of so close a friend would have invited comment, so she went to Tresserve, a place of safety, where she

---

57 The Moores are one of those fantastic families where nothing was ever thrown away. Charlotte Moore's 2010 bestseller *Hancox* (Penguin), includes much about her great-grandfather Norman.

58 Frankly, another of her 'grand statements'. In later years Ellen Willmott liked nothing better than loudly complaining about her situation.

and Gian had once been happy. That Princess Mary Adelaide suddenly died the day beforehand was a complication neither of them could have foreseen; but at least in November Ellen could use her mother's illness as an excuse to avoid Attempt Two. She sent the bride a gift though.[59] It, too, is now lost, but was recorded in the newspaper reports:

A jewelled cigarette case.

---

[59] There was nothing for George Stephen.

Interlude:

The Queen of Spades

TWO PAIRS OF BOOTS

A heavily worn pair of leather Balmoral boots, well-patched, much repaired; and an equally worn, equally battered pair of wooden sabots. Low-heeled, lace-up and still sporting hobnails and metal toe-plates, the boots have, over many years, moulded to their owner's feet. Sabots, by their very nature, are less willing to bend to their wearer's will. There has been an understanding between these fur-lined wooden clogs and their keeper: years of service in return for the wearer's feet adapting to them.

ELLEN IS BACK at Warley. The winter is at its darkest. Her mother is dying. Her sister is leaving. Her particular friend has just married a man. And in the heady world of horticultural politics, someone else has just been declared the Queen of Spades.

It has taken nine chapters – just under forty years – to get to the most famous woman in gardening but there is no putting it off any longer. In truth, I think it took Gertrude Jekyll and Ellen Willmott much the same amount of time to figure out what they felt about each other.

One of the heaviest-trodden clichés about Ellen Willmott is a famous quote by Gertrude Jekyll, describing her as 'the greatest of all living woman-gardeners'. Such epithets make the whole Edwardian horticultural scene sound very cosy and collegiate. And, in many ways, it was. Gardeners did share their findings, plants and ideas, and there were many friendships, not least between the two 'biggest' women on the scene. It wasn't always as simple as that though, or at least not to start with.

There's no denying the quote – it's in Jekyll's 1908 bestseller, *Children and Gardens*, in a chapter about playhouses; accompanied by one of Willmott's photographs and a very clearly signalled nod to the women's friendship that would have gone way over any young readers' heads.[60] Reading against that well-worn grain, however, the statement becomes something rather different: a public olive-branch after an unspoken – how to put it – *mistrust* between the pair that might, without check, have soured a long relationship.

---

60 'The picture was done by my friend Miss Willmott, the greatest of all living women-gardeners, and given me by her for your book', *Children and Gardens* (Country Life Books, 1908).

'It is an unwritten rule for gardening writers that they can criticise anyone they like but they must not criticise Miss Jekyll,' writes the equally hallowed Dr David Hessayon.[i] I have no intention of breaking that tenet. Indeed, I am angry at finding myself pitting two fine women against each other rather than pitching either of their skills against those of any number of male gardeners, which is much more rarely done. I am happy to report the pair came to much the same conclusion. It's worth taking a look at their initial mutual wariness, though, as an illustration of how society has traditionally assumed there can only ever be one Queen Bee.

For once, although as usual we only have one side of the conversation, in this particular case the voice from the past is actually Ellen's, via letters to Dr Moore. Even better, we have another 'half-conversation': that of Gertrude Jekyll to Ellen Willmott, though it quickly becomes clear that fewer of her letters survive.

Despite a gap in their chronological years – Jekyll was fifteen years older than Willmott – there was less of a difference in their 'horticultural ages'. Born in 1843, Jekyll began her career as an artist. Despite a lifelong interest in flowers, she only began taking gardening seriously as her eyesight began to fail, as a way to continue making art on a broader 'canvas'. In 1876, the very same year that an eighteen-year-old Ellen Willmott arrived at Warley Place, Gertrude's father died and the Jekyll family moved to Munstead, Godalming, where she began designing the garden.

Ellen Willmott was brought up to be a plant lover above all other aspects of gardening; if we keep the art analogy, she was more interested in the paint than the picture. Her gardening was heavily directed towards grouping plants with others that required similar conditions or came from the same geographical region, rather than creating something 'artistic' with colour, structure and pattern. I have often heard people say she collected plants more for their curiosity, rarity and, frankly, their cussedness in growing requirements than for what they actually looked like. Some of her rarest plants aren't very exciting to look at but present the ultimate gardener's challenge: getting them to grow at all.

By contrast, while Gertrude Jekyll knew her gardening onions, *her* greatest pleasure was in creating 'images' with tonally pleasing palettes and structurally exciting design. She knew, both instinctively and from her artistic training, how to put together complementary plantings, combining flowers, colours and foliage. This intensified after a chance meeting with architect Edwin Lutyens in 1889. As the much younger[61] Lutyens' star rose, Jekyll's rocketed too; their talents fused to a mutual foil of taste and elegance. Together, they would create some of the most exciting gardens of the late nineteenth and early twentieth century. For anyone who chiefly wanted a garden to enjoy rather than a constant source of toil, Jekyll was the woman to call. Indeed, she created 400-odd such works of art. Ellen Willmott largely worked alone, especially after her sister's move to Spetchley, and rarely designed gardens for others, though she is often credited with 'advising' on gardens at country houses across Britain.

Jekyll wrote prolifically: many of her books are still in print and she wrote over a thousand articles for *Country Life*, *The Garden* and other magazines. She would become editor of *The Garden* in 1899. Ellen Willmott was not so prolific. In general, she preferred her photography and her plants to speak for her.

In many ways, then, although they were both 'in horticulture', Jekyll and Willmott followed different paths within it and weren't much of a threat to each other. They also had much in common. Both enjoyed photography and painting, both were interested in science and both enjoyed the creative process of craftsmanship.

Jekyll was older and more established than Willmott. She had been given the freedom to go to art school and had been encouraged to learn about science from a young age. She had worked with Ellen's hero

---

61 He was twenty, she was forty-six.

William Robinson since 1881, and contributed to the Willmott women's bible, *The English Flower Garden*. To Ellen, Gertrude was popular, knowledgeable and had a partner-in-gardening who was clearly going to be big. To Gertrude, Ellen was the brilliant young whippersnapper, more conventionally attractive, more physically active, with plenty of money and ideas, and rapidly gaining popularity and influence in the gardening elite. Both would have also been aware, even if only subliminally, of the 'one lady is decorative; two are an invasion' subtext.

We don't know when the two women first met, but I'm voting for some time around 1893 or slightly earlier, when the Willmotts commissioned Lutyens to work his makeover on Rose's house, Warley Lea. Perhaps they discovered the young architect through Jekyll; no one knows. It may, once again, have had something to do with that great mover and shaker Minnie Grosvenor. Warley Lea was a bread-and-butter job for Lutyens and he didn't spend long on it, but something seems to have happened during that time that set Rose Willmott and Minnie Grosvenor against Gertrude Jekyll.

We hear about it, obliquely, in 1900 when Ellen tries to explain to her friend Norman Moore why she doesn't actually like her 'rival', even though Gertrude is pleasant to her personally. Ellen is self-aware enough to realise that in many ways, the fault is her own. She writes, on 19 February 1900, replying to a (now lost) letter where he has, presumably, mentioned her and Gertrude in the same sentence:

> *I always feel that I am wrong in not <u>quite</u> liking Miss Jekyll. I do <u>not</u> actually dislike her & I admire her greatly in many ways & I have a high opinion of her capabilities. The true reason for my not liking her thoroughly is, I firmly believe, due to prejudice. My sister dislikes her greatly & my dear friend Lady H Grosvenor did so equally. They had both reason to do so for she had been at different times very rude to them.*

I have not real reason.

It is true that the first time I met Miss Jekyll she sat upon me, she probably believed I wanted sitting upon & put all her weight into it. I did not resent it although I felt a little hurt, however I did not show it. That was the only time I could take exception as to Miss Jekyll's manner or action towards me. I believe she realises that not in any particular whatever could I clash with her & that I have neither the wish nor the ambition to do so.

She always now speaks nicely of me & to me & that is all I wish of any one.

I ought not to be a partisan, it is not profitable & is often very inconvenient, but it is born in some of us like other faults & grows apace if not checked.
My sister & my friend had not been well treated by Miss Jekyll & naturally in feeling I sided with them.

What a rigmarole.

Even Ellen Willmott seems to secretly think she probably deserved 'sitting on' the first time the two met. It's easy enough to imagine her accidentally blundering into Jekyll's world, young, bright and cocky, ruffling the older woman's feathers. Perhaps Gertrude felt bad after the initial sitting-on; she may well have felt even worse after the whole 'Queen of Spades' thing. Certainly by 1899, she was trying to include Ellen, inviting her to contribute to *The Garden*:[ii]

Dear Miss Willmott,
You will no doubt have heard that the 'Garden' has changed hands – but perhaps not that I am on the new editorial staff.

The only changes, will be we hope, to its much bettering as to beauty of illustrations & general get up. As the old traditions will go on & we hope be always strengthened, it is hoped that all old friends will be faithful & even more assiduous than ever.

Your support is much wanted and any photographs of beautiful garden efforts or details with your own remarks will be as always of the greatest value.

I add my own personal request to that of the paper. The new issue begins with the New Year & the first numbers are already in preparation so that if you could send something may we have it soon? Straight to me here if you will, as I do not go to the office & anything that came from you would be in my department.

I only wish I had some of your fine strength for I am very keen about this work. People are all so much alive to the delights of good & beautiful gardening that some fresh vigour in the paper that takes the lead in that way ought to be appreciated.

The old headings "Garden Thoughts" & "Notes of the Work" will go on, so that quite small notices of anything of beauty or interest will also be always welcome.

Yours sincerely

G Jekyll

This is three months before the 'sitting on' letter; we now see why Ellen was hedging her bets. She feels loyalty to her sister and her dead friend, but Gertrude *is* being very nice to her.

Or is she? There is a little passive aggression between the above lines, and it was to intensify. In 1901, Gertrude writes what is, on the surface, a perfectly friendly letter.[iii] Sent from home, it uses *The Garden* headed notepaper, showing Ellen exactly who's in charge.

It starts out with a compliment: 'Many thanks for the capital photograph of your Iris, I hope we shall be able to make a good block of it,' but immediately adds, 'though it is a pity that it happened to be so close to other foliage of Daffodil and Grape Hyacinth, all so much of the same type'. She continues with what looks like a piece of friendly advice: 'Did you ever notice in photographing that if you can secure a distinct effect of light and shade without sunlight that it is greatly to the benefit of the picture? Sunlight makes a hard glitter on every shiny leaf that often makes a fussy effect of what would otherwise be a good picture.' Ellen Willmott would have found the remark patronising at the very least. She had already told Norman Moore 'Miss Jekyll's expression was very rude I thought' a year previously. Alas, the 'rudeness' on that particular occasion is lost.[iv]

The letter continues. After asking Willmott to employ a new artist Jekyll has discovered, telling her Miss Charters is 'better than Moon, except at his very best' (Henry Moon had just painted *Narcissus* 'Ellen Willmott'), Jekyll goes on to try to transfer Ellen's invitation for *her* to visit Warley to someone else. She does at least have the grace to admit it's a bit of a cheeky ask: 'I told him that entrance to the Warley gardens was a very difficult matter.' This carefully worded letter, with equal quantities of flattery and 'sitting on' acknowledges the magazine needs Ellen's work – 'I hope your P.S. about Mr Hanbury's Anemones means that we may have the use of one of the photographs' – but makes it clear who is in the driving seat. It ends promisingly, though: 'I wish I had the pleasure of seeing you a little oftener. I think you know how welcome your visit would be to me at any time though . . . I hardly venture to ask you to come.'

Gertrude's 'suggestions' for improving Ellen's photography were not taken well. 'I do not think the manner in which she teaches is attractive,' Ellen wrote two months later, ostensibly talking about her rival's new book but clearly still smarting over Gertrude's more personal remarks.[v]

Not that the pair didn't occasionally come together for a little mutual snippiness. 'Many thanks for letting me see Mr Wilks's[62] letter. I have written him my "groan" about Mr Hall,'[63] wrote Jekyll, at the back end of 1901, adding, 'without, of course, any hint that I have seen his letters.'[vi] The unknown irritation by Mr Hall continued into January 1902. 'Many thanks for sending [illegible]'s letter. I am glad that the dissatisfaction exists also among the tradesfolk where one scarcely looks for taste,' sniffs Jekyll. 'I wrote rather strongly to Mr Wilks (of course not saying I had seen his letter to you) but have not heard anything from him. I sent him a private note saying that my strong letter was <u>official</u> if he thought it could possibly do any good, but that he could suppress it if he thought it better to do so.'[vii]

Any cosy backbiting and political plotting between the two did not lower Ellen Willmott's guard. On 16 Feb 1902, she wrote to Norman Moore: 'The other day a friend was dining with the Jekylls & Miss Jekyll said something complimentary about me. Lady Jekyll said, "Well, I am surprised, I thought you did not like Miss Willmott, you have always run her down." Miss Jekyll was most indignant & protested she had always liked me very much. I was amused.'

And yet, slowly, the women's relationship sweetened. The letter just quoted is the last I know of, from either woman that, in any way, badmouths the other. From spring 1902, they appear to have not only made their peace, but to have found much to champion in one another. Gertrude was invited to design a garden at Tresserve, albeit for a couple Ellen didn't get on with, and when Henry Correvon visited her there, Gertrude told him she had never known a gardener of Ellen's worth. Before long the women were quite the mutual force.

It would be easy, lazy and frankly untrue to claim that Ellen Willmott and Gertrude Jekyll's relative fame, then or now, was the result of one

---

62 The Reverend William Wilks, famous for the Shirley Poppy.

63 Probably Alfred Hall, Principal of Wye Agricultural College. We have no clue as to his crime.

October afternoon back in 1897. Gertrude Jekyll was the Queen of Spades long before Dean Hole announced it to the gardening world at the Victoria Medal of Honour ceremony, and there are many reasons why she is more famous than Ellen Willmott today, not least the relative amounts of the two women's surviving physical evidence.

My objects for this interlude are two sets of gardening footwear, as different in nature as the women that wore them. Miss Jekyll's boots are presented to us today as a loving 'portrait' of a woman that would not waste valuable daylight hours posing for an artist. Sir William Nicholson famously used the time he waited while Miss Jekyll dug her garden to paint her old boots, making his 'real' portrait of her by artificial light. Those boots have come to represent a busy mind and a hard-working woman. I can't help wondering if they had been Ellen Willmott's they might have been differently interpreted as a sign of wilful self-importance; of someone 'wasting' someone else's time. The painting is inspired and the boots themselves are in Godalming Museum. I rejoice in that as much as I mourn Ellen Willmott's long-gone wooden sabots, probably chucked in a bin while her house was being cleared. All we have is a little note from the clog-maker – A. Garrouste, of 4 rue d'Aurinques, Aurillac, informing her that her latest pair of fur-lined sabots will cost 11fr. 26.

Chapter Ten:

Picking Up the Pieces

A SILVER-HEADED KEY

A large, metal house key; its shank pock-marked with age, its teeth as angular as an Aztec temple. The original bowhead has been hacked away and replaced with a quatrefoil finial in silver, its centre perforated like a church window. The flower-shaped hole is filled with a curling silver scroll bearing the name 'Miss Willmott' in a fancy, serif font. Its accompanying silver ring, almost as large as the object itself, is wrought in solid silver to form a coiling capital letter: 'E'.

THE WARLEY PLACE visitors' book, while an admittedly useful resource, can be as much of an unreliable narrator as its former owner. Not that it lies on its pages, of course. There are no false entries or fake visitors. Its sin is of omission and there is no way of knowing just how big the transgression is. Entire years go by without a single recorded visitor when it's clear from even what correspondence we have that the house enjoyed plenty of comings and goings. In 1898, however, I am inclined to believe the paucity of names scrawled across its pages.

Although she would never look back on 1897 with undiluted pleasure, it was 1898, the aftermath of the *annus horribilis* that would become Ellen's real dark year of the soul. Her letters that spring reveal a pressure cooker of nerves. She suffered constant headaches, her back was playing up again and it was obvious to all that her mother was dying. Rose was pregnant, Henry Correvon was in Switzerland, George Engleheart was banned and Léon Brachet was seriously ill. He would not see out the year.

Ellen hid herself away, tending her mother to the point where people began to worry. In years to come she would brush off those 'lost' months, saying merely that she had 'been ill', but her physical symptoms hid a growing depression and profound loneliness. In March she tried a little respite break to Plymouth. It was hopeless. She told Dr Norman Moore, 'I was so melancholy there alone that I was too thankful to come back home,' admitting, 'I still have the same sort of headache, and at the back of my neck as well.'[i] Her letters ache with loss, ostensibly talking about a frail old lady in pain – 'she had scarcely 4 hours sleep last night' – but she is also describing herself.

A cabinet full of fat, leather-bound medical casebooks at the Moore family home in Sussex reveals how Dr Moore treated Ellen during that difficult time, and beyond. Moore's notes regarding Ellen Willmott in 1898 do not describe much in the way of physical illness. His patient is not sleeping, but her heart is good, her chest does not rattle, her knees jerk properly and her pupils react just fine. She is 'much thinner', he observes, however, having lost nearly a stone 'since Aix' – four, perhaps even three months ago. She suffers from headaches and boils, and her tongue is 'much furred'. She is also extremely weak. Moore insists on bed rest and that she is 'not to rush about'. He prescribes 'blue pills'.

'Methylene blue' was the world's first-ever fully synthetic drug. Created in 1876 by German chemist Heinrich Caro, by the 1890s it was being used in the treatment of depression. Today, some use the drug as a placebo; whether or not this is how Moore prescribed it then is unknown. The pill's most obvious effect is in staining its user's urine bright blue, which makes them think 'something' is happening. Ellen Willmott mentions several times how pleasant she finds her medicine.

A man wise beyond his era, Norman Moore was an early exponent of treating the whole body rather than the ailment and he recognised that Ellen was not just suffering physically. 'I am so pleased with the book,' writes Ellen, as it becomes clear that she has found the latest in her pattern of intense, platonic friendships with men. In the same letter she says, 'I do hope Mrs Moore continues to improve surely. It would be such a pleasure if she were able to come and see our Daffodils,'[iii] proving that, contrary to reputation, Ellen Willmott was not against eminent men's wives in principle.

Alas, for all his medical prowess the doctor could not save Mrs Moore; Amy would pass away in 1901. Norman would marry his wife's cousin Millicent (he stayed at Warley for three nights before the wedding) and conduct a discreet affair with another woman, but as with all her relationships with men, Miss Willmott was only ever a friend.

Death finally took Mrs Willmott on 31 May 1898. Her passing was hardly a surprise, but Ellen was completely floored. 'The only thing I seem to realise is that I am quite broken-hearted.'[iii]

Grief now compounded the previous autumn's stress. Ellen took to bed. Her brother-in-law, Robert Valentine, alerted the doctor: 'You ought to know that Miss Willmott's temperature last night was 101.2. This morning it was 99.6. She only slept for 3 hours from 12.30 a.m. to 3.30 a.m. The night before she was walking about the house all night.'

There is an odd flurry of correspondence that shows just how distressed Ellen was in June 1898. Thanks to the Willmotts' friendship with the Petre family, Mrs Willmott was not buried at Brentwood Cathedral with her husband but interred at the Petres' private chapel in nearby Thorndon Park. Ellen asked if she might move her father's remains there too; the implication being that Ellen herself might lie there in time to come. Lord Petre gave his formal assent. There follows much paperwork as Ellen jumps through various governmental hoops to gain a Licence for the Removal of Human Remains – including the document itself – yet Frederick Willmott's grave is still, apparently, at Brentwood. Is he in it – or by his wife's side at Thorndon? Hers is a double plot, the Home Office papers are intact, but Fred's name is not on the stone and there are no extant church records. Was he moved? If not, why did Ellen go through all the distressing red tape of getting a licence, then not follow through? If she did, why did she not have her father's name added to the memorial? Whatever happened, there's an empty grave somewhere, which probably says more about Ellen's state of mind in 1898 than any piece of paper, and would have been my 'object' for this chapter if I could work out which tomb didn't contain a body.[64]

---

64 Probably Thorndon, though alas, the present Lord Petre has no more idea than I have.

One of the reasons Ellen was in such a state should have been a happy one. Rose had given birth to a son on 23 April, just in time for his grandmother to briefly greet him. Yet another Robert Berkeley, he would be known as 'Rob', and came as something of a relief since, despite plenty of sons in the current generation, there was a distinct lack of male Berkeley heirs in the next, either in the Spetchley branch of the family or the titled line at Berkeley Castle. Rose, in her innocence, invited Lord and Lady Mount Stephen to be godparents. We don't know if Ellen was also godmother, but even if she didn't have to stand next to Gian at the font she could hardly have avoided the christening.

Gian, who perhaps had never seen her relationship with Ellen as anything other than temporary, seems to have been oblivious to any personal awkwardness. She had often visited Mrs Willmott and wrote of her the way she might describe her own mother. Gian sent a telegram to Ellen at 8.55 a.m. the morning after Mrs Willmott's passing.[iv] 'Am too shocked (and) most deepest grieved my heart and thoughts with you darling entirely. God help you. Gian.' It would be her last-known communication for ten years and was probably not much solace.

Ellen's mental health continued to deteriorate. Rose wrote to Dr Moore, confiding her fears: 'She was scarcely in bed all last night, walking about the house all the time. I am very worried for her.'[v]

Probate was granted on 21 June. Ellen Willmott was finally mistress of Warley. She was also entirely alone.

The rest of 1898 seems to have been a blur. Ellen travelled a little and did a few gardening things. There was a nice piece in *The Garden* about her orchids. She became a founder member of the Midland Daffodil Society,[65] whose council was an encyclopaedia of the narcissus world, including John Bennett-Poë, William Wilks and Robert Sydenham. Even George Engleheart and Peter Barr lay aside their metaphorical hatchets to join the committee. The initial meeting

---

65 It would eventually lose its regional moniker to become the grander-sounding Daffodil Society.

took place in July. If Ellen was present it's unlikely she had her mind entirely on daffs.

The months dragged by. 'I have been down in the depths again,' she wrote to Norman Moore. 'Miss Hunter told us last afternoon that Rosy had told her . . . that she & Robert had decided to go to live at Spetchley.' Ellen, as ever, held her head high. 'I did not let her see that I minded & I only made a casual remark about it.'[vi]

The impending loss of her sister sent her into further spirals of despair, but perhaps finally recognising Rose and Robert Valentine's inevitable move was what brought this woman of such infinite resource out of herself.

New Women of the 1890s are often depicted in art with a latchkey, symbolising their independence. No man could prevent a woman's coming and going as it took her fancy if she held the key to the door. One of the first things Ellen Willmott did when she finally became mistress of Warley Place was have the top sawn off the house's front door key. It was replaced with a silver head, *Ellen Willmott* emblazoned across its centre, complemented by a huge silver keyring in the shape of a letter E.[66] She would later commission an engraving of the Warley house and pleasure garden executed in the style of those eighteenth-century 'Kip and Knyff'[67] topographical prints that haunt the back corridors of National Trust properties.

Staggering in its detail, this anonymous masterpiece includes every last sundial, cabin, dog and tree – even Miss Willmott herself – though curiously, fails to disclose that Warley is on a steep hill. It was duplicated for distribution, with the best copies hand-tinted. She also had a map drawn of the entire estate, including Warley Lea, Well Mead and the newly completed Home Farm. In full colour, it is exquisitely detailed with scrolls and snails and flowers, even a dubious coat of arms acquired

---

[66] Le Lievre suggests it was the (equally proprietorial) key to a new safe.

[67] Jan Kip and Leonard Knyff made their names creating detailed 'birds-eye view' topographical engravings of the great eighteenth-century estates, collected like trading cards by members of the gentry.

by Fred Willmott[68] back in the day and bearing the motto *Garde ta Foy*: Keep the Faith. It's hard to imagine a more on-the-nose way of stamping one's ownership on a property, especially when it comes with a range of stationery including vignettes from the map. It was now 'Warley Place, the Seat of Miss E. A. Willmott'. In the same fashion her sister would soon be signing herself 'Mrs Berkeley of Spetchley', even in personal letters to close friends and, on occasion, her own sister. Lady Catherine would not have been amused.

By November Ellen was up to proper visiting – in this case the Reverend Charles Wolley-Dod at Edge Hall, in Cheshire – and reassured Norman Moore, 'I have felt so much stronger in mind since you came to see me & I think this little change, too, will make the good permanent. In any case I shall try to make a fresh start tomorrow when I go home.'[vii]

※

In early January 1899, Miss E. A. Willmott of Warley Place took a tour of Cornwall, staying with her great friends the Falmouths at Tregothnan. Letters from this time begin to show a shift in tone from the formerly sweet, pliant Ellie. She admires the zeal of the impressive restoration and building work at St Michael's Mount, for example, but while admitting the St Aubyn family are 'pleasant people', she can't help worrying 'the house is more like a town'. She does not hold back that it is 'not to my taste, it is not serene enough to suit the situation & position', or hide her disappointment that the St Aubyns have not gone down the wild-garden route for the grounds. Instead 'they have made attempts with shrubs & trees etc. entirely unsuited to the conditions & because they have naturally failed, they have given up the idea of gardening'.[viii] There is the very faintest tone of a later, 'imperious Ellen' in her next sentence: 'I think I gave them a few ideas . . .'

---

68 The coat of arms is for *a* Willmot (sic) family, not necessarily *our* Willmott family, and has traditionally been considered an 'overstretch' by Ellen herself, but we found 'licence to hold arms' renewals by Mrs Willmott. This one's on Fred.

Ellen was beginning to emerge from her grief – Norman Moore notes on 20 January that 'she has gained a stone and is in every way better' – but travelling was not yet working. 'I am much less inclined to leave Warley,' she confided.[ix]

Gradually, she began to receive visitors and meet new people. In March, Norman's son Alan Moore introduced her to his Eton housemaster. Alan's photographs of the pair in 'my tutor's garden' only show Ellen from behind, but the body language says it all: a cool, composed, slight figure waits graciously as an eager-looking gent in his best hat hurries to open the gate for her. In Henry Elford Luxmoore she had made yet another conquest. Around a hundred letters from him still exist; there would have originally been many more. H. E. Luxmoore's garden still exists at the school, though it appears largely to have gone over to greenery, a far cry from his early twentieth-century floral-fest, filled by many years of plant-swapping with Ellen Willmott.[69]

A mass of nigh-on illegible, faint-pencil scrawl, Ellen's many remaining plant notebooks are almost impossible to read by non-experts in Victorian botanical terminology (like me). What is clear, however, is the command she held over everything that went on in her gardens. Every variant is noted, every success celebrated, every mutation earmarked, either as an exciting new sport or the next addition to the compost heap. 'Lucifers ought to be replanted and not so thick, only the largest bulbs'; 'The rest on this bed not to be lifted'; 'Moonstone must come next to Moon Ray'; 'Mrs Bowley makes the bed too crowded'.

The new energy pulsing through Ellen Willmott seemed to peak with the new century. As well as the Warley estate, she had inherited £70,000 from her mother, well over £9m today. She could lavish not just time and energy but money on the best plants the world could offer and the best people to look after them: Head Gardener James Preece, Alpine Foreman Jacob Maurer, Herbacious Foreman Thomas Candler. Mr

---

69 I may be wrong about the lack of flowers. The garden is private and I have only seen pictures on the internet.

PICKING UP THE PIECES

Goodwin headed up the rose section; Mr Dyer the chrysanthemums. An entirely different team tended the vegetables. It was around this time that Warley's complement of gardeners reached its peak of 104[70] and there's no doubt Ellen Willmott directed everything. Everyone wore the Willmott-designed uniform: straw boaters with a green band; knitted green silk ties and navy-blue aprons.

For someone so dependent on her workers, Willmott was not a generous employer, or at least not financially. Like most gentry she paid the going rate and no more. Worse, unlike most gentry, she worked among her staff. They were never alone; never knew where the Chatelaine of the Silver Key might pop up and have something choice to say about their efforts. What she *was* well-known for, however, was her patience in teaching journeymen who wanted to learn (those who didn't show enough interest were swiftly shown the garden gate). Ellen often personally oversaw the young men who would later turn up as head gardeners of the great country houses and botanic gardens across the land and, on occasion, the world.

The gardeners must have whooped with joy when she disappeared, visiting those country houses and botanic gardens. The same might be said for at least one of her neighbours. Sometime in the very early twentieth century,[71] Count Lescher of Boyles Court, the estate-next-door, built a row of cottages overlooking her garden, and, for a while, things got a bit out of hand. We'll never know exactly what happened, but it looks as though he was insensitive in his siting of the dwellings and she was less than diplomatic in objecting to them. There is no doubting Warley's peaceful existence was threatened by Lescher's building placement and Fred Willmott would probably have worked it out with his old friend and neighbour, man-to-man. Man-to-woman didn't work so well. Although she later told the story of this almighty ding-dong to

---

70 As recalled by James Robinson to the housekeeper Annie Cotterill in the 1920s.

71 The precise date is unclear.

the young Russell sisters as an amusing anecdote, it is clear from Ellen's letters to Norman Moore that Lescher seriously spooked her, even at one point threatening to shoot her on sight. She admits several times her distress at having to share space in church with her trigger-happy neighbour, though there's no way she would have shown it. Ellen was no diplomat and would have covered her anxiety with belligerence. She eventually built a giant, ivy-clad privacy wall, supported by iron railway sleepers. They're still there (as are the cottages) but it would be years before the neighbours were back on speaking terms. Did she care? Probably, yes. She needed all the friends she could get, but Ellen Willmott had her pride, and her status as a silver-key-holding landowner to protect. She did have *one* up on Lescher: she was receiving some impressive visitors, including a large percentage of the Royal Family, but at what cost? At the end of every day, she was rattling around Warley Place alone (albeit with an impressive coterie of liveried servants).

At Tresserve, too, she went yomping into the Alps by herself, often starting out at 5.30 a.m. or even earlier, and not getting home until 9 p.m.

'The Chaplain & the few peasants who live in the Hospice[72] were greatly astonished to see me,' she wrote of one such trip. 'They had had no visitors for a month & did not expect to see any but the poor foot travellers until next July, when the snow disappears. It is rare at this time of year that the snow has not already come to stay. The Chaplain does not shave from 15 Sept to 15 July & he apologised to me for his month's growth of beard. He lets it grow because it saves trouble & keeps him warm.'[x] The Chaplain was "amused at my appearing . . . for ladies rarely travel for pleasure alone".' Ellen was still smarting that her sister hadn't wanted to come with her, as requested, but does herself no favours in the way she phrases things, making it quite clear she's glad she hadn't had to suffer the 'silliness, dullness and narrow-mindedness'

---

72 The Petit St Bernard, an eleventh-century traveller's hospice.

of the individual her sister had suggested she went with instead. Perhaps she has a point when she explains to Norman Moore that any potential companions (other than Rose) would have been 'bored to death'. In a world where women were brought up on chit-chat and pleasantries, Ellen was always going to be irritated by anything that wasn't in-depth and to-the-point. Her letters, often containing classical quotations, scientific quandaries, musical appreciation and historical debate reveal a serious mind that isn't going to score at parlour-gossip. If someone was worth talking to, she talked to them, whoever they were; Amy Moore, for example, and any number of her female gardening and musical pals. She especially enjoyed the frank, curious conversation of children, who she treated with respect and courtesy. She just couldn't bear vacuous tittle-tattle – from either sex – and unfortunately for her reputation, was unable to let things ride.

In 1904, a First Class Certificate – for *Narcissus* 'Great Warley' (another Willmott/Engleheart collaboration) – saw the start of a spectacular winning streak at the RHS that included four consecutive years of gold medals. In November 2021, we unearthed around fifty staggeringly beautiful watercolours of Ellen's prize-winning daffodils, commissioned from botanical artist Ella Williamson. Worthy of publication, Ellen seems have done nothing more than keep them in a folder to enjoy for herself.[73]

Her fellow RHS members might no longer see her as the sweet little girl they could treat like a precocious grandchild, or even wholly trust her, but they had to admit Ellen Willmott could rear a plant. And take a photograph. She swept the board in the 1900 *Gardening Illustrated* Photographic Competition, winning first prize in five classes: Country Houses, Flowers & Shrubs, Indoor Flowers, Picturesque Effects and Garden Structures. Looking at her extraordinary images of pumpkins and gourds from around the same time, I am only surprised she didn't win the veg class too.

---

[73] There are thirty-five Williamson watercolours of Willmott's irises 1904 to 1908 in the RHS Lindley Library.

The sheer amount of horticultural and intellectual pies Ellen Willmott had her leather-gloved fingers in is staggering. In August she became a founder member of the Railway Banks Floral Association, formed with the laudable ambition of beautifying Britain's tracksides.

Yet things were still not smooth. This new, no-nonsense Ellen was, on occasion, beginning to take out her frustrations elsewhere on folk that did not necessarily deserve it. She had stayed in piecemeal contact with George Engleheart, even if he did finish every missive with 'Please answer by word of mouth', 'Do not answer this' or even 'Burn this'. His predicament had peaked in June 1899 when he had to tell Ellen that although he'd promised to name a new daffodil she had chosen for her sister, 'it is best not to let any Warley names be written or current here'. [xi] *Narcissus* 'Incognita' would become one of the Great Edwardian Daffodils; I only hope Mary Engleheart did not speak Latin.

Given their consistent – and persistent – closeness, it's still difficult to work out what on earth happened between Willmott and Engleheart at the 1900 Truro Daffodil Show. It appears she accused him of the kind of sharp practice they had gossiped about in others. A long, injured letter of 17 April protests his innocence: 'I assure you the words stung me quite as much as ever an enemy could have desired.' Over several pages George takes Ellen, step by step, through the alleged offences in an attempt to prove she is wrong in what do sound like pretty outlandish charges. Why did she lash out at him in such a public fashion? I can't stand up for her here; the palpable distress of the letter and the careful laying-out of his situation convince me she was in the wrong. The matter had blown over by July and they were firm chums again, but this is just the sort of odd behaviour that starts to crop up from now on. The incidents are few and far between, but when they come, they are big, and they do nothing for the reputation that Ellen Willmott had accidentally begun to cultivate in October 1897.

Ellen's grumpiness would have had at least something to do with her chronic rheumatic pain, which had kicked in again, and badly.

Dr Brachet had died in 1898; she was forced to look elsewhere for treatment. She tried out Dr Zander's Institute of Mecanotherapy, which had just opened its doors in Aix-les-Bains. Many of Zander's mechanical exercise machines look remarkably like something you might find in a gym today. The women demonstrating them in promotional photos are swathed in corsets, padding, petticoats, tight jackets and thick overskirts, but they have at least removed their hats. Ellen thought them hilarious: 'You will be amused to hear about the Zander exercises which my sister and I have been doing,' though she admitted they were 'first rate, particularly for strong people with rather stiff joints.'[xii] Perhaps not feeling strong enough, she didn't become a regular client and would continue a quest for miracle cures for the rest of her life.

The visit wasn't entirely wasted. Ellen was an honoured guest at the opening of her old friend Monsieur Bernascon's glamorous new, deluxe Hôtel Bernascon. She enjoyed what looks like a free season ticket to the Casino des Fleurs too, but demons whispered in her ears. She missed her mother. She missed her dead sister Ada, she missed happy days gone by at Tresserve, and although her letters do not mention anything (or any*one*) else she might be missing, the air was heavy with loss. To Norman Moore she admitted a friend had told her 'that I was a failure & a disappointment to all my friends & that I ought to "buck-up", that was her word'.[xiii]

'Bucking-up' means going out and meeting people, right? Joining in, making friends. Ellen went out and met gardening heavyweight Canon Ellacombe for the first time. The canon nearly missed her at the station, as he expected someone older. Ellacombe showed her around the Botanic Gardens at Cambridge; Sir Michael Foster's house was pointed out in the distance. Both men would become close to Ellen, the former as a lifelong friend, the latter as a would-be collaborator. Sadly, Foster died before they could work on the *Genus Iris* together, which Ellen had offered to finance. She met plantsman (and pro-suffrage campaigner) Arthur Bulley, and toured Ireland, taking in Trinity College, Dublin, and the National Botanic Gardens at Glasnevin. Among her regular trips to Europe, she visited the Botanical Gardens at Munich, later moving on to Vienna, constantly broadening her network of personal and horticultural contacts.

At the celebration of the bicentennial of the arrival of sweet peas on British shores, Ellen became the only female founder member of the Sweet Pea Society. She joined the Chrysanthemum Society, the National Dahlia Society, the Tulip Society, the Carnation and Picotee Society, the Essex County Rifle Club, the Brentwood & District Choral & Orchestral Society, the London Library, *le Société Francaise Roséristes*, *le Société Nationale d'Horticulture de France* and any number of smaller institutions. Just attending the meetings of that lot would be exhausting, but she often also took organisational positions. Ellen Willmott has been 'accused' of being a 'committee woman', as though this were some kind of crime. Most people run a mile from the cut-and-thrust of club politics, but the Ellen Willmotts of this world – the folk who thrive on being at the centre of the melee – are much needed. Today, we have one particular reason to be grateful for Miss Willmott's committee-mania . . .

Mr G. F. Wilson had form in trying to get the RHS to take over his gardens. There are no pictures left of his first attempt, an 'experimental garden' called Heatherbank, which is a shame, since I'd have paid good money to see a photograph of his 'Wilson Raft' in action. From the line drawing, this floating bog garden, an invention of his own design, looks like it might actually have worked. Wilson tried to offer the estate to the RHS in 1870, not an ideal time in the Society's history. Nothing came of the suggestion. At his second garden, Oakwood, in the village of Wisley, Surrey, Wilson was able to experiment with an even bigger range of plants, creating a garden much admired by the likes of Henry Correvon and George Engleheart, who both stayed there. Ellen Willmott visited on a near-annual basis from 1894 onwards and corresponded with Wilson on a number of subjects. His range was 'bewildering'; his nursery so divided by scrim-covered iron hurdles that 'it could be mistaken for a sheepfold'.[74][xiv] Wilson was generous with his garden, allowing members of the public to visit, albeit at designated times so as not to tire out his staff.

Both garden and access were threatened in 1902, when Wilson died. The RHS committee was, as usual, divided. Some thought Society funds should be used exclusively for the grand new headquarters being built in Vincent Square; others wanted some cash hived off to pay for a new garden – after all, wasn't that what the whole thing was about? Ultimately, there wasn't enough money to successfully complete both ventures.

Ellen Willmott had been running to catch up ever since the Victoria Medal of Honour incident, doing her bit at shows, turning up to meetings and show-judgings, donating prizes and going all-out to impress with her gardening prowess. In 1903, perhaps in another bid to fit in, Ellen persuaded her old friend Sir Thomas Hanbury to buy – and donate – Wilson's garden at Wisley to the Society.

Ellen Willmott was now respected, had even influenced the direction of Britain's premier horticultural institution, yet she was still not completely loved. When the Society decided to build a gigantic rock garden at Wisley, her offers of help were politely declined, telling her the project had already been put out to tender. She swallowed the snub and donated rare alpines to populate the spectacular 'mountainside', constructed in Pulhamite, rather than her suggested Backhouse boulders, but each little turn-down rankled. She would not have been human not to wonder if her gender might have something to do with it. Would her directness have seemed less threatening if she had been male? There were many men in the Edwardian horticultural world only too well known for their 'difficult' manner; Irishman William Gumbleton and Reverend Henry Bidder of St John's College, Oxford, for starters,

---

74 This source also includes a fascinating account of the acquisition of Wisley.

and, of course, William Robinson himself, who fell out with pretty much everyone on a regular basis.[75] Then there was that young-Turk rock gardener with a chip on his shoulder, fire in his belly and a deft line in devastating put-downs: Reginald Farrer was as dangerous as he was amusing. Half the horticultural world had some kind of *contretemps* with someone, but most of them were in a club that Ellen could never join. For all her committees, donated prizes and hours of legwork, Ellen Willmott was one lonely woman.

If women had not been allowed into a group, Ellen had supported the female alternative – for example, the Empress Club, and the similarly ambitious, if short-lived, Ladies Athenaeum. In 1901 she was delighted to join Gertrude Jekyll and William Robinson as Trustees of Frances Wolseley's new gardening school for women at Glynde.

Where societies did allow women, she joined them and did her best to fit in as fully as possible – witness her role in the RHS. In 1904 Ellen Willmott was elected a life Fellow of the Royal Institution, one of the few major learned societies that allowed female members. For all the Institution's liberality, however, women were not allowed to hold office or give papers. Even the great Marie Curie was obliged to sit and watch her husband Pierre tell Fellows about the couple's joint work. When Henry Jamyn Brooks painted *Sir James Dewar Lecturing on Liquid Hydrogen at the Royal Institution* in 1904, the Institution initially declined to purchase the picture; one of the given reasons being there were too many women in it.[76] Yet it was lionised for allowing women to join at all. Most did not, and by the end of 1904, Ellen Willmott had had enough. She decided to join a small band of women meeting the learned societies head-on.

---

75 All three were very good friends of EAW.

76 Happily, the Institution now owns the painting.

Chapter Eleven:

Flying High

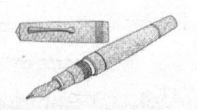

AN APPLICATION FORM

A single sheet of foolscap paper, pre-printed as a Form of Recommendation for a Fellow of the Linnean Society of London. Rubber-stamped 4 Feb 1908, it has been carefully filed in the Society's archives at Burlington House. It has been less carefully filled in, proposing a Mrs Marian Farquharson. Certain details have been scratched out and feminine pronouns hastily superimposed over masculine forms, but since such an application is unlikely to be oft-repeated, it has been deemed hardly necessary to alter the printer's instructions for a whole batch. It bears six signatures. The largest scrawl, in bold black ink, reads 'E Willmott'.

THE NEW WOMAN, after taking a brief dive back undercover in 1897, was once again beginning to emerge – into something new, something militant. Ellen Willmott was looking more like one of Charles Dana Gibson's 'Gibson Girls' every day. Rosina Mantovani Gutti's 1901 pastel study[77] depicts a confident Ellen with a direct gaze and a smile on her lips. Her hair, fashionably bouffant, tied back with chiffon in a white-grey haze, is artistic fancy, since a group photograph taken five years later at a conference at Horticultural Halls shows her as a vision of (probably yellow)[78] satin, frills and black lace, with the same huge hair, neither white nor grey.

Despite the big hair and direct gaze, one path Ellen Willmott does not seem to have followed is the call for women's suffrage. She counted suffrag*ist* Laura McLaren, Lady Aberconwy, and suffra*gette* Ethel Smyth as friends; and other women, such as choir buddy Mary Venables, felt happy enough to send her postcards depicting the banner of the Oxford Women Students' Society for Women's Suffrage. Ellen herself, however, seems to have stopped short of joining in. She did not, apparently, take up the request we found to become President of the Brentwood branch of Millicent Fawcett's National Union of Women's Suffrage Societies, and while she carefully preserved a personal invitation to a meeting of the Women's Political and Social Union (Mrs Pankhurst's suffragettes),

---

77 Originally sketched in charcoal. Ellen was way ahead of the curve, commissioning portraits of herself and Rose four years before the artist shot to fame. Gutti's most famous work, *The Peacemaker*, would later be used, apparently without irony, to sell war bonds.

78 Her favourite colour, as remembered by the Russell sisters. Yellow was also the colour of the New Woman.

there's no evidence she attended that or any other gathering. Perhaps her involvement with the politics at Kew Gardens, which was attacked by suffragette arsonists, divided her loyalty. In a straight fight between voteless women and helpless plants the greenery won every time. It would seem strange, however, for Ellen to have kept something she didn't agree with.

There were many ways to fight for feminist values apart from the suffrage cause célèbre, however, and it was along this infinitely more subtle road that Ellen Willmott would travel. In 1904, having tasted the joys of belonging to one major learned society, The Royal Institution, her ever-enquiring mind looked further. Mrs Marian Farquharson had been conducting a one-woman campaign to allow female members into one of the oldest and most important societies of all, the Linnean, and her dignified, direct action caught Ellen's attention.

The incident is all but forgotten today, but the admission of women Fellows at the Linnean was a big deal at the time; a small but important triumph in the march of feminism. It's worth remembering just how misogynistic Victorian society was. Even the usually charming J. M. Barrie, writing anonymously about a new Literary Ladies dining club, had scoffed that the women 'didn't even know how to operate a Vesta box, vulgarly lighting their cigars at candles on the table'. He added that several of the ladies present 'had contributed to the leading waste paper baskets of the day'.[i] Catherine Furley, who had spoken for The Spinsters at the inaugural dinner, took the insult as encouragement: 'Things are not ridiculed when they are sufficiently trivial to be ignored.'[ii]

The Linnean would find that ignoring their 'female problem' wasn't going to work either. Based at Burlington House, home to several stuffy institutions, the Society boasted an august membership of learned gentlemen, many of whom were closely involved in the science of horticulture and botany. They were not in the business of diluting their worthiness by admitting women.

Miss Marian Ridley's work on mosses and ferns, including three books, had been enough to allow her to become the first female Fellow of the Royal Microscopical Society, albeit she was banned from attending meetings. Even after her marriage, however, the truly grand institutions had shown Mrs Marian Farquharson closed doors. Now widowed, she decided to do something about that. Farquharson wasn't flashy like the suffragettes. Her agitation for women's rights was less easily dismissed as 'shrill' by the patriarchy, but she would be just as vilified in her own circles. On 18 April 1900, Farquharson formally petitioned both the Linnean Society and the Royal Society. If women were 'duly qualified', she argued, they should be eligible for membership and, if elected, they should not be forbidden to attend meetings.

Her applications were thrown out. Numerous times. She quickly realised the Royal Society was a nut too hard to crack alone, and filed away the challenge for later, but within the Linnean she found one or two sympathetic ears. John Lubbock's pointing out there was nothing actively barring women in the constitution, for example, failed to endear the former president to his peers. Old duffers found every possible excuse to declare each of Marian Farquharson's applications ineligible. If they couldn't find anything to complain about, they filibustered until there was no time left to consider her petition. She was making powerful enemies, but by January 1903 news of Farquharson's one-woman campaign was beginning to gain notice. Among the women who decided to join in by applying for membership too, Ellen Willmott threw her enormous feathered hat into the ring.

She turned to her friend (and LS Fellow) Henry John Elwes (1846–1922). Entomologist, ornithologist, lepidopterist and botanist, Elwes's 1880 monograph *Genus Lilium*[79] was a horticultural standard and he was currently working on his magnum opus, *The Trees of Great Britain and Ireland*. There are well over fifty letters from Elwes in the Spetchley archive, written between 1896 and 1925, and Ellen Willmott recognised

---

79 Written with J. G. Baker of Kew, another of Willmott's close associates.

FLYING HIGH

in him a kindred spirit. Anyone that could wear out two cars just going to look at trees was her kind of guy, and the admiration was mutual. In 1899 Elwes received an RHS Award of Merit for his *Nerine* 'Miss Willmott'. *The Gardeners' Chronicle* deemed it 'one of the showiest known', which seems to sum up both breeder and muse. Elwes was more than happy to sign Willmott's Linnean Form of Recommendation but, he warned, she might be better off finding a member of the Council to propose her, 'in view of there being a few malcontents who may make it their business to blackball every lady'.[iii]

Ellen entertained high hopes for the support of Sir William Thistleton-Dyer, director of the Royal Botanic Gardens, Kew. He was a strange old stick, variously fierce and charming – around the same time as he was arranging for Ellen to meet useful contacts at the botanic gardens in Munich and Vienna under his letter of introduction, for example, he was leading the opposition to her suggestion that the RHS acquire Wisley – but he was no misogynist. He had even hired three female gardeners at Kew back in 1896, albeit insisting they wear men's uniform so as not to distract their colleagues.

Ellen's nomination-petition to Thistleton-Dyer seems to have failed, though his Principle Assistant Otto Stapf's signature does appear alongside that of the faithful Elwes.

There were a few sour faces at the Society's meeting on 15 December 1904. Vice President Professor Vines was highly dubious about this new-fangled idea of not only allowing the weaker sex into the club but – heavens! – allowing them to attend meetings. He pronounced himself 'not altogether free from apprehension as to the future', while telling the gentlemen present: 'we are making a somewhat heroic experiment, with no precedent, no working hypothesis to suggest to us what the results are likely to be'.[iv]

'It was rather an ordeal,' admitted Ellen later. 'Mr Stebbing gave a paper upon the Crustacean & he brought a serpent to exhibit. One of the Fellows during the discussion got up to say that it was a curious coincidence that serpents and women should have been admitted to the Society on the same night.'[v]

Ellen Willmott is often miscredited as being the first female member of the Linnean Society. I don't find her big moment any less important for being one of the first *fifteen* female members:

Margaret Benson, D.Sc. Lond. – Botanist
Catherine Crisp – Micrologist and Horticulturist
Laura Embleton BSc – Biologist, Zoologist, Suffragist
Grace Coleridge Frankland, FMRS – Microbiologist
Maria Matilda Ogilvie Gordon, Ph.D Munich – D.Sc Lond.
Gulielma Lister – Botanist, Mycologist
Mary du Caurroy Russell – Aviator and Ornithologist
Ethel Sargant – Botanist and Cell biologist
Sarah Marianne Silver[80]
Constance Sladen – Artist and Natural Historian
Annie Lorrain Smith – Lichenologist and Mycologist
Mary Anne Stebbing – Botanist and Botanical illustrator
Emma Louisa Turner – Ornithologist and Photographer
Lillian Jane Veley, DSc – Biologist and Siamese cat breeder
Ellen Ann Willmott, VMH, Horticulturist

There is one name missing. Marian Farquharson was well and truly blackballed, and continued to be. As soon as they were able to, the women who had benefitted from her determination and personal sacrifice got together to force through the election.[81] Six names appear on the form, including Ellen Willmott's, but by this point Marian Farquharson was seriously ill. She would never formally add the letters FLS after her name.

There is a painting of the ceremony that is as odd as the event itself.

---

80 I am shocked to say I can find nothing about this scientist, either unmarried as she was when admitted, or later as Mrs Sinclair.

81 6 February 1908.

Not only is it huge – the only place large enough to take it at the Society's headquarters at Burlington House is the well of the great staircase – but *The Linnean Society of London First Formal Admission of Women Fellows* has a truly peculiar composition.

Lilian J. Veley signs the membership book at the front. Catherine Crisp receives 'the hand of friendship' from a wary-looking Society President while Treasurer Frank Crisp looks on from the shadows. Some other ladies crowd around the extreme left background behind another gentleman's head, almost out of sight, watched with weary resignation by a chap seated in the middle. So far, so normal. The rest of the foreground, however – a good third of the painting – is taken up with an unremarkable wooden desk and a random empty armchair, painted by what looks like an entirely different hand. Which it is. Very old reproductions of what cannot have been James Sant, RA's finest hour even when first painted, reveal a *slightly* more pleasing composition, including two other figures and no armchair.

The work was commissioned by Sir Frank Crisp, a wealthy lawyer and passionate microscope addict. Another larger-than-life character, Sir Frank was in turns avuncular, generous, a bit of a joker – and very thin-skinned. He would become yet another of Ellen's great male friends, but I'm willing to bet that she didn't know him before she became a member of the Linnean Society, not least because she does not appear in this most peculiar of paintings. I am certain that, had they been acquainted, he would have insisted on her being included. Some years after the event, Sir Frank fell out with the couple depicted in the painting's foreground and had them erased from the picture.[82] I am told that, in certain crepuscular light, two ghostly shapes reappear in the brushwork.

Ellen would become very good friends with another Fellow met that day, mycologist Gulielma Lister. We have only very recently found most

---

82 I have no idea why; all papers between the parties are lost. Stebbings was a fervent Darwinist but I can't see Crisp, a scientist to the core, being anti-Darwin.

of her letters to Ellen; long, interesting, interested, they range across a wide variety of subjects, though Lister's first love was slime mould. She lived in Leytonstone, then part of rural Essex, about twenty miles from Warley, and was an enthusiastic member of the Essex Field Club. Ellen joined the Field Club at the same time as Gulielma; both women hosted talks and events, and went on and led regular organised rambles across the county.

It is clear from her involvement with women from the Linnean Society that Ellen Willmott enjoyed conversing with anyone that would partake of good conversation, whatever their gender, yet she has gone down in history as some kind of ogre when it came to her own sex and, in particular, learned men's wives. Much of this goes back to her desperation to impress one of those learned men, Professor Charles Sprague Sargent. Trying to save her own reputation, Ellen appears to trample all over another woman's, ultimately damaging both when the letters became public property.

Professor Sargent was one of the most powerful players in the early twentieth-century horticultural world. As Director of Harvard University's Arnold Arboretum, Boston, he controlled vast reserves of academic research, acres of land, and globally important botanical collections. He was in charge of horticultural trials, scientific experiments and a large workforce. Importantly, he could also say yea or nay to plant-hunting expeditions across the world. Traditionally, such trips had been made either by individual gentleman adventurers or professionals sent by commercial growers looking for fast bucks rather than any deeper understanding of the botanical world. Sargent was interested in the academic possibilities and scientific rigour of exploration and the cultivation of its results. Luckily for us, he was also very organised, not only keeping many of Ellen's letters, but carbon copies of many of his own. More have recently turned up in Ellen's correspondence, giving us a clear image of their relationship.

Sargent first wrote to Willmott in 1904, introducing himself: 'I have heard so much of your skill and enthusiasm as a gardener and of the beauty and interest of your garden that I am most anxious to see the gardener and the garden.'[vi] We don't have her reply to that first letter, but their relationship appears to have been a bit of a horticultural whirlwind.

Ellen was repeating her habit of intense, platonic friendship, but the relationship also fits Sargent's own pattern of taking on promising young female horticulturists. These would later include landscape architect/gardener Beatrix Jones, barred from becoming a student because she was female and taught personally by Sargent, and botanist Susan Delano McKelvy. He can sometimes come across as a little over-ardent: 'I only wish that I had had the pleasure of knowing you ten years earlier,'[vii] which may have put Ellen on her guard, but generally the tone of the sixty-five-year-old Sargent's letters are more those of a father figure.

Ellen shared her hopes and dreams with her new penfriend, not least of the books she wanted to write. As well as the doomed work on irises she'd planned with Michael Foster, she had, for some time, been nursing her scheme for a definitive volume on the rose. Her fantasies of creating a modern version of Redouté's *Les Roses* may have been born when she met Alfred Parsons all those years ago in Aix. Now they were slowly turning to reality. Under Ellen's commission, Parsons was painting all the varieties at Warley and Tresserve; she showed thirty of them to the Linnean Society in 1905. Sargent was impressed by her passion and happy to help in any way he could. Instinctively recognising her 'girl's education' had left her short, he realised she was floundering with the basics, and gently steered her towards layout conventions. 'I have also asked my publishers to send you the first (and only volume yet) of a work prepared here at the Arboretum on trees and shrubs,' he writes.[viii] 'I am sending it principally to show you how a book looks when the illustrations follow the text.'

Willmott and Sargent's correspondence reveals some of our best information about Willmott's life at this time. She provides him with detailed news about improvements and new plants in her gardens; he persuades her to start a collection of *Crataegus* (hawthorns) and introduces her to American growers such as the Californian nurseryman Carl Purdy, whose catalogues are stunningly beautiful even for a time when *all* garden catalogues were stunningly beautiful. The Sargents become regular visitors to Ellen's gardens at Warley and Tresserve; he constantly presses her to return the favour.[83] The only reason I can come up with why she didn't take up the offer of a trip to the States is that she was just too darned busy. She certainly had the money.

Perhaps because of the physical distance between them, Ellen could be more candid with Charles Sargent than anyone in the intense, incestuous hothouse that was the British gardening world. It is through her letters to him that we glimpse her sometimes 'distant' role within it. She was no longer snubbed for that 1897 no-show, but neither was she particularly welcomed. She had sincere individual friends but, as a whole, the horticultural world seemed to keep its distance. 'I wish you were here this spring,' she wrote. 'I am quite alone with nothing to think about but plants and gardening.'[ix] For a woman who publicly declared that plants were all she lived for, this is quite an admission.

By this point in her life Ellen Willmott had decided that if she was going to be alone, she would be entirely self-sufficient. She held her head high, and she knew her mind. Charles Sprague Sargent seems one of the few people she holds in awe; to whom she shows humble deference. At times she appears genuinely nervous about his opinion of her work; keen, perhaps even desperate to prove herself, especially when it comes to commissioning plant-hunting trips by expert adventurers.

Ernest Henry 'Chinese' Wilson was a journeyman working at the Royal Botanic Gardens Kew when James Veitch asked Sir William Thistleton-Dyer to recommend a useful young chap the company could train up as a plant hunter. The would-be explorer, latest in a long and

---

83 Le Lièvre suggests EAW was snippy about Mrs Sargent. Reading the same evidence I can't draw the same conclusions. Vive la différence.

distinguished line, would be charged with discovering and collecting plants the company could sell from their premises at Coombe Wood.

As a wealthy customer and erstwhile regular visitor to Coombe Wood, Ellen Willmott would have been an obvious part-sponsor of that first trip. She had form: when the van Tubergens brothers of Haarlem sent plant hunters Anton Kronenburg and Paul Sintenis to Persia, Armenia and Turkestan, Ellen had taken a £25 stake. Nursery director John Hoog later upped the offer to her spending £200 per year for a four-year expedition (the company would only be stumping up £150). We don't know if she actually took up Hoog's opportunity, but she certainly leapt at Veitch's offer. Wilson left in 1899, returning in 1902. 'I succeeded very well with Wilson's first expedition,' Ellen tells Sargent. Indeed she did, not only in plants brought back for her but one, a now super-rare peony, was named for her: *Paeonia obovate ssp. willmottiae*. She then reveals something interesting: 'but of the second I was not asked to take a share . . . so I have nothing he collected then'.[x] A quick look at the dates reveals why, and we're right back to that *annus horribilis*. Veitch had gathered sponsorship for Wilson's first expedition before 1897. By 1903, when Wilson left for China again, his triumphs had guaranteed sponsors aplenty; Veitch wouldn't have needed Ellen's ever-so-slightly tarnished support.

Charles Sargent had met Wilson on that first trip; Wilson had travelled via the US and dropped in at the Arboretum for advice and training, albeit with strict instructions from Veitch to ignore all requests from the University to do anything that smacked of research. This was a commercial expedition; he was expected to bring back goodies people would actually want to buy. No ugly stuff, okay? Wilson had obeyed, much to Sargent's disappointment, but he had made a profound impression at the Arboretum. He proved himself a superb collector, sending back nearly 2,600 plants and hundreds of bulbs and seeds on his first trip, even more on his second.

Sargent determined to send Wilson again; this time to Western China, 'now the great field from which new plants are to be introduced',[xi] and collecting directly for the Arboretum. It appears he cooked up the idea while visiting Ellen Willmott at Warley in early 1906. The idea was that the Arboretum would pay for most of the expedition and a few selected individuals, such as Willmott, would be invited to contribute financially in return for a share of the spoils.

There was one problem: Wilson himself. Those years spent in the Chinese hills had seen him brave appalling living conditions, searing heat, freezing cold, torrential storms, pounding rapids, bubonic plague and the Boxer Rebellion. He had a nice, secure job now, at Kew. His wife, Ellen 'Nellie' Wilson, had already endured the stress of waiting at home while her husband undertook two perilous journeys. They had a daughter. This kind of thing had to stop.

Sargent realised Wilson was serious and, on the wrong side of the Atlantic, decided to bring in the big guns. After his customary chiding Willmott for not writing often enough ('When you drove away from the London hotel that April afternoon you seemed to have disappeared into another world'), he gets down to the Wilson business. 'He seems very shaky about going to China again,' he writes, 'and I had hoped that you would have seen him and urged him to undertake this new expedition. As you know, China is still full of novelties and there is no one but Wilson who would make a success of a collecting tour there.' Finally, piling on the pressure, he threatens: 'I feel half-inclined to run over to London this summer for the purpose of talking with him on the subject and I might do it now if it was necessary.'[xii]

Ellen's uncharacteristically swift reply has gone some way to securing her sour reputation as a 'woman-hater'. She begins with repeated and frankly excruciating apologies for pretty much everything – her abominable behaviour in not writing enough, her failure to thank him for some plants, her lack of success so far in persuading Wilson, her embarrassment at not being able to fulfil her part of the agreement. She uses the oldest chestnut in the book: 'Strange to say I had another appointment with Wilson fixed for today, your letter came just as I was starting to motor up to London to the R.H.S. Hall where Wilson was to come according to his promise.'[xiii] She then uses a series of excuses to explain her situation, including some that may actually be true. 'I have waited nearly all day and he has never appeared, no doubt his wife prevented his doing so.'

It is the rest of the letter that becomes difficult for a reader today.

'You have no idea of the difficulty which besets this affair,' Ellen writes. 'Every time I have talked to Wilson I have left him in a tolerably satisfactory state and have felt myself that if there was one thing I could do, it was to roll a stone to the top of a hill and make it stay there.' Then she drops the brick. The evil genius behind nice, decent Ernest Wilson's refusal to risk life and limb for two years in a dangerous country collecting roots is . . . Mrs Wilson. 'If there is one class of person impossible to trial with it is the lower middle-class woman,' sniffs Willmott.

Does Ellen have any idea what she is saying here? Without luck and her father's boundless ambition to enter into the middle-middle-class, she too might have been perilously close to Mrs Wilson's position. 'As a rule she [the lower middle-class woman] has a plentiful crop of all our faults, failing and foibles, a bad enough foundation, then defective education which is far worse than none,' Willmott continues, skimming over – or deflecting from – her own imperfect schooling.

Perhaps Nellie Wilson's worst crime in Ellen Willmott's eyes, however, is a lack of adventure. In her next accusation: 'an entire absence of the intelligence which would enable her to appreciate the great possibilities existing in certain circumstances which come in her way', Ellen seems to imply that, far from forbidding Ernest to go, Nellie should be gagging to accompany her husband. She finishes the section with a wistful 'chances which many wait for all their lives in vain'. Is Ellen actually jealous here? Jealous of an opportunity she herself might have liked and unable to understand why any woman might turn it down? I have always wondered why an adventurous woman like Ellen

Willmott, with such reserves both of energy and money, restricted her own plant-hunting to alpine overnighters and have never come up with a satisfactory answer.[84]

The only – tiny – saving grace in this sorry character assassination is that Ellen freely admits: 'I do not know Mrs. Wilson and she may not be like this very usual type,' though even then she can't help adding, 'but her actions are certainly exactly the same outcome.' Ellen buys a little time, making it clear she is now in charge of the situation: 'I have arranged for someone to entertain the wife whilst I turn my attention to Wilson,' before throwing the ball back into Sargent's court: 'In my opinion the matter now lies thus, that if the remuneration could be made tempting enough Wilson would put his foot down and accept and disregard his wife's objections.'

What can a Willmott apologist do with such evidence? I can't stand up for her, save to suggest that here is a woman desperate to be part of the big boys' gang and blaming someone not present for the predicament she finds herself in. It's unedifying, uncharitable and certainly not in the spirit of the sisterhood she seems to have been happy enough to perpetuate within her own (adopted) class. I am pretty sure it was meant for Sargent's eyes only, but that does not absolve her. This kind of prejudice was only to be expected in certain *men* of the day, but a woman should have known better. Nellie Wilson's situation should have secured Ellen's compassion. It was badly done, indeed.

The truth is, that Wilson *was* flattered by the attentions of such learned individuals – and the cash. Veitch had paid him £100 plus expenses, which came to around $10,000. Wilson asked for $12,000, perhaps in the hope that he'd be turned down, but in the unlikely case it was accepted, with careful budgeting he could come away with decent money. By August, Willmott's work was done. Sargent was able to report that 'his financial demands do not seem unreasonable or impossible and the money for

---

84 Perhaps ironically, Mrs Wilson did accompany Ernest on later trips to Japan.

the two years has been guaranteed . . . I do not see very well how he can withdraw now'.[xiv]

The once-fanciful notion now became a flurry of organisation. Wilson was to leave England on 1 December. 'I feel sure that without your aid he could never have been persuaded,' admitted Sargent.[xv] There was much to do before departure. Sargent asked Willmott to give what sounds like a still-not-sure Wilson a pep talk 'about those things which you are specially interested in and which you want him to collect. This would stimulate his interest I am sure and would, on the whole, be more satisfactory than if I talked to him more generally on the subject.'

Most previous plant-hunting expeditions had been a 'grab what you can and get out' affair. This time Sargent wanted scientific rigour, and this meant photography. 'I am very anxious that he should take a good series of photographs and I have already written him on the subject. Please impress the importance of his doing this and of providing himself with the very best possible camera without regard to its cost. I wrote him, too, to take lessons in photography, and this is another thing which I hope you will insist on with him. Even if he is to delay starting for a week or two it would be best for him to be thoroughly equipped as a photographer.'[xvi]

Miss Willmott was just as thrilled, pledging £200[85] and reassuring Sargent that Wilson is 'cheerful and full of enthusiasm for the future'. She couldn't help adding 'perhaps the victory over his wife may have contributed somewhat . . . The opposition of his wife was almost insurmountable.'[xvii] Perhaps Ellen genuinely believed that 'it is very sad that such a promising man should be hampered by such an ignorant short sighted wife at such an early stage of his career', but her feet of clay tread heavy here.

Sargent's excitement was palpable. 'I feel that it is the most interesting thing I have ever been connected with,' he wrote in December.[xviii] Wilson

---

85 Which would take some prising out of her; she definitely got her money's worth.

had arrived in America, and was making 'a most excellent impression here'.[xix] He left for San Francisco on 31 December, set steamer on 8 January 1907 and arrived in Shanghai 1 February, armed with two cameras, the best lenses money could buy, lessons from one of the best professional photographers in America, and a zoological assistant called Zappey.[86]

On 14 June 1907, Charles Sprague Sargent was able to write a hurried, triumphant note:

'My dear Miss Willmott:

Here is a part of the first package of seed sent by Wilson. If this cherry does not succeed in England it certainly will in your Italian garden.'

---

86 Walter R. Zappey, from the Harvard Museum of Comparative Zoology, sent to find wondrous birds and animals of Asia.

Chapter Twelve:
Riviera Nature Notes

AN IRRIGATION SYSTEM

Two cisterns, both alike in dignity, in fair Ventimiglia where we lay our scene. Nestled into a vertiginous Italian cliff-side a shady pool of undulating margins and hosts of waterlilies teems with goldfish, eyed by a weathered stone cherub peering through the spikes of razor-sharp Puya. The gnarled branches of an elderly Judas tree still produce a flush of shocking-pink blossom each spring, radiant against a deep, forget-me-not sky. The second 'tank' hardly merits such title at all, being a shallow cavern hewn from the cliff face. Perching on its rocky wall, the visitor may admire the grotto-like hollow and tough Mediterranean plants.

E VERYONE HAS SOME kind of passion. Most of us pick an interest or two then stick to them. Then there are the polymaths: the 'renaissance folk' that see no problem in concurrently following a ridiculous range of diverse, disparate interests, equally brilliantly, all at the same time. Ellen Willmott was a plate-spinner, juggling hobbies – and gardens – with the practised ease of a fairground contortionist, seeking the next thrill even as she enjoyed her applause from the last. In September 1904 she revealed to Charles Sprague Sargent that two gardens were not *nearly* enough for her gargantuan horticultural appetite.

'I spend the greater part of my time among my plants either in Savoy or in Essex,' she wrote. 'I am in great hopes soon of having a third [garden] it will be on the Italian shores of the Mediterranean. I am in treaty for a good piece of land with a kilometre of shore.'[i] The garden in question, complete with that kilometre of shore, belonged to Villa Boccanegra, just outside Ventimiglia on the Italian Riviera.

Ellen had been visiting her great friends Sir Thomas and Lady Hanbury for years (the same Sir Thomas who had donated Wisley to the RHS), admiring what they had done with their own ruined 'villa' over the past thirty-five years. Ellen adored the romance of the turreted palace majestically presiding over the sparkling Mediterranean. She luxuriated in La Mortola's cool marble balconies, its square, no-nonsense lookout, creeper-clad walls and, above all, its dense, deep, cliff-side garden packed with exotic plants, mysterious groves, spectacular vistas and secret nooks.

RIVIERA NATURE NOTES

Ellen's photos capture La Mortola's towering pines, lush roses and burgeoning pergolas in almost monastery-like isolation. Although the secluded effect was achieved more through planting than distance from the nearest towns,[87] it's worth remembering that the now-busy road outside still appears as a mud track in Willmott's photos. Inside, the estate's high walls, spiky succulents and fringed palms shaded ancient wells and weathered stone stairways. Cliff plunged to rocky beach via a series of deep terraces, dotted with stone-cut benches and graceful arches, all of which were squirrelled away for later via Ellen Willmott's ever-clicking shutter. Several of her images appeared in a book, *Riviera Nature Notes* by Charles Casey.[88] Ellen was deeply in love. She had to have an Italian villa of her very own.

Even as Sir Thomas Hanbury began to persuade his elderly neighbour to sell Villa Boccanegra, a couple of miles down the road, Ellen was dreaming big. 'If I succeed in getting it I hope to garden together all the Flora of the Meridional, even to the animals,' she wrote to Charles Sprague Sargent.[ii] 'This has never been done before in the way in which I think of doing it . . . It will not look like the usual garden but the plants will be growing just as they would be naturally as far as I can make them. Near, I [will] have a vineyard with plants along side of the paths. I [will] have an ark for any Iris species and forms which I can lay my hand upon.'[iii]

This seemed quite a lot. Ellen had neglected to mention Boccanegra's considerable olive groves, citrus orchard or even the villa itself, but Charles Sargent knew a money pit when he saw one.

'There are, of course, great horticultural advantages in having gardens in different regions and climates,' he replied, 'but isn't a garden a good deal like a home, and is it possible for one person to create in a lifetime more than one really good garden any more than it is possible

---

87 La Mortola is roughly equidistant from Menton, France, and Ventimiglia, Italy.
88 1903.

for one person to make more than one real home?'[iv] Writing ten months after their first correspondence, Sargent's candour is well-meaning but may have come across as patronising, especially when he followed up with 'is it not true that one may have a dozen houses in as many different countries and be able to put one's best thoughts and feelings and affections into only one?'[v]

However awed she might be with the professor, Ellen wasn't going to surrender romance to practical advice from a man she'd never even met. The estate was bought and the spend-fest began.

❦

Boccanegra is yet another of the great Willmott gaps. Ellen rarely writes about it in any detail, her planting schemes and plans are gone, and only about fifty plant tags survive. Even these may come from a later period; they're in leather and nothing like ones found at Warley. Some of her specimens remain; gnarled giants belligerently clinging to the arid, stony ground. Plants grow slow, hard and big in these parts.

Today the estate is worked by Ursula Salghetti Drioli Piacenza. With her husband Guido, she has laboured for nearly forty years trying to understand what Boccanegra was like in its heyday, using fragments of letters, photographs, mentions in magazines and diaries, and good old-fashioned archaeology. Guido's distant family bought the estate in 1956, but by the time he inherited it in 1984 it had been derelict for thirteen years.[89] Together they have brought the garden back to life and still labour to reveal its secrets.

One thing the Piacenzas are particularly grateful for is Ellen Willmott's first move: bold, ambitious – and punishingly expensive. If Warley is on a hill and Tresserve on a sharp incline, shelving away to the still waters of the *Lac Bourget*, Boccanegra is positively vertiginous.

---

89 Le Lièvre describes it, romantically, as *'abbandonata'*.

The views from the tippy-top of that lookout tower are staggering. To the west, Willmott's ancient olive grove, cypress sentinels and La Mortola; to the east, her citrus orchard, woodlands, rocks and path to the sea. Straight ahead, the port city of Livorno and hillsides of Tuscany loom grey against the glittering waters of the Mediterranean. Seventy miles away, Corsica is fainter still. In spring the vista is further spangled by ropes of white-pink *la follette* roses, romping through the cypress, sorbus and olive trees. Jasmine, pine, lavender and rosemary perfume the air. There's one problem: gardening vertically is no fun in forty-degree heat when you're the one in charge of the watering. While a 54-metre cliff face would make a spectacular backdrop for the global exotics she already had her eye on, without serious infrastructure Ellen was destined to be the queen of tinder-wood.

We know about Ellen's elaborate plans for Boccanegra's irrigation system, thanks to some perpetual excuse-making to Charles Sprague Sargent. She *would* offer more money towards Ernest Wilson's China trip, she tells him, except 'my Italian garden is taking so much to start it'.[vi] She goes on to explain she is 'making water tanks in different places where during rain the mountain torrents descend. I mean to engineer my path over these and pile up the soil in natural forms against walls, then at leisure the rest can follow.' She admits: 'I am rather laughed at for doing such uninteresting work first and likewise the most costly part,' which comes across as something of a humble-brag, but does at least prove she knew what she was doing. This was a serious plantswoman doing the groundwork before going mad at the garden centre. Her paths zigzag down to the sea, just wide enough for wheelbarrows, sturdy enough for hard graft without being speared by the lethal spickles of the aloes that thrive in Boccanegra's heat.[90] Crucially, they follow the channels carved out by the region's occasional heavy rainstorms, rather than attempting to counter them. Her 'tanks' – about as far from regular visions of rusting

---

90 After 115 years the paths are much narrower, and those spickles rather larger than in Willmott's day.

metal hulks as can be imagined – still do sterling service today.[91] Guido has also discovered a third, smaller 'tank', disguised as a rock pool; ideal for dipping a watering can. All are designed to be seen and enjoyed as well as perform a vital function.

We don't have the receipts for the major earth-moving or irrigation but the work, which involved fifty men, would have cost as much or more than the £12,950[92] Willmott had already paid for Boccanegra itself.[93] Who cared? She had plenty of money. Besides, now she'd taken the pain of the building work came the fun bit: the planting. The Banksian rose was already doing nicely, clothing those high estate walls snaking along the road, punctuated by solid stone gateposts with their terracotta urns, at the entrance. The only public-facing part of the house would be pretty enough with that, and if it gave a 'Sleeping Beauty, keep out!' feel to it, that was all for the better. Willmott welcomed visitors, but the best the riffraff could expect was that Banskian climber.

Sir Thomas supplied her with hundreds of rare plants but, as usual, Ellen could not resist horticultural tradesfolk, local or otherwise. She opened an account with Hickel Brothers at Beaulieu-sur-Mer – a *Phoenix dactylifera*[94] that has now reached prehistoric proportions came from them – and began to spend. Vast sums passed through the Hickels' hands; Willmott's 1906 statement from them ran to three and a half quarto pages, setting the pace for the next few years. She was a difficult customer, however, constantly changing her mind, leaving plants half-bought at the nursery to go back to tend her own at home, and, increasingly, failing to pay her bills in full. This is hardly surprising since the total for the next three years' worth of plants from local suppliers alone came to £2,000 – £250,000 in today's money. Furnishing

---

91 One is currently under repair, revealing its simple square-sided construction.

92 It is hard to know which currency the sum refers to but the amount in lira would have made the estate ludicrously cheap.

93 She tells Dr Moore she is project managing herself, which may have saved some money but involved much stress instead.

94 Date palm.

indoors cost a similar amount, and that doesn't even begin to account for what she was spending elsewhere. Ellen had just added an octagonal, raised and roofed veranda at Tresserve to complement her ever-burgeoning collection of antique furniture and religious *objets d'art*, including a set of stained-glass windows Henry Correvon had found in a Swiss chapel. In memory of her parents, she had also built a roadside shrine in the chateau's garden wall and constructed a *petite chapelle* in a nearby meadow.

Warley, Ellen had decided, needed redecoration throughout. She brought in swanky Chelsea experts Amédée Joubert & Sons to refurbish the main rooms. They installed new cabinets, an antique marble chimney piece, wall hangings, silk curtains and an enormous carved and gilded mirror. Joubert replaced Ellen's music room ceiling with a lofty ornamental dome and created a new organ fascia that filled an entire wall, gilding the pipes while they were about it. The bill came to £1,131; about £140,633 today. She was still spending on plants at Warley too. A photo from around this time shows a baby *Camellia* 'Middlemist Red'[95] and an equally small magnolia[96] nestling against one of Ellen's garden rooms. The summerhouse is long gone today, but I'm happy to report that both camellia and magnolia are still doing fine some 120 years on.

It may have been around this time that Warley's network of sunken hothouses was built.[97] Ruined, moss-clad walls whisper of boiler-fired opulence. One rectangular pool still holds water, the super-rare *Sabia latifolia* still romps across broken brickwork. At some point the boating lake was given serpentine walls and great stone slab steps.

It's unclear whether, when selling his holiday pad to Ellen Willmott, Biancheri had fully explained a compulsory purchase made by the Italian

---

95 Not yet officially confirmed but very likely.

96 Probably the *Magnolia x soulangiana* cv Amabalis Wilson brought back.

97 The blueprint for the nearby peach house has just turned up and is considerably earlier, if rather better-designed. The sunken hot houses are much more basic.

State Railway to build a new line along the bottom of his garden. She certainly knew the line was there, as it appears out of a tunnel directly below the citrus grove, but the rest of her 'kilometre of beach' remained gloriously private. Even the bit of Boccanegra open to the railway goes by in a flash; the angle of the cliff makes it impossible to see much at all. Most travellers would be looking the other way anyway. This spectacular line still runs along the entire coastline, dipping in and out of tunnels – there's one running under La Mortola too – right next to the sea itself. Ellen had clearly thought the whole thing was done and dusted. It wasn't. Out of the blue the railway company announced it was doubling the line and would be expropriating more of Boccanegra's garden to do so.

Ellen Willmott was officially Unhappy. It wasn't just the loss of land or privacy. Open coal fireboxes and dry-as-dust plants were a recipe for disaster. It mattered little whether it was a cigarette butt, carelessly tossed from an open window or burning coals shovelled from an engine cab to slow down the approach to Ventimiglia; either spelt disaster for the trackside brush.[98] It was a safety thing. Obviously.

The dispute went on for months. Ellen fought with all her might, but, in a fight between one woman and the Italian State Railway, even Ellen Willmott was going to come away bruised. Furious, she did the only thing she could: she planted another privacy wall, this time a row of fast-growing Eucalyptus, famous for its fire-resistant qualities in its native Australia.

Ironically, Ellen Willmott had been availing herself of the very same railway for years, visiting Sir Thomas and Lady Hanbury from Nice, or continuing east, further into Italy. For a woman on the move all the time, trains were easily the fastest mode of transport. She began a routine, visiting each of her gardens as it came into season. She'd begin the year in March at Boccanegra as the daffodils exploded into the

---

[98] Indeed, there have been two major incidents in the Boccanegra garden over the years.

dazzling clarity of the Italian spring. After a flying visit home to enjoy the bulbs at Warley, by May she was in Tresserve for the clematis, irises and roses – and a little remedial back treatment. Thence back to Warley for the RHS summer season before once more trekking to Tresserve for a few more punishing *bains-douches* and the grape harvest, ready for bottling by Robinson the butler. November caught the last rays of Boccanegra sun before Christmas at Warley or Spetchley.

Poor old Robinson had an even tougher time of it. He travelled ahead of his mistress, opening each house in anticipation of her arrival with whichever friends she'd invited along. His French was shaky, his Italian non-existent, but that was his lot. He, too, travelled by train, with all the baggage and whatever staff could be spared. By 1906, however, the iron horse was beginning to look old-fashioned.

All manner of rumours sprang up when Ellen Willmott arrived at Warley not only chugging inside a chain-driven *Charron* motor carriage, but with a livery-clad, black chauffeur from Mozambique in the driver's seat. Monsieur Frédéric, some whispered, had once saved Miss Willmott's life and she employed him as a way of repaying the debt. Others sniffed that she must have hired him in the South of France, where there were plenty of cheap arrivals from Africa. I'm not convinced by either of these rumours. We have one solitary letter from Monsieur E. Frédéric,[99] alas sporting a giant rot-hole in the middle. If she did acquire his services in Ventimiglia, it's clear he was no bumpkin off a boat. His hand is strong, his French perfect, his manner dignified. This man is both educated and skilled. He is also pretty upset.

Frédéric's letter is polite, but insistent. It is eight days since he arrived in England, and he still has nowhere fixed to sleep. The bothy (the unmarried gardeners' quarters) is filthy and untidy; he is not a *gouja* (bruiser) used to sleeping in such places. He has as much right to decent surroundings – and sheets! – as anyone else and is unaccustomed

---

[99] We do not know his first name.

to being laughed at by her staff. He will work out his month, then he will leave.

Such boldness from any servant in those days was rare, but it is clear M. Frédéric knows his worth and is not going to put up with any old nonsense. The rest of his letter shows us why he is confident enough to speak to Ellen as he does. He clicks into professional mode, explaining he is arranging for repairs to the car, mainly damage inflicted as a crane winched it from the boat at Dover. There is further work needed, on the brakes and the headlamps. It will take around eight days, so she should find a time when she won't need the car and take it into Hoopers. There is no ultimatum, no threat; M. Frédéric merely informs her he is unhappy and will be gone in a month.

The letter must have put the willies up Miss Willmott, for M. Frédéric not only stayed on, he brought his (white) wife over from France. The couple would become respected pillars of the local community; after all, the village was used to having foreigners arrive at the Warley gardens; experts who knew personally the regions where her plants came from. Mme Frédéric taught French in the village; M. Frédéric drove Ellen around the country in the Charron and its somewhat more reliable successors. He enjoyed a reputation for driving at breakneck speed; the Charron could reach a dizzying 28mph. We have one photo. In his chauffeur's breeches and boots, cap in hand, M. Frédéric poses by the fountain at Spetchley Park, accompanied by Rose's three children.[100]

I've always been a bit surprised that Ellen didn't drive herself. Perhaps she did and it's just not documented; perhaps the kudos of employing a chauffeur overrode any feminist tendencies. An article in *Lyon-Horticole* describes a motor car journey around the Ventimiglia countryside with the Willmott sisters, where Ellen's 'exotic' chauffeur seems to have made as profound impression on the reporter as her extraordinary

---

[100] Rose's youngest, Margaret Elizabeth, 'Betty', was born in 1902

garden.[101] Miss Willmott and her motor car became a familiar sight in the streets of London and made even more of an impact when she arrived at Tresserve. Hers was the high life and it wasn't going unappreciated. At least one young man was dazzled.

Johann Bernhard Mann was born in 1880,[102] the son of a merchant. Unusually for the time, his parents separated in 1892, largely due to financial pressures. Lost and lonely, in 1897 young Johann became a cadet in the German Imperial Navy. He took to sea life immediately, touring the West Indies, Central and South America. By the time he met Ellen Willmott, Johann Mann was a handsome, twenty-five-year-old lieutenant, commanding ever-more important battleships. He seems to have had little in the way of self-esteem, however, and, like Ellen, suffered excruciating rheumatic pain. The summer of 1905 saw them both at Aix-les-Bains. Johann's jaw dropped at this beautiful, strong, exciting *raconteuse* who knew everyone, presided over the best garden in the region and lived like there was no tomorrow. Generous, natural and ever-enthusiastic, Ellen took the shy young man under her wing, spent time with him and introduced him to her friends, much as Lady Whalley had done for her fifteen years earlier. It probably didn't occur to her that he might be 'interested'– she was literally old enough to be his mother; his own was born in 1859, one year after Ellen herself.

Johann couldn't believe his luck. On the way back to his ship he stopped off in Paris and wrote from the Hotel du Louvre with great excitement, thanking his new friend for the trouble she had gone to for him. 'If I may reckon the days I spent at Aix to be the best of my life, I think it was you who made them so. When I came to Aix I was rather afraid to have three long dull weeks before me without any friends or acquaintances and now I have got so many good friends!'[vii] Back in Kiel,

---

101 Jacques Vilmorin. The copy for the undated article, with corrections, probably in Ellen's hand, was clearly never returned to the editor.

102 Great-uncle of authors Heinrich and Thomas Mann.

he wrote again. Paris was grand, but would have been better in Ellen's company. He had told his mother and sister about Ellen and shown them her portrait; they were suitably impressed. For now he must return to active duty, but those days in Aix were, he reiterated, the best of his life.[viii]

The letters continue. It is through Johann we know Ellen now travelled to Boccanegra by car: 'I hope you had a fine way down to Ventimiglia, I think it must be the nicest thing of the world to make a journey in the motor, to hop wherever you like and look at all places and things you take an interest in.'[ix] Mann himself is back at sea, with attendant bad weather, mist, rain and snow, and remembering with ever-rosier-tinted spectacles his time in Aix. He imagines Ellen, at home at Christmastime, hoping that 'you too will have some kind remembrances in that direction'.[x]

By 10 January 1906, poor Johann can stand it no longer:

Dear Miss Willmott,

Now a quarter of a year has gone since we parted but in all this time my thoughts have been much with you – and now that such a long time has past [sic] *and I have spent it to think about the matter I am going to write of, you may believe that it is not a feeling which came suddenly and will pass the next day, but a passion that has grown strong and deep within me.*

I must tell you that I love you and I must ask you the question whether you too will love me and whether you will give me your hand.

Don't be angry for that and don't believe me silly, but I cannot help it. I know that I only am a poor lieutenant who cannot offer anything to you except himself, I know that you are a lady in a life high and rich with interests and spirit, but my love is strong and I know we should be happy together.

Dear Miss Willmott, when I left you I tried to suppress my feelings and drown them in my duties, for I thought it was impossible to ask you this question, but my love grew stronger from day to day and it did not give me any rest. I know it is you I love and only you. Do forgive me if I trouble you with this letter but I could not but write you this and ask you this question.

I told you the other day that I could not come to London in January – but I think I can, if you tell me to come.

Please give me an answer, dear Miss Willmott.
Yours, very truly
Joh. Bernh. Mann.

Now here was a pretty pass. It's clear from the six pages of crossings out, alternative versions, possible phrases and tortuous half-thoughts – all that remains of her draft reply – that for once even Ellen Willmott was utterly stumped. He was twenty-five, naive and lost; she was forty-seven, a woman of the world and possibly uninclined towards men in the first place. She was not, however, cruel. The excruciating agonies of the resulting scribble, trying to let down this sweet, overeager puppy as gently as possible, reveal the compassion of a woman who knows only too well what it is to love in vain. She desperately tries to avoid platitudes, tries to be straightforward, and just ends up tying herself in greater knots. She is 'proud to have won the love of such a man', 'a warm man and one who stands very high in my regard'. She is 'grieved that after your blessed letter to me mine to you must give you pain' and tries to tell him 'everyone is the richer for having a loving friend'. She assures him she 'hopes that ~~circumstance~~ will give your hand & make your wife as happy a woman as she will be a fortunate one' and that he will remain 'always my dear friend'. For her part she will be 'following every X̶X̶X̶X̶X̶ of your life with X̶X̶X̶ & affectionate interest' and 'look forward to your letters, & to seeing you i̶n̶ ̶E̶n̶g̶l̶a̶n̶d̶ X̶X̶X̶X̶ when your duties allow', but she is quite firm: 'this is irrevocable'. Every word drips with the misery of knowing how lame it all sounds. Oddly, the one thing that might have got her off the hook – his fervent Protestantism versus her profound Catholicism – goes unmentioned, but she nears the truth in another crossed-out phrase: 'I shall never marry, the reasons it is not necessary to give.'[xi]

Johann's reply was dignified and resigned. Although he was 'very sorry, more than I can tell you', and could not regret his 'expression of a noble feeling', he accepted 'your irrevocable opinion' and promised never to speak of it again.[xii] He would remain besotted. He wrote regularly, from command of ever-more-impressive ships, wistfully telling her his news, loneliness piercing every word, even as his professional star ascended in the German Imperial Navy's firmament.

Ellen kept in touch with Johann, albeit in a somewhat more guarded way, but by now those plates were spinning faster than ever. She was at the peak of her game, and nothing could have spelled out her position in the Edwardian horticultural world more clearly than the tenth edition of William Robinson's *English Flower Garden*, the very book the Willmott women had pored over in 1884. This impression included photographs, some by Ellen herself. Along with her usual harvest of prizes, certificates and gold medals, the book kept her firmly in the eye of every gardening journal.

She cannot have been unaware of someone else firmly in the eye of the regular press. News of the glamorous Lady Gian Mount Stephen appeared in newspapers from *The Times* of London to the *St Paul Globe*, Minnesota. She launched ships, made society appearances and engaged in charity work; even founding a canteen near Brocket Hall in 1905 when she realised the local schoolchildren had nowhere to eat. Gossip columns ooh-ed and ahh-ed as the Mount Stephens regularly entertained the entire Royal Family at Brocket,[103] always deftly pointing out that Lady Mount Stephen had once been a lady-in-waiting. The papers confided that she shunned publicity (not that they took any notice of her requests) but they did not pry enough to pick up on what might have caused the reticence. In 1900 Gian had given birth to the only child she and George Mount Stephen would ever conceive. It was stillborn.

Did Ellen know? Probably. Rose kept in touch with Gian and, if she ever wondered why she and her sister never spoke, we have no record of it. Ellen was never one for tittle-tattle, anyway, and she was Moving On.

※

The year 1906 saw the RHS International Conference on Genetics and Hybridisation.[104] Anyone who was anyone attended, and Ellen Willmott was literally in the front row. She appears in the event's group photo, taken in the newly completed RHS Horticultural Halls, a vision in satin, lace and opera gloves. She joined at least twenty-one new societies, including the British Astronomical Society, the *Société Dendrochronologique de France*, Oskar Fleischer's *Internationale Musikgesellschaft* and three different automobile associations, while still juggling all the other subscriptions, memberships to learned institutions, facilities such as the London Library and a wide range of (often Catholic) charitable subscriptions. Fascinated by the 'rediscovery' of 'folk music', she joined Cecil Sharp's English Folk Song Society in 1905. Ellen photographed the Countess von Armin[105] for Gertrude Jekyll's forthcoming book *Children and Gardens*, possibly in Jekyll's garden; more likely, the countess's castle in Pomerania. Perhaps her 'really busy' excuses to Charles Sprague

---

103 There are photos of such visits in the Royal Collection.

104 Actually the third of its kind, but the first one everyone took notice of.

105 Author of *Elizabeth and Her German Garden*, charming, self-deprecating and fabulously gossipy.

Sargent for not getting round to talking to Ernest Wilson about going to China again were genuine – though Wilson also appears in the group photo at Horticultural Halls; she could have cornered him then if she'd really wanted to.

If all this is sounding pricey, it was. By now Ellen Willmott's spending had spiralled out of control. She had inherited millions in today's money, but it was mainly in capital and the cash was dwindling. Any investments were what was left of her father's canniness; her own were piecemeal to non-existent. The letter to Sargent telling him she can't contribute more than £200 to the Wilson expedition is Ellen's first written indication that the cash was running out, but there had been other signs. Payments to tradesfolk had always been notoriously late, even when she was genuinely loaded. In 1904 even the great Alfred Parsons had had to remind her she owed him sixty guineas for a watercolour. Some take this as meanness; I suspect it was more unthinking. Ellen was not a miser; indeed, she was the exact opposite – an out-and-out spendthrift. She'd had more money than she could spend since her seventh birthday. Or so she had believed. Now it was beginning to look like she had been up to the task after all.

On 22 March 1907, she crossed a line. The great heiress Ellen Willmott borrowed money. Fifteen thousand pounds, from two senior partners at her father's old firm. It was all fine, it was only 4 per cent interest, and secured against Warley Place, Warley Lea, Warley Place Farm, the Headley Garden and some cottages. She could pay it back. No one need ever know.

Perhaps the loan came with the death of her great friend Sir Thomas Hanbury. People had been looking forward to Sir Thomas's seventy-fifth birthday shindig for over a year. One hundred and fifty of the greatest horticulturists in the world had contributed their autographed likenesses towards his present: a magnificent, folio-sized photo album. As usual, Ellen Willmott was the only woman included. Alas, Sir Thomas never saw it; he died on 9 March, three months before his birthday. The album was presented to his widow, then did a 110-year vanishing act, only turning up again, at the *Istituto Internazionale di Studi Liguri*, in 2017.

Hanbury's death left Ellen Willmott with more than just another empty space in her heart; it left a potential hole in her finances too. Sir Thomas had agreed to take a £200 share in the Ernest Wilson expedition. It hadn't yet occurred to Professor Sargent to ask her for the shortfall, but perhaps it was part of her thinking behind the loan. Equally, she could just have overspent. Her plant bills were spiralling, and Wilson's wasn't the only expedition she was funding. Among other, smallish contributions, Gerald Davidson of the South African Cape Orchard Company had been collecting rare pelargoniums for her since 1899.

At least it was all beginning to pay dividends. By autumn 1907 the parcels from the Arboretum were arriving thick and fast. One shipment, sent on 4 September, contained 116 packets of seeds, on top of many more specimens Wilson was sending direct to Warley. On that particular morning, however, Ellen Willmott's mind was not on plants.

Chapter Thirteen:

The Slow Fall of Icarus

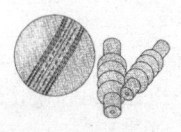

A VILLAGE SPORTS DAY PROGRAMME

A small piece of card, folded book-style, easily tucked in a pocket by both spectators and competitors attending the Great & Little Warley Cottage Show and Village Sports Day. Its cover includes a handsome sepia photograph of Warley Place by Miss E. A. Willmott. The show will take place on the field in front of the house, and since there is currently no master at Warley, Mr R. V. Berkeley will once again travel from Spetchley Park to stand in as captain of the festivities. Who will win the fancy-dress Slow Bicycle Race or be the last man on the Greasy Pole? Who will get drenched when the bucket tilts? It's a packed schedule but there will still be ample time to wander into the marquee for the fruit, vegetable and flower displays. All is well; all is as it ever has been. God Save the King.

A WARM, ALPINE-SUMMER night. Tresserve slumbers in the stillness. Deep in the valley, the *Lac Bourget* mirrors a waxing alpine moon; the distant peaks of the *Dent du Chat* loom charcoal-grey.

Suddenly, the church bell clangs to life, shattering the silence. It rings again, beyond the one o'clock chime, then again, and again. This is no marking of the hour. The relentless peal is joined by others: smaller, tinnier, grimmer, racing through the night. Bleary-eyed locals gape as *pompiers* from every fire brigade in the area battle the flames rapidly engulfing the smartest building in the village.

Ellen Willmott had one thing to be grateful for at Tresserve that fateful night, 2–3 September 1907. She wasn't there. She was en route, travelling overnight to her French villa, looking forward to a month with her sister and brother in-law. Rose and Robert Valentine had already arrived, however, and were fast asleep in bed. They managed to fling themselves free from the fire; there would be no human casualties that night. The same could not be said for the chateau.

Ellen arrived at six o'clock that morning to learn that the cheerful blaze laid to air her room had turned – first to an inferno, now to a blackened ruin that would smoulder for a week. Dazed, she retreated to Hôtel Bernascon, where the news spread fast. Local paper *L'Avenir d'Aix-les-Bains* was first on the scene: the 'sumptuous residence of the Misses Willmott', a 'true museum' that had been host to royalty had fallen entirely prey to the flames.[i] The story quickly saturated the British press, too. The letters of sympathy began the day of the disaster, first with local friends, radiating across continents over the following days.

Scores reached out to Ellen in her misery, from princesses to gardening doyens, neighbours and servants to celebrities and societies, sometimes helpfully enclosing whichever bleak newspaper cutting from which they'd discovered the news, as though this might help.

Many plain didn't believe the stories, or hoped the papers were exaggerating. Gertrude Jekyll was among the first to send her best wishes: 'the shocking news met me almost at the same moment that I was unpacking the box of plants you so kindly sent'.[ii] Johann Bernhard Mann, now in command of the Navy's latest destroyer,[106] was distraught, admitting that his thoughts still 'too often – perhaps every day – wend back to Aix' and mourning 'all those things that spoke of old times, of beloved persons'.[iii] Alfred Parsons, the Revd. Engleheart, William Wilkes ... there's a whole fat packet devoted purely to fire condolences in the Spetchley archive. Norman Moore wrote practically every day. Knowing Ellen's dark sense of humour, he related grisly anecdotes about great fires of history to keep her spirits up.

One F. Pouligon went to survey the damage and supervise the transportation of anything that might have been rescued. There was precious little. A few sticks of furniture, some curtains and soft furnishings wrenched from their fittings as master and servant fled. The roof was consumed; the walls were ready to collapse. The sheer amount of wooden relics, flame-bait books and tinder-dry textiles had been partly responsible for the fire taking such a hold so quickly. Ellen's priceless library was gone, as were most of the contents of her music room. Happily, the antique organ had been away for repair at the time.

The fire at Tresserve was a shock from which Ellen would never fully recover. She had lost more than a house; she had lost a time: of happiness, of giddy youth and opportunity. A time when her parents had still been alive, when money had flowed like the water in her alpine

---

106 SM *Torpedoboot*, G133.

ravines, when Rose had been her partner-in-gardening and when Ellen herself had enjoyed the frisson of love. 'The happiest time of the year by far to me is the time at Tresserve,'[iv] she told Dr Moore, trying to explain why it was hitting her so very hard. 'The rest, grandeur and peace. It has been mostly here that I have done my reading, thinking, botany and music. Every year I have learnt some fresh subject or some author I knew nothing of before. The feeling of the Channel & several provinces between me & the mad neighbour[107] is such a relief and has counted for a great deal.' This unusual opening-up of emotion was Ellen's way of paving the ground for her next revelation: Tresserve must rise again.

'That afternoon I began the plans for rebuilding,' she would tell Charles Sprague Sargent a couple of weeks later. 'It was of no avail to sit moaning and groaning.'[v] Jules Pin was commissioned to rebuild the broken villa, bigger and better than ever. Two days after the fire, Ellen was ordering furniture; three days after the fire, she was therapy-shopping in earnest. After all, what was a home without a solid silver antique mustard pot and two salt dishes? It would all be fine; the insurance would pay for everything.

It's hard to know exactly what went on in the ensuing insurance debacle. Ellen Willmott's status as unreliable witness reaches its peak whenever she talks about money. It seems she had believed Tresserve to be insured, but the contract had been incorrectly drafted by her father's clerk, Mr Dixson. Her story is further complicated in that there appear to have been several companies involved, in both France and Britain, and which bits of the house/contents/personal effects were insured by which policy were muddled. It's also unclear which sister was insured for what. Further complicating matters, Ellen admits, elsewhere, that she had known the place was underinsured and claims she had instructed her company to increase the amount, but the fire

---

[107] The unpleasantness with Count Lescher and the Dark Lane Cottages was clearly rumbling on.

had beaten her to it.[vi] Whatever the truth, the result was the same: the company refused to pay out.

The situation was only slightly less opaque then than it is now, but that was good. That meant leeway. Neither sister was going to let first refusal go unchallenged. Rose, who history sometimes forgets had her own backbone of steel, went first, pestering the directors of her British insurers, with decent results: £1,300 compensation for her lost clothes and jewellery. Relieved that Rose had something, Ellen, who had stood aside so her sister could have a clear shot, got stuck in herself: 'I wrote to every one of those I happened to know and to the relatives of friends of the rest. Many of them were people I had given plants to or helped in some way.'[vii] Her results were more modest, around £200 – a fraction of the value of even her immediate personal effects. She needed to fight harder.

At this point, somewhat unforgivably, Rose and Robert Valentine went home to England, leaving Ellen to deal with the smoking remains. We don't know why – the sisters' letters are lost from this period – but it may have had something to do with Rose's increasingly peaky health. To be fair, both she and Robert had also suffered a life-threatening shock. Ellen was understandably hurt, confiding to Dr Moore, 'If only they would have stayed over a little it would have been everything for me.' In the only instance I can think of where she admits she could have used some patriarchal muscle, she adds, 'Just Robert's presence would have been some help in struggling with the Insurance Companies and the authorities here.'[viii] She was exhausted from fighting, organising and replying to the scores of well-wishing letters: 'the same story over and over again only in different words'. The pressure was beginning to add up in small ways, too: 130f on stamps alone, bought and – the *indignity* – stuck on by Ellen herself.

That Ellen even mentions the amount of money she's shelling out on stamps signals a subtle but significant turn in her priorities. For the first time she is beginning to notice the pennies disappearing, even if she still can't quite believe the pounds have been trickling through her fingers for years. Something will happen to make the big stuff go away like it always has in the past, but how come the little things are so expensive?

Flinging the pennies to the back of her mind, Ellen plunged into her building project, meeting the architect and builders every day, poring over blueprints and using micromanagement as her passport from grief. By 29 September, Tresserve's dodgy walls, teetering chimney stacks and charred beams had been cleared or stabilised. Ellen was confident that a roof could be installed by the end of November, a good job since all that antique furniture was piling up. On her days off from builder-supervision, dealers variously sold her entire suites of Louis furniture, mirrors, tables, ornamental frames, a Louis XIV grandfather clock, some medieval brass plates and a gothic statue of the Virgin Mary.[108] She made 'a hurried journey' into Switzerland, Italy, Germany and Austria, shopping for architectural salvage, taking the opportunity to inspect Boccanegra and attend the funeral of the Grand Duke of Baden. Winter was setting in, the weather was appalling, but the experience seemed to reignite her passion: 'Having to think entirely for myself & act by myself has, I believe, been the best possible thing for me,' she wrote, adding just a little wistfully, 'although I could not help wishing it were otherwise.'[ix]

The exhilaration was, indeed, short-lived. By now the season was over and Ellen had Hôtel Bernascon to herself. The party town was closed. The loneliness in her letters punches across the decades. Everyone is nice enough and the waiter never comments that the hotel's only guest isn't eating the horrible food but, she confides to Dr Moore, in all the weeks she's been there just one person has dined with her.

Her name remained in the press – both *The Garden* and *Curtis's Botanical Magazine* dedicated their 1907 volumes to her – but on a

---

[108] Geneviève Frieh-Giraud describes in detail both the fire and Ellen's frenetic spending spree.

personal level, now the sympathy letters were out of the way, no one knew what to say. By December, still at Tresserve, still standing over workmen, still palpably lonely, she is asking Norman Moore if he has encountered various friends who have suddenly gone very quiet. Ethel Smyth, for example, has taken to only sending the occasional postcard.

Among the scores of letters of sympathy there is one that raises a curious eyebrow. A telegram, sent the day after the fire: 'We are so grieved. Anxious to hear how you are. Gian Mount Stephen.'[x]

It was followed the next day by a hurried note. Were the rumours of Tresserve's destruction true? 'We are both so grieved,' she wrote.[xi] 'I can only hope it is exaggerated.' The letter is written on Brocket Hall notepaper, and while it is unlikely Gian was consciously reminding Ellen she was a married woman now, it somehow comes across that way. Lady Mount Stephen commiserated wholeheartedly; fire must be 'one of the worst blows that can happen to one'. One of the worst, yes, indeed.

Ellen sat down and wrote a long letter. We don't have it, but we do have the reply, in Gian's typical, gushing, artless voice. She talks of her sadness for Ellen's loss and the horror that must haunt Rosey and Robert after their ordeal. It seems Ellen had failed to go to a pageant the Mount Stephens had held – presumably an invitation that had come via Rose – and Ellen had assumed Gian would be angry for avoiding her. Gian chooses to take Ellen's frankly lame excuses for not turning up at face value and pleads with her to visit. 'I don't think you realise how dreadfully I want to have you stay with me,' she writes, 'or you would have come before.'[xii] It is hard to tell exactly what she means when she adds 'there is so much I always long to talk to you about', though, in the understatement of the century, she also hopes they will not be 'drifting apart again'. Even as Gian spends several lines babbling about nursing her ageing husband through his first illness in fifty-three years, her mind drifts back to earlier days. 'I am thinking of you all the time & wish I was with you that I might try & comfort you somehow. I think of all the blessed days I had with you at Tresserve & it does make me sad.' The letter ends: 'please tell me how you are & tell me that you love me the same & that you don't want to drop me out of your life. Your Loving Gian.'

What was Ellen to do with such mixed messages? She had been hurt once; instinctively she knew how vulnerable she was now. As far as we know she did not reply. Soppy stuff was for an earlier incarnation and self-pity would not rebuild a dream. 'I am working away and keeping the workmen up to their work & the house is beginning to rise above the embers,' she told Dr Moore, even though 'the smell of burning and charred wood is still more powerful than the scent of the flowers.'[xiii]

Rebuilding Tresserve as a four-storeyed, fantasy-gothic pavilion was probably not the very wisest decision Ellen Willmott ever made, especially not the way she went about it. She simply didn't get the concept of economy, and worse, she didn't get that she didn't get it. She would tell Dr Moore, completely straight-faced, 'it has been my bringing up, I suppose, which makes me feel that business is duty & must be attended to first'[xiv] – before going out to order more antique tapestries and silk damask curtains.

Tresserve's new layout was glorious, including an octagonal viewing-turret sprouting from the covered veranda, reached by an open stonework staircase. Alas, medieval *Rapunzel* towers didn't come cheap, and the insurance didn't come through. Although Ellen told Dr Moore the furnishing would be simpler than before, somehow it didn't work out that way. She did try to economise. She was very proud, for example, that the wood panelling she had sourced was ornament in itself. It was a shrewd move, she said, because she wouldn't have to buy any expensive decorations. This was theoretically true, but said panelling came out of an old monastery and hadn't been a total bargain, and the baubles were purchased anyway.

By December 1907 Ellen was taking out her second loan, this time borrowing £3,000 against Shenfield Lodge, one of the Warley buildings she hadn't already mortgaged. Perhaps unknown to her at the time, her father's old Borough partners spread the risk with others, including the same Mr Dixson who had just made a mess of Tresserve's insurance.

Ellen kept the arrangement very quiet, mentioning it to no one, not even Rose. Especially not Rose. The witness signature on the agreement was that of James Robinson, her butler, who could be relied upon in such matters. Equally discreetly, she began making enquiries about selling one or two musical instruments, but now her immediate worries – roof and cash flow – had subsided, she was ready to go home. She returned to Britain for Christmas, looking forward to better times as she skated on Warley's frozen pond and unpacked crates of horticultural goodies sent by Ernest Wilson from the wilds of China. Money problems only ever consumed her in the short term; as soon as an immediate gap was plugged, the threat wafted from her mind.

❦

From the previous few pages it may appear that Ellen Willmott spent the back end of 1907 entirely consumed by building work and spending sprees, but this would not account for the sheer energy of an ever-fevered, polymathic mind. We get a hint of what she was also up to in a letter to Charles Sprague Sargent shortly after the fire. After riffing on the horrors of the inferno – 'the big old beams, falling upon each other descended through each floor and finally continued burning for days in the cellar' – she suddenly turns on the proverbial sixpence to the meat of her letter: 'Now, about Pritzel . . .'[xv]

Georg August Pritzel was the renowned nineteenth-century keeper of the Royal Library at Berlin, famous for creating directories that might actually be useful to scholars. As well as a comprehensive list of 40,000 works of literature in the great libraries of Europe and an index of common German plant names, Pritzel's 1855–66 *Iconum Botanicarum Index locupletissmus* was an invaluable register of botanical illustrations.

It was also hopelessly out of date. Ellen Willmott had, for some years now, been compiling an updated version for her own use, but it was also a godsend for her friends. Richard de Candolle, keeper of the Bossier herbarium at Geneva, had made a copy, and Charles Sprague Sargent constantly referred to it. Several years earlier Sir William Thistleton-Dyer had suggested Ellen write an official supplement and, earlier in 1907, talk began seriously.

Sir Michael Foster, with whom she had planned to write that definitive work on Iris,[109] had just died, leaving the work unfinished, and she 'only' had her magnum opus on roses to work on. She felt a gap in her schedule. Charles Sargent encouraged her, sending her suggestions for inclusions and talking to potential publishers and sponsors stateside, from individuals to the Carnegie Institution.

Alas, the Pritzel supplement would never happen. Despite Ellen's working on it during those cold, lonely nights in Hôtel Bernascon, *sans* her botanical library at Tresserve, and despite Sargent's writing that various people were very enthusiastic, it seems Kew suddenly got cold feet. 'Is it possible that Dyer is in any way mixed up in this opposition?' wondered Charles Sargent.[xvi] 'Can it be that he thinks that he would like to do this work himself sometime in the remote future?' Worse, news filtered through that a German botanist was working on an entirely new *Iconum*, rather than a mere supplement and, separately, Ellen discovered the RHS was planning its own revision. Without her. They didn't yet have the money, but committees were being mobilised. Committees she was not on. *Index Londonensis* would eventually appear in 1929. Ellen Willmott's early twentieth-century list is not acknowledged, despite its almost certainly being heavily consulted.

---

109 Foster and Willmott's notes were passed onto Ellen's erstwhile friend William Dykes. Ellen was outraged when Dykes approached publisher John Murray with a letter from the usually Willmott-friendly Otto Stapf at Kew, saying her work with Foster was unpublishable. She was incandescent when *Genus Iris* was finally published under Dykes's name in 1913, the preface implying that Michael Foster was disorganised, and Ellen's own contribution had been limited to 12 'rough' notebooks. This is entirely possible, but hardly cricket, and further fuels the general gardener-eat-gardener world of Edwardian horticultural politics.

The whole affair would be galling and cost much time, effort and shoe leather, but I struggle to see that it really upset Ellen. She talks about Pritzel to Sargent because he's so excited about it but rarely mentions it to others, and while she is flattered that de Candolle was impressed with her work, and even more so that Sargent had such faith in her, I get the impression that in her mind she was already done with it. She had created enough data for her own use, was prepared to share it with others and even to continue with it as long as there were no obstacles, but as a project it just didn't consume her. Ellen had only one true literary love, the much-vaunted *Genus Rosa*, first imagined some fifteen years earlier and inched towards ever since. There were signs of this bias from the get-go, of which Sargent was all too aware. 'Don't think of the Rose book until the Pritzel is finished,'[xvii] he would plead, in vain. 'I'm afraid you are a little too sanguine about the Pritzel matter,'[xviii] he would tell her later, when it all started to fall through, and he would be right – but so was she, for letting go.

Tresserve Mk II was deemed ready for partial habitation in May 1908. Rose and Robert Valentine came over for the season but chose to stay at Hôtel Bernascon, as the first-floor rooms were not ready. Ellen herself slept in what would eventually be servants' quarters: 'a tiny room in the roof with sloping walls. It is clean and airy and in the middle there are 3 or 4 feet where I can stand upright.'[xix] The garden was magnificent, though. The indoors might be 'dust, disorder and chaos', but outside was 'beautiful and the flowers never better'.[xx] We can't be sure of the exact dates she took a series of early-colour Autochrome shots at Tresserve, but it must have been around this time.[110] Ellen became a founder member of Aix-les-Bains Golf Club that season but she spent most of her waking hours among the roses, slowly working on her life's passion, *Genus Rosa*.

---

110 While EAW took a great many Autochrome and Sanger-Shepherd images, only about fifteen survive, mainly of Tresserve, plus a couple at Spetchley. The Museum of the History of Science at Oxford also holds some colour slides.

Once back at Warley, the whirl began once more. Some friends she met in person; others wrote from afar. Johann Bernhard Mann, by now *aide-de camp* for Vice-Admiral Zeye, enclosed a photograph, handsome as ever, mounted on a shining black horse. Ellen, perhaps wisely, doesn't seem to have replied, but this was not necessarily anything personal. Even Charles Sprague Sargent, who was supposed to be helping her on the rose book, had to admonish her: 'Whatever your other virtues may be, and no one admires them more than I do, can you flatter yourself for a moment that you are a good correspondent? It must be months since I last wrote you about the Rose book and I never have had a word in reply. Do you think this is friendly?'[xxi]

The trouble was that, once more, Ellen Willmott had taken on more than she could manage. The sheer amount of her correspondence was staggering – hundreds of letters sent in any one year – she couldn't help getting 'into arrears'. There were other arrears, too, but she had to keep up appearances, juggling visits to friends and family, increasingly expensive trips into London from Warley, subscriptions to clubs and societies and plant purchases against the mounting debts and spiralling wages bills. Hiding her worsening financial problems with outward show, she wore her most glamorous jewellery and rarest flowers on trips up to town. She fought to keep her finger on the horticultural pulse, strove to be at the centre of everything new and creative. At her various homes, the beneficent Chatelaine of the Silver Key did everything she could to secure the impression that all remained as it ever had been.

At Tresserve, where she had always felt closest to her Catholicism, Ellen continued a tradition begun many years earlier. Every June the entire village processed to Ellen's magnificent outdoor altar for the feast of Corpus Christi. Set upon an antique carpet, the altar was variously decorated with reliquaries, crucifixes, palm leaves, flowers, lace and candelabras. Back at Warley, the garden was opened for a day each spring, young Jim Robinson the butler's son collecting the sixpences in a tin.[111] Naturally, the money went to charity: Brentwood Cottage Hospital. Obviously Miss Willmott *herself* had no need of extra money.

In late summer came the village's Event of the Year, yet another way to demonstrate the largesse of Warley's mistress. The Spetchley collection holds several *Great & Little Warley Village Show and Sports Day* programmes, in various states of decay. The one at the top of this chapter almost certainly dates from 1908. Everything about this tiny piece of card stamps Ellen Willmott as the Lady of the Manor, including the photograph, by her, of her house. The field is lent by her, the prizes are donated by her. The programme itself may even have been printed by her. Ellen's brother-in-law – from 'real' aristocracy – will preside. All is normal. All is as it should be.

Warley's annual fixture, including a flower show, was hugely popular and photographs of the displays rival anything held at Horticultural Halls. Bowls of perfect fruit, ludicrously large bunches of table grapes and swags of exotic greenery decorate the canvas marquee walls. A picture postcard reveals just how large the marquees were, dwarfing the ogling masses. We don't have any pictures of the various sports, which is a shame since they included ladies' chase-the-greasy-pig, tug-of-war on donkeys and 100 yards on all fours, not to mention pipe-smoking, skipping and roll-eating contests. It was a rare break when Warley's gardeners could let down their hair, enjoy a pint and gossip about their employer. Was she really as mean as they grumbled about, or only the same as every other landowner out there? Voices of dissent were quiet, but they were there. Self-educated fan of Bertrand Russell and Arthur Koestler, Thomas Candler, Ellen's Herbaceous Foreman, had long suffered a knot of righteous indignation at Warley's unvarying wages and long hours.

Although on its inauguration in 1904 the British Gardeners' Association had insisted it was *not* a trades union, it agitated for wage

---

111 In 1908 those sixpences added up to a very respectable £5 2s 7d; approx. £400 today.

increases and improved conditions, and wanted to impose a closed shop, all of which outraged employers up and down the land.

Candler was not just a founder member of the BGA but served on the executive committee. He was also, for the present, keeping this fact very quiet from Miss Willmott. Other employers had forced members to make a straight choice – the Association or their jobs – and Thomas Candler had a young family. As conditions got worse, however, it was getting harder to keep silent. The Old Age Pension, introduced on 1 January 1909, should have made things easier for elderly gardeners but, on the shop-soil, nothing really changed. Ellen Willmott merely deducted the sum paid out by the Government from her older workers' wages. This bizarre-seeming behaviour probably came from an initial misunderstanding by some employers that the pension had been brought in as a way of subsidising jobs that might otherwise have been lost due to a reduction in output. That doesn't make it any easier to defend today. It was just one of many indignities the British Gardeners' Association was battling against across the country, and the louder their voices, the harder it was getting for Candler to stay under the radar. In France, Ellen faced out-and-out insurrection: 'Pierre has left for good,' she told Norman Moore. 'I expected him to strike me he was so violent, he raised his arm, but I looked him full in the face & was perfectly cool & the moment passed.'[xxii] In England things were, on the face of it, calmer, but the anger of ordinary jobbing gardeners up and down the land simmered below the surface.

Ellen Willmott's penny-pinching was beginning to be noticed elsewhere, too. Bills were taking longer than ever to pay, even to non-tradesfolk: 'Speaking of Wilson, you are indebted to the Arboretum to the extent of £6 10s 3d,' wrote Charles Sargent, 'being the amount prepaid by Wilson in China on the cases sent to you in the two years.' Since she was currently doing a very good job of covering her tracks, her friends still took this as forgetfulness. 'Sometime when you think of it, will you send me a draft for the amount as I want to settle up

THE SLOW FALL OF ICARUS

the accounts of the expedition,' Sargent continued cheerfully, little suspecting the coffers were empty.[xxiii] Others took a less charitable view and rumours began to circulate that Miss Willmott, despite having legendary wealth, was turning into Ebenezer Scrooge. After all, she had just rebuilt that chateau in France, and filled it with priceless antiques – again! She was winning all those prizes, both in France and at the RHS shows in the Temple Gardens. She was constantly on the move between *three* properties. Her Warley garden was a paradise of expensive exotics, secluded grottos, mountain torrents, disporting goldfish and rustic chalets. She was writing the rose book to end all rose books. How could she possibly be short of cash?

Yet there she was, making small economies (alas, not large ones) and eagerly snapping up the opportunity to use a free ticket to an opera box owned by Lady Mount Stephen, who wasn't able to go because the Princess of Wales was coming to visit today instead of tomorrow. Ellen and Gian were in (very) infrequent contact, but theatre trips were a rare treat these days and an opera box was an opera box.[112] It would take her mind off things, and not just her own cares. Her sister was poorly. Again. Just the usual aches and pains, but even when Rose managed to get away from Spetchley Park for a while, she took too many *bains-douches*, too fast, giving her fevers, and any relief from an unspecified 'discomfort and worry' returned as soon as she did. The cause of stress at Spetchley was obvious enough to Ellen and her friends not to have to spell it out in letters, so we remain unenlightened.

Ellen herself was back in pain and, as usual, trying out the latest miracle cures. Bodybuilder Eugen Sandow had found fame taking on all-comers in the World's Strongest Man competition, 1889, including Charles 'Samson' Sampson, Frank 'Cyclops' Bienkowski and Henry 'Hercules' McCann. He bested them all. Sandow broke chains, lifted people with his bare hands and posed in very little clothing at the 1893

---

112 This is their only communication I know of from this period; the invitation may have come via Rose.

Chicago World's Fair before joining Florenz Ziegfeld's travelling show and making a quarter of a million dollars. Back in England he founded the Sandow Curative Institute of Physical Culture. In 1909 Ellen Willmott took out a subscription, gambling some of her dwindling resources trying to find any relief from rheumatic misery through a programme of exercise and cod liver oil which lasted at least two years.

If chronic pain sometimes made her grumpy and financial problems made her look miserly, there is, nonetheless, a raft of evidence that Ellen Willmott was neither constantly irascible nor irredeemably mean. Among many small kindnesses she ensured visitors to her gardens never left without sacks of plants and bulbs;[113] if she was a visitor herself, she sent her hosts photographs she'd made on the trip. Friends in trouble could count on her to wade in on their behalf; when RHS secretary William Wilks found himself in danger of losing his garden, Ellen wrote letters and made cases in high places. She even stood guarantor for the landlord of the Thatcher's Arms pub (next door to Warley's front gate), an act of generosity that backfired since he defaulted, leaving Miss Willmott liable for the cash.

Ellen's biggest fan, Johann Bernhard Mann, stayed loyal despite the fact that it had now been three years since they had met. 'Sometimes I feel like an engine, working from morning to night, without seeing anything of the surroundings, only speaking to people on duty,' he wrote sadly.[xxiv]

Platonic friend Norman Moore also saw Ellen's many good qualities. 'Where my dearest friend is there is always a delightful glow, radiant from her,' he wrote on the way home from a long trip to Egypt.[xxv] 'It will indeed be delightful to spend an evening with her again. Yes, how

---

113 This is contradicted in a statement made by the Russell sisters from late in Willmott's life, saying she was mean with plants and only gave away 'fearful spreaders'. The body of evidence against the first is overwhelming. In defence of her second crime, people tend to give away plants they have too many of and these can turn out to be the horticultural thugs. Ellen's gifts would usually be newly introduced plants, used to dealing with tough terrains. Given care and attention, they sometimes turned out to be horrors. Even monsters like Japanese knotweed were once considered delightful garden gems.

much to talk of, how much to see in her bright eyes & dear face – always so full of all that is gentle, tender & intelligent.'

At home, she hosted rambles for the Essex Field Club, often in conjunction with Robert Miller Christy, another polymath, of energy surpassed only by Ellen Willmott herself. With him, Ellen led walks to Tyler's Common and Upminster Mineral Spring. Without him, she hosted club visits to Warley, usually consisting of a guided tour followed by a slap-up tea and a show-and-tell of some of her antiquarian books/ instruments/weird artefacts. A long write-up from one of these visits is the best description we have of any of Ellen's gardens.[114]

For someone who claimed to be chained to her desk writing her beloved rose book, and who we now know was virtually skint, Ellen Willmott spent an awful lot of time doing other things. In 1909, between travelling to her various gardens, winning prizes at horticultural shows (including 'Flower of the Show' at the National Tulip Show), playing Lady of the Manor and visiting friends from Scotland to Heidelberg, she somehow managed to find time to publish her first book, which was, of course, *not* the expected volume about roses.

Warley Garden in Spring and Summer is, in many ways, a frustrating book for today's readers. Willmott includes virtually no text in the large-format folio of forty-one collotype plates, interleaved with tissue and produced in no-expense-spared fashion. Thanks to archaic printing techniques, to the modern eye the images can appear 'muddy' and, being largely close-ups of Willmott's plants rather than the garden as a whole, it's hard to get much sense of what the place looked like, even using the very sparse captions. The lack of text did not go unremarked at the time. *The Field* felt 'the album would have been improved if Miss Willmott had written a descriptive note about each of the pictures; we certainly would like to know something of the picturesque house, and particulars of the garden, one of the most

---

114 J. C. Shenstone, 'The Gardens of Warley Place, Brentwood, Essex', *Essex Naturalist*, 1912–13.

famous in the south'.[xxvi] The reviewer also felt the images were taken 'to impress the gardener rather than the artist; consequently, only few of them are really pictures'. *Ouch* – though Ellen Willmott would have taken that particular barb as a compliment. Most reviewers, however, seemed to consider the book a triumph. Gertrude Jekyll described it as 'sumptuous', declaring that 'each scene of border, rock and wild garden, pool and water margin, speaks for itself'.[xxvii]

Bernard Quaritch almost certainly published the volume at Ellen's own expense and, sumptuous as may be, there was a limited audience for such a finely produced, expensive[115] work on so narrow a topic. Well into the 1920s, *Country Life* would carry a small ad in its back pages from a remainder company, flogging a 'new edition'[116] of a 'charming Xmas gift book' comprising 'views of the most noteworthy garden in England' at 10s 6d.[117] They were quite successful at getting the news out, even managing to get a review for the fifteen-year-old book.[118] All told, *Warley Garden in Spring and Summer* made Ellen just £7 1s 8d.[119] She didn't care. She was nearly ready to present her magnum opus to a grateful world, and that would solve all her problems.

---

115 Twenty-one shillings, approximately £80.

116 Not a new edition.

117 Approximately £22.

118 *Manchester Guardian*, 15 Sept 1924, treats the book as a novelty nostalgia trip in sepia and white, about an old-fashioned garden which, by then, it was.

119 Approx. £550 today.

Chapter Fourteen:

Digging Holes

GENUS ROSA

A thick book with heavyweight pages, bound in tan leather, roughly 30 cm x 40 cm in size, this is first of four such volumes, each with deep-tooled spine and gilded lettering. 'Genus Rosa' is a twenty-part, definitive exploration of the rose family in the early twentieth century. Each of the 132 entries includes a full Latin and scientific description, select bibliography, 500-word prose description and botanical illustration.

'PROBABLY ONLY A strong-willed, distinguished, intellectually eminent and rich man could have found favour with her, but she never met her Napoleon.'[i] Renowned twentieth-century botanist and garden historian William T. Stearn was convinced Ellen Willmott had a Napoleon complex, but I can't help thinking that while she admired Corsica's most famous son, her real passions matched those of his consort.

It had been nearly twenty years since the idea of recreating the book commissioned by Empress Josephine for a modern audience had sparked Ellen's imagination. Ever since those carefree times at Aix-les-Bains admiring Redouté's *Les Roses*, she had been slowly inching towards writing her own definitive work on the subject. Admittedly the 'writing' largely manifested as scribbled pencil memos in random notebooks, but she *had* commissioned Alfred Parsons to paint 140 watercolour portraits of her own specimens.[120] By 1901 forty portraits were complete and Ellen had interested John Murray, publisher to the stars, in bringing them to the world.

Genus Rosa's journey to publication was long, tortuous and, eventually, toxic. Murray failed to come up with a contract until 1909, which kept Ellen dangling, but an overeager buyer at Hatchards bookshop jumped the gun anyway. After she showed some of Parsons' watercolours at the Linnean Society in 1905, he announced the imminent arrival of the book, leading to an embarrassing climbdown when it became clear not

---

120 There would eventually be 132 paintings.

DIGGING HOLES

a word of it was written. Uncharacteristically, the usually genial Alfred Parsons would not wreathe himself in glory either, publicly insulting Murray's choice of printing firm with the apparent intention of hiring a company in which he had a secret financial interest. When the smear failed, he sulked.

For her part, Ellen dithered, deferred, demanded and procrastinated. I know how she felt. Every book is perfect before an author puts pen to paper. To witness it emerge from one's fingers as a shadow of the imagined paragon is the heartbreak of being a writer. Behind every act of public belligerence – rude letters, imperious demands and constant deflection of blame[121] – she festered with crippling self-doubt. Today we would label it Imposter syndrome.

It is now 1910. Ellen is working round the clock to complete her first draft, engaging help from the Reverend Engleheart (for general Latin terms), John Baker of Kew (writing the technical descriptions), Norman Moore (more Latin and comments) and Charles Sprague Sargent (everything else). It's all getting a bit heated. Ellen's behind with her letterpress, Alfred Parsons is moaning about the print quality and John Murray is fielding grumpy letters from both on a daily basis. It has been decided that the work will come out in twenty-four parts, to be bound in two, cathedral-Bible-sized albums. Even the wealthiest customers cannot be expected to afford a single volume of such size as a one-off. This presents new problems, not least when, and which, reviewers should be allowed to see it. What will happen to sales of subsequent parts if the notices are bad? What if subscribers drop out? When are the royalties due? Will there actually be any royalties? Who's paying for all this anyway? There were no easy answers to any of the above.

Ellen was sure of one thing – no corners were to be cut. She was bankrupting herself financially, physically and mentally; she expected nothing less from her beleaguered publisher. 'This Rose book has cost

---

[121] Sometimes the fault did actually lie with other people.

me so much in time and money that I am anxious not to leave any stone unturned in order to improve it or in any case to avoid trivial or careless shortcomings,' she explained to Charles Sargent.[ii] Sargent himself was on the floor, saying that he was ready to retire to a sanatorium for the rest of his life after working on Ellen's book. He may not have been joking.

Everything about *Genus Rosa* would be painful, strung-out and unpleasant but it is unlikely Ellen Willmott ever fought harder for anything. She accepted harsh criticism from Sargent, Moore and Engleheart with meekness, wincing every time one of them pointed out a schoolboy error in her self-taught science or dictionary Latin. All three made allowances; they were men enough of the world to know she had never been a schoolboy, but standards were standards. She had sunk everything into *Genus Rosa*; it *had* to be a success. By proposing a 'definitive work' on something that can never be definitive, however, she was making a rod for her own back.

The tragedy was that Ellen *had* done the reading. She knew all about, even espoused modern thinking. In her mind, however, *Genus Rosa* harked back to a golden age, of Josephine, Shakespeare, chivalry and romance. She deliberately chose traditional, nineteenth-century botanical conventions, of description from observation alone, making the merest of nods to the work of geneticists such as Gregor Mendel or modern 'hybrid tea' breeders, whose results she considered vulgar.

Even sticking to her own parameters, Ellen's material was getting out of hand. Vast amounts of often conflicting data, conflicting opinion, conflicting history and conflicting science somehow had to be condensed into a cohesive argument and she felt inadequate to the task. 'I worked my hand at the Rose M.S. all the time I was in Italy and put together all I could think of under the observations,' she wrote to Sargent, admitting, 'I am afraid a good deal of what I should consider rubbish.'[iii] Sargent ignored Ellen's fishing rod, merely replying with more corrections.

Dark clouds appeared on the horizon even as the manuscript neared completion (or at least the parts John Murray needed for the 1910 releases). Ellen had been bumbling around her various gardens, much as she did any spring, save for a quick trip to Holland where, in a true coals-to-Newcastle moment, she had been invited to join the bulb jury at the Great Exhibition at Haarlem. She was getting nice reviews for *Warley Garden in Spring and Summer*. Mrs Theresa Earle, author of the famous *Pot-Pourri* gardening series, had told her 'everyone knows about England's greatest gardener'.[iv] She was climbing the ranks of interesting clubs and was about to be made president of the Sweet Pea Society, but something wasn't sitting right.

Perhaps attending King Edward VII's funeral on 20 May brought back morbid thoughts of lost loved ones; more likely a car accident reminded her of her own mortality. We don't know much about the smash, save that it totalled the vehicle, a fact only discovered after expensive – and ultimately unsuccessful – uninsured repairs.

What really did for Ellen that spring, however, was the sudden coming home to roost of some financial chickens. If we are to believe her, Ellen had left her business affairs in the hands of Henry Dixson – the chap she claimed had messed up the insurance at Tresserve – while she wrote *Genus Rosa*. It does appear that Dixson invested in some dodgy schemes, and Ellen later claimed that he had managed to manipulate Warley's mortgage commitments to himself, under a different name, which is hard to verify. However incompetent or wheeler-dealer-ish Dixson may have been, I really can't see that Ellen's finances could have been ruined by him in such a short time. It's unlikely she only took her eye off the economic ball during *Genus Rosa*. She hated anything to do with money and had always trusted her father's old firm to do it for her, even as the individuals running it changed, and Dixson wasn't the only man in the company. She treated cash like confetti and made no effort to check there was rice enough left to throw. Her father had not taught her even basic economic wisdom, but Ellen Willmott was not a stupid woman. She must have seen the runaway train steaming towards her.

Consulting her best friend Norman Moore was not the action of a stupid woman. The doctor listened soberly, went away, thought about it, then suggested a plan of action.

Ellen needed to know exactly what she owed at her various residences. She needed to get rid of her butler, 'the Frenchman' (M. Frédéric the chauffeur) and possibly Eliza Burge, Ellen's lady's maid since the early 1890s. She should keep only a cook ('of low degree'), a parlourmaid and housemaid.[v] Norman wrote to Dixson on Ellen's behalf, in an attempt to get a straight answer on the true state of her estate. 'You cannot state things too clearly to Miss Willmott at present,' he pressed.[vi]

The results were a tangle, which Norman Moore boggled at, then put into a chart for Ellen, including outgoings and debts against her dwindled capital and modest income from rented cottages. If she could rent out Warley Farm, Well Mead Garden and Warley Lea (the former home of her sister and brother-in-law), she could begin to pay off her debts, he told her. This would, however, leave her with just £137 a year to live on.[122] By relocating to Tresserve, Ellen could live comfortably on that; on her visits to England, she could stay with friends who, he added gently, would be *more than glad* to have her. Pre-empting Ellen's distress at losing her English garden, Moore suggested William Robinson might be interested in purchasing Warley.

There was one more thing: Ellen must tell her sister everything. Rose and Robert would surely be able to help. Moore ends his humane, tough-love approach by reminding her that these are mere suggestions, from an 'unskilled' friend; the choice is, ultimately, hers. 'You could be happy at Tresserve & would feel you had faced your difficulties & would never get into any more,' he wrote. 'If you do nothing, things will get worse every month.'[vii]

Ellen was devastated. 'I am not sitting down crying although I feel pretty bad.'[viii] She did a couple of things, such as packing off one of her

---

[122] Approx. £16,500 today.

cars to Spetchley, along with poor M. Frédéric, and offering the other vehicle to Alice de Rothschild for £500.[123] But the garden! 'If I send off all the men I shall be losing hundreds of pounds worth of plants . . . which could be sold advantageously,' she told her friend, hinting that if 'someone' who didn't need an immediate return on their money might just take over Warley's mortgage and let her stay on, it would be a sound business bet for the future. Equally, in ten years' time Boccanegra would be worth a *huge* amount. The local building frenzy and railway line she had fought so hard against were now selling points. *Genus Rosa* was, she had calculated, going to make her £13,860 (just shy of £1,700,000 today) minus publisher commission. While she waited for that boat to come in, she could, she supposed, stoop to writing some gardening articles for magazines. Oh, and she had just remembered some land in town her father had owned. That would soon be valuable, too, as London County Council would have to buy it in order to build the new bridge that was all over the newspapers.[124]

In what would become a Willmott pattern, Ellen also came up with a get-rich-quick scheme: lodgers. The plan was to contact all her friends who had lost husbands and invite them to become paying guests at Warley. 'I only want two rooms myself,' Ellen burbled, imagining a house full of interesting women and a debt-free existence.[ix] It would be better than losing Warley. 'I never realised how I loved every tree & stone until the thunderbolt fell.'

The lodger wheeze was a nice idea, but ultimately, Ellen's widowed friends were either comfortably off and didn't need to bunk-in with others, or they were even poorer than she was and unable to afford such luxury. William Robinson wasn't keen on purchasing a second property either, somewhat tactlessly informing her: 'The way to get into trouble

---

123 Alice was clearly embarrassed. She refused the car, but sent her friend a cheque for £500, making it clear it was a gift – '<u>I never lend money</u>' – and telling her to visit, when they could chat about anything – except finances. Ellen did not get the hint and pressed for advice; Alice told her to find a proper businessman and said it was probably best they did not meet for the present after all.

124 For London fans, this is Southwark Bridge. Ellen owned the warehouses on the southside approach; some of the original wall still stands.

is to have several homes. I have always been greatly impressed by your expenditure and thought that only a millionaire could afford it.'[x]

John Murray, snapping at her heels for her manuscript, suggested Ellen hire an editor. She replied that she had already spent huge amounts of money on *Genus Rosa*, thank you very much, and would rely on her own editorial skills.

Part the First was finally published on 15 December 1910, to a collective sigh of relief from all involved. The sections were to be collected into two gigantic green-cloth binders, tied with tape. Ellen's personal leather-bound copy, described at the top of this chapter, is even more impressive. It now lives in the RHS Lindley Library, bought and bequeathed by Ellen's friend, Reginald Cory. It is magnificent, not least because the reader can compare both original watercolour and printed plate, bound together on opposite pages, separated by wisps of tissue.

Genus Rosa is, undeniably, beautiful. Even today the colour plates seem to glow from the pages, even if the print quality could have been better. Alfred Parsons' griping may have had dodgy origins but that didn't mean he was necessarily wrong. After his hissy fit, Parsons washed his hands of the process, but it would have benefited from his (unbiased) supervision. Early copies show a slight 'yellowness' in the chromolithography, which impacted sales. It was also, alas, a book out of its time. Ellen Willmott's romantic approach encapsulates a moment – the nineteenth century – when everyone, including Willmott herself, lived in the fast-moving, scientific twentieth. Even this shouldn't have been a deal-breaker, though. Many people enjoy a little nostalgia. *Genus Rosa's* main problem was its price. An entire collection would set back a purchaser the equivalent of nearly £2,500 today. It was just too darned expensive.

Ellen's attempts to shift copies cannot be faulted. She went into overdrive, getting volumes sent to friends (who sometimes had the embarrassment of sending them back when they found out the cost), writing to all and sundry and even manning stalls at flower shows. Distribution was a serious problem. The Army & Navy Stores kept

DIGGING HOLES

their 'display copy' locked away for fear of its getting dog-eared. Most couldn't afford to stock it at all. Due to its piecemeal publication, reviews were staggered, sometimes not appearing for years. Gertrude Jekyll's authoritative praise in the *Quarterly Review,* for example, wouldn't arrive until October 1914, when most people would have their minds on rather more pressing matters.

Things were getting desperate. Ellen was forced to reveal her circumstances to someone else: Lady Mount Stephen. I can't see that Ellen and Gian had been in contact since the Tresserve fire, save for Ellen's snapping up of that spare opera box a year earlier. Her writing to Gian out of the blue, offering to sell her a series of sketches of Bulwick Hall, home of their lost mutual friend Minnie Grosvenor, seems to have come as a surprise. Gian replies with kindness, yes, she might be interested, though wall space is short and she could only take a couple (Gian had two giant properties, Brocket Hall in Hertfordshire and a town house in Carlton House Terrace; there was plenty of 'wall space'). She ends with a polite enquiry after the rose book and vague hopes to meet again.

The letter marks a handbrake turn on the women's relationship. Once very much the junior partner, in awe of Ellen's two houses and vast spending power, Gian is now Lady Mount Stephen, wife of one of the richest men in the land. She regularly entertains the King and Queen and appears in the society columns. It's hard to tell how she views her former confidante in straitened conditions. There's pity in her characteristic scrawl, yes, but there's something else too. Condescension? Wariness? Or just a friendship that has run its course?

Gian bought two sketches, and commiserated with her friend, hoping that she wouldn't have to part with all her lovely things, especially that 'spinet' of hers. The harpsichord Fred Willmott had bought for Ellen's birthday was one of the finest instruments in the world. Ellen had treasured and played the instrument ever since, also occasionally loaning it to museums for exhibitions. Gian remembered it fondly. Yes, losing that would be awful. Though if, by any chance, she ever *did* think of selling . . . she would tell her old friend Gian first, wouldn't she?[xi]

Of all the things Gian could have suggested Ellen part with, this would have touched the rawest of nerves. In a belated birthday letter ('I wish I had known,' Gian writes artlessly, having celebrated Ellen's birthday many times in the past), she just happens to mention the matter again. 'I hope I have made it clear about the harpsichord, which is how gladly I will buy it if you decide to sell.'[xii]

Ellen's draft reply is undated, but from the crossings out it's clear it was no snap decision. 'I cannot say I do not prize it,' she writes, 'but if I have to part with it there could not be any way that I would rather see it go.' Recognising the change in their relationship status, she adds humbly, 'It is very kind of you to make it as easy as possible for me.'

Things then suddenly go quiet between the two women. A new knight in shining morning suit has entered the scene; a new straw to clutch at.

❧

We last met Sir Frank Crisp in 1904, in that strange painting at the Linnean Society where he watches in the background while his wife Catherine is accepted as one of the first female Fellows – the one where Sir Frank fell out with the couple in the foreground and then had them painted out. Ellen isn't in the picture at all; she remained only a passing acquaintance with the Crisps until later when 'merest chance' brought them back into her life. The incident is not recounted, though their new friendship must have had something to do with the equally idiosyncratic garden Sir Frank was creating at Friar Park, Henley-on-Thames. Ellen was sending vast amounts of plants to Friar Park around this time, and she and the Crisps became very close, very quickly. Sir Frank was as loyal to his friends as he was scourge to his enemies, and when Ellen got into trouble he dropped everything to help her.

A lawyer by trade, he delved into her financial affairs and concluded things weren't so very awful. Contradicting Norman Moore, he advised Ellen not to tell her sister; it would only worry her. She joyfully tells Norman that 'Sir Frank is going to find the money to keep me going here. I have nearly halved the weekly cheque. The great thing now is to sell the cottages & all the property east, this may possibly pay off the whole of the mortgage on this place. You can imagine the relief after the agony of mind I have been going through. I weigh a stone less than I did 2 months ago & I am sure if that awful strain of mind had gone on I should either have been in my grave or the asylum.'[xiii] Norman's eyebrows must have raised, given this is pretty much the same advice he had given her a month or so earlier in somewhat less-varnished language, but he was probably just relieved not to be dealing with the mess alone. Ellen babbles on: 'He was most cheering, his last word was, "I have no fear of not pulling your affairs round & I mean to save Warley for you."'

Ellen is spinning Sir Frank's words here, choosing to taste only the sugar with which he delivers the same bitter pill Norman Moore prescribed.[125] I have never seen such claims in any of his communications. Like so many men, Moore included, Sir Frank was dazzled by the intoxicating mixture of fierce independence, voracious appetite for knowledge, determination to achieve, and 'damsel-in-distress' that Ellen Willmott radiated. Was she even conscious of playing the 'little girl lost' card? Of allowing such men to indulge their chivalrous fantasies by 'helping' her? Was it some kind of guerrilla tactic in a war against patriarchy – or merely learned behaviour, dating back to the days when she and Rose, devoid of legitimate 'agency', had still managed to wind their father around their collective little fingers? However it happened, Sir Frank fell for her charms (not sexually, as far as I know, which is even more intriguing). For the moment, at least, he had plenty of sugar to help that medicine down.

By September Ellen was teetering back into her old ways. Asking Norman Moore his opinion on the preface for the next part of *Genus*

---

125 The same advice was also given by Alice de Rothschild, before withdrawing herself from the conversation.

Rosa, she glibly told him that Sir Frank 'says I have cut down quite sufficiently now, at any rate for the present and says I made a great mistake in giving that motor to the Berkeleys'.[xiv]

Things calmed a little. The world spun on. The 1910 Japan-British Exhibition changed perceptions of the Orient in the popular mind. Three times the size of the 1900 Paris Exposition, its White City[126] site was so vast that visitors needed a mile-long monorail to get around.

Most spectacular were two enormous Japanese gardens, built using authentic structures, bridges, boulders and exotic plants. Importing living things from halfway around the world had been a trial. To prevent the cherry trees bursting into bloom in the middle of the tropical Indian Ocean, all living exhibits were sent across America under harsh conditions of the opposite variety. Only the Japanese, however, knew how plant-reduced and overcrowded with ornament the exhibition gardens were. To the eight and a half million visitors (nearly a quarter of Britain's entire population) the result was breathtaking, and boosted a burgeoning craze for oriental horticulture well beyond the dreams of the Veitch Water Gardens at Coombe Lodge.[127]

Ellen was far too bound up with *Genus Rosa* and looming bankruptcy to be involved in organising the exposition, but we regularly find unused exhibition postcards among her papers, mainly of women in kimonos enjoying pagodas, bridges and wisteria-framed rock-gardens. She also purchased plants a-gogo from the Yokohama Nursery Company, putting faces to the stunning catalogues she had been ordering from since 1894. Perhaps the most useful connection she made at the Japan-British exhibition, however, was the Vicomte Foukouba, Director of the Imperial Palace Parks and Gardens, Tokyo. Foukouba visited Ellen at Warley and, on his return to Japan, the pair began a system of plant and news exchange, communicating in French.

---

126 West London.

127 One of the structures, a scale model of the Chokushimon (Gateway of the Imperial Messenger), lives out its days in the Japanese gardens at Kew.

DIGGING HOLES

It was some respite from the ongoing financial train wreck at home. January 1911 brought the usual greetings from Johann Bernhard Mann, now commander of SMS *Sleipner*, the Kaiser's personal yacht, and hoping to hook up with Ellen when the German Emperor stopped in Portsmouth. The idea was attractive, and Johann's letter had found her in reasonable spirits. 'My affairs are not so bad as that statement showed,' she tells Norman Moore around the same time. 'Sir Frank has every hope of bringing everything round.'[xv] She is still suffering the stress of 'knowing there was no one in the world I could turn to for help and advice' – a rich statement from someone who absolutely *did* turn to someone: the very man she is writing to, plus at least two others, and who has still chosen not to share her problems with her sister. Ellen has convinced herself that 'the missing money' has been found, in investments that may yet pay out. The next part of *Genus Rosa* is coming out any day now; its status as bestseller is only a matter of time. The real moustache-twirler is Henry Dixson, who 'has muddled everything frightfully & feathered his own nest & from not having a penny in the world except his salary he is now a rich man'.

Convincing herself of Dixson's villainy didn't actually pay Ellen's bills. Instead of selling one or two properties, as suggested by everyone she asked, she dickered around the edges, selling odd bits and bobs and relying on the sales of a few seeds and bulbs, which took more manpower and expense in creating and printing the lists, and packing and sending the items than they attracted in returns. Selling her finest blooms to upmarket florist Pipers in Bayswater, who picked and chose what they fancied and paid what they pleased, brought little return for such hard-won riches. They sometimes didn't pay on time, either, giving her a small dose of her own medicine.

With what must have been the heaviest of sighs, Ellen wrote again to Gian Mount Stephen, this time specifically about the harpsichord.

Gian's plan from the start, Ellen discovered, had not been to buy the instrument for herself but as a surprise coronation gift for

Queen Mary. Ellen swallowed the fact that her friend didn't want her precious instrument and just pronounced herself grateful that at least it wouldn't end up in America like all antiques seemed to these days. She had originally suggested Gian buy it for £300 but now 'just happens to mention' that there are 'other interested buyers' who have offered her £400 and that she's heard it might fetch an even higher price, thanks to the Princess Amelia connection. She has refused of course, but might Gian give her the £400 anyway?[xvi] Gian wonders if 'the other party' might be the Queen herself, who is on a drive to collect royal items, and dodges the £400 question by saying that she hopes Ellen won't regret selling the item to her at £300 when she could have got more. In a clumsy second attempt to up the price, Ellen replies that thanks to some undisclosed jiggery-pokery from Sir Frank Crisp she now doesn't need to sell the item; she's only doing it because it's for her friend Gian.

Her friend Gian, clearly beginning to lose patience, tells Ellen it's never been an issue of money, and if Ellen doesn't want to part with it, she can easily find something else for the Queen. Her husband doesn't think it a suitable gift anyway.

No, no, replies Ellen hurriedly. 'I had quite made up my mind to its going & in fact had looked upon it as no longer mine . . . Will you not reconsider, you will be doing me a real kindness & I will never trouble you again about anything of the sort.'[xvii]

The harpsichord ping-pong bats on. Ellen gets herself further into trouble by mentioning the confidential matter to Queen Alexandra's ancient retainer. What's worse is that as she's standing in his garden at Windsor Castle discussing the issue, the King and Queen turn up. Ellen doesn't actually admit she let the cat out of the bag, but Gian's next letter is close to losing it altogether. 'I think it was a pity to have spoken to Sir Dighton about an entirely private matter between you & me these things get talked about,' she writes, finally coming to a decision. 'I am sorry it has all come to nothing in the end.'[xviii]

DIGGING HOLES

It couldn't come to nothing. It mustn't come to nothing. The bill for last year's car smash had just arrived and Ellen's coffers were empty. The desperation in her next flurry of letters is pitiful; the steel in Gian's replies excruciating. April 25th 1911: 'Dearest we have quite decided that we will not think of the Harpsichord . . . it will be more pleasing to us to give the Queen something more personal.' April 28th 1911: 'If . . . you would like me to have the Queen told privately that it was to be had I would do so with pleasure.' May 1st 1911: 'I wish I had never mentioned the subject.' May 2nd 1911: 'If you want it so much I will take the Harpsichord as originally settled. Can you send it to me either Thursday or Friday. I hope the Queen does not know anything about it as I should not like it to have got about. I also hope you will not repent selling it for £300.'

The indignity of it all is palpable – and it wasn't over.

May 12th 1911: 'Dearest, I must tell you that there is rather a blow about the Harpsichord. I have found out quite privately that the Queen does not want it as she has no room to put it.'

Gian presents her friend with two options. Ellen can take it back or keep the £300 'but I must tell you – that if I buy it, I shall sell it'.

After all that humiliation, nothing. Ellen decided to take her beloved sixteenth birthday gift back but, in one final mortification, couldn't afford the removal fees. Gian agreed to temporarily house it in her boudoir 'which I never use'. The matter had soured not just Ellen's finances but any possibility of future reconciliation with Gian.

So far Ellen's problems had been kept relatively quiet. Selling bulbs and seeds was normal for horticulturists, and any other sales had been more or less under the radar. She was now forced to make public economies, starting by asking James Preece, her head gardener of nearly twenty years, to find another position. This is a truly baffling decision. Preece was respected by both his workforce and the wider gardening world. His opinion was valued by experts at Kew, and he won prizes under his own name. There is no indication of any disagreement between him and his employer. Ellen might have sold practically anything in her museum of a house before getting rid of him. Yet Preece was out. He would eventually set up a commercial enterprise in the Headley Garden, a neat solution for both parties; a business for him, rent for Miss Willmott, but it was one odd move on her part.[128]

In an even odder move, Ellen's brilliant money-making solution to Preece's departure was to hire a chap called Fielder,[129] who was, like Ellen herself, the holder of a Victoria Medal of Honour. Practical, capable, a member of the RHS Floral Committee, examiner for public park employees and weekly columnist for the *Gardeners' Chronicle* – how on earth could such a man have been cheaper than James Preece? Admittedly, Fielder was a part-timer, but that came with attendant cat-away-mice-play issues that I can't see Ellen Willmott putting up with for long. With Fielder came a rash of high-profile prizes, though. Perhaps by appointing a VMH and by being seen to introduce award-winning plants Ellen was metaphorically nailing a fig leaf over the most exposed parts of her finances.

Another gardener left Warley in 1911. Herbaceous foreman Thomas Candler had always been a little disaffected with life at Warley, but he was positively angry when he found himself another job and Ellen Willmott refused to give him a reference. He had been with her for years and felt he had served her well. For her part, Ellen had helped Candler find a job for his brother-in-law and, it appears from his postcards, given Candler himself time off when required. It also looks as though she originally agreed to provide a testimonial when Candler found a new post. She baulked, however, on discovering that he hadn't needed the reference to get the job. Instead, he wanted it as something to keep in his back pocket to produce at some unspecified date in the future. For years the incident has been taken as cussedness on Ellen's part. I now believe she had reason for her refusal. Her draft reply is basically several ways of

---

128 Inexplicably, the business didn't take.

129 Initials 'CM', there is no record of his first name.

Top left: Warley's daffodil bank in spring.
© *Berkeley Family and Spetchley Gardens Charitable Trust*

Top right: Narcissus 'Ellen Willmott', as painted by Henry Moon for *The Garden* 1897.

Bottom: The formal lawn at Warley Place. The agapanthus-filled Versailles planters are some of the batch that enjoyed a holiday at Hampton Court Palace in 1919.
© *Berkeley Family and Spetchley Gardens Charitable Trust*

Ellen photographed by Numa Blanc, Aix les Bains, 1894.

© *Berkeley Family and Spetchley Gardens Charitable Trust*

Ellen's photography ranged across many disciplines, including plant portraits.

Top left: An unknown orchid, one of Ellen's very few surviving early-colour Autochrome shots.

Top right: An unknown daffodil.

Bottom: Ellen and (probably) her painting tutor, Helen Green, perhaps taken with Ellen's spare camera.

© *Berkeley Family and Spetchley Gardens Charitable Trust*

Top left: Miss Gian Tufnell, from a photograph in the Royal Collection. Only a detail of the photograph is shown here. *Royal Collection Trust / © Her Majesty Queen Elizabeth II 2021*

Top right: Gian and another lady pause on the bridge at the Water Gardens, Kingston on Thames. *© Berkeley Family and Spetchley Gardens Charitable Trust*

Bottom: The music room at Warley Place.

© Berkeley Family and Spetchley Gardens Charitable Trust

Villa Boccanegra,
Ventimiglia, Italy.

© *Berkeley Family and Spetchley Gardens Charitable Trust*

Right: Johann Bernhard Mann.

© *Berkeley Family and Spetchley Gardens Charitable Trust*

Bottom: Anne Hathaway's cottage, Stratford-upon-Avon.

Top left: Ellen c.1907.

Top right: Ellen dressed in 18th century fancy dress for her nephew Rob's grand 21st Birthday Ball, April 1919. The guest of honour was absent, still serving abroad.

Bottom: Ellen judges a local garden competition, late 1920s.

© *Berkeley Family and Spetchley Gardens Charitable Trust*

Top: Warley's ruined conservatory today, surrounded by wild flowers and woodland.
© *Sandra Lawrence*

Right: Investigating a trunk, 2019.
© *Karen Davidson*

saying 'you got a job without bothering to get a reference from me this time, why should I give you one to use as currency for the future?' but there is something odd about its tone. She has not only drafted in advice from her brother-in-law for what should be a pretty straightforward employer/employee spat, but consulted her friend Robert Vyner too. To me there can only be one explanation: Ellen discovered Candler had been an active member of the British Gardeners' Association for years. She assumed he had been responsible for any and all dissent in the ranks since 1904 and was not going to recommend a union man to her friends.

It wasn't all doom and gloom. Ellen kept herself busy and active, and discovering new things in between slogging through new parts for *Genus Rosa*. She had to end subscriptions to several clubs; sometimes via excruciating resignation letters, more often by simply failing to pay subs, but she joined others, including the Bach Choir, via its founder Herbert Jekyll, Gertrude's brother. Ellen would find comfort and camaraderie in the choir to the end of her life, moving hell and high water to attend practice sessions, and if she missed the last train home after rehearsals, she didn't mourn the comfy bed that would once have awaited her at the Empress Club. She was not above hunkering down on a bench outside St-Martin-in-the-Fields for the night. After one concert in Oxford, she discovered that the friends she'd hoped to stay with were away. Undaunted, she curled up on the steps of the Judge's Lodging. On being woken at 2.30 a.m. by a bobby on the beat, she accepted his offer of a night in the station cells. She didn't care what anyone might think of the incident; indeed, she told the anecdote herself. It became quite a habit. Henry Luxmoore wrote a worried note the day after she'd visited him: 'I should not be very much surprised to hear that a waiting room table or a travelling horsebox was your only refuge!'[xix]

The humiliations she had already undergone brought out a new, hardened Ellen – one who had seen everything and now just took life as it came. It's likely the policeman had taken her for a tramp; gone were her days of accounts with Parisian couturiers. Rose sent her a red dress to wear when people came to visit the garden, yet even scruffiness seems, in its way, to have been a disguise. Ellen delighted in watching the reactions of people who had taken her for a nobody as they suddenly realised she was (still) somebody. She wore her growing eccentricity like a carapace; Ellen Willmott did all these unfathomable things because she chose to, okay?

Some of the unfathomable things were acts of surprising generosity. As a Trustee of the Royal Botanic Gardens, Kew, Ellen sent hundreds of plants for use there, including an important collection of sempervivums she'd originally been planning for a monograph. The 30,000-specimen *Herbarium Warleyense* she donated in 1911 was also a straight gift, at a time when she might have been forgiven for selling it. Admittedly it took until 1921 for the work to arrive, and it would seem from the resulting palaver that Laurel and Hardy were subcontracted to transport it across town.[130]

At home despite – or perhaps because of – Warley's head gardener shuffle, things were thriving. Charles Sargent was delighted at how successful Ellen had been with the seeds Ernest Wilson had sent from China. Indeed, he noted a fair few of her successes that no one else, including himself, had managed to germinate. At the RHS the ongoing *Genus Rosa* manuscript treadmill retained her status; perhaps even lent mystique to this unfathomable woman. After all, who could fail to be impressed by an author whose work is so important no one can afford to own it?

In December 1911, still unaware that his friend is teetering on bankruptcy, Charles Sargent asks for cuttings of a Helwingia and a Sabia he's been unable to germinate, cheerily wishing Ellen the compliments of the season and joy for 1912, adding: 'I hope you are taking better care of yourself than you used to and that you are not working too hard.'[xx] She was doing neither.

---

130 Originally the Bonnet Collection. She had already donated another herbarium, the Jordan Collection.

Chapter Fifteen:

A Funny Thing Happened on the Way to Chelsea

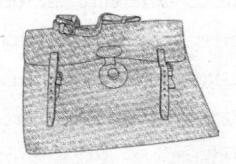

A LEATHER SATCHEL

Fashioned from thick, no-nonsense, chestnut-brown hide, this folio-style briefcase was designed for heavy wear. Its chrome lock is supplemented by two leather straps with buckles. A separate flap reveals three sturdy pockets, inside which, still connected by a piece of string, hides the satchel's rusted key. The strap, once extendable for use as a shoulder-bag, has welded into a solid mass of stiffened leather, seized metal fittings and a rainbow of multi-coloured fungus. Clouds of spores explode into the atmosphere whenever the object is touched. The legend, stamped in plain black letters, is still legible:

E.W. Warley Place.

HOW DO RIVALRIES begin? An accidental comment? Simple misunderstanding? Financial dispute? Intellectual clash? Jealousy? That last accounts for many a tiff, but one thing is sure. Enmity can only fester between parties that actually care about something, and passions ran nowhere more obsessively than in early twentieth-century horticulture. Friends could turn to enemies overnight; feuds might run for years then, equally rapidly, halt, as adversaries made peace in order to fight a common foe. There was just too much at stake. Practitioners studied their subjects to distraction. To imply, therefore, that new-kid-on-the-plot Reginald Farrer existed only to stir up trouble would be ridiculous. Farrer knew his subject. But he did love a punch-up. For him, Ellen Willmott represented a hostile establishment wilfully obstructing his quest to be crowned top maverick. Worse, she was a woman.

Born in 1880, Reginald John Farrer had been something of a boy-wonder. He became obsessed with botany as a child and built his first rock garden in an abandoned quarry, aged fourteen. Oxford educated, Farrer dreamed of exotic exploration. His first trip, to Japan and the Far East, was seminal; he fell in love with the culture, the gardens – and luxury travel. His expectations were curtailed when his family reined in the expenses, perhaps after seeing the array of colourful costumes he brought back to parade around in, which went down less well in his native Yorkshire than he might have hoped. Farrer's early travelogues and garden volumes were a hit, at least; his novels and poetry attracted more mixed attention.

Farrer had very definite opinions, especially on rock gardening. He wrote several books on the subject; always deeply personal, always dictatorial, always bitingly funny. He ceded no quarter to anyone failing to live up to his own exacting standards, sniggering at middle-class wannabes whose alpine gardens resembled 'almond puddings', 'plum buns', 'devil's lapfuls' or even 'dogs' graves'. A wrong choice of stone was a 'drunkard's dream of noxious cement blocks'.[i] Perhaps fatally for Farrer, however, he didn't stick to taunting faceless, weekend gardeners. He took pot-shots at horticulture's great and good. In *My Rock Garden*,[ii] the alpinums of Kew, Warley – even the saintly Charles Wolley-Dod – blistered under Farrer's gaze, yet he employed such a turn of phrase the book stayed in print for forty years.

It was pretty much a given that Ellen Willmott and Reginald Farrer were going to hate each other. I have always wondered, however, what triggered their at least ten-year enmity; a mutual dislike that would periodically sputter into action, cause a to-do then fizzle out until the next jibe (usually on Farrer's part; Ellen seems only to have reacted when poked).

Farrer clearly knew Warley, so they must have made an effort to be nice at first. We don't know when he visited, once again Warley's *Livre d'Or* lets us down, but it may have been with his friend E. A. Bowles. Sweet, charming, gentle and generous, Edward Augustus 'Gussie' Bowles was about as far in temperament to Farrer as could be imagined, but somehow they worked. They met at the RHS in 1909 and instantly agreed to meet up on an alpine plant-hunting trip a few weeks later. Farrer's resulting book, *Among the Hills, A Book of Joy in High Places*, was dedicated *Avem Crocum Omnium Rex Imperator Paterculus Augustus*[131] – a nod to the pair's nicknames for each other.

Gussie Bowles had known Ellen Willmott for years. Farrer was supremely jealous of their friendship, at one point snapping that Gussie should 'marry the cankered Ellen at once and save further trouble'.[iii]

---

131 *Hail, King and Emperor of Crocuses, Little Father Augustus.*

Both Audrey Le Lièvre and Bowles's biographer Mea Allen wonder if Reg had good reason; if Ellen had set her cap at lifelong bachelor Bowles, who had been horrified at her 'awkward' advances and run a mile, I doubt it. Ellen's letters to Gussie are cheery and enthusiastic but don't, to me at least, carry flirtation, clumsy or otherwise.

How did Ellen get so 'cankered', then? Who knows, but one 1910 review of *Warley Garden in Spring and Summer* can't have helped what seem to have been already strained relations.

Two Modern Gardens is a double-feature in *The Saturday Review*.[132] In an attempt to compare literary apples and pears, the Hon. Mrs Evelyn Cecil metaphorically pits Reginald Farrer's textural tableaux against Ellen Willmott's picture-album. The only thing the two books have in common is that they are both books. Farrer's latest sizzler, *In a Yorkshire Garden*, is another on-brand, first-person description of a landscape – his own – comprising 316 pages of passion, pith and personal flamboyance. *Warley Garden in Spring and Summer* is a large-format photographic collection that doesn't total a hundred words. In her 'review', Mrs Evelyn Cecil chooses to compare not just the two authors' books, but their respective gardens. One is found distinctly wanting.

Mrs C begins with Warley Place: 'Nothing could give a better idea of the luxurious growth in a modern garden,' she gushes. Miss Willmott 'is well-known as one of the most expert of gardeners,' she continues, adding, 'her knowledge is not new-born of the present craze' but 'the ripe result of real study and experience.' After waxing lyrical on Warley for a good three more paragraphs the review turns to the young whippersnapper of the present craze.

'Mr Farrer personally conducts his readers round his 'Yorkshire Garden' to which he has already admitted the public in his earlier and more valuable works,' writes Mrs C. 'Although from time to time he gives some useful horticultural experiences, much of his discourse . . . is

---

[132] 5 March 1910.

entirely irrelevant. Gardeners will,' she sniffs, 'be wearied by such digressions.' Grudgingly admitting Farrer's garden is 'attractive', and that he has hit on some good ideas for growing alpines, in her last line she delivers her verdict: 'there is no more vivid example of a beautiful garden of the British Isles than Warley in spring and summer'.

There is no way this review would have gone unnoticed by either author or, indeed, the wider gardening world. It's worth knowing that 'Hon. Mrs Evelyn Cecil' is just one of several aliases employed by Alicia Amherst: author, *Times* columnist, saviour of the Chelsea Physic Garden, co-worker (with Gertrude Bell) for the British Women's Emigration Association[133] and 'Mother of Garden History'.[134] 'Allie' Cecil had also been a paid-up member of Team Ellen for years. Perhaps I've got this wrong, perhaps I'm reading too much into one review, perhaps these are Cecil's genuine thoughts on two simple gardening books, but there seems to be an agenda here to which we are not party. Could it be belated payback for a comment in *My Rock Garden*, where Farrer describes Warley as 'a trifle too violent to be altogether pleasant', or some more recent slight that has not filtered down the decades?

Two years later, the feud had, temporarily, calmed down, though storm clouds still loomed. January 1912 saw Farrer abroad again as Ellen read the latest missive from Johann Bernhard Mann. She had yet again failed to hook up with her young admirer. When Mann arrived in February, now commander of Troop Destroyer G175, in spite of a flurry of letters and telegrams, the best he managed was afternoon tea with Lady Falmouth at Tregothnan and the hope that he might meet up with Miss Willmott on the return trip in May. We don't have Ellen's replies to Johann's telegrams and letters trying to make arrangements, but they're easily imagined. How could she tell her most ardent admirer that she

---

133 Founded to find employment for domestic servants abroad and protect them on their travels between positions.

134 AKA Lady Rockley of Lytchett Heath and the Dowager Baroness Rockley – she was the author of *A History of Gardening in England* (Bernard Quaritch, 1895).

couldn't afford the fare to Cornwall? No, best be 'too busy' to make it. To some extent it was true. *Genus Rosa* rumbled on, needing letterpress for seemingly endless forthcoming parts. The imagined riches from the already-published segments still showed no signs of materialising. Later that year, Johann would write again, this time brimming with joy: 'I have found the love of a dear soul who agreed to go the way of life together with me.'[iv] Now personal assistant to Groß Admiral Alfred von Tirpitz, Johann would be deskbound for the next three years but at least he'd be able to enjoy married life.

❦

Ellen's nomadic lifestyle between three gardens was no longer practical. It's not clear when she visited Boccanegra for the last time, but it was probably less than seven years after she bought the place and blew a fortune on it. Not that she could bring herself to sell; instead, she decided to rent to people she knew personally. At home she developed new ways to conceal the worst of her indignity, arriving at major events in billows of lace and gigantic 'statement' hats, dripping with jewellery. A cheap way of making her mark while confirming her horticultural expertise involved wearing a buttonhole of a different rare flower each time; defying experts to identify it. Miss Willmott made sure she was seen – and photographed – in good company. She explored the National Rose Show with Queen Alexandra and Princess Victoria in 1912; in 1913 she visited the first-ever Chelsea Flower Show flanked by the Duchesses of Wellington and St Albans. Her hard horticultural work was finally paying off. She won an Award of Merit for a *Corylopsis multiflora*, a member of the witch hazel family, from seed sent to her by Ernest Wilson. Wilson himself named a martagon lily for her.[135] The hugely influential *Société d'Acclimatation de France* presented her with its highest accolade, the *Grande Medaille Geoffroy Saint-Hilaire*. She was humbly invited, by an

---

135 *Lilium davidii var. willmottiae* E. H. Wilson. Ella Williamson's stunning 'actual size' botanical illustration is slightly silverfish-nibbled but still bright and includes a one-eighth size sketch of the entire plant.

A FUNNY THING HAPPENED ON THE WAY TO CHELSEA

all-star committee, to be Patron of the International Botanical Conference to be held in a couple of years' time. Miss Willmott's recommendations were sought for anything from head gardeners to botanical illustrators, by anyone from the Duke of Wellington to the Royal Botanic Gardens, Edinburgh. Baron Burdett-Coutts solicited her for his garden at Holly Lodge, Hampstead.[136]

Rudolph Barr (son of Peter) offered to act as agent for a commercial deal with a prospective client in New Zealand.[v] This potentially lucrative proposition, which would have allowed Ellen to dispose of surplus specimens grown from Wilson's seeds, appears to have been swiftly nixed when William Bean of Kew got wind of it. Without naming names, he fired an almost Mafia-like warning shot across Ellen's bows, hinting heavily 'it would be a pity to let them go to anyone whose soul does not rise above a cherry laurel or a privet'.[vi] She stood down. Much as she needed the cash, Ellen's status within the horticultural elite came above everything else. Just at the moment she needed it more than ever, that annoying ankle-snapper Reginald Farrer was beginning to win big prizes for his alpines, including a rock garden he designed for the 1912 Royal International Horticultural Exhibition. He was even stealing Ellen's thunder by donating awards, sometimes vulgarly naming them after himself, as with the Farrer Cup for Rock Plants. It must have rankled that Ellen's own days of silver-cup largesse were long gone.

She kept herself busy, advising her friends Robert and Nelly Vyner on their extraordinary and, ultimately, doomed fantasy rock garden at Newby Hall, Yorkshire. The three had become very close. Robert sent Ellen game; she sent plants that made the head gardener's 'eyes bulge' and mushrooms that don't seem to have gone down quite so well.[137] Even as the magnificent rock garden flourished, however, Nelly Vyner diminished.

---

136 Alas, now lost under the famous faux-Tudor Holly Lodge estate.

137 Robert Vyner to EAW, 22 Oct 1913. Re. the mushrooms, Vyner's wife and friend 'were not as complimentary as I had hoped'.

In December 1912, a devastated Robert Vyner wrote to Ellen, who he called 'the kindest woman in the world', that his Nelly had passed away, having 'suffered much'.[vii] More bad news arrived. Robinson the butler (who, contrary to Norman Moore's advice, Ellen had not got rid of) wrote with a confession. He'd had an accident in the car (the one she had failed to sell), and although all that had happened was that a horse had backed into him and put a tiny dent in the mudguard, and although both the chap riding the horse and a passing constable had decided the horse was unhurt, he had just received a court summons claiming the accident had turned the horse lame. Robinson swore he did not injure the horse; even that it wasn't injured at all. He had gone to see the owner – Mrs Gray, licensee of an unknown local pub – and seen the horse being exercised with no problems at all. He was told the animal had injured its front leg, but everyone knew it had backed into him. He put the whole thing into the hands of the AA, intending to fight what he suspected was a fraudulent claim.

As 1914 dawned, things looked a little rosier. Audrey Le Lièvre talks of an unsubstantiated story – an invitation by the Emperor of Japan for Miss Willmott to design a garden for him. Emperor Meiji had become quite a gardener in his old age, creating a wonderful iris haven for his empress, but he had died in 1912. His son was now on the throne, and appears to have been 'odd' – to a point where he was a bit of a PR disaster. Perhaps Vicomte Foukouba thought a nice new garden would make for a good image.

Ellen declined the invitation as she 'had far too much to do in Europe'. In the past this has been added to her list of 'crimes' as an act of conceited rudeness. The refusal surprises Dr Le Lièvre as 'she certainly could have done with a replenishment of her resources'. I'm less convinced that money would have been part of the deal in the first place. Designing a garden at the Imperial Palace would have been considered an honour, not a paid gig. Being 'too busy' may have been Willmott's most elegant way out, even if it appeared discourteous.

A FUNNY THING HAPPENED ON THE WAY TO CHELSEA

The Emperor of Japan anecdote is undated but the only time I have ever come across Ellen planning anything beyond Europe is in a letter from Gian Mount Stephen in early 1914. Replying politely to a sympathy note following a burglary at the Mount Stephens's town house, Gian congratulates Ellen on a forthcoming trip 'around the world'.[viii] Ellen could have put together one hell of an itinerary. Charles Sprague Sargent had been badgering her to visit for years; she was at the height of her communications with Carl Purdy in California, had already pencilled in a tour of Holland and been invited to a reception marking the bicentenary of the Imperial Botanic Garden in St Petersburg. She had a cousin in New Zealand. Why not stop off at the Imperial Palace in Japan while she was about it?

It all came to nothing. Just a few days later Ellen was floundering in debt again. It must have been particularly galling to hear Reginald Farrer boasting about his forthcoming expedition, to be bankrolled by the RHS and various of Ellen's own friends, none of whom, she may well have fumed, saw to helping with *her* problems. Not that she'd told them about her affairs, of course. Reports now circulated of her 'legendary meanness',[138] of her squirrelling away vast wealth while refusing to pay bills, employees and tradesfolk, and penny-pinching every last copper in dealings with friends. What else could she do? To admit the truth would be to lose face; at least an 'eccentric miser' had gravitas.

She made efforts at cutting back, even if she still didn't get 'economy'. She went to great expense creating printed booklets advertising her properties for sale or let, complete with tissue paper between the photographs. No one was nibbling. One prospective tenant said he might be interested if Ellen installed electric lights. Since this would involve installing a generator (Warley village didn't get mains electricity until 1947), the lease fell through. She received a compensation demand from

---

138 A phrase that often crops up in the biographies of her contemporaries, such as, here, that of Francis Younghusband.

a gardener who had injured himself on duty. Repayments on the Warley mortgage seemed to come round on an ever-more frequent basis.

For once, Ellen did something drastic: she sold one of her Amati violins. Then another. The proceeds didn't even touch the sides of the hole. She wrote one of her famous I-want-to-sell-I-don't-want-to-sell letters to Charles Sprague Sargent, sending such mixed messages about antique books that she might/might not be prepared to part with that no transactions happened. Most of the time she ignored the mounting debts, managing to present enough of a front to the world that people generally thought she was still loaded and only didn't cough up because she was obsessed with getting 'even more' money. Nobody knew that Warley Place was now reduced to two working areas, the morning room and conservatory. At Boccanegra Ellen's retainer Clodoveo, who she had tried in vain to get rid of, was selling off her possessions to pay his wages.

Ellen had recently sent that sympathy note to Gian, presumably in the hope of opening up relations again, but she didn't quite have the front to face her former confidante. She wrote directly to the man with the money. Lord Mount Stephen deputised his wife to deal with the problem anyway. Gian wrote in consternation; what was all this about losing Warley? What did Ellen need? The draft reply gives us Ellen's interpretation of her troubles. Her money problems had all started with the fire (not entirely true) and from then on events had conspired against her. She had recently nearly sold Tresserve but the buyer backed out (stretching the truth), but if she can just sell Warley Lea all her problems regarding Warley Place will be solved (not true). It will be easy to sell up (not true); the foreign properties alone are worth £40,000 at least (not true) but by then it would be too late (that bit is correct). Ideally Gian would buy Tresserve, but if not, could she take over part of Warley's mortgage? Ellen will pay her back when she sells something. The last part of *Genus Rosa* comes out next week and she's working on three other books including a history of Warley for which a publisher, Edward

Arnold, has offered very good terms (the only offer of publication we have ever found from Arnold is for a single magazine article). She ends 'The helping hand would be my salvation.'[ix]

Salvation was not forthcoming. 'My dear Ellie,' Gian wrote, as kindly as possible, 'I am afraid it is too big a thing for me to undertake.' Even if Ellen got the money for the mortgage, the money would only pay back the mortgage, leaving nothing spare, and 'your foreign properties seem to be unsaleable'.[x] A further plea yielded similar results a few days later. 'Alas I fear I cannot be any use nor can I think of any play by which I could help'[xi] – as did one final, forlorn entreaty: 'My dear Ellie, I am not allowed to pay the interest on the mortgage for the next two or three years as you suggest . . . I am very sorry to have to say no again.'[xii]

Gian was only spelling out a situation that, by now, Norman Moore, Frank Crisp and a merry-go-round of solicitors had been trying to explain to Ellen for some time. In April, Sir Frank Crisp took a step onto a very slippery slope, buying his friend some time by lending her money. Ellen's gratitude knew no bounds. Alas, her method of showing it could have been better thought out.

♣

Sir Frank Crisp had been building a veritable theme park of a garden ever since he had rebuilt his country estate at Henley-on-Thames as a fantasy-gothic mansion. The theme was 'fun'. Visitors could enjoy anything from ye Woods of Merriment to ye Gloomie Glen; ye Water Caves to ye Fountain of Perpetual Mirth. There was an electric generator ('where they make ye lightning'), a menagerie of topiary 'beestes' between the paths of Love and Thyme, and a maze ('for losing ye bodies'). It couldn't be further from the serious, science-based grounds at Warley, but Ellen enjoyed a laugh[139] and Crisp's planting was solid. There was one feature missing. By way of an apogee, Sir Frank now took the concept

---

[139] She often copied out the lyrics to comic songs and poems that had tickled her, sometimes printing them up to share with friends.

of miniature alpine gnome tableaux, so lovingly espoused by Charles Isham, to its logical conclusion. Almost certainly on Ellen's advice, he commissioned Backhouse of York, and Mr Richard Potter, to build him a rock garden.

In many ways Sir Frank was only doing as Reginald Farrer suggests in his wildly popular how-to, *My Rock Garden*: 'Have an idea and stick to it. Let your rock-garden set out to be something definite, not a mere agglomeration of stones,' Farrer writes. 'Let it be a mountain gorge, if you like, or the stony peak of a hill, or a rocky crest or a peak.'[xiii]

Frank Crisp did exactly that. He built a scale model of the Matterhorn.[140] He committed completely, using coloured gravel 'scree', large expanses of massed alpines and even cast-iron *chamois* mountain goats. His three-acre Alpine Garden took 7,000 tons of stone and 4,000 plants, and involved waterfalls, pools, mountain paths, log cabins, bridges, caverns, precipices – even a 'glacier' with an 'ice grotto'. It stood between thirty and forty feet high; crampons would not have been without their uses to visitors on the higher slopes.

He had had his idea, and he stuck to it. So far, so Farrer.

Perched on the precipice of kitsch, the garden received a mixed reception. Henry Correvon loved it, as did William Robinson in *The Garden*. Others found it irreconcilably naff. Poor Sir Frank's baby was even the subject of an unflattering cartoon in *Punch*. The criticism was, in many ways, unfair. It is clear from the way he presents his garden – complete with comedy gnomes and visual gags – that his tongue was firmly in his cheek, and a wonderful illustrated guidebook he wrote for visitors is nothing short of (deliberately) hilarious, but the reception from some quarters was so very hostile he suddenly became sensitive about the whole thing. Sir Frank seems to have taken criticism of his kitschy settings with good humour, but he drew the line when his choice

---

[140] This was not a new phenomenon. In the 1830s Lady Broughton recreated an entire Savoy mountain range in her back garden at Hoole House, near Chester, using local red sandstone for the rocks and grey limestone quartz for *La Mer de Glace*.

of plants was attacked by people comparing his masses of alpines to the hated-by-the-gardening-elite Victorian carpet-bedding.

In 1913 Gussie Bowles invited Reginald Farrer to write the foreword to his new book, *My Garden in Spring and Summer*. Farrer gleefully accepted, but instead of waxing lyrical about his friend's daffodils and crocuses he used the platform to tear a strip off certain individuals who thought they knew about rock gardening. Farrer stopped short of mentioning Sir Frank's name but made it abundantly clear which dodgy alpine monstrosity he was referring to. He further twisted the knife by implying the unnamed garden's owner was not, somehow, a 'proper' plantsman.

Sir Frank snapped.

Apoplectic with fury, he asked William Robinson to print a tirade of his own in *Gardening Illustrated*. Robinson, who had also been at the pointy end of Farrer's pen, agreed, perhaps without considering that Sir Frank's intemperate rant was actually directed, by name, at poor, innocent Gussie Bowles. In eight, close-typed pages of bile, Reginald Farrer's name doesn't crop up once. Still steaming, Sir Frank reprinted the article into pamphlet form and Ellen Willmott stood outside the gates of the second-ever Chelsea Flower Show with a large leather shoulder-satchel, handing out copies to anyone who would take them.

I am not suggesting that the large leather shoulder-satchel at the top of this chapter is definitely *the* Satchel of Unpleasantness. Despite its considerable size, it may have just been a writing case; after all, much of Ellen's day was taken with correspondence, and this whole storm in a gardener's tea-mug was conducted via the written word. We found it in one of the disintegrating trunks, festering between layers of rotten letters from the exact time period, and it somehow sums up her life at this most fractious time. She can't have been unaware of how bad standing outside a flower show handing out leaflets badmouthing a friend must look, but by now, hurt and confused by her clumsy dealings with Gian Mount Stephen and facing financial ruin, Ellen's world was spiralling. It's traditionally suggested that she did it after her amorous advances were rejected by Bowles. I don't believe it for a moment. By insulting Sir Frank's alpine wonder, built by the same people – indeed, the same *man* – that built her own ravine all those years earlier, when *she* had been the young maverick, and populated by plants from her garden, Farrer insulted her. In her mind Ellen owed Sir Frank for helping her (just about) keep Warley. It was the least she could do.

The 'Crispian Row' did little for the reputations of any of those concerned. Gussie Bowles was mortified, Frank Crisp looked foolish and bombastic, and Miss Willmott branded herself a shrew. The only figure who seems to have come out of gardening's biggest literary punch-up without so much as a dent was Reginald Farrer himself, who quietly skipped town to go on his plant-hunting trip.[141]

Not that anyone had much time to dwell on one of the worst character assassinations in horticultural history because, one month later, real history assassinated the Archduke Ferdinand.

---

141 Farrer continued the feud in his 1919 book *The Rock Garden* with an acidic, backhanded compliment. After describing *Primula magaseifolia* as 'a rather chilly and bitter tone of magenta-lilac (suggesting an acid old maid crossed in an unseasonable love affair)', he gleefully announces, 'it was introduced by Miss Ellen Willmott in 1901'. He didn't have long to enjoy the remark. He died the following year, aged just forty, while on a plant-hunting trip in Burma.

Chapter Sixteen:

The Most Hopeful Work...

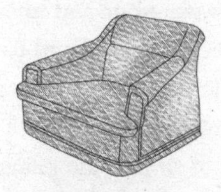

A COUCH

The small, austere cubicle, with plain walls, patterned carpet and large, curtainless window, contains just three items of furniture: a large, leather armchair, circular side table and a long, padded leather couch.

IT IS 1 JANUARY 1914, and Johann Bernhard Mann writes with good news. Finally! He's getting out from behind a desk and going back to active duty! The only thing that will make life better is if he and Ellen can meet up for that long-awaited *wiedersehen* this summer. Johann encloses snapshots: himself, handsome as ever, if a little sea-grizzled, his twenty-two-year-old wife, sweet and smiling in white lace, and their little dachshund. All three sit relaxed and happy on a garden bench in Charlottenburg, Berlin. Johann's New Year greeting would be the last Ellen would ever hear from him.[142]

Today, the final part of *Genus Rosa* being published in March 1914 seems symbolic of a last hurrah for a soft-focus, fantasy Edwardian summertime, filled with straw boaters, waxed moustaches and afternoon tea. If that rose-festooned, golden age of Empire ever existed, however, it had disappeared long beforehand. If it hadn't, perhaps more copies of Alfred Parsons' glowing watercolours and Ellen's earnest prose would have been sold. Perhaps Ellen wouldn't have been writing to Norman Moore, Frank Crisp, Gian Mount Stephen, *anyone*, for money. Perhaps her frustration wouldn't have manifested so illogically in hitting out at poor Gussie Bowles at the Chelsea Flower Show.

It's all moot. On 28 June 1914, as Ellen's English roses bloomed and Johann Bernhard Mann entertained the British Navy at a German Regatta, an obscure Serbian anarchist was assassinating a prominent

---

142 Mann would play a pivotal role in the First World War, but like so many combatants on both sides, war hardened him. Disillusioned by his own commanders and government, this once-sweet young man would become a true believer in German Nationalism and die fighting in the Second World War.

THE MOST HOPEFUL WORK...

Austrian archduke. The murder kicked off a chain of events that, exactly one month later, saw the Kaiser declare war. It was all over the papers. Everyone was talking about it – except Ellen Willmott.

Her letter to Dr Moore of the very same date – 28 July 1914 – speaks of a much closer tragedy: her sister has cancer. Rose had been feeling peaky for years, but everyone had put it down to overwork and stress. 'It has quite crushed me,' Ellen writes.[i] 'I wanted to start off at once for Spetchley but have not done so for it may only upset them more.'

Dr Moore describes Rose's tumour as a small, 'dense carcinoma' in her right breast, recommending it be removed as soon as possible. His casebook also reveals another patient: Ellen herself, who has turned up at his practice with her oldest niece Eleanor, nigh-on hysterical, pleading to 'know the worst' and whether she can be in London 'when it takes place'.

The 'it' Ellen speaks of was pretty radical stuff. Dr Moore's friend Anthony Bowlby, surgeon to Kings Edward VII and George V, performed a risky operation to remove the tumour. It was successful, but inevitably the infestation returned. Cancer was a death sentence in 1914 but there was (small) new hope.

Rose would be one of the London Radium Institute's earliest malignant cases (when the doors first opened in 1911, doctors mainly treated benign, rodent cancers). She would have spent hours lying on the couch described at the top of this chapter, recovering after various experimental procedures. The armchair would be occupied by Robert Valentine or Ellen herself. The hospital didn't take in-patients, so Rose and Robert stayed overnight at Claridge's on a variously regular basis. No one had yet discovered the true extent of any danger attached to the miracle cure; at one point Ellen even asked if radium could do anything for her chronic back pain. Medical research was going at a phenomenal pace, however, and stepped up as casualties began to appear from the Front.

Everything Ellen Willmott does from this moment on needs to be seen via the spectre of Rose's Big C. She is not exaggerating when she tells Norman Moore, 'You know my sister is the only person in the world for me.'[ii] Rose's diagnosis could not have hit harder if it had been Ellen's own. She threw herself into taking care of her nieces and nephew at Warley, taking them to cricket and tennis, garden parties and Friar Park, with its caves and 'beestes' and practical jokes. She allowed them ice creams, as much fruit as they liked and free access to her musical instruments; took them to see shows and performing dogs. If the aeroplanes and airships gathering ominously overhead spooked them, Auntie was always back from their mother's bedside in time to tuck them up at night.

There was no way Ellen was going to burden her sister with money troubles now. That didn't stop the final demands, writs and threats, including an impending lawsuit from the building firm still working (for the present) on the rebuild at Tresserve. Her gardener had already taken her to court for unpaid wages, as had a Mme Foucard, for unpaid rent. At the very same time Ellen heard Rose's devastating news she also discovered her father's former solicitor had gone bankrupt. By now everything was so muddled I can't really see that this dumped her much further into the financial soup than she already was. Happily, Lord Lilford, husband of a friend of Ellen's, had recently taken over the mortgage on Warley Place, so she didn't become 'an asset' in the windup, but it did add another layer to her already tangled affairs.

It didn't help that she was receiving visitors from the United States at the same time as all this was happening. Charles Sprague Sargent had arrived with an itinerary that would be optimistic even for someone whose sister hadn't just been diagnosed with cancer. The fabulously wealthy industrialist Henry du Pont also turned up to meet his gardening heroine – after two abortive attempts at meeting, Ellen waited in so she could show him around.

War waits for no one. On 3 August 1914, Albert, King of the Belgians, refused to allow the Kaiser's troops passage through his lands to attack

France, waving the Treaty of London as proof of neutrality. On 4 August, the Kaiser declared the Treaty a *'chiffon de papier'* (a scrap of paper) and invaded Belgium anyway, gathering an outraged United Kingdom into a rapidly expanding war snowball.

In the days that followed, Britain was on high alert. All foreigners were to leave the country immediately. Professor Sargent got out in the nick of time; Henry du Pont was booked on the last liner home. Ellen's maid raced across a panicked London with a large parcel of rare bulbs, hoping to catch him before departure.

Even as the Americans left, others were arriving. The Belgian Refugee Crisis of 1914 is one of the least-documented aspects of World War One, but it was huge news at the time. Thousands of displaced families crammed onto any cross-channel vessel they could find, often with little more than the clothes they stood up in, inspiring a mania of British volunteering. Ellen, still in deep shock for her sister, took in her share of refugees. It was the patriotic choice and, as a Roman Catholic, she would have been moved to help others in need, especially those of the Faith. We don't know how many she took; various accounts tell us twenty-five, thirty and 'a colony'.[iii] We don't know where they were housed, what they did, how they were fed or even what gender they were, though some at least were women. Official records were patchy at best, scattered or destroyed after the refugees went home and the 'Belgian problem' was over. Perhaps more surprisingly, we don't have any pictures either; a former Ellen would have lined them all up for a welcome group-photo.

In many ways, hosting the Belgians gave Ellen an elegant excuse for poverty, much as war provided a legitimate reason for not visiting Tresserve or Boccanegra. She could also legitimately sell seeds to various American horticultural societies in aid of her Belgians, though this seems to have worked more for morale than cash.

Back home, Warley Lea and Shenfield Lodge were requisitioned by the army. Ellen was relieved the trouble of maintenance and could make a fuss about getting repairs done – but she also couldn't liquidise her assets. She regularly saw Rose, who had taken in four Belgians herself despite continuing to visit the Radium Institute. It was now rumoured the war might last two years. Ellen felt powerless. 'I have come very near to losing heart,' she confided to Norman Moore, given 'my sister's illness and the awful dread which has taken possession of me.'

The bills continued to mount, though small glimmers of hope sparkled. In October, Colonel Prain of Kew wrote with the welcome news that the Chinese plumbago seeds Ernest Wilson had sent to various people, but that only Ellen had managed to germinate, were indeed a brand-new strain. To this day every specimen of *Ceratostigma willmottianum* grown in Britain can trace its roots back to two seedlings: one at Warley; one Ellen sent to Rose at Spetchley Park.

By 1915 the glimmer faded. Sir Frank Crisp was wealthy but he could not continue to bail Ellen out of her latest crisis with his by-now regular 'loans'. He wrote to Lord Mount Stephen 'with considerable reluctance' informing him that Lord Lilford still held Warley's £18,000 mortgage, repayable when Tresserve could finally be sold, but that 'we are now left with the much lesser problem to solve of keeping Miss Willmott going week by week'.[iv][143]

Sir Frank's letter minces no words. He tells George Stephen he has lent Miss Willmott £2,500, but, what with the war and everything, he's running out of funds. Could the Mount Stephens stretch to £480, which would keep her ticking over for a year? It wouldn't be a gift, but a loan, against Boccanegra. Such a gesture would act as encouragement to her other friends, who Sir Frank is also discreetly approaching; already William Robinson has agreed to join in helping their friend.

George Stephen once again left his wife to respond. Gian's reply boils down to '£200, that's my final offer, let me know how you intend to get Miss Willmott out of the fix', signalling the sputtering end of a long,

---

[143] Crisp is not lying; he, too, is now struggling financially.

complex relationship that had started with such tenderness. Poor Sir Frank was also beginning to reach the end of his tether: 'What a lady you are,' he wrote. 'I have written ten letters to Robinson. The result of the first four was to get an offer of £1 a week. The result of the next six was to get an offer of £1,000 – only extracted by entreaties and wailing – and now you ask me to get him to 'make it £2,000.'[v]

I have no idea how Ellen managed such front; how she could be so self-unaware. She must have known – as her friends did, only too well – that she sat on a fortune: three properties, a vast library of rare manuscripts, walls full of old masters, salons full of exquisite antiques and vanity cases brimming with jewellery. Yet, emotionally incapable of parting with even one item, she had the chutzpah to demand money from friends as though it was their duty to support her. Even more unfathomably, they gave it to her. Those eyes that gaze so steadfast, so unflinching from photographs and paintings, even from childhood, must have held the allure of Rasputin in real life. Her friends could write rude letters as much as they liked when out of her company, yet still they came back, time after time. Even later, after the financial scales had fallen from their eyes, few of Ellen's friends ever completely deserted her; they just went back to writing gushing letters of greetings and bonhomie, never mentioning the money they'd lent/given her in the past.

The exodus of young gardeners meant Ellen could cut down on staff without obvious culling. She was also able to get rid of men she could no longer afford by recommending them to friends across the country looking to replace gardeners who'd taken Kitchener's shilling. Of those that marched off to war, many never returned.

Her friends, acquaintances and staff seemed to be dropping like the proverbial flies: Robert Vyner, who had never got over the loss of his wife, never enjoyed his beloved rock garden either. It was completed three weeks after the declaration of war; he died shortly afterwards. Young Henry Russell, son of Ellen's friends Champion and Isobel, fell at the Somme. The loss of Eliza Burge, Ellen's lady's maid and old friend, in 1916, would have held particular poignancy: Lalla died of cancer. She was not replaced. Canon Ellacombe also died that year, leaving his head gardener 'absolutely unprovided for'.[vi] Ellen wrote to Gussie Bowles[144] in the hope of finding some financial aid for the chap. It's clear from her letter that she is writing to others, too, at the same time she is about to lose her own home. She may have been self-centred and self-pitying from time to time, but she was not without a heart. Generous as ever, Bowles obliged with a cheque, which Ellen matched, from funds unknown.

The very same day her solicitor, Arthur Forster, of Frere Cholmeley & Co,[145] wrote with stark news. Forster's letters are hard to read (not physically; for once they are typed). Time and again he tries to explain the severity of Ellen's situation; time and again she has obviously replied without comprehending a word of it. He is polite and, frankly, kinder than many would be, but his letters visibly lose patience. Surely, despite what she says, the final demand for £8,000 can't have *really* come out of the blue? She *must* have been served with writs from the banks – London Joint City, Barclays and Midland – that she hasn't told him about, and no, she can't use her London properties as security for more loans. Her father's old office is leasehold, and Lord Lilford has first dibs on those warehouses in Newcomen Street, due to be compulsorily purchased for the bridge. Will she *please* let him write to Mrs Berkeley? 'I could put matters in such a way as not to upset her much,' says Forster, weary resignation tingeing every syllable.[vii]

At this point Ellen has another lightbulb moment, another fantastic scheme. A gardening school for ladies, like that one at Glynde run by her friend Lady Frances Wolseley! Nice, wholesome young women, of the upper classes, of course, who will learn from Miss Willmott herself.

---

144 The pair had long patched up their friendship after the unpleasantness at Chelsea.

145 Dixson had disappeared; not even Forster could get a reply from him.

THE MOST HOPEFUL WORK . . .

There's a war on, don't you know? Women will be needed to work in the gardens of England. The students can live-in, thus providing rent, and their training will be – and this is the brilliant bit – looking after Warley's gardens. It will solve everything – the money situation *and* the lack of labour!

On 9 March, Forster writes again. Ellen has been hit with Supertax, presumably based on the on-paper value of her properties and, sorry, those Argentine Railway shares she's miraculously found down the back of the sofa won't fetch much in wartime Britain: 'Nobody in their senses would invest in Argentine Bonds,' he tells her.[146] Ellen has no income, only outgoings. Forster *has* discussed the gardening school idea with Lord Lilford, but will this be enough to save her? He tells her straight: 'I cannot see how you can possibly stay on at Warley.' The alternatives are either sale by auction – though her home probably won't make the money Lord Lilford's already put up for it – or selling everything in the house. He then drops a brick: he has told Rose of Ellen's troubles.

Rose, of course, had clocked the situation years ago. She told Ellen to rent out everything except Warley Place, Red House (her butler's cottage) and the two lodges (one of which housed her poor Alpine gardener Jacob Maurer and his family of nine). Rose could afford to give her sister some money, and in order for Ellen to save face, was happy to sell some of Warley's antiques out of Spetchley.

It doesn't seem Ellen listened to Rose any more than Arthur Forster, Frank Crisp, Norman Moore, Gian Mount Stephen or anyone else that had given her exactly the same advice. The gardening school came to nothing. Friends had thought it might work, with Miss Willmott's name in the title. She was still deeply respected in garden circles, had been the subject of the prestigious *Celebrities of the Past and Present* column in the 1915 Daffodil Yearbook and just been afforded a five-page

---

146 He was right. Ellen's broker sold the bonds for £3681.8s then stopped his own outstanding bills, leaving her with £45 7s 6d.

feature in *Country Life*.[viii] A school run by someone of her status *could* work. Ultimately, though, such a venture needed capital to start it and organisational skills to run it. Ellen majored in neither.[147]

She did take in some paying guests: former adventurer Sir Francis Younghusband, his wife and their fourteen-year-old, 'middle-aged' daughter. A proto-hippy, Younghusband was a free-love advocate. It must have been one weird household, and it's not surprising the arrangement didn't last long, though it seems that Ellen stayed on reasonable terms with the family after they left.

According to Garden Club of America bulletins, during all this Ellen also still had her colony of Belgians. I have no idea where; perhaps she put them up in the bothy Monsieur Frédéric had hated so much. The lack of available accommodation led to some unpleasantness among English folk, too. It appears Ellen told the wife of a gardener serving at the Front that she could stay rent-free in their cottage, then changed her mind. We know very little about the incident, save for an unpleasant article in *John Bull* magazine, headlined ESSEX LADY'S PIECRUST PROMISE TO A SOLDIER. Ellen did not reply, presumably because it would have involved admitting she was almost bankrupt and needed the cottage back.[ix] As usual, the world took her behaviour as miserly. Miss Willmott's tenants couldn't even count on her for minor things: 'Madam, I much regret to inform you the sanitary pail at this house has worn right through and has a hole in it. May I ask you to be so kind as to let me have one to replace it as I am in a very awkward position without one.'[x]

The outward lady of the manor was also bombarded with begging letters from war charities, some of which she helped with small amounts, some in kind, writing to friends and acquaintances with more disposable income than her or by arranging and performing concerts for wounded soldiers with the Oriana Madrigal Society. Music remained one of

---

147 She never intended to run it herself. The organiser would have been a mysterious Miss Scott.

Ellen's great solaces, even if her subs were outstanding. In between visits to the Radium Institute, Rose was also doing her bit, holding regular charity 'entertainments' at Spetchley in aid of disabled fighters.

Whatever her personal battles, Ellen Willmott's spirit rarely dimmed. The closest I have ever found to despair is in a letter she wrote to Mary Gilpin, William Robinson's nurse, the moment she learned her old friend was withdrawing his alleged £1,000 loan offer. 'When that awful letter came I went out weeding as the only way to bring me a little relief,' she wrote. Robinson's letter was a terrible blow, she revealed; now she faced a forced sale. She felt 'a wreck & not a soul in the world to raise a finger to help in any way. When I think of the hundreds I have helped in every way.'

It's hard to read a letter like this; hard to sympathise when Ellen blames anyone but herself for her misfortunes: 'Forster is my evil spirit,' she tells Mary Gilpin. 'He does not like me for what reason I have no idea.' Yet this is also a woman in pain; things *are* getting to her: 'Being RC,' she admits, 'the two ways that are so often chosen, making away with oneself or drowning misery in drink, are not allowed to us.'

❧

By now the war was in full swing. Letters from this time are filled with Zeppelin raids, brown beans to feed the masses and dreaded telegrams from the Front. Rose and Robert Valentine worry as their young son Rob is called up as a cadet – a serious fear, as he is the only male Berkeley heir. Ellen appears at a tribunal trying to save a gardener from conscription. She fails; Austin, too, marches off to war.

Ellen's correspondents' letters now took a more practical approach, discussing vegetable crops over flowers. RHS Chelsea, 1916, was a dismal event, fielding just one formal garden. After being threatened that any future displays of such luxury would be subject to Entertainment Tax, the society ceased all shows; growing and exhibiting for beauty alone seemed uncomfortably frivolous anyway.

The food problem was getting serious. The European potato crop had failed. Argentina's harvest boded ill and, like Australia and America, was inaccessible anyway, thanks to U-boats. Gloomy government forecasts estimated Britain had four months' worth of flour left. Rationing was a serious possibility. Ellen discovered the joys of a thick, salty meat extract diluted with boiling water to make 'beef tea'. She would become quite obsessed, sending it to all her friends as a supplement to the war diet, but Bovril provoked strong opinions for and against. After filling Spetchley's larders with jars and cubes, Rose gently but firmly asked her sister to cease and desist. Bovril-by-the-jugful would become a staple of Ellen's diet for the rest of her life; a marked, though apparently un-mourned change from the lobster and champagne of her youth.

Britain needed to be self-sufficient, but while farming had been a reserved occupation, many labourers were now being conscripted anyway. In times of emergency, it might seem obvious to use an abundant, available and willing workforce: women. Only after exhausting supplies of Belgians, POWs, interned aliens, old men, injured soldiers, anyone rejected for active service and even the hated conchies,[148] however, did Britain's farmers grudgingly consider female labour.

The Women's Farm and Garden Union (WFGU) had been around since 1899, promoting educational and employment opportunities for women working on the land. Ellen Willmott had been a member for years, but in 1915 she got 'the call' to help build what we now know as the Women's Land Army.

On 16 March, an announcement appeared in the *Standard*: 'May we make known that we wish to hear from farmers, market-gardeners and others wanting the services of women for work on the land?' It goes on to confirm these are women of good birth as well as those born on farms, adding, 'we have quite a good number who can and will milk'.

---

148 Conscientious objectors.

THE MOST HOPEFUL WORK . . .

The expected stampede never came. It wasn't just that farmers thought the 'lilac sunbonnet brigade' weren't up to the task. Men were deeply suspicious that women might take their jobs permanently or – shock! – demand the same wage. Women were weaker than men so, obviously, couldn't work as hard. Some suggested the women should work for free; most agreed their wages should be heavily reduced. Oh, and the classes should be divided – no one wanted nice girls getting caught up with toughs. Now the women were less keen. The idea stagnated, yet the shortage of workers wasn't going away. Someone had to bring in the harvest.

Eventually, David Lloyd George, Minister of Munitions, enlisted Emmeline Pankhurst's help. Between them they cannily changed the issue from 'the government needs workers, so sign up' to 'the government is denying us the right to serve, so sign up'. The counter-intuition worked. Thirty thousand angry women marched through London demanding the right to hard labour, and Lloyd George got his workers. It wasn't just men who needed convincing of women's efficacy, though. Princess Louise, who, as a sculptor herself should have known better, wrote a private letter to Miss Willmott, asking advice about taking on a young woman Ellen had recommended. The princess was dubious. Kensington Palace's current (male) head gardener was 'a worthy and respectable soul' albeit 'not very practical and lacking in method', but wouldn't a woman need a woman to look after her? Would she have to take on a *second* woman?[xi]

The Land Army faced competition from munitions factories, the fledgling Women's Royal Naval Service and the even-younger Women's Royal Air Force. It also sported the ugliest uniform in Christendom: a shapeless, khaki smock over breeches, dragged in at the waist like a sack of King Edwards; land girls would have to wait until World War II to get something halfway decent in the way of kit. Yet these pioneers began something special. They wore breeches, drove tractors, ploughed fields, even thatched roofs. By the end of the war the same men who had laughed at the idea of women on the land would petition to keep them.

Committee work was a good way of focusing away from the finances, but all the time Ellen was still receiving doom-laden portents from Arthur Forster. 'I have already explained to you that my firm cannot advance you any more money . . . You have plenty of things at Warley you can sell . . . Select one or two things of value . . . for such a sum as you may require to settle your taxes . . . You could do this tomorrow morning . . . I cannot understand why, under the present circumstances, you have such an objection to selling anything.'[xii]

No one else understood either. Today, there's probably some fancy syndrome attached to Ellen Willmott's pathological horror of parting with anything at all, but then it was just considered bloody-minded. All she sold were several hundredweight of Jerusalem artichokes, to Peter Barr & Sons.

Rose continued to visit the Radium Institute. Her letters, written on the backs of advertising fliers, food wrappers and old envelopes, thanks to the national paper shortage, are filled with air raids, fire-bombs and ambulances.

Eventually, painfully, Ellen agreed to sell something: the old Victoria coach Fred Willmott had shown off to the village in 1883. The Army & Navy Stores sent a curt reply: 'There is now no demand for this type of carriage.'[xiii]

Arthur Forster's politeness was wearing thin. 'I send you Landon's accounts. They are not paid as I have no money to pay them with.' Forster has been putting off creditors 'practically ever since you came here' but 'you have never seen your way either to allow a competent agent to manage your property or to sell anything'. He reminds her: 'you owe my firm a large sum of money for payments made on your behalf'. Lord Lilford is also getting edgy; it is likely he will foreclose.

THE MOST HOPEFUL WORK...

Oddly, by this point, Ellen seems beatific. She appears to cease writing panicked begging letters to all and sundry and to fully adopt head-in-sand mode. She exchanges cheery news of meeting with Henry Luxmoore's friend Montague Rhodes James in Cambridge.[xvi] She chuckles with Norman Moore over memories of Ethel Smyth smoking cigars while taking the sacrament ('She appears at her best in your company,' replies the doctor).[xv] She goes back to chatting with Frank Crisp about safer, gardening topics. She giggles with Rose over one of Spetchley's tenants marrying an 'awful-looking Belgian'. She attends all three days of the 75th Annual Congress of the British Archaeological Association.[149] She entertains the Essex Field Club with tea in the Warley garden until the light fails, then conducts a show-and-tell of antiquarian manuscripts in her still-magnificent library.[xvi] She badgers the Ministry of Food for extra sugar rations to preserve vast amounts of fruit that would otherwise spoil and consistently fails to come up with a promised chapter for a new book celebrating the late Canon Ellacombe.

Ellen worries about her nephew Rob, lost in action (later found safe in a hospital in Cairo), she worries about her sister's increasingly frequent visits to the London Radium Institute, and she worries about the new tenant taking over Warley Lea, but her creditors? They can whistle.

On 13 November 1918, Ellen's sixteen-year-old niece wrote to her aunt from Spetchley Park. The letter, on Betty's customary pink paper, is severely damaged; happily, ye olde tweezers-and-craft-knife combo separated the layers of crusted lace to reveal the gist: an elated teenager's account of Armistice Day. Bubbling with excitement, Betty describes hearing hooters and cathedral bells three miles away in Worcester. 'Almost immediately Mr Ostler started ringing our church bells,' she froths, 'then I went up and had a ring, and Mama [then] Dada rang.' The next part of the letter is eaten away, but we pick it up again

---
149 July 1918.

as the family flag is being hoisted over the portico. Another flutters from the church; there's even a little one in the yew tree. Miss Feltham the local teacher is ringing the school bell outside in the street and, at last, Spetchley fire brigade can sound its sirens for joyful reasons.

The war was over. Not much else was.

Chapter Seventeen:

Peaks and Troughs

A VERSAILLES BOX-PLANTER

The sturdy, iron-framed planter is in the classic 'Versailles' style, invented in seventeenth-century France. Filled with citrus trees, such troughs added elegance to the grand avenues and formal parterres at the palace of the Sun King, Louis XIV. This example is bolted together to allow its slatted wooden sides to be repainted or replaced. The current incumbents are a dark teal green.

SEVEN MONTHS AFTER she had written to her aunt of bells and flags and car horns on the very first Armistice Day, young Betty Berkeley's pink notepaper was out again. Now seventeen, she was abroad. In Paris! Her letters bubble with an excitement Ellen might have recognised in herself at the same age, describing the city to her godmother Helen Tasker. Betty is currently in Versailles for a few days, as are the most powerful men in Europe.

Betty's letter would have been a bright spot for Auntie. Peace was all very well, but with it came payback for pretty much everyone. The sheer loss of life, from four years of pointless war and an ongoing pandemic, was catastrophic. The ensuing financial crisis was felt not just by people who had been profligate in a former life. To read Ellen's correspondence from this period is to read blanket gloom. No one except young Betty is having a good time. Even those who haven't lost close relatives are struggling, from the introduction of new taxes for a once virtually immune landed gentry to shortages of wood, paper and basic foods for absolutely everyone. Ellen's friend Miller Christy faces bankruptcy. Charlotte Knollys and Sir Dighton Probyn, once respected royal courtiers, are reduced to filling up on Ellen's 'patent soup'[150] and, while hoping to see her soon 'at our frugal tea table', can offer only plum bread if she does turn up. Even supposedly joyful events carry a layer of gloom. In November 2021, we found photographs of a much-trumpeted fancy dress ball held at Spetchley in April 1919. It

---

150 Bovril.

was supposed to celebrate Rob's twenty-first birthday, but he was stuck in Germany, not yet demobbed, and it was too late to cancel. At first glance the *bal poudré* looks fantastic – everyone in original eighteenth-century dress, robbed from the mansion's attics. Ellen, now sixty-one, is radiant in powdered wig and panniers. Closer inspection of the hosts, however, cannot conceal the truth. Pain is etched across Rose's face. Her chest is entirely flat; her body stiff and stick-thin. Her husband's eye-bags look bigger than his gigantic moustache.

Henry Correvon, far away in neutral Switzerland, has managed to lose everything, including his once-ebullient spirit. His German investments are gone. His wife is old and frail, as is he. He misses the old days. A visitors' book, given to him by Ellen in 1902, 'talks to me every day of you. It is the moment to talk of Miss Willmott: "Oh! You know Miss W? She's a friend of my cousin!" or "She was a friend of my sister", or "I saw her once at the RHS", or even, "It is a very famous name in England".'[i] Henry keeps just two photographs on his desk: Ellen Willmott and Sir Frank Crisp. The loss of the latter, a few days earlier, is almost too much to bear.

Sir Frank's death hit Ellen hard, on a purely personal level. Both he and Norman Moore (recently knighted but much slowed down) had been poorly for some time, leaving Ellen alone with her finances. Her poverty was beginning to show to the world in general. Some whispered she had lost her money in German investments. It seemed plausible; so many had. There's no evidence Ellen Willmott ever had money in Germany, but it was a rumour she wouldn't have quashed.

Warley Lea was decommissioned by the army. Her friend Edward Hudson of *Country Life* suggested that, advertised to let along with the dairy and Warley Farm, it 'would bring the replies in'.[ii] It seemed like the thing to do, so Ellen put the word around that much of the estate was for rent. Enter, centre stage, for her grand, full-costume walk-down, Lady Angela Forbes.

Lady Angela is the sort of character the word 'socialite' was coined for. Ellen would have been aware of her through her friend, Angela's half-sister, Daisy, Countess of Warwick,[151] and, of course, from the press. Lady A had originally found fame as a 'society beauty' in high-class magazines of the 1890s. She married a chap because she liked his horse, divorced him and began a long, very public court case to take him to the cleaners. While she waited for the payout, she wrote four novels, none of which are classics. During the Great War, she became something of a forces' sweetheart when, at Boulogne, she witnessed soldiers in transit, stuck for hours on the quayside without food or drink. As anyone might, Lady A nipped to Fortnum & Mason and purchased some vittles for the troops. Later, she began a series of *Angelina's* canteens, and a high-profile charity to support them and promote herself. She started opening British Soldiers' Buffets further into France, this time charging for food to fund more. To her credit, she worked her stockings off, but she made few friends in the military. Details are scant but after a camp riot Lady A was ordered back to England by General Haig. All attempts at appeal failed, even in Parliament, where both her former and current lover spoke on her behalf. A century on, it seems to me that Lady Angela Forbes was guilty, at most, of thoughtless enthusiasm and attention-seeking rather than any kind of moral degeneration or malice. In what appears to have been a pattern with 'tall-poppy' women and the armed forces, however, Lady A was well and truly 'sat-on'.

She started looking for ways to help on the Home Front (and, frankly, to keep her name in the papers) and found the Silver Badge Soldiers. These were disabled men who had been honourably discharged from the army but whose injuries were not always immediately obvious. After several unpleasant incidents in which ex-servicemen were harangued in the streets and even given white feathers for cowardice, the Government had issued special silver 'discharge badges': 'For King

---

151 Daisy had been mistress to Edward VII. After holding a fancy dress ball at Warwick Castle, she was criticised for her lavish lifestyle by left-wing paper *The Clarion*, took it to heart and became a socialist herself. Daisy would later become a keen gardener at her country pile in Essex, which is how Ellen Willmott knew her.

and Empire, Services Rendered', to be worn on worthy civilian lapels. Lady Angela figured these brave men needed training for life in Civvy Street and, despite having zero experience herself, decided to start a farm to teach them agricultural skills. Her eye alighted on Warley.

Angela brought a reputation for self-serving abrasiveness[152] but Ellen often got on well with 'difficult women', and it seems that, at first, she was quite impressed with this fellow go-getter spirit. Lady Angela herself states that Miss Willmott 'was full of enthusiasm for the idea'.[iii] Ellen certainly needed the help – and the money. Hardly a day went by that there wasn't some new writ or claim on her non-existent wealth. Lady Angela moved in. Then came the pushback.

The missives begin with Col. David Prain, Director of the Royal Botanic Gardens, Kew. 'I understand that, with your usual public spirit, you have placed at the disposal of the department which undertakes the training of disabled soldiers, some portions of your garden,' he writes.[iv] 'Now, your garden, in spite of its being your private property, is, as I believe you yourself will admit, in some respects a public asset.' After listing some of the most important plants of which Ellen is the sole guardian in the Western world, Prain gets to the point. He fears that in 'making over your garden and nursery' beginners 'may not fully appreciate the great scientific value of the plants in your collection'. He hopes 'you have taken all the steps necessary to safeguard these plants from injury or loss while they are not under your control'.

Prain was concerned enough to send a round-robin to the horticultural brotherhood. The floodgates opened. William Wilks, of the RHS: 'We are greatly alarmed to hear that you have given up your nursery and part of your garden for training soldiers . . . on behalf of the Horticulture of this Country – indeed the whole world – I entreat you to let soldiers be trained elsewhere, on less valuable plants, and not on those which are so many of them irreplaceable.'[v] Isaac Bayley Balfour,

---

152 The novelist Marie Corelli warned Ellen that Forbes was an 'unprincipled coquette'. Ellen was good friends with both Corelli ('Queen of the Bestsellers') and her 'wife', Bertha Vyner.

Regius Keeper of the Royal Botanic Gardens, Edinburgh: 'What is all this I hear about the handing over of your garden . . . I shiver over the thought of your unique and rare plants being at the mercy of the ordinary run of gardener.'[vi] The letters pile in. Frederick Moore, keeper of the Royal Botanic Gardens, Glasnevin. Irwin Lynch, of the Botanic Garden, Cambridge.

What was to do? Ellen was broke and Lady Angela was the only game in town. How bad could an army of free labour be? She decided to go ahead but enshrine her precious plants within a highly modified contract, with multiple clauses specifically protecting the rarest specimens. Lady Angela, who had already moved in, signed it. The *Daily Mirror*, *Sketch* and *Tatler* then syndicated newspapers as far away as Lake County, Indiana, Tampa Bay, Florida and St Paul, Minnesota. All ran stories, the headlines trumpeting: SHE EMPLOYS ONLY DISABLED SOLDIERS TO WORK HER FARM alongside photographs of this smoothest of media operators in glamorous outfits surrounded by free-range geese or 'showing a poor soldier' how to feed cows against a backdrop of chicken wire and sheds. She even managed to get herself into a newsreel. Perhaps this should have rung a few warning bells but, for the moment, Ellen was getting a bit of money, and, in Warley's main garden, which she had not given up, she was able to sow some seeds newly arrived from the slopes of Mount Everest courtesy of the Royal Botanic Gardens, Edinburgh. She was even relaxed enough to have her head turned by national matters.

We know relatively little about Ellen Willmott's politics, save that they were, generally, right-wing and, generally, feminist. Emmeline and Christabel Pankhurst's short-lived Women's Party demanded equality in pay, marriage, divorce and parenthood, and for maternity and infant care to be subsidised on a sliding scale according to income. I can't see that Ellen was heavily entangled with the party, though she was involved enough to be asked to steward a meeting in 1918. She did throw herself headlong into another cause, though.

PEAKS AND TROUGHS

In retrospect, the case brought by the whistle-blowing ex-commandant of the fledgling Women's Royal Air Force was a century before its time. Miss Violet Douglas-Pennant had been relieved of her duties after uncovering sexism even beyond the lax standards of the day. Together with an army of (largely) women supporters, the worm fought back, calling out her wrongful dismissal. Ellen Willmott, who had known both Violet and her sister Hilda for years, became a valiant infantrywoman, writing to the newspapers, attending meetings, organising petitions and providing personal support.

Ultimately, the case failed. Too many stood to gain from a lone woman's character assassination – and to lose far more if the 'renegade' was found to be telling the truth. Violet Douglas-Pennant would assert her innocence for the rest of her life, loyally supported by a vocal but largely impotent following. For Ellen, the cause was as righteous as it was important; she may even have believed it reflected her own (less convincing) injustices. Her heavy involvement also reminded the world she wasn't done yet. Ellen Willmott was still a public figure, who still had something worthwhile to contribute.

A chance to make that contribution came in late spring, 1919, as Britain faced a new national scandal:

DOOMED FLOWER BEDS AT HAMPTON COURT!
71 out of 121 TURFED OVER!
MORE VANDALISM AT HAMPTON COURT!
DUTCH GARDEN IN DANGER![vii]

The headlines hit a nerve; a pinch-point in the national mood. Fair enough that everyone had gone through privations during the Great War. Fair enough that Britain's parks and gardens had been made over to vegetable plots and easy-maintenance grass during hostilities. But peace now reigned – or so they said. Could it be true that Hampton

Court Palace, Britain's National Treasure, was now to be marred by horticultural vandalism? Rumours abounded that the famous flower beds would not be reinstated at all. Some even said the ancient Dutch Garden, on the way to the Great Vine, was to be destroyed entirely. The only thing left, the papers raged, would be the pond. Worse, the evil deed had been cooked up undercover. 'The scheme was to have been carried out gradually so as not to alarm the public until in the end nothing but grass and trees remained.'[viii]

The Observer, Country Life, Daily Telegraph and especially *The Times* made the Hampton Court horrors a cause célèbre. HM Office of Works poured oil on the flames of a PR disaster by changing their story every time there was a new 'revelation', sending out spokesmen who used weasel phrases such as 'there is no intention at present' and insisted that whatever they did would ultimately *enhance* the gardens and was for the *greater public good* and no, they were not going to reveal what that would be, thank-you-very-much.

I have no idea why they didn't just refute what was, frankly, a piece of puff journalism. True, the cash wasn't there anymore, and the gardens had run to thistle, nettle and couch grass, thanks to a four-year war, but actually, some of the old-fashioned Victorian beds were either too close together for the kind of visitor numbers the palace now attracted or genuinely detracted from the landscape. Hampton Wick Council jumped on the bandwagon, foaming with righteous anger and demanding a U-turn in the unspecified plans. Was this the kind of thing those brave boys in the Somme had fought for? Matters got so heated there were questions asked in Parliament.

At this point Lionel Earle[153] at the Office of Works decided to put a lid on the fire. 'I dare say you have noticed a great deal of Press agitation in connection with the Gardens at Hampton Court,' he wrote to Ellen Willmott, adding, 'I need hardly say of a misleading and erroneous

---

153 Civil servant and son of garden writer Theresa Earle.

character.'[ix] He continues, 'The First Commissioner has decided to appoint a Committee to advise him on the whole subject,' hoping Ellen 'might possibly find time to give your valuable advice on the subject.'

For Ellen, beleaguered from every flank, this public call to arms was balm to a tortured soul. After checking exactly what the claims were, what the plans involved and that the Office of Works would actually take notice of any recommendations, she accepted. The press now had something different to talk about: the 'expert' line-up. Who was it to be? Would it be fair? Could it be trusted? Was it a set-up? *Country Life* reminded the ministry of 'the justifiable suspicion and hostility with which Press and public watch executive action on the part of all Government departments – arising from their wasteful bungling of their business'[x] but the *Observer* was convinced: 'Looking at the names of the Committee, one has good hope that the planting may become intelligent and artistic.'[xi]

At 11.15 a.m. on Friday, 13 June 1919, an all-star cohort met at the Palace gates to find out exactly what was going on. Headed up by architect and president of the Royal Academy, Sir Aston Webb, this heritage A-Team included Kew curator William Watson, designers Harold Peto and Robert Wallace, plant hunter Frederick Balfour and historian Ernest Law. Ellen Willmott was, as usual, the only woman. It was a convivial affair; these experts had a job to do and clearly enjoyed each other's company. Ellen took the task seriously, soliciting others for their thoughts, including Queen Alexandra, who couldn't be seen to get involved but wanted to hear all the gossip, and William Robinson, who was only too happy to wade in with his two-penn'orth.

I wonder whether a White Paper about garden design would attract fevered national anticipation today. Somehow I doubt it, but in 1919 the issue did not go away, as various papers speculated about what it might contain. On its release in August, however, this storm in a delicate china teacup fizzled out as quickly as it had flared up. The committee's solution was obvious stuff, but it had taken a committee to get to it: keep beds where they are appropriate, lose beds where they are inappropriate. Ditch anything sickly. Make the herbaceous borders *actually* herbaceous and, while it's all being done, how about some formal troughs to lift the spirits while retaining elegance?

The Times was particularly impressed with the speed in which said troughs appeared around the fountain and in the Dutch Garden. If they had visited Warley, they might have been equally struck by the lack of troughs in Miss Willmott's garden that year. I am not sure whether all twenty-seven of the Versailles planters I counted on the 'Kip & Knyff' print of Warley vacationed at Hampton Court that summer, but it's rather pleasing to see them at Spetchley today after, for a brief moment a century ago, they captured the spirit of a nation.

Both the *Observer* and *Country Life* were impressed with the team's no-nonsense spirit, and the union would cement further friendships. Sir Aston Webb told Ellen, 'No one could, I am sure, wish for a pleasanter & more reasonable committee to work with.'[xii] Ellen continued to work with Ernest Law as Hampton Court's Pond Garden and Privy Garden were restored. Just as she was basking in national glory, however, Lady Angela Forbes did a moonlight flit.

Even in her own memoir[xiii] Lady Angela admits her scheme lasted less than a year. She blames the farm's failure on Ellen Willmott's 'idiosyncrasies', that the extra clauses and 'impossible stipulations' Ellen added to the contract had doomed the project from the start. Yet Lady Angela signed that contract and Ellen had left her alone, as requested. Indeed, if we are to believe Ellen's side of the story (which in this case I am inclined to, since it is almost certainly a sworn statement for the court case that followed), when Ellen's gardener came in to do the tidying stipulated in the contract, he was ordered off the property without even permission to collect his tools.

Ignoring all of Miss Willmott's clauses, intended to protect some of the most valuable and rare plants in Britain, Lady Angela turned Warley Lea into a barren quagmire. 'All there is remaining on the ground are some stumps and blackened sticks,' wrote a heartbroken Ellen. 'All vegetation has been ruthlessly destroyed, herbaceous plants as well as iris, roses, paeonies, kniphofias and all shrubs.'

Sir Michael Foster's life's-work collection of Iris was wiped out. Ellen couldn't even start over, as 'the lead labels on which he has recorded the parentage of the seedlings have all been burnt'. The official damage report is, simply, jaw-dropping. Forty-one collections of botanical rarities and scores of mature specimen plants hacked to the ground. A 380-foot pergola ripped out and burned, the rare climbers growing up it reduced to stumps. Glasshouses smashed, their ribs torn away from the base; fruit trees infested with mealy bug or simply razed. Specialist equipment used for firewood. The veterans – who to be fair, were beginners and seem to have been in receipt of some truly weird 'training' by someone who hadn't a clue in either the agricultural or horticultural department – even annihilated the seventy-year-old collection of ancient roses started by Ellen's mother. Those same roses, Ellen pointed out, could have made the soldiers serious money simply by selling the blooms to local florists.

'We have twice visited the gardens since Lady Angela left and their present state baffles description,' she wrote in September 1919. 'The garden and lawns around the house [have been] given up to rearing fowls and ducks, right up to the drawing room window.' Warley's kitchen garden, which had been handed over bulging with produce, had nothing in it at all save a few self-seeded parsnips. 'The tragedy of the whole thing,' she keened, 'is that there is not as much ground under cultivation for vegetables as there was when it was taken over by Lady Angela. In more than one place the ground upon which grew the rare plants and shrubs and which was cleared of all that stood upon it is now covered with thistles and nettles and has not been used at all.' Ellen's distress is palpable: 'The border upon which were grown Dr Lowe's collection of ferns and a collection of ivies has not been touched since the plants were destroyed last year. Had the wholesale destruction of rare plants been followed by a well-cropped and cultivated vegetable garden there would have been some point in violating the conditions of tenure, but as it is that wholesale destruction is purely wanton.'

Part of Ellen's statement comprises extracts from the agreement, which clearly stipulate the care that was to be taken with extant plants and even makes provision for assistance from Ellen's gardeners, who were banned from the site.[154] Worse, her legal argument couldn't even be with Lady Angela, who had skipped town, but now had to be with her long-term lover, Hugo Charteris, 11th Earl Wemyss, who, it appears, had bankrolled his mistress after the money won from her ex-husband ran out.

The court would find in Ellen's favour (a measly £200, rather than the £2,000 suggested by the independent report)[155] but nothing could bring back those plants, or her reputation with the great horticulturists of her day, who at least did not outwardly queue up to say, 'I told you so'.

For decades the only publicly available version of the above tale was in Lady Angela's autobiography, where Ellen Willmott is depicted as a nit-picking, squawking eccentric, intent on ruining Lady A's dreams of charity. At least we now have the other side of the story. She was had – and we are all the poorer for the loss of some extraordinary, irreplaceable, historic plant collections.

❖

Ellen was back to square one – indeed, she had descended into negative squares. All context is lost around a letter sent that October by William Robinson, which starts out: 'The great mistake of our people is, I think, not teaching the girls the elements of business & so lead them to trust too much to others.'[xiv] He does not refer to Ellen's own predicament,

---

154 Reading between the lines of Lady Angela's memoire, I suspect Ellen's priceless plants had already been destroyed before the contract was signed.

155 £10,500 rather than £105,500.

and surely even Robinson, known for his forthrightness, would not have said something so blunt about her, to her, but he was right: Ellen was floundering.

She made vague stabs at economy, getting items valued, discovering it was a bear market and that she had paid well over the odds when it had been bull, and deciding to wait until she could get a better price. Despite recent privations, and the horrors at Warley Lea, her ornamental garden was still legendary. Ellen herself still held great sway in cultural circles, not least thanks to her recent hand in the 'saving' of Hampton Court's gardens. Against fierce competition she won the Peter Barr Memorial Vase for her services to daffodils – no woman would hold aloft the prestigious silver cup for another forty years.[156] Her advice was sought constantly, for example by her friend (and, she discovered, distant cousin), Sir Martin Conway.

Sir Martin, settling down after a life of derring-do exploration for the Royal Geographical Society, had been tasked with creating the new Imperial War Museum. Conway had already earmarked a section in the museum for women's contributions to the war effort, to be run by his daughter Agnes. He fired all his male gardeners after they turned out to be 'complicated and efficient thieves' and, apparently on Ellen's recommendation, the museum's first head gardener was a woman. Miss Carr 'hires the needed men and puts the fear of God into the whole place,' he told her. 'She has done more in two months than our previous folk in two years.'[xv]

The plaudits, grand openings and galas were little comfort as Ellen watched her personal life descend into wilderness. Not even her sister could help now. 'We have come to the conclusion that we must let Spetchley,' wrote Rose.[xvi] A month later, even letting was not enough. 'I have about £800 a year to live on and Robert has not one penny, he is over £1000 a year on the wrong side with these iniquitous taxes. We

---

[156] Helen Richardson, in 1960.

must sell part of Spetchley and then shall be not much better off. I cannot afford to keep any kind of menial but must do all myself.'[xvii]

Even as Rose was taking cookery lessons and cheese classes, blaming 'this vile servants' trade union', Ellen widened her circle of people in-the-know of her circumstances, writing a draft letter to William Wilks. 'I am in a temporary hole and unless I can find a helping hand it will be a permanent one.'[xviii] She sent similar missives to others: Isaac Bayley Balfour, Vicary Gibbs, Lord Ducie. All expressed sympathy with her situation but weren't going to touch Ellen Willmott's finances with the proverbial bargepole. Alice de Rothschild made a sensible suggestion – why not sell a painting? – but still Ellen seemed pathologically unable part with 'things'. She even tried to squeeze money out of her virtually estranged publisher, with the predictable no-dice. *Genus Rosa's* estimated production cost had been £5,275 (£635,000). Of that, Ellen Willmott had paid £1,500 (£180,000). John Murray swallowed the rest, which would have been okay if the project had made all those projected millions. By 1920, 740 of the 1,000 copies remained unsold. Ellen began a new campaign, trying to find different companies to take the copies. Murray told her that these days young people wanted motor cars, not libraries, which didn't go down well. An argument arose over who owned the unsold copies.

One day in March 2020 – exactly one hundred years after the debacle – John Cannell and I were going through some wrecked correspondence from this period. John announced he had found a bunch of irritated letters from John Murray demanding the return of unsold copies currently in Willmott's possession. We laughed at the bunch of missives I was concurrently turning up across the table from him: a series of gushing thank-you letters from worthy institutions up and down the country blessing Ellen for her generous gift: a copy of *Genus Rosa*. If John Murray wanted those books back, he'd have to pry them from the cold, disadvantaged hands of charity. Advantage: Willmott.

On 11 May 1920, several years after most people's resolve would have dissolved, Lord Lilford foreclosed on the Warley mortgage. Ellen went into overdrive, writing to gardening friends including Robert James and Reginald Cory, asking for assistance 'against my collection of books, my Napoleonic collection, my Napoleonic library, my musical instruments, including two Amatis, two harpsichords, my collection of [unreadable] my collection of Stuart miniatures, my Louis XIV writing table, my interest in [unreadable], my mortgage, my claim against Lord Wemyss, Tresserve and Boccanegra.'[xix]

She was finally prepared to give up everything. Just, please, *please*, let her stay at Warley.

Chapter Eighteen:

Down But Not Out

AN AUCTION CATALOGUE

Twenty-two thick paper pages, rough-cut and bound in dove-grey, the brochure advertises a long-rumoured Essex sale. 'Warley Place' appears in curled script; the 'd' of 'near Brentwood' printed with such flourish it might be taken for an engraving. The date has no such issue: '1920', in straight, no-nonsense numerals.

THE CLOSING MONTHS of 1919 brought Ellen one small shred of dignity. The Shakespeare Birthplace Trust, Stratford-upon-Avon, keen to avoid the negative publicity Hampton Court had attracted, put Ellen's committee-chum, historian Ernest Law, in charge of designing an 'authentic' Shakespearean garden at New Place. Law invited Miss Willmott to collaborate. As a lifelong Shakespeare obsessive, she was delighted.

Ellen's work at Stratford would mark a new – if short-lived – phase in the public eye. So far, her life achievements had been largely those of a private gardener. Her advice had been solicited by friends, family and even institutions. Her awards and work with the RHS and Women's Farm and Garden Union were well known in the horticultural world, and she saturated the gardening press on a weekly basis. Outside the hothouse world of horticulture, she was less well known. During the Hampton Court debacle, Miss Willmott's name had begun to appear in the national press alongside those of public experts, acknowledged as their equal. Being invited to collaborate with Ernest Law on a second national treasure would have helped see her through some very dark days indeed. Ellen's finances were in tatters, as were large areas of her gardens, not least thanks to Lady Angela Forbes's vanity project. Her friends were dying. Her sister was ill. Her house was threatened with repossession. What did that matter? The British Public needed her.

Law and Willmott set to with gusto, exchanging frenzied letters, sometimes twice a day, over five months. We have many of Ernest's missives, none of Ellen's. Law came up with 'Elizabethan' landscape designs; Willmott provided Shakespeare-specific planting plans. They sent the results to the appropriately named Mrs Flower. Charles Edward Flower, the famous Midlands brewer who had founded the Shakespeare Memorial Theatre, was long dead, but sundry relatives remained heavy hitters in the Trust. Mrs Flower had been appointed gatekeeper to Law and Willmott's project and seems to have kept a close hold on the keys.

From the start communications were poor. Ernest Law sent letters, blueprints and reminders; Mrs F did not reply. He and Willmott tried to meet Mrs Flower for site visits; she was unavailable. Occasionally she sent notes promising to reply in full, then took days to do so and sometimes still didn't answer any of their questions, especially anything to do with funding, which they were beginning to realise was 'limited'. Occasionally, random bulk batches of bulbs that neither Law nor Willmott had ordered arrived which, despite having nothing to do with Shakespeare, they were forced to incorporate. At first Ernest's letters mutter excuses about Mrs F being 'busy', but his annoyance slowly grows as the head gardener informs him that yet another one thousand tulip bulbs have been planted under a beech tree without reference to him or Ellen. Ernest had liked and wanted to keep the garden's old yew 'buttress' hedges – he felt they gave the garden structure – but was told there had 'been complaints' that they made the garden look 'short'. He and Ellen compromised by simplifying rather than removing them entirely – they're still there today – but they now had a new problem: the bard himself.

St George's Day, 23 April, has long been adopted as Shakespeare's birthday and the powers-that-be wanted a grand opening to coincide with the festivities. The pair now had to come up with a complete garden *and* a celebratory event by that date, approved by the elusive Mrs Flower and on a ridiculously low budget.

There was one solution: a national appeal. Ernest wrote an impassioned plea to the Great British Public to donate 'Elizabethan' plants from their own gardens. Flyers were distributed and articles published in *The Morning Post, Observer, Times, The Field, Country Life* and all manner of local papers. Ellen plundered her high-profile address book; Ernest asked his friend Lady Cawdor to supply some Macbeth-themed plants and wrote optimistically to people in Venice and the owners of Juliet's House in Verona. Ellen pragmatically suggested that if people couldn't send plants, cash was equally acceptable.

The idea of filling the Bard's back yard with flowers from one's own appealed to the British imagination. Donations rolled in, from lords and ladies sending entire shipments to ordinary folk sending what they could. The call was seemingly ignored, however, by other potential donors. A rude letter appeared in the *Morning Post* complaining that while even inner-London schoolchildren had coughed up, not a single thespian had responded to the appeal. 'From the actors themselves,' the letter griped, 'not a slip of gillyflower, not a rootlet of wild thyme nor even a sprig of rosemary for remembrance.'[i] After a few more choice comments about actors in general, the letter was signed 'A lover of Shakespeare' and it's a toss-up as to who wrote it. My money's on Ernest but Ellen would have been just as hopping mad. She and Rose had plundered Warley and Spetchley for suitable plants, but New Place was a large site, and they needed all the greenwood they could get.

The breakthrough came via Ellen's royal contacts. King George, Queen Mary, Queen Alexandra and Edward, Prince of Wales, all agreed to donate plants from their gardens, lending gravitas to the project. Ernest's centrepiece 'knott garden' could now be divided into quadrants with a royal rose crowning each section.

This was all very well, but basic plants were still missing. There was a 'difficult' patch at the end, too, cursed with dry shade and knotty tree roots. Ellen suggested a wild garden, but the only way they could get one to work was by raising the site nine inches, using soil dug out from a genius wheeze: making the knot garden 'sunken'.

The pressure was ramping up. The American Ambassador was to be guest of honour at the grand opening, making it an international affair. Ellen sourced some trees and crab apples from Harold Hillier, but even as late as 19 March, with one month to go, Ernest, blighted with constant ill health, had new cares, not least over which dignitary should ceremonially plant which royal rose. 'We could not have Lady Warwick to plant Q. Alexandra's rose!' he fretted to Ellen. Both would have been only too aware that the countess had once been one of King Edward VII's (Alexandra's husband's) less-discreet mistresses. The alternative was Lady Craven, a Yankee!

Alas, we leave Ernest Law's panic a couple of weeks before the big day; presumably he spent the time on-site with Ellen as there are no more letters. The *Illustrated London News* implies that the garden was not quite finished by the grand opening, but there was enough greenery in place to make a respectable British fist, and for Ernest Law to be able to lie down in a darkened room. Ellen had no such luck.

All the months she had been undergoing Shakespeare-related stress and writing heartfelt pleas for help with the Stratford garden, she had been receiving practically daily final demands and threats of litigation. Eighteen days after the grand opening of Willmott and Law's second national triumph in a year, Lord Lilford pulled that final toothpick and Ellen's eight-year game of *KerPlunk* descended into an avalanche of financial marbles.

She fought the mortgage foreclosure but, as her friend Philip Sassoon (cousin of Siegfried) told her, she had signed a contract that gave Lilford the power to pull the plug without allowing time to make arrangements or put her finances straight. It could be argued that Ellen had had eight years to 'make arrangements'; that the whole idea of the mortgage had been to allow time to put her finances straight. Not that she saw it that way.

Ellen received an offer[157] of £19,000 for Warley. Given Lord Lilford's share would be £18,000, that was nowhere near enough to pay off even a

---

157 We don't know who from.

few debts, let alone have anything to live on. There was nothing for it – her family home and beloved garden would have to be sold by auction. Even then she'd have to pray for a good day in the room.

No expense was spared in printing up the brochure. Thick paper, glossy photographic plates; this was going to be the sale of the century. The contents were to be sold first, by Sotheby's. Ellen couldn't believe that, in her younger days, she had paid over the odds for practically everything and kept upping the reserve prices until the auctioneer wrote in frustration, 'Yesterday the armour sold splendidly without any reserve. Cannot you please leave the furniture at the prices I suggested. It is a mistake to put these impossible prices.'[ii]

The big sale date hurtled ever closer. Bidding would begin at 2.30 p.m. precisely, Wednesday, 9 June 1920. Ellen Willmott, happy face to the world, attended the newly reinstated Chelsea Flower Show and even, it would seem, donated an important Tudor book 'to the nation'. This impressed her friend Norman Moore: 'I looked all through it & it reminded me of you and your books in the happy days of the past.'[iii] The identity of the book is unknown; neither do I have any idea why she didn't sell that, too. The 'nation' may have been the V&A, with whom Ellen had become very closely associated. She lent her beloved Kirkman harpsichord to the museum at the same time.

Meanwhile, back in the 'other' line of the Berkeley family, Lord Randal, 8th Earl of Berkeley, had long fretted over his lack of a son. In 1920 he bowed to the inevitable and made young Rob Berkeley (Rose's son, Ellen's nephew), his heir. Although the title would become dormant on the Earl's death, Rob would now eventually inherit Berkeley Castle as well as his father's estate at Spetchley Park. Perhaps it was in thinking of his newly named heir that Lord Berkeley now stepped in to Ellen's predicament. Eight days before the sale,[iv] [158] he offered to save Warley by purchasing Tresserve. He was, he said, happy to pay more than a

---

158 The letter is damaged, but the date seems probable.

mystery French buyer had offered. Ellen, I am ashamed to say, saw the lifeline and tried to make it a boat.

She immediately took Warley off the market, telling Lord Berkeley the Frenchman was offering her £26,000[159] for Tresserve, far below its 'real' value. Was she being greedy, or just desperate? Lord Berkeley had never visited Tresserve but was pretty sure that, in its present reported condition, it couldn't fetch even that sort of money. He did some digging.

In a remarkably calm, reasonable and generous letter Lord B gently but firmly tells Ellen he wants to help but he's not a mug. The French buyer has actually offered 40,000 francs, which translates as around £8,000.[160] He is happy to give Ellen slightly more than that, plus half-interest in any profit he may make later, reminding her, 'you must remember that I have no idea as to the real value of the property'.[v] Lord Berkeley's letter finishes: 'Please tell me what interest you have to pay the insurance company on the Warley estate . . . I might be able to help you in that matter.'

It was the best offer she was going to get and, wisely, Ellen stuck. Using some financial jiggery-pokery I've never been able to fathom (most of the paperwork is lost or damaged to the point of illegibility), not only Tresserve's deeds but Warley's mortgage now found their way into Lord Berkeley's portfolio. To the profound distress of Tresserve's ancient retainers Claude and Gasparine Meunier, the earl dispensed with all staff but a caretaker and, it would seem, visited the French property only once.[161]

Heartbreaking as it must have been, letting go of her French garden must have lifted a weight from Ellen's shoulders. She even managed to sell her father's old Borough High Street office – for a terrible price[162]

---

159 About £1,188,395,00 today.

160 About £365,500 today.

161 The estate fell into high-walled slumber. On Lord Berkeley's death legal complications made Rob's inheritance messy. Eventually, the estate was bought by the municipality; the house is now the local *Mairie*.

162 £1,600, about £73,000 today.

– which meant she could actually help her sister for once. The respite was temporary; creditors were already gearing themselves up for the next round, but Ellen could count herself lucky. She had so far kept her mental health, which was more than some of her friends had managed.

※

The First World War is notorious for the horrific mental scars suffered by returning servicemen. Less well chronicled is the cost to noncombatants. Before 1914, botanist, archaeologist, historian, folklorist and naturalist Robert Miller Christy was one of the most dynamic characters Ellen knew. He had been the joint owner of a successful printing firm and published scores of books, pamphlets and articles. Fellow of the Linnean Society, founder member of the Essex Field Club and the Morant Club, editor of *Essex Naturalist*, Christy's most famous works are on the natural world, including ornithology, botany and archaeology, especially of the built environment. To witness the fall of such a man must have been a severe shock.

We don't know the full details of how the Hayman, Christy & Lilly printing presses were commandeered by HM Stationery Office at the outbreak of hostilities. Christy never refers to it as anything less than common theft. That in itself, however – and even the later compulsory purchase of his entire works, machinery and equipment, bringing the company's bankruptcy – should not have brought a man of such energy to his knees. *Something* happened. It isn't explicit in his letters, as Ellen was clearly party to the story already,[163] but by January 1920, Miller Christy's friends were concerned enough to circulate a private letter, soliciting contributions for a fund that might enable him to live somewhere other than his brother's office in Temple. When she had money Ellen was generous to such appeals; it's probable that she helped when her boat came in, in the form of Lord Berkeley's purchase. The ramifications of

---

163 He implies a former colleague defrauded him while he was sick with Spanish 'flu.

such generosity, however, put her in a difficult position. Now in her sixties, Miss Willmott received a second proposal of marriage.

Jane Austen's Mr Collins could not have written a more gauche missive. After starting out with a few pleasantries, Miller gets to the point: 'From what you have said & from other things, I think I am not presumptuous when I infer that you would not be unwilling to consider the possibility of our marrying one another. Whether that is so or not, I see no harm in telling you exactly how I view the matter. For my part I should be delighted to marry you (far more, probably, than you have any idea of) for I believe we could get on admirably together, as we have so many interests in common, & I am sure we could be helpful to one another in many ways.'

Not a wildly romantic start, but passable so far. Alas, Christy feels the need to elaborate. 'Moreover, as far as I am concerned, existence has been, for the last four years (for reasons known to you), all but intolerable, & the only prospect now is that it will become <u>absolutely so almost at once</u>.'

He carries on digging: 'So you may believe me when I say that almost <u>any</u> change of the kind would be a relief', hurriedly adding, 'even if with a lady much less desirable than yourself', before feeling the need to clarify, 'though as a matter of fact there is none such in view.' Christy continues in the same vein for several more lines, even announcing, 'we considered the matter a year or two ago'. Given what was happening in Ellen's life 'a year or two ago', I simply don't believe they did 'consider' this, though I can imagine a situation where Christy aired the idea and didn't notice Ellen tactfully steering the subject back into safer waters.

He goes on to list his many and various financial problems but is adamant: he does not want to marry Ellen for her (non-existent, surely he knows that) wealth: 'I am not a silly young noodle seeking to marry & settle up.' He needs to fight a new case in the Losses Court 'without a halfpenny', but, he insists, he doesn't expect Ellen to pay for it, whatever sum he might later 'settle for' upon their marriage. After spending a further two paragraphs itemising his physical and mental health problems, poor Miller Christy closes: 'May I know your view?' He adds a postscript: 'In replying please mark 'private' and seal, as the only permanent address I have is my brother's offices & the clerks sometimes open my letters by accident.'

Unlike Johann Bernhard Mann, we do not have Ellen's draft reply to this heart-rending, car crash of a proposal. Her sorrow can only have been eclipsed by the knowledge that she had to reply to this lost soul in a way that would not crush him further. From later letters, it appears her excuse for refusal was general: 'the times'. No one should be judged on their weakest moment, and I am happy to say that though he never recovered from his financial woes or mental health issues, Christy did weather this multi-faceted storm enough to work on several archaeological projects.[164] We don't have any letters from him immediately after the proposal, but Ellen must have hit a kindly note as the pair was soon conversing again, this time about a much safer subject: primroses.

The *Primulaceae* family, which also includes cowslips, was another of Ellen's specialities but, in this instance, she was outshone by her sister. Rose had focused on an intense primrose breeding programme, crossing varieties for colour and, unusually, perfume. In *Country Life*, 1921, Henry Avray Tipping somewhat alarmingly claims 'in no detail has Mrs Berkeley neglected the eugenics of the primrose'. Rose has, he tells us, built on work done by Gertrude Jekyll on white and yellow strains to add orange, crimson, maroon, pink, mauve, purple and blue. Her flowers are 'massive, but not coarse', 'large, yet refined and shapely'. Some of the blooms 'very nearly reach a diameter of 3 inches'. Tipping praises 'the deft hand, the tasteful judgement that have enabled Mrs Berkeley to make Spetchley the home of the blue-blooded aristocracy of the primrose empire'.

---

164 Including Harlow Temple, Essex. Ellen would continue supporting her friend in every way she could (short of matrimony) to his death in 1928.

This didn't stop snobs holding forth on the vulgarity of 'modern' primroses, something Ellen, fiercely proud of anything her sister did, was very sensitive about.

'Dear Miss Willmott, I was amazed today when Mr Mudge told me what you had heard about my running down your sister's Primroses,' writes Peter Barr Jnr in March 1921, proving that horticultural snarkiness had not abated since Victorian times. Barr goes on to suggest it was probably his brother who had maligned the flowers, as *he* intensely dislikes non-self-coloured primulas.[vi] He ends the letter with the backhanded 'There is room for several classes of Primroses . . . and each should be judged in its own class.'

This may, at first, look like yet another ho-hum horticultural bickerfest, but this time the backbiting touched a nerve. As she watched Rose struggle with her worsening cancer, Ellen's pride had become obsession, a kind of pre-death grief, expressed through flowers. The radium treatment now seemed to be doing more harm than good, judging from oblique references to 'my wound'. Rose battled on, taking six straight days and nights of treatment at a time, and though at least it was now administered using portable equipment at home, she dreaded every session. In between, she struggled to care for and exhibit her primroses, each named for a different saint.

Ellen helped where she could, notifying nurseries when Spetchley seed was available (at a whopping five shillings a packet),[165] asking Kew to register new varieties and circulating newspaper cuttings about her sister's triumphs, asking her friends to return the articles so she could send them on. She also helped with the children, all three of whom were now young adults. Eleanor, who was becoming a proficient artist and photographer herself, came to stay. The youngest, Betty, received 1922's latest craze – a pogo stick – for an otherwise sombre birthday. Sadly, it has not made it down the past century, or I would have chosen

---

165 Approximately £7.50.

it as this chapter's object as an example of Ellen Willmott's continuing sense of humour, love for her family and choices in expenditure when all around her is falling to pieces.

Ellen even went abroad – to Paris, for the first-ever Iris Conference, in preparation for a major exhibition to be held in London that July – but her brief respite from money problems was beginning to fade. Her creditors were lining up yet again. Bills, writs, final demands, even the odd court summons;[166] *every single day* something horrid plopped through Pandora's Letterbox. Like Pandora, Ellen pounced on vestiges of hope. She still received invitations and letters from royalty and important horticulturists around the world; was still asked to use her influence. One proffered lifeline, however, she inexplicably refused.

Edward Hudson, proprietor of *Country Life* and now *The Garden*, had been on at her for years to write for him. Now he made a specific proposal: 'Cox[167] is going to edit the magazine and I want you to help him. There are very few people living with such a knowledge of flowers as you have, and in addition to this, such a knowledge of photography and what to photograph.' To avoid ambiguity Hudson assures her: 'I am writing to you of course quite as a matter of business, all the assistance you can give will be treated on a business basis.'[vii]

Ellen swerved the bait. Otto Stapf, of Kew, had a go next, suggesting she write for the *Botanical Magazine*.[viii] [168] The best he got was a selection of newly crossed plant specimens for Kew's in-house artist to paint. Hudson tried again: 'I know you would do this through friendship but I want to treat it as a matter of business,' pleading, 'why cannot you write for us? You know I should value it if you would. I am sure you would not get better mediums than *Country Life* and *The Garden*.'[ix]

Why not indeed? Her reticence baffles me. Ellen was not a bad writer, and she knew her subject better than almost anyone else out

---

[166] She habitually never paid rates; Le Lièvre says this was an attempt to avoid jury service.

[167] Euan Cox, previously deputy ed.

[168] Lillian Snelling made a painting of a new *Dictamnus caucasica*.

there. There was no shame in respectable ladies writing for money; some of her best friends were garden writers. Gertrude Jekyll had been doing it for years. Celebrity Editor of Britain's biggest garden magazine would have secured her status as one of the country's most eminent horticulturists. Yet still she demurred. Perhaps the not-unqualified success of *Warley Garden in Spring and Summer* and *Genus Rosa* had knocked her; I cannot think of a single other reason other than Imposter syndrome finally getting the better of her. Frankly, Hudson dodged a bullet; Ellen Willmott was incapable of recognising a deadline. Poor Arthur Hill had just worried himself to a near-early grave waiting for Ellen's chapter in a tribute volume to Canon Ellacombe,[x] though her writing, when it arrived, was perfectly up to standard. The money would have been useful, though. With numbing predictability, her creditors circled closer.

Ellen must have known for years that she needed to sell her Italian garden. Part of the reason she loved it was the lure of taming a difficult terrain, but a decade of neglect under its current tenant had tipped it well beyond anything she could hope to claw back.

Lady Susan Menzies and Ellen Willmott were cut from similar cloth. Lady M had once known great wealth, once been lauded in the society columns as she opened fêtes, appeared at garden parties and doled out prizes at farm shows. Like the rest of the world, however, Ellen would have read the titillating, blow-by-blow coverage of a ten-year court case brought by milliner Miss Eliza Pontz, claiming over £2,000 in unpaid hat bills against Lady Menzies' late husband's estate. Ellen sympathised at first and let both her foreign properties to Lady M and her daughter on an occasional basis, most often Boccanegra. As the years passed, however, Lady Susan turned from beleaguered friend to annoying tenant, constantly complaining and making demands. Her letters, once full of bonhomie and 'My dear Ellie' had distinctly cooled, and now

Susan wanted Boccanegra outright. She got her solicitor to write asking how much Ellen wanted for it.

Despite the fact that she desperately needed the money, that she hadn't visited in ten years and had told Alice de Rothschild she never intended to go abroad again, Ellen was adamant. There was no way Lady M was getting her paws on Boccanegra. This is probably due to Lady Susan's solicitor listing all Ellen's dead and dying plants and describing in detail the horrible neglect of both house and garden, then telling her that Lady Susan would put everything straight – for the right price. Ellen might well have asked Susan how Boccanegra had got into such neglect in the first place since she'd been living there during the years said neglect was going on. Luckily, she had another prospective buyer.

In direct contrast to Susan Menzies' confrontational approach, recently discovered letters from John Tremayne of Heligan are textbook examples of the correct way to persuade Ellen Willmott to part with something. Perhaps he really was in awe of her reputation, skill and gardens; it certainly reads that way. Even if he wasn't, flattering her with questions about the care of individual specimens and requests for original planting lists so he can replace those lost through wilful neglect are sure-fire door-openers. Negotiations began. Ellen needed the cash and Jack T needed somewhere to live. Heligan was, as we all now know, descending into elegant slumber.

British buyer and seller began trying to deal concurrently with Italian and English solicitors; various Italian legal and governmental bodies also needed fielding. Susan Menzies was incandescent that she had been overlooked and, perhaps missing the thrill of the courtroom, threatened to sue. Ellen's solicitors couldn't see what possible grounds she might have, but it still involved much to-ing and fro-ing of expensive letters and was an added worry at precisely the wrong time in Ellen's life: her sister was dying.

There was no pretending the radiation treatment was doing anything anymore. Rose had fought valiantly for eight years but now her only hope was the Little Flower of Jesus, St Thérèse of Lisieux. Patron saint of gardeners and florists, St Thérèse had known terrible illness and suffering, dying aged just twenty-four in Ellen's own *annus horribilis*, 1897. Young Betty Berkeley, especially, placed her ever-deepening faith in the young nun who had so heavily influenced Catholic belief in the previous century.

By July 1922, Rose was too poorly to stay at Spetchley. Pioneering Catholic hospice, St John and St Elizabeth's in North London, was at the vanguard of advanced palliative care; Rose would be in good hands there. Robert Valentine would stay nearby, visit every day and send Ellen updates on the days his wife was too exhausted to receive visitors. As his sister-in-law looked out for the young people and fielded Susan Menzies' legal threats, Robert Valentine took his beloved wife outdoors, to see the garden she had made at Spetchley one last time.

'I wheeled her only a few yards down and she asked to go back,' he wrote to Ellen later, 'she could not go any further... The last time before starting in the car for St John's & St Elizabeth she looked across the Park but made no remark... she knew she would never see it again.'[xi]

Chapter Nineteen:

The Grande Dame

A KNUCKLEDUSTER

Well balanced, mass produced and weighty, these classic 'T'-handle brass knuckles are made in the British style, with four oval 'stalls' (rings) and a shallow, rounded 'T' shape that fits into the palm. It is cast from solid, brushed brass with bevelled edges, allowing the piece to slide down to the base of the fingers for a firm grip. This weapon is no slugger. It is for keeping in a pocket and slipping on at short notice.

ROSE'S DEATH, ON 22 August 1922, was probably the single worst thing that ever happened to Ellen. The loss of her parents, the *annus horribilis*, the Tresserve fire, the money problems, nothing beat this. The horror of those last weeks in the hospice – the emergency operation, the near loss of a ravaged foot and exquisite pain – haunted her. At least a special Papal blessing had arrived in time for Extreme Unction.

The fallout was almost unbearable. Robert Valentine was inconsolable. Eleanor, Rose's oldest, suffered cold sweats. Rob failed his exams at Oxford. Betty, barely twenty, became suddenly and dangerously ill. Today, her condition would probably be diagnosed as broken heart syndrome; she spent many months in bed, her heart palpitations the cause of serious concern.

Ellen was tasked with writing an obituary for *Essex Naturalist*. It's a tough read, mainly for what it doesn't contain. It's clear she has had no chance to process her grief, and other, earlier losses churn through her mind. She pays homage to her mother who, she reminds readers, taught all three Willmott girls to break away from carpet bedding to seek new ideas. Ellen makes it clear it was Mrs Berkeley and not herself who made Spetchley the garden it is today. Her words are aloof, distant, almost those of someone who didn't know the deceased, admitting no emotion until the end, and the words of Omar Khayam:

> *The Moon of Heaven is rising once again;*
> *How oft hereafter rising shall she look*
> *Through this same garden after me – in vain.*

THE GRANDE DAME

Ellen and Robert Valentine had the verse carved into a stone alcove near the fountain. It is still there today, lonely, secret and sad.

The world spun on, but Ellen remained paralysed with grief, slipping into a depression she hadn't acknowledged since 1898. Scores of friends expressed genuine sorrow at the loss of her sister's quieter but in many ways equally talented life. Many remembered Ellen's own words of comfort when they had lost relatives. After the horrors of September, three of Ellen's dearest friends also fell that November: Henry Elwes, Sir Isaac Bayley Balfour and, most devastatingly of all, Norman Moore. No wonder her writing paper carried black borders for the next two years. One simple observation, made to the Russell family, sums up her loss: 'Now there is no one to send the first snowdrops to.'[i]

True to well-worn pattern, at the same time as Ellen's doormat filled with sympathy letters, there were others. Mainly creditors, but several from Jack Tremayne, still keen to buy Boccanegra, and from Susan Menzies' solicitor, threatening to sue if he did.

The whole thing had descended into the usual chaos. There were several extra flies in this particularly rancid ointment. Ellen's unwanted retainer Clodoveo and his thuggish son had now installed themselves in Boccanegra, taking what they liked. Tremayne paid Clodoveo 5,000 lire to leave. He didn't, but with 'a string of abuse' said he 'might' leave by June, if he got another 5,000 – and somewhere to live. Tremayne's letter is badly damaged, but his indignation at having to try to evict 'this horrible man' is clear. Appealing to Ellen's Achilles heel, Jack tells her he only wants to be able to tend the plants, 'and to protect your house and contents', especially the carpets, which he fears will be Clodoveo's next victims. He can only get the law involved, however, when he is the complete, legal owner of Boccanegra.[ii]

Ellen's problem was that she wasn't the complete legal owner, either. Her Italian property had been bundled up in the impossible-to-fathom financial stew she'd entered into with Lord Berkeley a couple of years earlier and she doesn't seem to have informed the earl she was selling it. Predictably, Lord Berkeley was furious and appointed a receiver to list her assets. Ellen vaguely realised she had annoyed him and drafted a humble-for-her apology. I don't know if it was ever sent. In another draft document from around this time, scribbled on the backs of old letters and titled 'Origins of Trouble', she scrawls frantic justifications for her current difficulties, none of them self-imposed, all of them the fault of others or of fate.

For all her show, Ellen's emotional state had always been brittle, her self-esteem not nearly as rumbustious as most believed. In her quiet way Rose had recognised this and had her sister's back in any way she was able. For the first time after thirty-odd years, Ellen's mail did not include that daily dose of non-judgemental sister-love. Her financial mentors were dead; her most recent saviour was foreclosing. In other such moments Ellen had delved deep into her soul and found new energy. Now the barrel was empty she dived again, into what little she had left, and resurfaced as something entirely different.

※

Ellen the Fierce was a heady combination of blue-sky creativity and wiry, naked determination to survive. Ellen the Fierce would show the world she still had it in her. Ellen the Fierce no longer hid behind a metaphorical carapace; she wore full body armour. Lord Berkeley must be paid, so Ellen invented the garden centre.

Of course, it wasn't actually called that; modern garden centres wouldn't appear for a good forty years, but the basic idea was very similar. In 1922, the only way of purchasing plants was through nurseries or market gardens. Ellen thought there must be a way to circumnavigate that. The physical condition of papers regarding the Amateur Gardeners' Society make it hard to work out exactly what it involved, especially as it's sometimes referred to as 'the syndicate'.[169] We

---

[169] Nothing to do with several earlier syndicates Ellen belonged to.

THE GRANDE DAME

know, however, that a fair few nurserymen were livid at Ellen's idea. They fumed that she was going to cut out the middleman by providing an 'experience' whereby the public could visit Warley Gardens, wander round an adjacent nursery purchasing plants they'd seen and then, perhaps, enjoy a cuppa in the tearooms. It sounds pretty regular stuff today but plantsman Walter Ingwerson, who had been invited to help run the show, was surprised at the ill will the rumour caused. We only have the right-hand side of Ingwerson's letter dated 15 Nov 1922, but it appears 'rumours' had reached RHS headquarters and 'certain people' were unhappy. When the idea was floated again, a year later, it had been modified to the status of a club and the reception was generally better.

The Amateur Gardeners' Society was a limited company, with £1 (£62) shares, that rented the buildings and gardens at Warley as its base, 'incidentally' keeping Ellen afloat. It was a genius wheeze on her part: it had a secretary, a billing address in Victoria Street, Westminster, a highly appealing brochure and credible officials, all of whom were solvent. Herbert Jekyll and noted horticulturist Reginald Cory became heavily involved. William Robinson enquired about shares, but was, like Henry Avray Tipping, put off by the price. Ellen was discreetly warned off asking Queen Alexandra to become patron, with the excuse that she didn't do clubs[170] – but do come over for tea.

The project began well, and money started coming in. Members seem to have been able to visit when they liked and buy choice plants reared at Warley. A library, lectures and even profits were dangled, too.[iii] Ellen could now submit a fair proportion of her garden expenses to the club, which doesn't smell too fresh, but details are almost impossible to glean now. Crucially, there are silverfish holes in some undated documentation which would reveal whether a particularly large sum of money is actually a loan, taken out against possible members' shares.[iv]

Ellen started looking for a head gardener. It seems word had got

---

[170] A poor excuse. Alexandra was patron of plenty of societies, including the Royal National Rose Society, whose events she went to with Ellen.

around – perhaps about her ability to pay, the general state of Warley or the way staff got treated – but maybe, just maybe, there was a little intimidation from nurserymen. An unknown number of candidates, initially very keen, subsequently declined the position. Ellen was forced to advertise and, from that moment on, confidence seems to drain from the project. Slowly at first, shareholders started asking exactly what they were getting for their money, then asking for it back. The Amateur Gardeners' Society took a long while to die; it was still limping on in 1928, but ultimately, Ellen's perfectly good idea was, once again, poorly administrated.

Not that she was worried about that just now, in 1923, the beginning of her project. Once more she had national fish to fry. A new sewer was being laid outside Anne Hathaway's Cottage and the Shakespeare Birthplace Trust asked Ellen to redesign the twelve-acre garden in 'sympathetic' style. This time she designed alone, though she did run her choices – plants mentioned in Shakespeare plays for the main garden and spring bulbs for the orchard – past William Bean from Kew. If the result says more about the early twentieth-century than anything Shakespeare would have known it was not for lack of diligence, study and effort on Ellen's part. Postcards of Anne Hathaway's Cottage after her transformation reveal a charming 'olde English' jumble, wildly popular with the public. A century later, it is being restored in her image, one of the very few 'Willmott' spaces we have left.

While she was in the spirit of reprise, Ellen wrote to the Office of Works at Hampton Court Palace, unhappy about the state the gardens were slipping back into. A couple of beautiful watercolour planting designs at the National Archives prove she couldn't resist putting her mark on the new 'knott garden' Ernest Law had just designed near the Great Vine. The layout involves some of Ellen's favourite plants, including, in memory of her sister, Spetchley primroses. She would have been particularly pleased when Gertrude Jekyll (now signing herself 'yours affectionately') asked how she could obtain some.[v] In January the following year Ellen herself was awarded the highest accolade in the Rose Universe: the Dean Hole Memorial Medal. I suspect that this time she turned up in person to receive the honour.

Meanwhile, poor Jack Tremayne was still in Italy, still battling with the recalcitrant Clodoveo and still trying to buy Boccanegra. Lord Berkeley was kicking up again, having had enough of Ellen's trying to buy and sell properties from under him, the latest being the Croft, a Warley cottage that she was offering to the Amateur Gardeners' Society.

At this point I have to admit defeat when it comes to Ellen's finances. The documents, found in the same batch as the Amateur Gardeners' papers, are often literally half-eaten and the complex web she had built was hard enough to understand by her own (multiple) solicitors. Even using Lord Berkeley's recently recovered correspondence we can only vaguely stab at what happened. It seems Ellen tried to reopen the Boccanegra deal by telling Berkeley some Americans were interested (I have no idea if this was true). She then decided to accept John Tremayne anyway, but had already taken out a sub-mortgage against the money she would get for the deal, seemingly oblivious to Lord Berkeley's share in the matter. It doesn't help that the documents are muddled up with other deals for several unconnected properties whose identities and addresses are missing.

There are no two ways about it – however bright she may have been, however talented, Ellen Willmott was a terrible businesswoman. Over and over, her solicitors *still* tried to explain that she couldn't repeatedly mortgage something already in hock to someone else. I don't know how *Proprieta Tremayne* was finally chiselled into the gates at Boccanegra, but someone – perhaps Ellen, perhaps Lord Berkeley, perhaps the man in the moon – accepted Jack's offer of £4,000 down payment and £6,000 mortgage.[171] Ellen sent him her garden notes and plant lists, probably more with relief than sadness, though at least

---

171 Roughly £618,000 today.

confident she was selling her tarnished dream to someone who really wanted it and intended to recreate its brief splendour. Lady Menzies quietly stepped away from the fray.

New onslaught arrived, a threatening letter from the Inland Revenue; Ellen got her solicitor to write saying that although, no, Miss Willmott had never filed a tax return, she *had* paid whatever was demanded and probably even merited a rebate. Amazingly, in this particular case, she did receive a small sum from the taxman, but her general financial situation did not improve. Apart from her occasionally disappearing into town with jewellery and returning home without it we do not know how she lived day-to-day.

It would be a mistake to believe that she was permanently miserable over all this. Indeed, I'd argue the opposite. Now in her mid-sixties, Ellen Willmott started wearing metaphorical purple. It was as though she had finally learned to roll with the punches and derive her characteristic black humour from whatever lumps life sent her. She powered through everything, energetic as ever, a battleaxe in the most positive sense. She continued to write twenty-odd letters a day, and receive a similar number, fighting for the causes she believed in – the Violet Douglas-Pennant case rumbled on – and keep up with a dizzying number of clubs, from the Hardy Plant Society to the Gilbert White Fellowship.

One by one, Warley's borders and hothouses were abandoned – the orchid house and walled garden last – but the alpine garden remained as magnificent as ever. Ellen still hybridised her roses, still experimented with novelties, still turned up to every RHS meeting and committee – 'a gracious, benevolent presence'.[vi] Part of the fun of committee reports was Sir William Lawrence's 'Miss Willmott wore . . .' section, in which he described Ellen's 'impossible' buttonhole. It's probably a good job Sir William didn't mention the rest of her clothes, which bore little resemblance to the stylish New Woman Ellen had once epitomised. Right up to 1921 she had at least remained curious about fashion, requesting (and keeping) a variety of fabulous catalogues with colour plates advertising the new, daringly short styles, even if she didn't buy much. After Rose's death, such frivolity no longer mattered. Apart from a collection of gigantic (and frankly hideous) hats, she now seemingly wore whatever she laid her hands on first each morning. Housekeeper Annie Cotterill was discreetly tasked by Ellen's nieces to keep an eye on the worst vagaries of their aunt's personal appearance after an unfortunate incident where, meeting Queen Mary, Ellen forgot her gloves. She borrowed a pair from a friend on the station platform which – horror! – turned out to have holes.[vii]

She continued to judge shows, from Chelsea to local school events, where she gave out seeds from her garden. Miss Willmott had always enjoyed the company of children and some of the best letters in the collection are from random kids writing excited missives to an elderly woman who understood their wonder at the world. My personal favourite is a young fellow called Hughie, to whom Ellen gave free reign of her music room.[172] Hughie sends her 'secret codes', drawings of her gas-powered organ, descriptions of his explorations and reassures her that he hasn't broken the hunting horn she lent him – yet. Ellen's replies haven't survived but would have been in a similar vein. For all the 'mean old woman' reputation she would acquire, especially after her death, the sheer number of letters from people who think she's great, even from this period in her life, is overwhelming. At the same time as Lord Berkeley – who had also enjoyed her company until he made the mistake of getting financially involved – was foreclosing on her, Ellen was getting letters from Colchester Museum, thanking her for a donation.[173] The Women's Farm & Garden Association thanked her for arranging a table at a show. A clergyman thanked her for congratulating him on his sermon. Gardeners thanked her for her generosity. Norah Lindsay, who would later become one of the great twentieth-century garden designers, was picking herself up after the collapse of her

---

[172] Possibly a member of the Tower family, South Weald.

[173] Some ancient keys she'd found in the back garden.

marriage, and facing financial difficulties. Ellen, perhaps understanding Norah's predicament more than most might guess, visited with advice then sent swathes of plants to start afresh.

Despite working with young journeymen, employing female gardeners during the war and flirting with the idea of a gardening school for women, Ellen had never really gone in for formal teaching. Now she took on an apprentice. Jaqueline Tyrwhitt was excited to be Ellen's protégée, but she was a young woman in an old garden. Set to work for the Amateur Gardeners' Society under Jacob Maurer, her interests were elsewhere. Ellen did what she could, but at Madrigal Society rehearsals told Mrs Tyrwhitt her daughter didn't have her mind sufficiently on gardening. Jaqueline later admitted: 'I was too young and impatient to learn all I could have and should have from Miss Willmott',[viii] and instead of resting after a day's work, sneaked up to town to meet her friends. Unfortunately, those friends were the British Fascists. After less than a year trying to secretly juggle Ellen Willmott's garden with BF meetings, Tyrwhitt left Warley. I am glad to say she was soon disenchanted with fascism and settled down to become an influential town planner, eventually building her own garden in Greece. During the Second World War, Jaqueline Tyrwhitt joined the Women's Land Army in 'loyalty to the kindness and charm of Ellen Willmott – one of the few women I've loved'.[ix]

Ellen doesn't seem to have had much luck with her protégées. She would, later, take on a second apprentice, Yella Bullion, about whom I can find virtually nothing save that, apparently, she went on to design a garden for Adolf Hitler at Berchtesgaden. Allied footage of the bombed Berghof, however, shows no signs of a lost garden, and even today the Biergarten at the Eagle's Nest restaurant doesn't have much in the way of plants. Ellen's taking on female apprentices does put into perspective one well-bandied anecdote, though. When Bach Choir chum Beatrix Havergal founded her famous Waterperry School of Horticulture, Ellen told her women would be 'utterly hopeless and unsafe in the borders'.

How anyone has ever taken this as anything other than a joke with an old friend baffles me, but it is often quoted to 'prove' Ellen was some kind of woman-hater.

Ernest Wilson wrote from the Arnold Arboretum, Harvard, where he had finally settled, happy and contented, with Mrs Wilson, as assistant to the now very elderly Charles Sprague Sargent. 'He is an institution rather than a man,' wrote Wilson, knowing the end was near for his old champion and mentor.[x] Ellen was only too aware of the fact. Her friends were dropping with frightening regularity. She'd lost the Revd. Bidder and William Wilks in 1923, Old Molly and Sir Dighton Probyn the following year. Poor Alfred Parsons, who had died in 1920, the same year as Ellen's old enemy Reginald Farrer, now seemed a lifetime ago. On 20 November 1925, just as Warley was getting ready for a visit from Queen Mary, Ellen received a telegram, cancelling the lunch due to the death of another friend, Queen Alexandra. A jewelled, ivory paperknife arrived at Warley soon afterwards as a memento. We have never found it. Ellen would later open Warley as part of the first-ever National Gardens Scheme event, in memory of Alexandra's love of flowers.[174] She continued to enjoy Royal visits well into the 1920s. One story I have never been able to prove talks of her arriving at Brentwood station to find a police constable trying to control a sudden crowd straining to see the King and Queen. On being told she could go no further, Ellen replied, 'But I must, they're coming to have tea with me.'

If her friends weren't dying, they were in mental distress. Robert Valentine was still in deep mourning in 1925, still fixating on the good times, when Monsieur Frédéric used to drive too fast to Lyon, Geneva and the Grand Chartreuse: 'What a pace he used to travel! It all seems now like a dream.'[xi] At Christmas his letter pleads with Ellen not to sever herself from Spetchley despite the sad memories. He needs her – and there *is* skating . . . Robert has not donned his own pair; it reminds

---

[174] June 1927.

him too much of dear Rosey, but 'do come, dear Ellie'.[xii] Miller Christy wrote obliquely regretful letters about what 'might have been' in between musings on planting primroses upside down into cowpats to turn them red.

On 6 February 1927, Ellen arrived in town for the latest Douglas-Pennant meeting, found herself early and decided to do a little shopping in the Veiling and Scarf department of Galeries Lafayette department store, Regent Street.[175] What happened next is unclear, but as she left, Ellen was stopped by the store detective and arrested for shoplifting a black and red scarf, value 13s 6d. Ellen protested loudly, to no avail. To be fair, the store was one of a number of high-end shops being targeted by an all-female shoplifting syndicate, the Forty Elephants, an offshoot of the notorious Elephant & Castle mob. Led by 'Queen' Diamond Annie, the gang's *modus operandi* was to enter stores dressed to the nines, ask to see a selection of big-ticket items, then quietly snaffle a few away in voluminous pockets. Ellen Willmott had, it would seem, done all of the above except, of course, the dressing-up-to-the-nines bit. She was escorted to the manager's office and the police were called.

Outraged, Ellen demanded her phone call. It was only when it became clear she was ringing Queen Mary that the manager twigged he was not dealing with a run-of-the-mill tough. He hastily retracted, but by now, Ellen had the bit between her teeth. She told the manager he had started this, and he must now follow through. She spent the night in a cell at Marlborough Street Police Station and was brought up before the beak the following morning. Back home, Robinson the butler was doorstepped by reporters. 'Clear off, I'm not talking to you,' he yelled, slamming the door in their faces.[xiii]

Ellen Willmott was defended by Sir Henry Curtis-Bennett, KC. Queen Mary's Private Secretary, the Lord Lieutenant and Chief Constable of Essex were her character witnesses. She was, naturally, acquitted then

---

175 More or less where Hamleys is now.

made a long, surprisingly 'lefty' speech: she was lucky to have friends – what if she'd been a poor woman with no contacts? She'd have been behind bars by now and no one would care!

She'd won, but there was no way Ellen Willmott was going to let the humiliation go. Defendant turned plaintiff, she now took the matter to the King's Bench, accusing Galeries Lafayette of false imprisonment and malicious prosecution. The papers loved it, and for good reason: the juicy details that came out in the witness box paint a vivid picture, though exactly what of is unclear.

Did she do it? Who knows. Just when I come to my own verdict, I change my mind. Ninety-odd years later, we only have the defence statement, not hers. Carefully worded, it claims Miss Willmott looked at the scarf, bought a cheaper one, said, 'I have paid you, haven't I?' before rushing out into the street and crossing the road 'at some personal danger'.[xiv] The unpaid-for scarf was found on her person. An anonymous customer said she'd never witnessed anything so brazen. Miss Willmott was even alleged to have 'committed a nuisance' on the shop floor.[176] Genuine mistake or grand larceny, it was great theatre.

The papers all carried the verdict – Ellen had been wrongfully accused – while rehearsing the sordid details one last time, just in case anyone hadn't already heard them. I am not sure what she would have made of the accompanying foggy mugshot accidentally being of Lady Suffolk.

To Ellen, victory was triumph. To the rest of the world, she just came across as pugnacious, and it is this Ellen Willmott, the angry eccentric, that reverberates down the decades.

One of the best-known 'funny Willmott' stories is that she carried a loaded revolver in her handbag. She once showed it to Annie Cotterill after the housekeeper suggested Ellen might consider not returning home at all hours wearing her favourite diamond brooch in her hat and sporting hands full of valuable rings. 'Whoever comes near me

---

176 'Committing a nuisance' usually meant public urination, but as EAW was in full capacity, I can't see this as a possibility. Perhaps it refers to spitting.

will get the worst of it,' Ellen confided.[xv] Ellen the Fierce knew how to use it, too; Warley included a rifle range as far back as the 1880s. It's a good job that poor, shocked Annie didn't look at what was probably in Ellen's pocket. I found the brass knuckles described at the top of this chapter nestling among layers of her correspondence, and although we can't be completely sure it was hers, there was nothing of anyone else's in that trunk.

Knuckledusters in the nineteenth and early twentieth centuries were not considered particularly sinister. Anyone could pick them up in hardware or sporting goods shops, and they were not expensive. There were even ladies' versions. The 'Brute Tamer', made by Winchester, came with swirling, solid-brass 'pyramids' over each dainty, girly-sized stall. Knuckles only became 'offensive' when they began being routinely used by gangsters like the Forty Elephants, rather than carried in pockets for self-defence, though their leader 'Diamond Annie' was notorious for just using her rings.

Miss Willmott's loaded revolver has always been giggled about as part of her notorious 'fighting spirit'. I confess I smiled myself when I found the brass knuckles. The idea of a would-be mugger discovering their little old lady victim is tooled-up to the gunnels is, frankly, funny. At first. In reality, it represents genuine, secret fear, of a modern world in which that little old lady no longer wields power. Ellen was seventy in 1928 when all this happened. She led an active life, singing in the Bach choir, attending committee meetings and visiting friends, and she talked the talk. So what if she got back to Brentwood station in the small hours? She'd walk home, like she always had. Yet she *was* seventy, and late at night in dark, deserted lanes, demons lurk. One evening, returning from a National Art Collections Fund reception in full satin splendour, her diamond tiara stashed in a brown paper bag, those demons got the better of her. Someone was behind her. There were footsteps. Spooked, Ellen shoved the tiara into a hedge and ran. Robinson spent the next day searching for it and bringing it back to Ellen's museum of a house.

THE GRANDE DAME

Museum of a house. Yes. Ellen had a mansion full of priceless artefacts, not that she seemed to remember that whenever she reached the next financial crisis. The nights were dark, and the entire neighbourhood knew she lived alone. The handbell kept by her bed to scare intruders was not enough and Robinson, whose wife did like to see him on an occasional basis, didn't always sleep at the house. Ellen could stand solitude, but still the shadows haunted. Warley had been burgled before, when there was a houseful of people; thefts from the grounds were a semi-regular occurrence. One of the last members of staff she let go was the nightwatchman and his dog, sacked for falling asleep on the job, but now, even though Warley had never had electricity installed and only had partial gas supplies, Ellen Willmott had a deafening alarm system fitted to every door and window. Another protected the strongroom, filled to bursting with gold medals, silver cups, canteens of cutlery and a complete, twelve-place silver dinner service that Robinson spent all day polishing whenever royalty visited. Outside, in another well-worn tale of Willmott eccentricity, she famously booby-trapped her prize daffodils to deter bulb thieves. This provided hours of amusement to the local kids, who used to throw things at the wires, hoping to trigger the airguns. Paranoid she might be, but just because you fear people are after you doesn't necessarily mean you're wrong, and judging from contemporary correspondence, plant theft was a serious consideration.

Ellen's energy, however, seemed irrepressible. She had become fanatically interested in archaeology and was a member of or regularly corresponded with fourteen societies.[177] She was a founder member of the Roads Beautifying Association, which carried the laudable aim of making Britain's highways look nice. She wrote the foreword to a retrospective lecture/article about Gertrude Jekyll and attended the wedding of her nephew Rob.

There were more losses: Charles Sprague Sargent, 1927, Miller Christy,

---

[177] A rough count shows her as belonging to or corresponding with 134 societies including historical, political, archaeological, arts-related, scientific and sporting.

1928, but, sad as they were, Ellen had steeled herself for these departures. Nothing prepared her for the next. Her beloved niece Eleanor, to her father's shock, ran away with the family chauffeur, an Irishman called John Brennan. She married 'the unmitigated scoundrel'[xvi] but died, three months later, in childbirth. For Robert Valentine, still missing his Rosey, life turned bleak indeed. For Ellen, the future turned black.

For many years she had treasured the idea that one of her nieces would take on Warley and its battered but brilliant garden. The first blow had fallen when young Betty changed her life. Instead of going home after a shooting party in Scotland, September 1926, Betty had travelled to Lourdes, writing to her father that she had felt a calling and now had to follow her heart. Robert Valentine's youngest child became a postulant on 1 November, was clothed as a novice in 1927 and professed in 1928. Never in the history of nun-dom has there been a happier, jollier, more fulfilled nun, but in forswearing the material world, Sister Marie Edward de Sion also relinquished the opportunity to continue her aunt's earthly garden. Now Ellen had lost her other niece who, the family later discovered, had been living with Brennan for the previous three years and running a pub in Droitwich. Warley would now pass to her nephew Rob who, with the prospect of Spetchley Park and Berkeley Castle to look after, was hardly going to have time to care for a rundown estate in Essex. A well-meaning letter from Mayfair jeweller Tessiers summed up the misery, somewhat tactlessly advising Ellen to pawn her best stuff as she now had 'no one in particular to leave it to'.

No way. Ellen's armour was complete – a carapace of bravado, pity and calculation – and it was going to be decorated. Lots. She may have no one to leave it to but Ellen still derived huge pleasure from her jewellery, wearing as much of it as possible, whenever possible, whatever the state of the rest of her attire. The Russell sisters remembered her at dinner parties, glittering with diamonds, seemingly unaware of the conversation around her. Suddenly she would pile in with a swift, devastating comment, then retreat, chuckling.[xvii] The same traits that have me throwing up my hands in despair, searching for 'what really happened' in Ellen Willmott's life, made her the ideal *raconteuse*. Wild exaggeration, constant reinterpretation and a bard's sense of narrative saw her murdering facts to create each perfectly formed, malice-studded anecdote, told with a relish that rendered it as innocent as it was cruel. Her target was just as likely to be herself as anyone else.

Ellen attended the International Horticultural Congress in London, was elected to the RHS floral committee. She attended garden parties at Eton and Harrow and private views at Burlington House. She was elected as an honorary life member of the Alpine Garden Society; no one mentioned that in former times she would have been a founder member. Annie Cotterill left to get married. When Queen Mary popped a button on a visit, poor old Robinson was the only person in the house who knew how to sew it back on.

In 1932 Ellen reached the pinnacle of French gardening, created *Dame Patronesse* of the *Société d'Horticulture de France*. She was elected to the RHS Lily Committee. Yet she was uneasy. When Herbert Jekyll died suddenly that September, Ellen had a gut feeling she should meet with his sister, and sooner rather than later. She managed to visit Gertrude at Munstead Wood one last time. Ellen and a now extremely elderly William Robinson attended the December funeral. She later told mutual friend Hebert Cowley, 'She was such a sensitive and great personality. I so thoroughly realised it, perhaps more than others.'[xviii] Ellen was right; she was one of the very few who had known the pleasures and pitfalls of being a high-profile female horticulturist in days when most were male.

The following May the newspapers announced another passing: Lady Mount Stephen. Since her husband's death in 1921, Gian had blossomed. George had never allowed her to join him on his frequent trips to Canada; now she had seen the mountain he named himself for, ridden his railroad and even tried her hand at his hobby, salmon fishing. The women's mutual friend Queen Mary would have kept both parties up to date with gossip, but I don't believe that Ellie and

Gian ever actually met each other again, perhaps not even since Rob's christening.[178] Much as this romantic biographer would like to imagine a heavily veiled woman in black standing mysteriously at the back of the church, Ellen would have been too poorly to attend her former confidante's funeral, even if she'd wanted to go. A bout of pneumatic bronchitis had become so serious that her imminent death was openly and heartbrokenly discussed by friends, neighbours and brother-in-law. She refused to see a doctor or go to bed but, despite dire portents, Robinson had finally been able to write that his mistress was recovering and enjoying jelly and champagne. Ellen wouldn't have attended the Sotheby's sale of Gian's effects, either, but she might have smiled at Lot 176, a portrait, by Lady Helena Gleichen, of a cheeky black Pomeranian dog called Chang.

Age was catching up, but Ellen wasn't done yet. She had defied rheumatism for nearly forty years; she was used to powering through pain. The generally acknowledged image of Ellen Willmott in her later years shows a bitter old woman seething in malevolent silence in her crumbling conservatory, and there *were* days when she did not go out. There were days when she hated the world. There were days when the bitterness struck, when the malice exploded and the eccentricity flared. There were more days when she'd stride down to the station in time for the first excursion-price tickets, ready for her next adventure.

Some say that, on 26 September 1934, seventy-four-year-old Ellen went up to London for a show, moved on to a dinner party with friends and arrived home close to midnight. Others claim she'd been ill to the point of immobility for months, though journal articles and letters from friends acknowledging visits – even thanking her for photos of said excursions – preclude this. All we know is that on the morning of the 27th, James Riches Robinson found his beloved mistress lying on her bedroom floor, dead.

---

178 Gian sent a brief condolence from Winnipeg after Rose's death, but there is no indication they ever physically met after 1898.

Chapter Twenty:

Renaissance

MISS WILLMOTT'S GHOST

Bought from the local garden centre, this small paper packet contains an average thirty seeds. There are several brands available; Eryngium giganteum, 'Miss Willmott's Ghost', is a staple for twenty-first-century gardeners looking for a spooky silver plant to bring structure to their borders and romance to their lives. Sales of this reputedly invasive silver sea holly are usually accompanied by a hilarious anecdote: of an equally prickly, otherwise obscure Edwardian gardener who carried pockets-full of the seeds to sprinkle in other people's gardens. These would emerge, phantom-like, a couple of years later. These days the story is always accompanied by the caveat: 'allegedly'.

EVERY NEWSPAPER CARRIED a slightly different version of Miss Willmott's demise; whether she crashed from her breakfast table or suffered a coronary upstairs in the bedroom hardly matters. Discovering his employer on the floor, Robinson must have known it was the end of an era. Ellen had been a woman out of her time for years. Almost all her friends were dead; of her family only the ever-grieving Robert Valentine and his son Rob were left.[179] It was more than that, though. Miss Willmott's death snapped another fibre in the thin thread connecting the straitened 1930s with the Empire's 'golden days'.

In her later years Ellen had, it has been said, developed resentment towards organised religion. 'If ever I get to heaven, it will be no thanks to the nincompoop along here,' she used to say, pointing to the Catholic church, 'nor,' she would continue, switching her gaze to the Protestant church along the road, 'to the lunatic down there.'[i] The comment is understandable enough, given the gloom of the past twenty-odd years, but I'm willing to wager it was just another of her famous melodramatic statements. The profundity of her Catholic beliefs had dictated her entire life; she wouldn't – couldn't – have totally given up now. Ellen's body rested at the 'nincompoop' church her godmother had built, her parents had decorated and she herself had been benefactress to. Holy Cross and All Saints is still sometimes called 'Miss Willmott's church'. On Monday, 1 October 1934, after Requiem Mass, the coffin was borne to Brentwood Cathedral to lie beside that of her father. No one was

---

[179] Betty lived in Paris as a nun.

RENAISSANCE

left to ask where her mother might be. Loyal to the end, Ellen's aged head gardener Jacob Maurer gathered Warley's finest flowers for the interment. Her equally loyal, equally aged butler kept up appearances for the benefit of a long list of mourners.

Two days later, a more opulent Requiem Mass was held at the Church of the Immaculate Conception, Mayfair. Among the sundry lords, ladies and viscounts a few of Ellen's old friends were still alive. Kew's retired Director David Prain came, as did current Director Arthur Hill. *Country Life* founder Edward Hudson paid his respects alongside the Courtney-Pages from the National Rose Society and Antoinette Vanderpant, of the Women's Farm and Garden Union. Agnes Jekyll attended in memory of her husband Herbert and sister-in-law Gertrude; Mary Hanbury in memory of various members of a family who had loved Ellen from her earliest years. Hilda and Violet Douglas-Pennant attended both funeral and memorial. At an extremely doddery ninety-four, however, William Robinson was forced to send a representative, as was eighty-four-year-old Princess Louise.

How Ellen was portrayed in those few days after her death has largely shaped the image we have been peddled ever since. Obituaries allow us to overstate someone's best aspects and insinuate their worst with weasel words of praise; the subject has no right of reply. Of the numerous tributes, from the *Telegraph* and *Times* to syndicated national and international newspapers, *Revue Horticole* to the *British Fern Gazette*, a few things were omnipresent. Invariably described as 'musician and gardener' – in that order – Ellen Willmott's 'boundless energy', which 'she retained up to the last, an astonishing vitality'[ii] was mentioned without fail.[180] At the top of every obit was the usual erroneous claim that her garden had originally been laid out by diarist John Evelyn. Of all her accomplishments it baffles me that absolutely every writer wasted column inches implying Ellen merely 'improved' someone else's garden.

---

[180] And this despite an operation in 1921, which we only know about via Alice de Rothschild and some hospital bills. Neuralgia is usually a debilitating condition. Ellen Willmott did not stop either side of the op.

Readers then and now, myself included, took and take what they please from such eulogies. We fashion them to our own arguments and the eye is always drawn to a nice, juicy, backhanded compliment. The most famous Willmott obit-quote comes from the *Gardeners' Chronicle's* 6 October edition: 'Faithful with an equal and emphatic fidelity to her likes and dislikes of people, Miss Willmott did nothing by halves,' writes the anonymous obituarist. 'She would, by her incisive judgements upon them, suggest to the mind a new version of the divine injunction "love your enemies", for she undoubtedly got a lot of enjoyment out of them.' This implication, that Ellen had more feuds than friends, just isn't true. Many loved her, almost disproportionately, and often in spite of her behaviour.

The official obituary in the same paper digs a little closer to the truth: 'Miss Willmott was not always loved by those who sat at ease in high places.' Down the years, many have chosen to stay with the 'not always loved' image, rather than delve into *why* certain bigwigs didn't like her. The rest of the article 'jokes' that Miss Willmott believed prospective committee members should 'pass an examination' before being admitted. In other words, she expected people in positions of power to have dedication and expertise rather than influential mates. The rest of the *GC* obit describes her courage, reminding us that 'the "slings and arrows of outrageous fortune" left her still bright and cheerful'. The writer remembers a typical garden visit:

'"You must have that," Miss Willmott would say, "it does well at Warley,"' until at the end of the walk the list of things that ought to be in the garden was longer than the owner's purse. But presently would come a great, untidy, bulking sack, full of all the plants Miss Willmott had said should be in the garden, and others besides, jumbled up, but precious. Her presents were always greater than her promises.'

The *Chelmsford Chronicle* reconfirmed in print something we already knew from countless letters and photographs: Ellen the comedian. 'She was brilliant as a companion, always seeing the humorous side, with a

RENAISSANCE

pretty taste in leg-pulling.' We're even given an example, quoting a time Ellen had been asked what a sermon had been about. 'She answered promptly, "about ten minutes".' I don't know who wrote the piece, it is merely attributed to 'a correspondent', but this is a highly personal tribute.[181] 'A fine intellect is gone,' it laments; 'her company was a great refreshment; her talk was so witty and well-spiced. In effect,' it sighs, 'she was a genius.'

Ellen had always hoped to leave Warley to one of her nieces, but with Eleanor dead and Betty behind the veil what was left of Ellen's broken fortune fell to her nephew Rob. Captain Robert Berkeley hadn't yet inherited either Berkeley Castle or Spetchley Park but he had been more or less running Spetchley for years, an uphill task in the 1930s. He did not need a mouldering house in Essex filled with mouldering antiques and mouldering memories. Immediately after his aunt's death there had been rumblings of Warley's garden 'going to the nation'. Even after the 'attentions' of Lady Angela Forbes and Ellen's own inability to keep up in later years it would have been worth it. In 1912 James Chapman Shenstone claimed 100,000 plant varieties at Warley.[iii] A newly discovered 1908 list suggests Shenstone is out by a decimal point, but even ten thousand specifically named species, varieties and cultivars in a single garden makes Warley one of the finest plant collections in Edwardian Britain. *The Kew Bulletin* hoped the National Trust would take it on. Another small cohort led by Daisy, Countess of Warwick, tried to get the RHS to designate it as an eastern outpost of Wisley: 'It would be a thousand pities if a place that should be the Mecca of all garden lovers were to pass into private hands and so be lost as an open and accessible example of a great botanical garden.'[iv]

Nothing came of it. For the second time in just over ten years auction catalogues were drawn up. Heartbroken, Jacob Maurer loaded Warley's

---

[181] My money is on local friend Champion Russell.

best specimens (and those Versailles planters) on to a Pickfords' removal van destined for Spetchley.

The sale took ten days: three for Sotheby's to clear Ellen's most valuable books and manuscripts, six for local auctioneer Kemsley to flog her possessions, one for her home. Crowds rocked up to see how 'the old woman' had lived. To poke at her furniture, peer into her bedroom, pry into cupboards and, perhaps, purchase a small souvenir from among the cheaper items at the end of the day out. After all, everything must go. Chippendale chairs, Queen Anne bureaux, Arabian bedsteads, Axminster carpets, lacquer screens, Persian rugs, Ming incense burners; enough travelling trunks for an Atlantic crossing. Ellen's world was laid bare, her daily intimacies exposed for the world to gawp at. Her cuckoo clock. Her stockpot. Her coal scuttle. Mrs Willmott's bath chair. That old Victoria carriage Fred had paraded around the village. For every Louis XV *chaise-longue* there was a Bathel's patent 'Roarer' blowlamp; every 'finely sculpted figurine' was balanced with 'five gallons of lubricating grease'. Ellen's porcelain took a whole day. Her musical instrument collection – trumpets, bassoons, zithers, alphorns (including a handy folding travel-model), lutes, cowbells, even a side drum alleged to have sounded at Waterloo – was balanced with items from outhouses: a croquet set, eight ladders, three alarm guns for anyone else that might fancy booby-trapping their daffodils. Right down to the very last knockings – Lot 2158: 'a heap of manure'; Lot 2159: 'a heap of leaf mould and a heap of manure' – it was one hell of a show.

There was only one real topic of gossip. Who would buy Lot 1, Warley Place itself? The lucky bidder was . . . drumroll . . . Mrs Eliza Annie Gray, licensee of that local public house. It has been whispered ever since that the purchase was an act of malice.

Enmity between pub landlady and lady of the manor dates all the way back to Chapter Fifteen, when Mrs Gray's horse backed into poor Robinson's car. Ellen took her butler's side and fought Mrs Gray's claim which, if Robinson's version of the incident is true (and he was a famously honest man), was fraudulent. We don't know what the verdict was, but the feud had festered ever since. Revenge-purchase or otherwise, the acquisition would prove catastrophic.

Mrs Gray left her prize unguarded, some allege, purposefully. Word spread quickly that millions of extremely valuable plants were up for grabs and folk arrived armed with sacks, spades and wheelbarrows. Looting, on a monumental scale, stripped the garden naked. The only plants that survived the wholesale destruction were either too large to remove, self-seeding annuals or bulbs that had disappeared deep below the spit of a spade. Even then, certain individuals returned the following spring to help themselves to Miss Willmott's daffs.

There was no way Kew, the RHS or the National Trust were going to be interested now. I may be maligning Mrs Gray here, the 'revenge' part of her neglect *is* only gossip, but it *was* neglect and however slim Warley's chances had been of being saved for the nation, that neglect stymied them all.

Miss Willmott's personal papers were bundled up, shoved into trunks and carted off to Spetchley. Perfectly understandably, when they arrived, no one knew what to do with them. Staff did what we all do with stuff that's too important to chuck but nothing we'll actually need: they piled them up in the cellar.

Mrs Gray held onto Warley just long enough to oversee its demise before selling it on. The new purchaser, property developer Alfred Joseph Traylen Carter, had big plans for the land, including a 'new village' of 35 houses and – downwind – a sewage works, all built on top of the once world-famous gardens. Detailed plans of his proposed scheme at Essex Record Office do, at least, specifically retain Ellen's alpine ravine.

The Second World War put a spanner in Carter's works. Knowing the British military's reputation for requisitioning buildings and failing to return them, he demolished Warley Place before the army could demand the keys.[182] The Luftwaffe finished the job, razing the stables to a thick layer of rubble.

Spetchley Park did not escape either, commandeered as a rest home for the 'Mighty Eighth' United States 8th Army Air Force division. Goofy, faded snapshots, an abandoned GI helmet and graffiti on the basement walls – *Tex, Chuck, Slim, Sparky, Hank, Frankie St Louis, Huey 'Frisco* – tell us all we need to know about those years. Everything was about survival; Ellen Willmott's personal effects, pushed to even damper, darker recesses, were the last thing on anyone's mind.

On Britain's return to Civvy Street a new, 'green belt' was placed around London with the intention of preventing urban sprawl. It put paid, once and for all, to Alfred Carter's development plans. He couldn't even sell up as the house was gone. Warley went to sleep, snug beneath an ever-thickening blanket of brambles, pernicious weeds and general undergrowth. It wasn't alone. Post-war country houses up and down Britain were being razed in their hundreds. In the new, jet-age of modernisation, space exploration and swinging youth, Heritage was a dinosaur.

Horticulture, too, had undergone a revolution, and was now a pastime for the masses. Who had room for blousy Victorian bedding and fussy Edwardian flounces? Even Gertrude Jekyll's memory was smothered in the streamlined '50s fascination for stripy suburban lawns and regimented rows of petunias. It was just too soon for the previous generation to have acquired a patina of charm. Just as today, many adore art nouveau and art deco while admitting brutalism still baffles, for mid-century gardeners, the old guard was as naff as the '90s.

Horticulture's 'new' stars had only known their predecessors in their older, diminished years; only remembered the likes of Ellen Willmott for the cranky stuff, not their early, pioneering work. Dr William T. Stearn is a typical example – an influential and important

---

182 Some suggest he just jumped the gun and started his project.

RENAISSANCE

modern expert who met Ellen Willmott as her powers were deserting her; who witnessed only the haughty, ageing Queen Bee and little of the genius behind the mask. Describing a 1920s book about *Curtis's Botanical Magazine*, Stearn describes how 'Miss Willmott, now a waspish old lady embittered by the loss of her money and the ruin of her celebrated Warley garden, declined to state her age and provided a portrait made in her twenties.'[v] The book, he continues, recalled a time when Willmott famously 'broke more hearts than lances',[183] which, Stearn sniffs, 'was certainly not true of her later'. I'm sorry – but what woman *d'un certain âge* has *not* been a little coy about their years and *not* supplied a younger picture of themselves for publication? Besides, it is entirely possible that the portrait Ellen did send had been painted in 1907, the year *Curtis's Botanical* dedicated their volume to her.

The tide was turning; just a little. Writing the same year as Stearn, Graham Stuart Thomas casually wondered the origins of the popular sea holly *Eryngium giganteum*'s varietal name, 'Miss Willmott's Ghost'.[vi] No one knew, though it is interesting that the notorious story about Ellen's sprinkling its seeds in other people's gardens was not brought up.

Gertrude Jekyll achieved her renaissance in the 1960s, 'rediscovered' and presented as an unthreatening, uncomplicated old lady who lived in a pastel paradise before the H-bomb. Jekyll hit a perfect storm: the rise of second-wave feminism, women's studies and a new nostalgia that saw young people wearing junk-shop Victoriana with platform boots and Union Jack miniskirts, hankering for hazier, simpler times. A single woman without issue, Jekyll's papers, like Ellen Willmott's, could have become forgotten or lost if it wasn't for the bulk of them being acquired by American landscape designer Beatrix Farrand.[184] For many years they have lived at the University of California, Berkeley, for

---

183 Attr. Sir William Lawrence.

184 Another of Charles Sprague Sargent's acolytes.

the world to enjoy. Ellen Willmott's papers were in another Berkeley 'collection': the back of the cellar.

Part of that 'perfect storm' was a turn in the way people 'did' history. Young radicals challenged the traditional chronologies of 'great events' by 'great men' and began to look more deeply into other aspects that make our collective past. In the fledgling discipline of garden history, groups of like-minded folk started to uncover 'secret' gardens that had, like Warley, been lost for decades. In Norwich, volunteers began uncovering the lost Plantation Garden, built in an abandoned quarry in the centre of town. In Surrey, enthusiasts rediscovered Painshill, an entire landscape garden. At Warley, Alfred Carter's son Norman and *his* son Paul joined with small work parties trying to control the forest of weed sycamores, giant hogweed and Himalayan balsam. In 1977, Norman Carter leased the site to the Essex Naturalists' Trust (now Essex Wildlife Trust) as a nature reserve. I am delighted to report that Linda Carter (Paul's widow) and her children remain as interested in Warley as ever.

Audrey Le Liévre was first to relate the most famous tale of all, of that pernicious sea-holly scattered in other people's gardens. I don't know where she got it from but once told it quickly took root. There is *some* matter in it. Ellen did love *Eryngium gigantium*; even had Alfred Parsons paint its portrait. I am also assured the plant can be a bit of a pest though I've never had any luck growing it myself. I doubt anybody believes the story's literal truth but it works because it is the perfect shorthand for a prickly personality.

Crucially, the 'bad stuff' related about Ellen Willmott – the meanness, the sharpness, the poor treatment of her staff, the general 'eccentricity' – dates from after 1897, the year I am convinced everything changed in her life. It was only after she experienced the loss of both her particular friend and her mother in the space of a few months that she seems to have hardened into something else. There is one anecdote, however, from before that date. The worst story I have ever heard about her; it is also relatively new, only surfacing in the past five or so years. It is doing the rounds, though, and it would be dishonest to ignore it.

A few years ago, Mr John Borron[vii] wrote to me of an old friend, Theresa Carr-Saunders, who had once told him that Ellen Willmott 'should have been' her mother. 'Ellen was very much in love with Teresa's father,' Mr Borron wrote of Captain Edmund Molyneux-Seel. On one of the captain's visits, however, Ellen was, he told me, annoyed by a caged bird: 'It kept on singing so she took it out of its cage and wrung its neck. This so disgusted Molyneux-Seel that he never saw her again.'

There's no doubt Theresa's father existed. He's there in Fred Willmott's diaries and a bunch of Ellen's photos. He looks great fun, a handsome man with a cheeky grin and a penchant for fancy dress. Even given Mr Willmott's poor observational skills there does not seem to have been any serious spark between the captain and Fred's girls. We follow Ellen, Rose and Captain Molyneux-Seel to the end of 1889 but, alas, the diaries run out after that. The trail picks up again briefly in 1891 at Rose's wedding, then runs cold again.

Clare Carr-Saunders remembers her grandmother Theresa as the family raconteur; an unreliable witness who loved to embroider far-fetched stories for dinner guests. Clare's father (Theresa's son) now lives with dementia, but sometimes, when recalling the past, he remembers quite well and Clare spoke with him for me.

Theresa, Clare reported back, had grown up fantasising that her father, full of fun but who had died young, had been in love with someone else before his marriage to her mother, a dour woman. 'Dad didn't remember the name himself but when I suggested Ellen Willmott, he latched on to that name,' Clare told me. 'He didn't seem to know about the "budgie strangling" story. I'm thinking it might have got embellished over time.'

There's even a question over which Willmott sister Theresa fantasised about. One day Theresa took her son (Clare's father) to a grand house, where they looked over the wall at a beautiful garden. Theresa told him that the woman who lived there 'might have been' her mother. When Clare asked her father where the garden was, he replied 'in the Midlands somewhere'. This implies Spetchley Park, in Worcestershire, not Warley Place, down in Essex.

Who knows what the real story is here? Seeing the life ripped from a caged bird would not have endeared most people to a potential life partner, and Edmund Molyneux-Seel was a gentle soul. But did the incident actually happen? How did Theresa learn of her father's 'first love' in the first place? Would he really have told a very young child about such a gruesome incident? Perhaps it started out small: 'Honestly, I'm going to wring that bird's neck if it doesn't stop singing . . .' and became embroidered, little by little, into an avian horror-fest. Short of Fred Willmott's other diaries surfacing there is no way of knowing, and until then the jury remains, most uncomfortably, out.

What the anecdote tells me, however, is that Ellen's role as gardening bugaboo is alive and kicking. It kicked again in 2017. An article in the Italian *La Republica* implied that Rose married in order to get as far away as possible from Warley, that Ellen had relationships with her lady's maid and apprentice, that she was guilty of shoplifting, was 'caught' with a gun in her purse and thought to be autistic by her contemporaries.[viii] I have sometimes been asked if I think Ellen was 'somewhere on the spectrum'. I know very little about definitions but I'm pretty sure we're all 'somewhere' on the scale. Some of Ellen's behaviour *could* suggest autism or one of its relatives: the compulsive collecting and hoarding, the obsessive mastery of skills, the seeming inability to understand when behaviour is 'off' or, on occasion, see a situation from any angle but her own. Yet this must be balanced with a vast capacity for empathy and discretion, not least in her nuanced refusal of Johann Bernhard Mann's proposal and dogged support for Miller Christy in his hour of need. Generosity, sympathy, reason, humour; if this was autism it was high functioning to the point of invisibility.

RENAISSANCE

Of course, I could be accused of similar muck-spreading. And it's entirely possible I'm wrong – this story, like all history, is not yet done. I would love there to be so much new material turn up that I need to rewrite. My own work continues; if I've made a mistake, I will be the first to admit it. All I can do for now is suggest a current-best interpretation and show my workings-out.

So why, then, have later generations – and perhaps I – concentrated on the bad stuff, instead of celebrating what she has given us? My guess is that it's the easier option. Attempts to pinpoint her legacy have floundered partly because she was a polymath. Ellen Willmott excelled at a multitude of things; it is hard for posterity to focus on a merry-go-round of achievement. It doesn't help that few of her passions aimed at immortality. Unlike Gertrude Jekyll, who bequeaths us the physical – dozens of books and gardens to visit – Miss Willmott's contribution was ephemeral. Her gardens are (mainly) gone. Her work in Hampton Court was forgotten as soon as *The Times* and *Telegraph* became fish-wrappers. Her redesign at Anne Hathaway's Cottage and plantings for New Place have only been acknowledged very recently and their full extent is still to be researched. Without Ellen Willmott, RHS Wisley might not exist as a garden, let alone be open to the public – but persuading someone else to buy something and then helping to make it happen is hardly the stuff of legend and her contribution is rarely mentioned.

Ellen's uncanny ability to raise plants no one else could, from seed collected on expeditions she had part-financed, was remarkable at the time but is, frankly, esoteric today. Her own, prize-winning cultivars, so famous in their day, are now largely extinct. Even the prizes are largely lost: gone is the Warley strongroom filled with silver bowls and golden cups. Ellen was 'one of the pioneers in the cultivation of Alpine plants' whose garden 'was one of the first to be constructed on the grand scale and to break away from the dreadful "rockwork" of mid-Victorian times'.[ix] But that garden no longer exists and can only be 'seen' by someone actively seeking her. Pinpointing genius without evidence is hard.

Ellen considered *Genus Rosa* as her one true gift to the world. It remains a beautiful object, but so vanishingly rare few even know about it. Dr Charles Chamberlain Hurst, the first botanist to study the genetics of the rose, thought it exceptional: 'The welding together of the artistic and scientific elements into a realistic whole with a universal appeal were due entirely to the genius of Ellen Willmott, and her monograph on roses stands as a lasting monument to her artistic and scientific sensibilities.'[x] Alas, she was dead when Hurst wrote the accolade and most reviews while she was alive were less generous. I can't help feeling she was highly sensitive to that criticism. Her carefully disguised Imposter syndrome burgeoned when the book did not sell and finally burst into bloom when her baby was remaindered. It is the only reason I can think of that drove her decision not to write – or garden – for the public; something that might have provided a passport to lasting fame.

One potential 'passport' could be Ellen Willmott's photography. We have still not managed to wade through all her output, but of the circa ten thousand prints, plates and negatives we have looked at so far (around two thirds) the range and quality of her work is astonishing. Conservation and cataloguing will take years, but this extraordinary collection may yet prove Willmott one of the nineteenth-century's finest horticultural photographers. Ellen's 'thank-you' albums could reside in any number of archives, from any time between around 1885 and 1934, and may not even be labelled as her work.

Ellen's choices outside the horticultural world were hardly posterity-chasing either. By all accounts a highly accomplished musician, she was an amateur in the most positive sense of the word. She played for herself; sang for the sheer joy of communing with others. In the twenty-three years she was a member of the Bach choir, I've found no record she ever took a solo. Politically, she was a team player too, angry at injustice but content to take her place in the rank and file of unfashionable women's

RENAISSANCE

issues rather than force herself into the spotlight. The Women's Party ultimately failed. Violet Douglas-Pennant's wrongful dismissal case was mercilessly crushed, yet it is due to valiant, fallen foot soldiers like her that women battled further into the twentieth century. Ellen Willmott never stopped battling either and, despite claims to the contrary, not always for herself. She added her name in the most literal sense to the cause for women to join all-male societies. She threw herself into what would become the Women's Land Army, content to be a backroom girl, attending meetings and committees rather than hogging the limelight. Ellen may not have achieved her gardening school for women, but she supported others, like Frances Wolseley and Beatrix Havergal, in theirs.[185]

❧

I called this book *Miss Willmott's Ghosts* because it recalls a world that no longer exists, populated entirely by shadows. A grainy, black and white world in which even major players have become phantoms, sometimes without even a monochrome snapshot to their once-famous names. However unreliable, Ellen Willmott is a go-between to the different country that is the past. Her connections are deep and wide; she knew pretty much everybody in a certain, rarefied level of Edwardian society. I am less convinced they knew her – and I am absolutely sure she did not know herself. Perhaps I should have called it *Miss Willmott's Demons*.

Countless times I've puzzled what to make of this unwittingly self-destructive woman who burned so brightly in a riches-to-rags blaze of tarnished glory; asked myself what I can take from her story. Her tangible legacy is thin – some Latin plant names, broken gardens, exhibits in museums; several dozen collapsed bankers' boxes full of mouldering correspondence. Yet she inspires many, and with each year seems to inspire more. While Warley slumbers on, every spring it becomes a riot

---

[185] Head gardener Rob Jacobs tells a marvellous, possibly apocryphal tale of Miss Willmott arriving at Waterperry in a chauffeur-driven, open-top car with gigantic tree-of-heaven seedling sticking out of it.

of colour, a joy to the thousands that turn up to see Miss Willmott's prize daffodils run wild. Ellen's French fantasy-villa is now Tresserve's *mairie*. The new village hall has been named *Salle Ellen Willmott*. Guido and Ursula Salghetti-Drioli-Piacenza have made Boccanegra's garden their life's work. In 2018 Ursula received the Veitch Medal, the highest RHS award available to someone outside the UK.

The Gardeners' Chronicle claims Ellen was not just a 'great gardener'. 'She was more,' it tells us, 'a great personality. That rare and magic quality alone can make those that have it immortal in our memories. Others are remembered for this or that gift, but Personalities are remembered, as living beings.'[xi] Ellen Willmott had that 'something', even in her day. As people discover Ellen today, they often feel inexplicably drawn to her. Undiluted charisma is not always appreciated. It invites the strongest feelings; individuals burdened with it endure the extremes of love and hate from those around them. Even the wearied inhabitants of Warley Village, who saw Miss Willmott at her least glamorous, were fascinated by her.

For me, Ellen Willmott's horticultural and other achievements, especially in those early, maverick days, pale in comparison with her later determination while under fire, never to give up, never to break. Reading her correspondence in chronological order is harrowing stuff from around 1914 onwards. Every day brings new indignities to her finances, health, loved ones and even her garden. Yet Ellen's daily mailbag also sparkles with gems. Letters of love, from friends, relatives and people she hardly knows. Replies to her requests for help for others. Up-to-the-minute horticultural debate, in which the correspondent genuinely wants to know her opinion. Invitations to the latest important events, which she will move heaven and earth to attend. So what if excursion-rate trains have replaced that lost fleet of carriages? So what if park benches now stand in for that comfy Empress Club bed? There is life out there, to be lived. Ellen Willmott remained a contender right up to the end.

It's very trendy to write about 'difficult women' of history at the moment. Ellen Willmott might have been born for the moniker. Complex, brilliant and confrontational, she did 'difficult' things, in both the physical 'hard-to-accomplish' and metaphorical 'hard-to-justify' meanings of the word. She refused to accept the traditional female role as a decorative homemaker, yet neither was she the uncomplicated, pure-of-heart, pioneering role model; the 'rebel-girl battling against marginalisation' it's fashionable to lionise today. Indeed, some might ask whether anyone born into such privilege could even be considered 'marginalised'. Perhaps our own twenty-first century privilege has already allowed us to forget the restricted lives *all* women, of whatever class, lived before some decided to get up and change things. Ellen Willmott could afford to stake her claim as a New Woman. That doesn't make the stake any less claimed.

I like Helen Lewis' idea that a 'thumbs up, thumbs down approach to historical figures is boring and reductive'.[xii] Her argument that we should not try to 'sand off the sharp corners on the movement's pioneers' hits home for me. Ellen Willmott should not be a role model for anyone, but she has much to teach us all. I find myself returning to that pocketful of seeds she may or may not have walked around with. The 'Miss Willmott's Ghost' story is, probably, a myth. Instead, we are haunted by something less palpable but vastly more powerful: Miss Willmott's spirit.

Epilogue:

Mouldlarking

A MAGIC LANTERN SLIDE

Black and white on glass, this photographic slide depicts a thickly wooded alpine hillside. At its summit an austere chateau oversees a meadow of rare summer flowers filling the foreground. The subject is interesting enough, but the slide is very curious. Measuring roughly three and a half inches by ten inches, it is three times too long to fit a regular magic lantern.

It is autumn 2022, six months since *Miss Willmott's Ghosts* was first published, and a year since I delivered the manuscript. I always knew Ellen's story would remain a major part of my life long after any book came out and, indeed, I cannot see a time when she and I will be done. Evidence left over from that first 'new cache' of letters, photographs and other documents found in 2013 still needed (and needs) transcription but, more pressingly, Berkeley and Spetchley Estate Archivist Karen Davidson and I still had a small mountain of those third-hand bankers' boxes filled with our own cellar exploits to plough through. Rescuing disintegrating documents cannot be hurried, not even for a book deadline. Even on an initial 'what's in the box?' basis, there are months – years – of work left, let alone the enormous task of conserving the material or asking in any depth what it means.

If anything, the search for Ellen has become even more intense since *Miss Willmott's Ghosts* first appeared. New avenues of enquiry are opening across the world. One of the most joyful things has been the huge response I have had from people who feel a personal connection to Ellen. These may be the grandchildren or even great-grandchildren of her former employees, or former residents of Warley, people who have acquired odd pieces of Willmott memorabilia that have bubbled up from the 1935 auction, or who have found intriguing references to her in archives or gardens I didn't know about. I am still hearing from people, from New Zealand to Canada, France to America, and the novelty never wears thin.

MOULDLARKING

As I write, in October 2022, the pile of boxes is going down, but there is still much to uncover, and it's getting harder. Admittedly we're now down to the true grot. We have become mould-larks, a name shamelessly adapted from 'mudlarks', pauper-children who scavenged the shores of the River Thames for lost treasures in Victorian London. Like the original mudlarks, we dip a cautious hand into the Willmott tombola, with no idea what it may retrieve. Rusty pins, broken paper clips, fused treasury tags, seized paper fasteners and unidentified sharps turn up more often now; the piles of spores and shredded paper left over at the end of a day's mouldlarking are thicker and dirtier. Yet this is still triage, an initial pre-sort before embarking on a much more thorough conservation job. Not a single scrap with anything at all on it is thrown away; the smallest fragment can reveal secrets. One tiny, tattered shred, once a letter, was headed 'Munstead Wood', identifying it as a missive from Gertrude Jekyll. Not a word remained of its contents but the salutation 'Dear Ellie . . .' written in the now-familiar hand, was different to every other letter we'd ever seen, each of which began with the more formal 'Dear Miss Willmott . . .' Thanks to that scrap, we now know that in their later years, these two great doyennes of gardening had become close enough to call each other by diminutives.

Even the humblest item can speak down the decades. I am particularly enamoured of the ivory-backed, *EAW*-monogrammed hairbrush found at Red House, the former home of Ellen's butler James Riches Robinson. I was charmed by this deeply intimate object above all the other bits and bobs discovered there. Fred Willmott's binoculars, a little wooden reading stand (probably turned by Ellen herself), and even what is almost certainly one of Ellen's own cameras; all are practical items, and I can understand why Robinson kept them.[186] It is unlikely he would have taken a battered hairbrush to use himself, however, and I can't imagine his wife would have thanked him for a heavily worn, second-hand brush

---

[186] These would have been purchases or gifts from his employer. Robinson was far too honest to have stolen anything.

monogrammed with someone else's initials. I can only believe that, for all the tittle-tattle about Ellen's making his life extremely difficult, James Robinson preserved this most intimate of objects in an act of pure love, a memento of someone he would genuinely miss.

Sometimes I've been able to put two and two together to finally make the four I've been searching for. Karen and I had been finding small but elaborately personalised gifts to Ellen in various states of disrepair for some time. Almost certainly Christmas presents, the leather-backed, silver-tipped notebook, diaries and propelling pencils bore Ellen's initials, and each was stamped with a strange squiggle that was clearly someone's signature. It was not dissimilar to Gian Mount Stephen's scrawl, and Karen and I wanted to believe they were from her, but something sat wrong in our collective gut.

On 25 January 2022, one of those weird wake-up-in-the-middle-of-the-night moments made me get out of bed to check a snapshot I'd taken of the flyleaf of one of Ellen's books, now held at the RHS Lindley Library. The catalogue of Norman Tower Garden, Windsor Castle, was dedicated to her by its author. We briefly met Sir Dighton Probyn, Queen Alexandra's (very) ancient retainer, in Chapter Seventeen, gossiping over his garden wall about Ellen's harpsichord. The strange squiggle on the flyleaf was exactly the same as that on the gifts, making me realise that Ellen was much, much closer to Sir Dighton – and his beloved mistress – than we had previously thought. This was compounded by the discovery of a delicate silver tea strainer, presented to Ellen at Christmas 1913, engraved with Sir Dighton's wobbly cipher and handwritten motto: *Thank God for tea*. A few days later my hand pulled out a disintegrating photograph of all three. The queen is in mourning, accompanied by her faithful servant, his beard reaching almost to his stomach, and by Miss Ellen Willmott, sporting a ridiculous hat with giant wings that look as though she is planning to take off.

The tea strainer was found in Spetchley's strongroom, which was not affected by the renovation works, and had not, therefore, been included in our four-day rescue mission. It is slightly more at leisure, therefore, that we can explore Ellen through personal objects that never made it to the 1935 auction. Each has a story. A christening cup, engraved to 'Helen' Ann Willmott, implies that Helen Tasker had been under the unfortunate misconception that her goddaughter would be named after her instead of Ellen's mother. A bag full of staggeringly beautiful mother-of-pearl gaming chips, engraved with oriental scenes, no two the same – did Ellen add that monogram herself? Two enormous matching travel dressing-trunks by Asprey of London, one for each sister. Everything inside, from a selection of hair tongs to portable oil lamps, is monogrammed on silver, tortoiseshell and green leather for Rose, red leather for Ellen. Both have heavily worn canvas covers. What must it have been to travel in such luxury? A delicate, blue cloisonné watch, also by Asprey, bears a confident, jewelled 'E' on its reverse. Alas, the velvet-lined, heart-shaped case for Ellen's tiara now contains only two tortoiseshell-and-silver securing combs and an enigmatic, handwritten note from jeweller Edward Tessier: 'There are 12 stones missing from this ornament'. Could it be worth checking the hedge Ellen so hurriedly stuffed the tiara into in Chapter Nineteen?

Teetering on a stepladder, I spied a black umbrella. Puzzled as to what a dusty, ordinary-looking gamp was doing in the silver cupboard I took it out, then burst into laughter. Its handle was a carved ivory skull on a silver base. At the back a small button worked its jaw, revealing a skeletal grin and bright red tongue; its empty eye sockets rolled ghoulishly. They probably once held precious jewels. Engraved 'R Willmott, Warley Place, Great Warley, Essex', it exactly fits Ellen's sense of humour – and her budget. I am certain it was a gift to Rose from her sister in the late 1880s, a time when both girls became interested in the supernatural, even joining the Society for Psychical Research. A full set of SPR journals from 1882 to 1900 wait patiently in around twenty-five as-yet-unsorted boxes of important, mainly horticultural publications, signed to Ellen by their illustrious authors. Ellen would later communicate with the society regarding some spooky occurrences in Sussex in 1899, and Karen has tracked down photographs where Rose carries the creepy brolly, reminding us of the sheer sense of fun the girls had in their early years.

A gigantic silver rose bowl, also in the cupboard and bedecked with medals, comes from a point in Ellen's life where she was winning so many prizes that she had to resort to drilling holes in them and hanging them from a single trophy. More medals remain in their boxes alongside a remarkable number of prizes awarded to Rose, who is coming into her own. Ellen's photographs not only reveal her sister's plantings at Spetchley Park Gardens, but they also prove Rose was highly revered in her own right. I am still trying to figure out which year Ellen took a series of grainy shots of the garden her sister made for the Chelsea Flower Show, filled with the Spetchley primroses Gertrude Jekyll coveted so much.

Ellen never produced a Chelsea garden but she was an important RHS judge for around forty years, and it was pleasing to find, along with her official's tag, information about what is expected of her, the days she can get into the show free and some (surprisingly unused) luncheon tickets. These would have been from later in her life, but it is equally exciting to find evidence from her earlier gardening years showing just how ahead of the curve she was. For example, I have had to revise my dating on her relationship with the Yokohama Nursery Company. Formed in Japan in the early 1880s, the firm's name was only formalised in 1893/4. The YNC would become famous in 1910 when they took a prominent stand at the Japan-British Exhibition (see Chapter Fourteen). I had been pleased to announce that Ellen had been buying exotic lilies from them since 1907. I was astonished, however, when two YNC catalogues turned up in the dust dated 1894, thirteen years earlier than the date on the first Yokohama receipt we have found – so far. It is always 'so far' with Ellen's papers and we have not yet begun serious work on her bills and receipts. A little digging revealed that British nurserymen Veitch & Sons had used YNC plants in building that Japanese showcase in Gian's Tufnell's back garden at Coombe Wood in Chapter Eight; I am now certain that that is where – and when – Ellen discovered them. The catalogues are exquisite. What looks at first to be staining on their covers turns out to be brushed gold. Inside, each variety is illustrated in glowing, full-page, hand-drawn colour. The Yokohama Nursery Company is still trading in Japan but lost their archive in an earthquake; these may be some of the only examples left.

We are still discovering Ellen's relationships with plant hunters, beyond Ernest Wilson's first (Veitch) and third (Arnold Arboretum) expeditions and trips by explorers for the Dutch company van Tubergen. Ellen Willmott National Collection holder Nick Stanley alerted me to an intriguing dedication in little-known naturalist Antwerp Pratt's 1906 *Two Years among New Guinea Cannibals* . . . where he particularly thanks Miss Willmott, 'without whose help the expedition could not have been undertaken'. We are hoping some newly tracked-down letters may reveal exactly what such 'help' consisted of.

Answers to some questions turn up when least expected. My puzzlement at the colour and size of Ellen's hair in Chapter Eleven, for example, was at least partly answered in a fat batch of receipts between 1904 and 1912, from a 'Mr Charles' who worked for G. Sutterlin, Court Hairdresser – 'Specialist for Hair Colouring and Artistical Wig Maker'. Over eight years Mr Charles lists in detail Ellen's many, *many* hairdressing requirements: nets, lotions, *papiers poudres*, manicures, pin curls, hair pads, dyes, 'bunches of curls', dressing, crimping, back combing and more than a hundred 'side pieces' alongside sample cards for a new hair switch asking Ellen if she would like to go the newly fashionable grey or stay dark haired. The sample switches are now sadly missing.

We turn up thousands of postcards. Most are unused, souvenirs of places Ellen visited, but each needs to be checked they are not always just views of British beauty spots, European cities, old master paintings or funnies that have tickled Ellen's ribs. A couple, for example, that we initially took for regular views of some cattle in a landscape, reveal that she bought a herd of highland steers so important that a set of commemorative cards was printed to celebrate the purchase. A sneaky peek into the top of the box I have earmarked for my next visit seems to show a complete series of Warley Farm accounts, each year carefully folded into crisp bundles, so hopefully we will learn more about the mysterious beasts. More postcards, nearly a hundred of them, are mementos of Ellen's visit – nay, pilgrimage – to Malmaison, home of her beloved Josephine Bonaparte. Ellen would not have seen the empress's by-then-ruined rose garden as a premonition.

While much of the material harks back to Ellen's heyday, there are vast amounts of letters, plant lists, receipts and, I am sorry to say, bills, from her later years. These make for much more sober reading. The 1920s seem to have been bad news for all save a few gilded, bright young things, but the sheer quantity of final demands, letters from creditors and direct requests for overdue subscription payments that are still turning up in almost every handful must have made even more of a daily onslaught of woe than I had previously imagined. Her attempts to clear the debts are equally heartbreaking, from trying to send in the bailiffs to a long-vanished Lady Angela Forbes to desperately attempting to sell her once-priceless musical instrument collection, most of which is now so badly eaten by woodworm and damp there are no takers. My eyes filled at a handwritten draft of a letter to an unknown recipient, scribbled in pencil on the back of a discarded letter telling Ellen she has been unsuccessful in the ballot for tickets to the annual general meeting of the Primrose League. In her familiar, almost unreadable scrawl she admits: 'Losing my sister has left me with only my garden to love. I am now thought of pityingly . . .' In August 2022 I found a small roll of Irish Sweepstakes tickets for the 1934 Derby, folded around a postage stamp-sized picture of Jesus.

Yet all this must be taken into account with the sheer number of positive things Ellen was doing in the 1920s and early '30s. This woman was in constant pain from chronic rheumatoid arthritis, overwhelming debt, crippling grief and ceaseless worry (a heartrending 1930 appointment diary kept by her brother-in-law Robert Valentine recounts the death in childbirth of her beloved niece Eleanor), and yet there she is, judging shows, attending openings, visiting friends, eating out and founding new societies, even as she is being kicked out of others (often quite brutally) for non-payment of subs. She continues to correspond with the gardening great and good. I was initially disappointed to find a large stash of empty envelopes, until I realised why Ellen had saved them: for the stamps. The missives come from across the globe; their return addresses and postmarks give us some idea of the breadth of minds with whom she was discussing horticulture. From Russia (later, the USSR) to New Zealand, Venezuela to Lithuania, Norway to Canada, Japan to Nigeria, including every European country, even empty envelopes can tell us that Ellen Willmott was in communication with practically every great botanical institution in the world, right up to her death.

It was no surprise to confirm that Ellen was unafraid to plough into new controversy, such as the museum-soup being concocted by the bigwigs at the Ashmolean, Oxford. I don't know (yet) how she met controversial curator Robert T. Gunther, who was trying to establish what is today the History of Science Museum and facing stiff opposition from all-comers. Ellen recognised an embattled character when she saw one – her unswerving support for causes such as that of Violet Douglas-Pennant are testament to that. Her correspondence with Gunther in the late 1920s, when she was in her early seventies, will hopefully explain more about the museum's acquisition of important antique scientific instruments and objects, not least for the jealous gossip about (and from) other institutions including the V&A who also want to get their paws on the loot. Gertrude Molyneux, from Ellen's Gian days, with whom she had never been close and who had not been in contact for forty years, now wrote chummily with the transparently ulterior motive of acquiring Ellen's best stuff for the Worshipful Company of Turners, while warning her off dealing with the Old Ashmolean. For reasons we can never know but certainly guess, Ellen chose Gunther, and although she sold some items, most seem to have been donated, showing astonishing generosity from someone under the constant threat of bankruptcy. We knew the History of Science Museum held her famous Holtzapffel lathe, described in Chapter Seven, but I had no idea Ellen had owned *two* world-class lathes, the other being a rose, a specialist geometric machine for detailed work, as used for engraving the die for Penny Black postage stamps and Fabergé eggs. Both now live in the museum along with some truly exceptional antique nautical instruments and timepieces.

For me, however, the most important and exciting thing emerging from those filthy boxes – and elsewhere – is the vast body of Ellen's photographic work. We initially estimated c.10,000 glass plates, negatives, prints and published works, but even last year we were realising this was a conservative estimate. The prints, especially, just keep on coming, in conditions ranging between near-perfect and 'doily', but all tell us something about her world and even early twentieth-century social attitudes. Without my glasses, I initially took one very small print to be a WWI soldier returning home with his kit bag, hailed by villagers. Specs on, magnifying glass poised, the photograph turns out to be Ellen's Mozambican chauffeur, Monsieur Frédèric, arriving for duty seven years earlier, in full livery. Every Warley inhabitant has come out onto their doorsteps for a gawp. The man himself remains elusive. We still do not know his first name.

More pictures of M. Frédèric playing with the Berkeley children around the Spetchley fountain have fetched up, however, among Ellen's many images of her sister's garden. Five new glass plates show Spetchley in glorious autochrome, sending present-day Head Gardener Chris Miller straight to specialist plant nurseries. And, in mentioning Ellen's colour work, we finally reach my object for this chapter.

I had always been intrigued by fleeting mentions of her magic lantern lectures but assumed that they stretched only as far as the famous shows she used to give the village children at Christmastime. After visiting the History of Science Museum at Oxford, I have been forced to re-evaluate. The archive holds around a hundred lantern slides, all that is left of a collection that once numbered thousands. Not all of the images are by Ellen, and one or two are clearly from somewhere else, a confusion that probably arose in the 1940s when the then curator turfed out Ellen's slides from their fancy 'Warley Place' cases to house his own. Some were made in colour, using the complex Sanger-Shepherd process introduced in the early twentieth century. Others have been hand-tinted with varying degrees of skill, ranging from professional quality, through 'decent amateur' to blobby examples probably coloured in by Ellen's young nieces and nephew (which may be why she saved them). Odd, single slides are sometimes part of commercial sets, which can be dated from catalogues or their subject matter, showing the long period over which Ellen worked. 'Will-o-the-Wisp', for example, is from *Natural Phenomena*, a 36-part lecture series for children from 1890. An image of Queen Victoria (*Longest British Reign – God Bless Her*) probably comes from 1897, perhaps purchased to go with a show based on those jubilee procession images Ellen snapped on 22 June that year.

Ellen mentions her magic lantern presentations quite casually in her letters, in a voice that makes it clear they are a regular part of her life. Many of the remaining slides are of her plants and gardens, and she certainly gave lectures about both up and down the country, but she also covered other topics, including fine art and architecture. I have no idea what the programme would have been when Ellen told her friend Gussie Bowles, 'Was doing a Magic Lantern for the Soho Girls Club last night & not in bed until 1-30-am', but I'm pretty sure endless close-ups of plants wouldn't have cut it for the young working women staying in the Greek Street hostel; I'm guessing comedy or ghosts. It does, yet again, however, show that Ellen didn't care about venturing alone into the less salubrious parts of London by night. At the other end of the scale, in 1920 she was humbly invited to give a scientific talk in the brand-new, state-of-the-art Ashmolean lecture theatre, Oxford. Perhaps this was where she first met Robert Gunther.

Willmott scholar Paula Sewell sent me a clipping from the *Essex Naturalist* showing that by 1915 Ellen was so skilled at the extremely complicated Sanger-Shepherd colour system that she was able to give the club a show about it:

> *Many of the slides were exceedingly beautiful and realistic and gave an excellent idea of the capabilities of the process. Miss Willmott made comments on the pictures and recounted the difficulties and triumphs attending the taking of the views and subjects . . . The apparatus and the process appeared to be expensive and difficult, but the exhibit showed that in skilful hands this method of coloured photography was quite in the front rank of this wonderful and most useful invention.*[187]

Using the auction catalogues of 1935, we can see why Ellen's magic lantern work has been overlooked: it (nearly) all got sold. Dozens of lots, including thousands of slides, mechanical slides with moving parts, screens, stands, special effects and no fewer than four magic lanterns show us only what Ellen had in her possession when she died; she was known to buy and sell photographic equipment throughout her life. One of the projectors is very interesting indeed. The Newtonian Universal Science Lantern was invented in the first years of the twentieth century, 'devised with a view to producing an instrument that shall be extremely portable and which shall yet be capable of producing with a minimum of trouble and rearrangement, most of the experiments required by lecturers on light, photography, colour and similar subjects'[188]. It cost £18

---

187 *Essex Naturalist*, Vol. 18, 1915.

188 Catalogue, Newton & Co., 1906.

in 1906 (£2,328 today). There were not many made and only someone very interested in presenting scientific lectures – and a lot of them – would invest in kit as expensive and specialised as this. I can think of at least one use Ellen would have put it to . . .

There are seven very curious slides in the museum's collection, including the one described at the top of this chapter. These are anomalies: exactly three times as long as a regular slide, depicting three identical-looking black and white images. They threw me. If they had been doubles, I'd have taken them for 3D 'stereoscopic' images (and yes, of *course* Ellen indulged in the nineteenth-century stereoscope craze) – but *three* identical pictures? Richard Crangle, from the Magic Lantern Society, solved the puzzle. Despite their appearance, these are extremely rare early *colour* images. The photographer would take three simultaneous monochrome photographs of the same scene, using a special camera fitted with three filtered lenses: red, green, blue. They would process the resulting glass plate normally before showing it through a three-lensed, three-filtered projector where the image would magically transform into colour. I am told the hue is eerie, almost psychedelic in its vibrancy.

We don't yet know whether these slides are from Ellen's Sanger-Shepherd years or from an earlier 'Kromskop' process known as the 'photochromascope'. If they are Kromskop – and the subject matter implies that they may be – these remaining seven slides could tell us that Ellen was dabbling with colour photography as early as 1895, an extraordinarily early date. There is just one (known) working example of a Newtonian Universal Science Lantern left. My dream is, at some point, to project Ellen's magic slides through it and experience her world in weird kaleidoscopic colour, as she would have seen it.

At the other end of the scale, we have uncovered some of Ellen's last photographs. Probably taken with a simple Box Brownie, these are little more than snaps, mementoes of visits to friends (she was still sending those photographic thank-you gifts) or of group holidays organised by a local club. A set of pictures of Norwich, for example, comes from the early 1930s, quickly and somewhat carelessly snapped, then contact-printed (directly from the negative, so the same, small size as the neg) by a local developer. It is interesting, but perhaps a little cruel to compare them with similar 'visitor' images of Bradford-on-Avon or York from the 1880s, carefully composed, processed and enlarged by Ellen herself. By this point, of course, with her financial world falling around her ears, it is surprising Ellen was photographing anything at all, and such pictures speak to us of her tenacity. She was determined to get out there, to do whatever she could, however straitened her circumstances. These tiny two-inch squares are miniature declarations of defiance, and I love her for them.

❖

I am relieved to have found little to contradict most of what I wrote this time last year, though I have made one or two revisions in the text, where new evidence has turned up. For example, I always knew there was an 1881 diary written by Frederick Willmott somewhere in the boxes of tat, but, back in 2019 when I'd put it in there, I had not noticed the appalling condition it was in. I could have cried in August 2022 when I realised the shredded cover was the best-preserved thing about it. But Willmott giveth even as she taketh away, and underneath was a second near-intact journal neither Karen nor I had noticed on our four-day rescue frenzy. We now know Fred started his journal on 8 March 1877, almost exactly one year after he and his family moved to Warley Place and four years earlier than we had previously known.

The only real 'mistake' I have found turned up very recently indeed, in a letter from an obscure monsignor to his bishop that I don't feel too embarrassed to have only just discovered, by complete accident. The archivist at the Roman Catholic Archdiocese of Birmingham wins the Sandra Lawrence Award for Speed in Supplying Archival Evidence, turning my initial enquiry into a digitised document in less than an hour.

MOULDLARKING

The letter addresses in detail the friction that Karen and I had 'felt' between Mr Robert Martin and Lady Catherine Berkeley and their oldest son Robert Valentine and his wife Rose. We had noted that after the wedding in 1891, the young couple were hardly seen at Spetchley for years, and that Rose never appeared at any family gatherings. It turns out our instinct was correct – there was indeed unpleasantness – but our reasoning for it was wrong and we had mistaken just who was staying away from whom. Anyone who has read the hardback version of this book will notice a difference in Chapter Six as I deal with the consequences of reading a single letter after a book has been published.

I am still trying to figure out what all this means. I continue to work with John Cannell, Paula Sewell and the sturdy group of Warley volunteers, transcribing and analysing material that is turning up more quickly than we can deal with it. Even as I was writing this chapter, eight previously unknown 'slipping' (moving) magic lantern slides surfaced at the History of Science Museum. At Spetchley Park, Karen and I work with Mr Henry Berkeley to figure out what Ellen did with weird objects that still turn up on a regular basis – the latest being a monogrammed travel candleholder, which can be attached to the side of a trunk or the spine of a book. Do not try this under the bedclothes at home. I have a shopping list of other items to look out for, not least that jewelled paperknife from Chapter Nineteen, bequeathed to Miss Willmott by Queen Alexandra, and the oil painting of Ellen, dressed 'poet' style, at her horticultural zenith. There are numerous black and white images of it, but no colour, which implies the portrait was lost some time ago, but if the Willmott project has taught me anything, it is not to give up hope. Neither have I given up on finding the key (probably some kind of ledger-style book) to the code numbers on the back of many of Ellen's photographs, which would unlock so much about her life, friends, plants and gardens.

Then there is the largest Willmott gap of all: the Victoria Medal of Honour itself. This should not be missing. It is solid gold, and hugely important to Ellen and the Berkeley family; neither she nor they would not have let go of it lightly. It is not with her other medals or valuables, so where is it? Did she ever even receive it? Tantalisingly, the RHS has no record either. There is at least one locked box at Spetchley that Karen and I have singularly failed to pick, and a locked cupboard that I have only ever heard of, never seen. That VMH could be anywhere, in anyone's collection. Even as I write I can hear its faint cries, calling from . . . somewhere. It is out there – I am convinced of it. As all the best academic papers say, More Research is Needed.

Sandra Lawrence, October 2022

Acknowledgements

They say it takes a village to raise a child but literary babies sometimes need a town. Or even a city. The sheer number of people who have bent over backwards to help me on this extraordinary journey of discovery is both impressive and humbling in that they were so willing – and keen – to help me achieve a dream. If there are mistakes or misconceptions within these pages, the fault will be entirely my own.

Where to start when so many have been so very generous? Certainly this book would not exist without my wonderful agent, Ella Khan, who didn't just place my baby with the right publisher, but stood by me every step of the way. Without her, I certainly would not have found my equally brilliant editor Susannah Otter. Susannah immediately 'got' what I wanted to do, then did everything within her power to enable me to do it. Ellie Carr provided sage feedback at critical points in the book's progress and Kerri Sharp made the most sensitive copy edit I have ever received. Nikki Mander, Jenna Petts and Jessica Tackie formed a powerful publicity triumvirate.

The Berkeley family have borne my intrusion into their lives with patience and kindness. I must particularly thank Mr Henry Berkeley for allowing me into his home, for granting unfettered access to such extraordinary material and for trusting me to tell Ellen's story as I saw it. My thanks also extend to Mr Charles Berkeley, Mrs Berkeley and the staff at both Spetchley Park and Berkeley Castle, in particular the lovely people in the estate offices, especially Josh Nash and Sarah Bird. A generous grant by The Stanley Smith Horticultural Trust UK helped to facilitate travel and accommodation during the rescue of the Willmott papers.

I must also acknowledge 50 odd years' worth of researchers, each working with one metaphorical hand tied behind their backs. Of these, Audrey le Liévre, Ellen Willmott's first biographer, reigns supreme. Thanks to her diligence I have not had to reinvent many too many wheels.

This book would have been simply impossible to write without my great friend and accomplice, Berkeley Estate Archivist Karen Davidson. Having the faith to grant me access to documentary riches when they were so raw and vulnerable was extraordinary in itself, but Karen threw herself into the project, too, often on her own time, working with me, discussing with me, delving with me, frothing with me and, occasionally, yuckking with me when the finds just got too gross. I thank Megan, too, for sharing her with me.

John Cannell has been my other 'partner in Willmott'. John's knowledge and meticulous attention to detail made him invaluable but his company, integrity and sense of humour during hundreds of hours of Willmott Tombola has been a personal joy. Shirley Cannell provided support and friendship throughout. Indeed, without all the volunteers at Warley Place, I would be nowhere. Ailsa Wildig's stellar encouragement came with powerful plant knowledge. Paula Sewell, as well as being an expert on EAW's photography and a great transcriber, is also one of the finest – and most generous – winklers-out of information I know. Without Dr Michael Leach's insights and

ACKNOWLEDGEMENTS

expertise, I would have often been way-off mark. Thanks too, to Jills Plater and Payne, Mick Hedges, Annabel Davenport and, indeed, the entire Warley volunteer community.

Fiona Agassiz was kind enough to introduce me to the 'real' Warley village and its wealth of residents, all of whom shared their homes, time, tales and tea. Steve and Christine McAllister, Eileen and David Fife, Dean Maylon, Helen Burgess, David and Freddie Wellings, I thank you. The families of Ellen's Alpine gardener, Jacob Maurer, and butler, James Robinson, helped enormously; in particular Trish Kilpatrick and Christine McLaughlin. Linda Carter has been invaluable in helping me figure out what happened to Warley after Ellen's death.

Transcribers-extraordinaire Maggie Thorpe, Fiona Tittensor and Melanie Dymond-Harper squinted at many pages-worth of horrible Victorian handwriting. At Berkeley Castle, Jill and Peter Barlow spent literally years listing the original 'new cache' of Willmott documents under the supervision of David Smith. Peter Yardley's patient counsel was matched only by his sterling photography, ably assisted by Jim Pimpernell. Rachel Wales must have gone cross-eyed staring at blank glass plates, while Catherine Witchell spent too much of her young life copying prints.

Ellen Willmott was both a 'visitor' and a 'joiner' and there is a huge list of country houses, gardens and institutions I must thank for access, information and enthusiasm. In particular, Ken Briggs, Historian at Newby Hall, John Page from the Alpine Garden Society, Jane Harrison at the Royal Institution, Peter Harvey at the Essex Field Club, Alasdair Moore at Heligan, Tom Coward and Celine Leslie at Gravetye Manor, Rob Jacobs and Pat Havers at Waterpenny Gardens, Annabel Watts at Mustead Wood, Penny Snell at the National Gardens Scheme, Mark Iles at the Water Gardens, Dianne Long and Caroline Keep at the Devon Gardens Trust, Peter Crook at Henley-on-Thames.org, Anne Tweddle at the National Collection of Engleheart Daffodils, Nick Stanley of the National Willmott Plant Collection, Mrs Harrison and the staff at Friar

Park, Tom Ruffles of the Society for Psychical Research, Nicola Steele at the Grosvenor Estate Archives, David Rae of the Royal Botanic Gardens, Edinburgh, and Glyn Jones, formerly of the Shakespeare Birthplace Trust, who spent much time discussing Willmottiana over coffee and walks around Anne Hathaway's Cottage garden. Staff at the Lindley Library, the Royal Botanic Gardens, Kew, Essex Record Office, John Murray Archive, Linnean Society, Magic Lantern Society, Milestone Society, and the Royal Collection went out of their way to help my research, while Lord Petre dealt patiently with numerous queries. Ellen Willmott was a longstanding member of the extraordinary London Library; I have been delighted to conduct much of my own research there too, and gratefully acknowledge my Carlyle Membership.

Individual experts in their fields who have been supremely kind with their time and knowledge include Ian Dunnigan (photographic curiosities), RHS authority Brent Elliott, Patricia Fara (Gulielma Lister), Mr Gerald and Mrs Joan Gurney (the Willmott fan), Graham Harper (Latin translation), Derek Holwill (legal precedents), Fiona Kilpatrick (Catholic ritual), Sue Lee (Victorian *frou*), Sotheby's expert David MacDonald, Carmen Mangion (Victorian Catholic girls' education), John Phibbs (landscape history), Sophie Piebenga (Alice de Rothschild), Brian Pike (all things *Eryngium*), Twigs Way (garden history guru), and Chris Roberts, who solved the Southwark Bridge Mystery. Thanks, too, to Mr John Borron for the 'terrible' story – and to Claire Carr-Saunders and the Molyneux-Seel family for their help trying to fathom it out. I owe a particular debt to Charlotte Moore, who gracefully shared the Norman Moore letters and medical notes, alongside warm hospitality and wise insight. I would also like to thank members of the Department of History, Classics and Archaeology at Birkbeck University of London, especially my MRes supervisor, Julia Laite and fellow students Richard Scurfield, Anne Pegram and Tom Marshall.

Much of my work has involved friends-in-Willmott abroad, some of whom I was forced to meet on Zoom. I hope this will not always

ACKNOWLEDGEMENTS

be the case. In France, I must thank Geneviève Frieh-Giraud for a superb book and many, *many* kindnesses but especially for her help in local research when covid prevented me leaving the UK. In Italy, I extend my thanks to Ursula Salghetti Drioli Piacenza at Boccanegra and Caroline Hanbury at La Mortola, also to Charles Quest-Ritson for an illuminating conversation. In Switzerland, Pierre Boillat at the Conservatoire et Jardins Botaniques, Geneva, was very helpful regarding Henry Correvon. In America, I must thank Maureen O'Brien of the Massachusetts Horticultural Society, Paige Trubatch and Anne Myers from the Garden Club of America, Jenny Rose Carey and Marjorie Nailor from the Garden Club of Philadelphia, Tess Frydman at Wyck, and Heather Clewell and Linda Eirhart at Winterthur. Lisa Pearson at the Arnold Arboretum Horticultural Library, Harvard, provided superb material and cheery support. My thanks also to the Embassy of Japan for fielding some very odd enquiries.

And then there are the many, many people who encouraged me in the writing of this book, including – in no way exclusively – Robert Bevan, Simon Caney, Linda Eggins, Mark Fielding, Clare Foggett, Don Gallacher, Helen Griffin, Frances Hardinge, Neil Heathcote, Monica Herman, Karim Kronfli, Jessica Lutkin, Veronica Lysaght, Kitt Price, Jill Pritchard, Kay Stopforth, Karen Storey and David Townsend. My sister Mary and father Charles shared Warley every step of the way, always remembering my mother Pat who would have if she could. Timandra Harkness's constant support, shoulder and champagne will never be forgotten.

Finally, I must also thank Lady Antonia Fraser, whose pioneering work *The Weaker Vessel* inspired me to study women's history in the first place. Many years later, her kindness, advice and hospitality helped mould the way I write it. I was both astonished and proud to receive the Society of Author's Antonia Fraser Award; I pray I can live up to the honour.

There are so many people who have helped *Miss Willmott's Ghosts* come to life; I am sure I have missed someone out and the moment the book goes to print I will be horrified to remember their contribution. Whoever you are, please accept my apologies – and profound thanks.

Endnotes

INTRODUCTION
i   Audrey Le Lièvre, *Miss Willmott of Warley Place: Her Life and Her Gardens* (Faber & Faber, 1980).
ii   Dawn McLoed, *Down To Earth Women: The Who Care for the Soil*, (William Blackwood, 1882).

CHAPTER ONE
i   Brent Elliott, *The Royal Horticultural Society: A History 1804–2004* (Phillimore, 2004).
ii   Dawn MacLeod, *The Gardeners' London: Four Centuries of Gardening, Gardeners and Garden Usage* (Duckworth & Co., 1972).

CHAPTER TWO
i   Le Lièvre, *Miss Willmott of Warley Place*.
ii   Carol Dyhouse, *Girls Growing Up in late Victorian and Edwardian England* (Routledge & Kegan Paul, 1981).

CHAPTER FOUR
i   Ellen Ann Willmott (EAW) to Countess Tasker (CT), 23 September 1875.
ii   *Lyon-Horticole*, 1908.
iii *The Garden*, 3 March 1894.

CHAPTER FIVE

i   As quoted in Stéfan D'Arve, *Les Fastes du Mont-Blanc: Ascensions Célèbres et Catastrophes*, 1876.
ii William Wakefield, *Baths, Bathing and Attractions of Aix-les-Bains* (Savoy, 1886).
iii RW to EW Snr, 13 May 1890.
iv EAW to EW Snr, dated 'Sunday'; possibly 29 September 1889.
v   EAW & RW to EW Snr, 25 April 1890.
vi EAW to EW Snr, 16 May 1890.
vii Queen Victoria's Diary, 12 April 1885.
viii EAW & RW to EW Snr, 18 May, year unknown.
ix EAW to EW Snr, undated but probably 14 April, either 1889 or 1890.
x   EAW to EW Snr, 13 April, year unknown but either 1889 or 1890.

CHAPTER SIX

i   Fred Willmott's Diary, 12 October 1888.
ii RW to EW Snr, 25 April 1890.
iii RW to parents, undated, probably 30 April 1890.
iv RW to EW Snr, 4 May 1890.
v   EAW to EW Snr, undated, probably 4 May 1890.
vi RW to EW Snr, 4 May 1890.
vii EAW to EW Snr, date unknown (postmark 26 April, which does not make sense, so perhaps it was returned to the wrong envelope).
viii EAW to EW Snr, undated.
ix Stephen Scanniello, 'Cuttings; When Malmaison Celebrated the Rose's Beauty', *New York Times*, 31 March 1996.

CHAPTER SEVEN

i   George Engleheart (GE) to EAW, 19 December 1894.
ii GE to EAW, 10 December 1894.
iii GE to EAW, 20 November 1895.

CHAPTER EIGHT

i   Tracy J. Collins, 'Athletic Fashion: Punch and the Creation of the New Woman', *Victorian Periodicals Review* (Johns Hopkins University Press, 2010).
ii E. Lynn-Linton, 'The Girl of the Period', *Saturday Review,* 1868.
iii GE to EAW, 25 March 1894.
iv Le Lièvre, *Miss Willmott of Warley Place: Her Life and Her Gardens*, probably via Jim Robinson, James's son.
v   Kinloch C. Cooke 'The Private Diary of the Duchess of Teck', A *memoir of her Royal Highness Princess Mary Adelaide, Duchess of Teck* (1900).

ENDNOTES

vi   Rudyard Kipling, 'The Betrothed', (1886).
vii   *The Girl's Own Paper*, 1898, as quoted by Matthew Hilton in 'Smoking in British Popular Culture 1800–2000' (Manchester University Press, 2000).
viii   Margerie Russel Sedgwick, Pamela Russel and David Rolt, 'Memories of Miss Ellen Willmott 1858-1934', circa 1970s, held at Essex Record Office.

CHAPTER NINE

i   GE to EAW, 29 March 1895.
ii   GE to EAW, 30 May 1896.
iii   GE to EAW, 8 February 1897.
iv   Lady Wolseley to Lord Wolseley, 21 April 1897, as quoted by Heather Gilbert, *The End of the Road* (Routledge, 1978).
v   *The Boudoir*, November 1903.
vi   *Daily Telegraph*, 4 May 1897.
vii   EAW draft letter to GE, undated.
viii   *St James Gazette*, 3 July 1897.
ix   Garnet Wolseley, as quoted by Heather Gilbert, *The End of the Road* (Routledge, 1978).
x   Hon. Lady Phipps to Queen Victoria, 27 November 1897.

INTERLUDE

i   D. G. Hessayon, *The Bedside Book of the Garden* (Transworld, 2008).
ii   Gertrude Jekyll (GJ) to EAW, 28 November 1899.
iii   GJ to EAW, 11 May 1901.
iv   EAW to Norman Moore (NM), 7 April 1900.
v   EAW to NM, 30 June 1901.
vi   GJ to EAW, 21 December 1901.
vii   GJ to EAW, 2 January 1902.

CHAPTER TEN

i   EAW to NM, 20 March 1898.
ii   Ibid.
iii   EAW to NM, 2 June 1898.
iv   Telegram, Gian Mount Stephen (GMS) to EAW, 1 June 1898.
v   RB to NM, 1 June, probably 1898.
vi   EAW to NM, 10 December 1898.
vii   EAW to NM, 29 November 1898.
viii   EAW to NM, 10 January 1899.
ix   Ibid.
x   EAW to NM, 12 October 1899.

xi   GE to EAW, 27 June 1899.
xii   EAW to NM, 1 October, probably 1900.
xiii EAW to NM, 2 June 1900.
xiv Brent Elliott, *The Royal Horticultural Society, A History 1804–2004* (Phillimore & Co Ltd., 2004).

CHAPTER ELEVEN

i   The Literary Ladies' Dinner, *Scots Observer*, 8 June 1889.
ii   *Scots Observer*, 15 June 1889.
iii   H. J. Elwes to EAW, 28 January 1903.
iv   Presidential Address, Linnean Society, 15 December 1904.
v   EAW to NM, 26 January 1905.
vi   Charles Sprague Sargent (CSS) to EAW, 30 January 1904.
vii   CSS to EAW, 6 August 1906.
viii CSS to EAW, 17 April 1906.
ix   EAW to CSS, 31 May 1906.
x   EAW to CSS, 26 October 1906.
xi   CSS to EAW, 14 July 1906.
xii   Ibid.
xiii EAW to CSS, 24 July 1906.
xiv CSS to EAW, 30 August 1906.
xv   CSS to EAW, 18 October 1906.
xvi CSS to EAW, 6 November 1906.
xvii EAW to CSS, 27 November 1906.
xviii CSS to EAW, 11 December 1906.
xix CSS to EAW, 24 December 1906.

CHAPTER TWELVE

i   EAW to CSS, 29 September 1904.
ii   Ibid.
iii   Ibid.
iv   CCS to EAW, 3 November 1904.
v   Ibid.
vi   EAW to CSS, 24 July 1906.
vii   Johann Bernhard Mann (JBM) to EAW, 14 October 1905.
viii JBM to EAW, 25 October 1905.
ix   JBM to EAW, 4 December 1905.
x   JBM to EAW, 1 January 1906.
xi   Draft letter EAW to JBM, undated.
xii   JBM to EAW, 20 January 1906.

ENDNOTES

CHAPTER THIRTEEN
i   *L'Avenir d'Aix-les-Bains*, 5 September 1907.
ii   GJ to EAW, 5 September 1907.
iii   JBM to EAW, 17 November 1907.
iv   EAW to NM, 15 September 1907.
v   EAW to CSS, 26 September 1907.
vi   Ibid.
vii   EAW to NM, 29 September 1907.
viii   Ibid.
ix   EAW to NM, 10 October 1907.
x   GMS to EAW, 4 September 1907.
xi   GMS to EAW, 5 September 1907.
xii   GMS to EAW, 10 September 1907.
xiii   EAW to NM, 10 October 1907.
xiv   EAW to NM, 8 December 1907.
xv   EAW to CSS, 26 September 1907.
xvi   CSS to EAW, 26 December 1907.
xvii   CSS to EAW April 1907, exact date unknown.
xviii   CSS to EAW 5 April 1909.
xix   EAW to NM, 29 May 1908.
xx   Ibid.
xxi   CSS to EAW 23 August 1909.
xxii   EAW to NM, 29 May 1908.
xxiii   CSS to EAW, 23 August 1909.
xxiv   JBM to EAW, 2 November 1909.
xxv   NM to EAW, 7 January 1908.
xxvi   *The Field*, 18 December 1909.
xxvii   *Country Life*, 12 November 1910.

CHAPTER FOURTEEN
i   W. T. Stearn, 'Ellen Ann Willmott, Gardener and Botanical Rosarian', *The Garden*, June 1979.
ii   EAW to CSS, 29 March 1910.
iii   EAW to CSS, 29 March, year unknown.
iv   Theresa Earle to EAW, 7 May 1910.
v   NM to EAW, 6 August 1910.
vi   NM to Henry Dixson, 7 August 1910.
vii   NM to EAW, 7 August 1910.
viii   EAW to NM, 10 August 1910.
ix   EAW, 9 August 1910.

x   William Robinson to EAW, August 1910.
xi   GMS to EAW, 10 August 1910.
xii GMS to EAW, 21 August 1910.
xiii EAW to Norman Moore, 24 August 1910.
xiv EAW to NM, 3 September 1910.
xv   EAW to NM, 24 January 1911.
xvi EAW to GMS, 2 April 1910.
xvii Draft letter EAW to GMS, undated but from April 1911.
xviii GMS to EAW, 20 April 1910.
xix H. E. Luxmoore to EAW, 17 July 1918.
xx   CSS to EAW, 27 December 1911.

CHAPTER FIFTEEN
i   Reginald Farrer, *The Rock Garden, Present Day Gardening*, undated.
ii   Reginald Farrer, *My Rock Garden*, 1907.
iii Quoted by both Le Liévre and Allen.
iv   JBM to EAW, 24 December 1912.
v   Rudolph Barr to EAW, 8 August 1912.
vi   W. J. Bean to EAW, 19 September 1912.
vii Robert Vyner to EAW, 21 June 1914.
viii GMS to EAW letter, 1 Febuary 1914.
ix   Draft letter EAW to GMS, undated but March 1914.
x   GMS to EAW, 8 March 1914.
xi   GMS to EAW, 12 March 1914.
xii GMS to EAW, 19 March 1914.
xiii Reginald Farrer, *My Rock Garden*, 1907.

CHAPTER SIXTEEN
i   EAW to NM, 28 July 1914.
ii   Ibid.
iii Garden Club of America bulletin, 1915, 1916, 1917.
iv   Frank Crisp (FC) to Lord Mount Stephen, 15 May 1915.
v   FC to EAW, 9 July 1915.
vi   EAW to EA Bowles, 14 February 1916.
vii Arthur Forster, Frere Cholmeley & Co., 23 February 1916.
viii H. Avray Tipping, 'Warley Place in Springtime', *Country Life*, 8 May 1915.
ix   *John Bull* magazine, 22 January 1915.
x   E. L. Glover to EAW, 15 November 1917.
xi   HRH Princess Louise to EAW, 3 July, probably 1917.
xii AF to EAW, 30 March 1917.

ENDNOTES

xiii Army & Navy Stores to EAW, 14 January 1918.
xiv   HEL to EAW, 17 July 1918.
xv   NM to EAW, 5 May 1917.
xvi   EFC Journal, 5 October 1918.

CHAPTER SEVENTEEN

i   HC to EAW, 8 June 1919.
ii   Edward Hudson to EAW, 7 February 1918.
iii   Lady Angela Forbes, *Memories and Base Details* (Hutchinson, 1921).
iv   David Prain to EAW, 15 October 1918.
v   William Wilks (WW), 14 November 1918.
vi   Isaac Bayley Balfour, 17 November 1918.
vii   *The Times*, 14 April 1919, 20 May 1919, 21 May 1919, 15 May 1919.
viii *The Times*, 19 February 1919.
ix   Lionel Earle to EAW, 24 May 1919.
x   *Country Life*, 14 June 1919.
xi   *Country Life*, 14 June 1919.
xii   AW to EAW, 24 September 1919.
xiii Angela Forbes, *Memories and Base Details*, op. cit.
xiv   WR to EAW, 5 October 1919.
xv   Martin Conway to EAW, 10 February 1920.
xvi   RB to EAW, 30 November 1919.
xvii RB to EAW, 27 January 1920.
xviii Draft letter EAW to William Wilkes, dated 1920.
xix   Draft letter EAW to Robert James and Reginald Cory, 12 May 1920.

CHAPTER EIGHTEEN

i   *Morning Post*, 16 February 1920.
ii   Auctioneer to EAW, May 1920.
iii   NM to EAW 13 April 1920.
iv   Lord Berkley to EAW, 1920.
v   Lord Berkeley to EAW, 19 August 1920.
vi   Peter Barr to EAW, 23 March 1921.
vii   Edward Hudson (EH) to EAW, 29 December 1922.
viii Otto Stapf to EAW, 22 May 1922.
ix   EH to EAW, 21 February 1923.
x   Henry Nicholson Ellacombe, *A Memoir*, ed. Arthur Hill, *Country Life*, 1919.
xi   As remembered by RVB to EAW, 29 May 1926.

CHAPTER NINETEEN

i   Margerie Russel Sedgwick, Pamela Russel and David Rolt, 'Memories of Miss Ellen Willmott 1858-1934', circa 1970s, held at Essex Record Office.
ii   Jack Tremayne to EAW, 12 April 1923.
iii Peacock & Goddard, 31 January 1928.
iv   Burch & Co (probably) to EAW, around February 1923.
v   GJ to EAW, 5 January 1925.
vi   The Revd. James Jacobs, as quoted by Le Liévre.
vii As quoted by Le Liévre, *Miss Willmott of Warley Place*.
viii 'Jaqueline Tyrwhitt', *RHS Journal*, November 1981.
ix   Ellen Shoshkes, *Jacqueline Tyrwhitt: A Transnational Life in Urban Planning* (Taylor & Francis Ltd., 2016).
x   EW to EAW, 27 January 1925.
xi   RVB to EAW, 19 August 1925.
xii RVB to EAW, 6 December 1925.
xiii As quoted by Le Lièvre, *Miss Willmott of Warley Place*.
xiv Defence statement, High Court of Justice, King's Bench Division, case No. 1142.
xv   As quoted by Le Lièvre, *Miss Willmott of Warley Place*.
xvi EAW to Rob Berkeley, 30 March 1930.
xvii As quoted by Le Lièvre, *Miss Willmott of Warley Place*.
xviii Le Lièvre, *Miss Willmott of Warley Place*.

CHAPTER TWENTY

i   As quoted by Le Lièvre, *Miss Willmott of Warley Place*.
ii   *Country Life*, 6 October 1934.
iii Essex Field Club, 1912.
iv   Frances, Evelyn Warwick, *Daily Telegraph*, 14 March 1935.
v   *RHS Journal*, 1966.
vi   *Gardeners' Chronicle*, 31 August 1966.
vii Kindly forwarded via Dianne Long at the Devon Gardens Trust, 10 December 2018.
viii Rosella Sleiter, *La Republica*, 12 May 2017.
ix   *Kew Bulletin* vol. 1934.
x   *Nature*, 1934.
xi   *The Gardeners' Chronicle*, 6 Oct 1934.
xii Helen Lewis, *Difficult Women: A history of feminism in eleven fights* (Jonathan Cape, 2020).

Index

A

Aberconwy, Lady 164
Adolphus, Prince 107, 109, 118
Aix-les-Bains, France 47, 57, 58–9, 61–9, 105–6, 159, 189–90
    see also Tresserve, Willmott family villa in
Aix-les-Bains in Savoy (L. Brachet) 57, 59
Albert of Belgium, King 250–1
Albert, Prince 14
Alexandra, Queen 238, 271, 282, 283, 299, 305
Allen, Mea 236
alpine blooms 46, 50–1
Alpine Garden, Warley Place 3, 47–51, 77, 78–9, 89, 92, 235, 236, 302, 319, 325–6
Alps, the 45, 46, 56, 156
Amateur Gardeners' Society at Warley 298–300, 301, 304
Amati musical instruments, EW's 87, 242
Amédée Joubert & Sons 185

Amelia, Princess 27
Amherst, Alicia 130, 237
Among the Hills, A Book of Joy in High Places (R. Farrer) 235
Angelina's canteens 266
Anne Hathaway's Cottage garden 300, 325
Anning, Mary 17
archaeology, Warley Place 5
archive sources 6–10
Argentine Railway shares 255
Armistice Day 261–2
Army & Navy Stores 222–3, 260
army regiments, Warley Barracks 33, 39–40
Arnold, Edward 242–3
Arts & Crafts movement 77
    Exhibition (1896) 112
Atelier Muegle studio, Thoune 43
auctions, Warley Place 279, 284, 318
autism 324

B

Bach Choir 231, 326
Baker, John 217
bal costumé (1897), Duchess of Devonshire's 129
Balfour, Frederick 271
Balfour, Isaac Bayley 267–8, 276, 294
Balmoral boots, Gertrude Jekyll's 137–46
Barr Jnr, Peter 289
Barr, Peter 'Daffodil King' 94, 99, 151
Barr, Rudolph 239
Barrie, J.M. 165
Bath Spa 52
Battersea Dogs' Home 37
Bean, William 239, 300
Belgian Refugee Crisis (1914) 251–2
Bennett-Poë, John 130, 134
Berkeley (nee Willmott – EW's sister), Rose 6, 151, 225
   Aix-les-Bains, France 61, 63, 64–5, 67, 68–9, 72–6, 80, 91, 104, 105, 198, 201, 207
   death and burial 29, 296–7
   dislike of Gertrude Jekyll 141–2
   family background/lifestyle 24–5, 35, 37, 38, 40, 45, 52
   First World War 242, 257, 260, 261
   friendship with Lady Mount Stephen 135, 193
   health 211, 249, 252, 265, 289, 292–3
   marriage to Robert Valentine Berkeley 80–3, 87, 91, 130, 148
   move to Spetchley estates 152
   personal financial troubles 275–6
   pregnancies and births 104, 135, 151
   primrose breeding programme 288–90, 300
   receives Papal blessing 296
   relationship with Maurice Berkeley 53–5
   sister's financial difficulties 220, 231, 254, 255
Berkeley, Betty 261–2, 264, 289–90, 293, 296, 310
Berkeley Castle 284, 310
Berkeley, Eleanor 88, 135, 296, 310
Berkeley family 52–3, 80–3, 130, 151
Berkeley, Juliet 8
Berkeley, Lady Catherine 52–3, 81–2, 130
Berkeley, Lord 284, 297–8, 301, 303
Berkeley, Maud 52, 80
Berkeley, Maurice 53–5, 81, 82
Berkeley, Robert 'Rob' 151, 257, 261, 265, 284, 296, 309, 310, 317
Berkeley, Robert Valentine 80–3, 87, 130, 150, 197, 198, 201, 207, 231, 249, 257, 265, 275, 293, 296, 305–6, 309
Berkeley Snr, Robert 52–3, 130
Bernard Quaritch publishers 214
Bernascon, Monsieur 59, 74, 91, 105–6, 159
Biancheri 185–6
Bidder, Revd. Henry 161, 305
Birmingham Narcissus Show (1895) 97
Boccanegra, Ventimiglia 181–7, 190, 221, 238, 242, 252, 291–2, 297–8, 301–2, 328
Boer War 122
Bonaparte, Empress Josephine 58, 73, 79–80, 216
Bonaparte, Napoleon 45, 58
Borghèse, Pauline 58
Borough High Street property 22–3, 129, 285–6
Borron, John 323
Botanic Gardens, Cambridge 159, 268
Botanic Gardens, Vienna 160, 167
Botanical Gardens, Munich 160, 167
Botanical Magazine 290
The Boudoir magazine 127
Bovril 258, 264

INDEX

Bowlby, Anthony 249
Bowles, E.A. 'Gussie' 235–6, 245–6, 254
Boyles Court, Brentwood 155–6
Brachet, Dr Léon 57, 59–61, 62, 63–4, 66, 67–8, 69, 73, 74–5, 93, 148, 159
Brentwood Cathedral 88, 150, 314–15
British Archaeological Association 261
British Fascists 304
British Fern Gazette 315
British Gardeners' Association 209–10, 231
Broughton, Lady 244
bulbs, trade in daffodil 89–90
Bulley, Arthur 159
Bullion, Yella 304
Burdett-Coutts, Baron 239
Burge, Eliza 220, 254
Burlington House, London 165, 169
butler, Willmott family 90–1, 114, 155, 187, 205, 220, 240, 306, 308, 311, 312, 318–19

C

cabinet cards, Victorian 43, 45
calling cards, Victorian 27
Candler, Thomas 92, 154, 209–10, 230–1
Cannell, John 5, 30, 276
Carr-Saunders, Clare 323
Carr-Saunders, Theresa 323–4
Carter, Alfred Joseph Traylen 319–20
Carter, Norman 322
cartes de visite, Victorian 27
Casey, Charles 181
Casino Ancien Cercle, Aix-les-Bains 65–6, 91
Casino des Fleurs, Aix-les-Bains 55, 159
Catholic Directory 25
Catholicism 23, 33, 208, 293, 296, 310, 314
Cawdor, Lady 282
Cecil, Evelyn 236–7
Ceratostigma willmottianum 252

Chang, pet dog 113, 312
Charron motor, EW's 187, 188
Charteris, Hugo 274
chauffer, EW's 187–9
Chelmsford Chronicle 316–17
Chelsea Flower Show 238, 245, 257, 284
Children and Gardens (G. Jekyll) 138, 193
China plant-hunting expeditions 173–8
Cholmeley, Arthur 254
Christy, Robert Miller 213, 264, 286–8, 306, 309–10, 324
Church of the Immaculate Conception, Mayfair 315
cigarette case, EW's 101, 119
cigarettes/smoking 118–19
Clodoveo (Villa Boccanegra retainer) 242, 297, 301
clothing/fashion 102–3, 114–15, 122, 137, 146, 164, 231–2, 238, 302–3
coat of arms, Willmott family 153
Coke, Lady Katherine 134
conservatory, Warley Place 3, 242
Conway, Sir Martin 275
Coombe Wood 105, 114–15, 173
Corpus Christi feast, Tresserve 208
Correvon, Henry 50–1, 77, 78, 88–9, 93, 112, 145, 148, 160, 185, 244, 265
Cory, Reginald 222, 277, 299
Corylopsis multiflora, EW's RHS award for 238
Cotterill, Annie 155, 303, 307–8, 311
Country Life magazine 140, 214, 256, 270, 271, 272, 282, 288, 290, 315
Courtney-Page family 315
Crisp, Catherine 169
Crisp, Sir Frank 169, 224–5, 227, 243–6, 252–3, 261, 265
Curie, Marie and Pierre 162
Currey, Frances 90
Curtis-Bennett, KC, Sir Henry 306–7
Curtis's Botanical Magazine 202, 321

D

Daffodil Yearbook (1915) 255
daffodils 2, 4, 85, 89, 93, 94–8, 99, 112, 117, 125, 126, 144, 151–2, 157, 158, 186–7, 255, 275, 309, 328
Daily Mirror 268
Daily Telegraph 5, 127, 270, 315, 325
Daudens, Jacques and Marie-Françoise 73, 74
Davidson, Gerald 195
Davidson, Karen 6–7, 8–10, 52, 53, 106, 119
de Beauharnais, Hortense 58
de Broc, Adèle 58
de Candolle, Richard 206, 207
de Rothschild, Alice 221, 276
de Sion, Sister Marie Edward *see* Berkeley, Betty
Dean Hole Memorial Medal 300
Delano McKelvy, Susan 171
Devonshire, Duchess of 129
Dickens, Charles 22
Dighton, Sir 228
Dixson, Henry 200, 205, 219, 220, 227
dogs, pet 37, 113, 114, 312
douche-massage therapy 61–3, 69, 211, 315
Douglas-Pennant, Violet 269, 302, 327
Down to Earth Women (D. McLeod) 4–5
du Pont, Henry 250, 251
Ducie, Lord 276
Dyer (Warley Place gardener), Mr 155
Dyhouse, Carol 27–8
Dykes, William 206

E

Earle, Lionel 270–1
Earle, Theresa 219
education, EW's 25–6, 28–9, 40
Edward, Prince of Wales 282
Edward VII, King 219, 283
Ellacombe, Canon 159, 254, 261, 291

'Ellen Willmott' *Narcissus* 97, 98, 125, 126, 144
Ellis, Havelock 122
Elwes, Henry John 166–7, 297
Empire, dominance of British 122
Empress Club, London 126–7, 162
Engleheart, Mary 97–8, 124–5, 158
Engleheart National Plant Collection 98
Engleheart, Revd George 92, 93–8, 110, 111, 117, 124–6, 128, 148, 151, 157, 158, 160, 199, 217, 218
English Flower Garden (W. Robinson) 35, 192
engraving of Willmott estate 152–3
Essex Field Club 170, 213, 261
Essex Naturalist magazine 296–7
Essex Naturalists'/Wildlife Trust 322
Essex Regiment 40
etiquette, social 27
Eton College 154
Evelyn, John 33, 315
eye witness reports 6, 8

F

Falmouth family 153
fancy dress ball (1919), Spetchley Estate 264–5
farming/agriculture, WWI 258–60
Farquharson, Marian 163, 165, 166, 168
Farrand, Beatrix 321–2
Farrer, Reginald 162, 234–7, 239, 241, 244, 245–6, 305
Fawcett, Millicent 164
fern grotto, Warley Place 3, 49, 106, 112
The Field magazine 213–14, 282
Fielder, C.M. 230
fire at the Tresserve villa 198–201
First Class Certificates, RHS 85, 97, 126, 157
First World War 249, 250–1, 253–4, 256–62, 266–7
aftermath 264–5, 286

INDEX

Flower, Charles Edward 281
Flower, Mrs 281
food supplies/rationing 258, 259, 261
Forbes, Lady Angela 265-6, 268, 272-4
Forster, Arthur 254, 255, 257, 260
Forty Elephants shoplifting syndicate 306, 308
Foster, Sir Michael 159, 171, 206, 273
Foukouba, Vicomte 226, 240
Frederic, Monsieur E. 187-9, 220, 221, 305
Friar Park, Henley-on-Thames 224, 243-4
Frondes Agrestes (J. Ruskin) 112
Furley, Catherine 165

G

Galeries Lafayette, Regent St 306, 307
Garden Club of America 256
garden gnomes 47, 244
The Garden magazine 35, 67, 95, 124, 125, 126, 140, 142-3, 151, 202, 244, 290
Gardeners' Chronicle periodical 167, 316, 328
Gardening Illustrated magazine 35, 67, 95, 157, 245
Gentlewoman magazine 91, 92, 104, 106, 134, 135
Genus Iris project 159, 171, 206
Genus Rosa (E. Willmott) 171, 206, 207, 215-18, 221, 222-3, 227, 232, 237, 248, 276, 326
Geological Society 17
George, David Lloyd 259
George II, King 27
George V, King 105, 118, 282
'ghost' photographs, EW's 53
Gibbs, Vicary 276
Gibson, Charles Dana 164
Gilpin, Mary 257
Glynde College of Lady Gardeners 162, 254

'Golden Bell' *Narcissus* 98
Goodwin (Warley Place gardener), Mr 155
Grand Tour, Willmott family's 54, 55
Grande Medaille Geoffroy Saint-Hilaire, EW awarded 238
Gravereaux, Jules 80
Gray, Eliza Annie 318-19
Great & Little Warley Village Show and Sports Day 197, 209
Great Warley, Brentwood 32
'Great Warley' *Narcissus* 157
Green, Helen 42
Green, Nathaniel Everett 129-30
Grosvenor, Lady Dora Mina 'Minnie' 92, 104, 105, 106, 110-11, 141-2
Grosvenor, Lord Henry 92
Gumbleton, William 134, 161
Gumley House, Isleworth 25-6, 29
Gutti, Rosina Mantovani 164

H

Haig, General 266
Hampton Court Palace gardens 269-72, 280, 300, 325
Hanbury, Mary 315
Hanbury, Sir Thomas 161, 180, 181, 184, 186, 194-5
harpsichord, EW's Jacob Kirkman 27, 87, 223-4, 227-9, 284
Harvard University's Arnold Arboretum 170, 173-4, 210-11, 305
Havergal, Beatrix 304, 327
Headley Garden, Brentwood 88
Herbarium Warleyense, EW's donation of 232
Herbert, Philip 52
Hessayon, Dr David 139
Hickel Brothers, Beaulieu-sur-Mer 184
Hight, George Ainslie 40
Hill, Arthur 291, 315
HM Office of Works 270-1

HM Stationery Office 286
Hole, Dean 133
Holly Lodge, Hampstead 239
Holtzapffel lathe, EW's 87
Holy Cross and All Saints church, Warley 98, 314
Home Farm, Brentwood 88, 152
homosexuality 109–10, 122
Hoog, John 173
Hoole House, Chester 244
Hôtel Bernascon, Aix-les-Bains 159, 198, 202
Hôtel de l'Europe, Aix-les-Bains 59
Hotel Windsor, Westminster 14, 15
Hudson, Edward 265, 290, 291, 315
Hurst, Dr Charles Chamberlain 326
hysteria malady 59–60

I

Iconum Botanicarum Index locupletissmus 205–6
Illustrated London News magazine 23, 283
Imperial Botanic Garden, St Petersburg 241
Imperial War Museum 275
In a Yorkshire Garden (R. Farrer) 236–7
'Incognita' *Narcissus* 158
Index Londonensis (Royal Horticultural Society) 206
Ingwerson, Walter 299
Inland Revenue 302
Institute of Mecanotherapy, Aix-les-Bains 159
International Botanical Conference 239
irrigation system, Ventimiglia 179, 183–4
Isham, Sir Charles 47, 244
Italian State Railway 185–6

J

James Backhouse & Son, York 48, 244
James, Montague Rhodes 261
James Pulham & Son 47–8

James, Robert 277
Jamyn Brooks, Henry 162
Japan-British Exhibition (1910) 226
Japanese garden, Coombe Wood 114
Jekyll, Agnes 315
Jekyll, Gertrude 4, 16–17, 18, 129, 133, 138–9, 140–6, 162, 193–4, 199, 214, 223, 291, 300, 309, 311, 321–2, 325
Jekyll, Herbert 299, 311
John Bull magazine 256
Jones, Beatrix 171
Journal of Horticulture and Cottage Gardener 15
Jubilee, Queen Victoria's Diamond 13, 14, 15, 123, 126–7, 128–9

K

Kew Bulletin 317
Khayam, Omar 296
'Kip and Knyff' topographical prints 152
Kipling, Rudyard 118
Knollys, Charlotte 264
knuckledusters 295, 308
Kronenburg, Anton 173

L

La Mortola, Ventimiglia 180–1, 186
La Republica 324
La Villa Fleurs, Aix-les-Bains, France 65, 159
Labouchere Amendment (1885) 109
Ladies Athenaeum 162
The Lady magazine 127
Land Army 259–60, 304, 327
latchkey 'New Woman' symbolism 152
L'Avenir d'Aix-les-Bains 198
Law, Ernest 271, 272, 280–3, 300
Lawrence, Sir Trevor 15–16, 123
Lawrence, Sir William 302
Le Lievre, Audrey 5–6, 10–11, 83, 236, 240, 322
leather satchel, EW's 233

INDEX

Les Roses (P. Redouté) 73, 171, 216
Lescher, Count 155-6
Lewis, Helen 329
Lilford, Lord 250, 252, 254, 255, 260, 277
Lincolnshire Chronicle 131
Linn-Lynton, Eliza 104
Linnean Society of London 163, 165, 166-9, 216
Linnean Society of London First Formal Admission of Women Fellows (J. Sant) 169
Lister, Gulielma 169-70
Little Ice Age 38
Liverpool Street station, London 32
London Scottish Royal Volunteers' Drill Hall 15
Louise, Princess 259, 315
Lubbock, John 166
Lutyens, Edwin 18, 83, 140, 141
Luxmoore, Henry Elford 154, 231
Lyon-Horticole magazine 49, 188-9

M

Malmaison *rosaraie*, Empress Josephine's 73, 79-80
'Manly Maiden' cartoon, *Punch* 103, 104
Mann, Johann Bernhard 189-92, 199, 208, 212, 227, 237-8, 248, 324
Married Women's Property Acts (1870) 93
Mary Adelaide, Duchess of Teck 105, 106, 107, 115, 116, 126, 127, 129, 130, 134, 136
Mary, Queen 228, 282, 303, 305, 306, 311
Maurer, Jacob 51, 92, 154, 255, 304, 315, 317-18
May of Teck, Princess 105, 109, 131
McLaren, Laura 164
McLeod, Dawn 4-5, 11
Meiji of Japan, Emperor 240
Menzies, Lady Susan 291-2, 293, 297, 302

methylene blue medication 149
Meunier, Claude 78, 90, 285
Meunier, Gasparine 90, 285
middle class socialising, Victorian 27
Midland Daffodil Society 151-2
'Miss Willmott' *Nerine* 167
'Miss Willmott' *Paeonia* 173
'Miss Willmott's Ghost' *Eryngium giganteum* 313, 321, 322, 329
Molique, Anna 29-30
Molyneux, Gertrude Eleanor 'Gem' 111, 117-18
Molyneux-Seel, Captain Edmund 323-4
Moon, Henry George 126, 144
Moore, Alan 154
Moore, Amy 149, 157
Moore, Dr Norman 135, 139, 141-2, 145, 148-9, 151, 152, 153, 154, 156, 159, 184, 199, 200, 201, 202, 203, 204, 212-13, 218, 220, 225-6, 227, 243, 249, 261, 265, 284, 297
Moore, Frederick 268
Morning Post 282
Morris, William 77
Mount Stephen, Lady *see* Tufnell, Georgiana 'Gian'
Mount Stephen, Lord George First Baron 126, 131-2, 134-5, 151, 193, 242, 252
munitions factories 259
Murray, John 216, 217-18, 222, 276
music 26-7, 33, 86-7, 114, 193, 256-7, 326
My Garden in Spring and Summer (R. Farrer) 245
My Rock Garden (R. Farrer) 235, 237, 244

N

Napoleon III, Emperor 58
Napoleonic Wars 79
Narcissi *see* daffodils
Narcissus Committee 99
National Rose Show (1912) 238

National Trust 317
National Tulip Show (1909) 213
National Union of Women's Suffrage Societies 164
New Women, Victorian 102-4, 110, 115, 118-19, 122, 152, 164, 329
Newby Hall, Yorkshire 239, 253
Northcote, Alice 131, 132

O

Oakwood Gardens, Wisley 160-1, 167, 317, 325
obituaries, EW's 315-17
Observer 270, 271, 272, 282
Oriana Madrigal Society 256-7

P

Pankhurst, Emmeline 164, 259, 268
Paris, France 44, 290
Parsons, Alfred 67, 73, 130, 171, 194, 199, 216, 217, 222, 305, 322
Peter Barr Memorial Vase 275
Petit St Bernard traveller's hospice 156
Peto, Harold 271
Petre family 150
pets 37, 113, 114, 312
Phoenix dactylifera 184
photography 40-2, 44-5, 52-3, 55, 59, 83, 95, 114, 116, 124, 129, 138, 140, 143, 144, 157, 177, 192, 193, 207, 213, 326
Pin, Jules 76-7, 200
Pipers florist, Bayswater 227
Place des Thermes, Aix-les-Bains 61-2
plant-hunting expeditions 172-8, 194, 195, 235
Pontz, Eliza 291
Potter, Richard 48, 244
Pouligon, F. 199
Prain, Colonel David 252, 267, 315
Preece, James 68, 92, 154, 229-30
Primrose League 104
primroses/*Primulaceae* 288-9, 300

Pritzel, Georg August 205
Probyn, Sir Dighton 264, 305
Punch magazine 103, 104, 244
Purdy, Carl 172, 241

Q

Quarterly Review periodical 223
'Queen' Diamond Annie 306, 308

R

Radium Institute, London 249, 252, 289
Railway Banks Floral Association 158
Redouté, Pierre-Joseph 73, 79
Revue Horticole 315
Reynolds Hole, Dean 16
rheumatism 42, 45, 52, 60-1, 69, 159, 189, 212
Ridley, Marian 165-6
rivalry and clashes, gardening 'big wig' 94-5, 99, 161-2
Riviera Nature Notes (C. Casey) 181
Roads Beautifying Association 309
Robinson, James Richard 90-1, 114, 155, 187, 205, 208-9, 220, 240, 306, 308, 311, 312, 318-19
Robinson, William 35, 47, 77, 95, 130, 141, 162, 220, 221-2, 244, 245, 252, 257, 271, 274, 299, 311, 315
Rome, Italy 55
roses 19, 73, 79-80, 301, 302, 326
  see also Genus Rosa (E. Willmott)
Royal Botanic Gardens, Edinburgh 239, 268
Royal Botanic Gardens, Glasnevin 160, 268
Royal Botanic Gardens, Kew 165, 167, 206, 232, 235, 239, 267, 289
Royal Horticultural Society 13, 85, 92-3, 97, 112-13, 115, 206, 232, 257, 267, 280, 302
  abolish Narcissus Committee 99
  Awards of Merit 167, 238
  EW's membership 13, 14-19, 92-3,

INDEX

112–13, 115, 124, 133–4, 157, 160–1, 162, 181, 193, 232, 238, 280, 299, 311
First Class Certificates 85, 97, 126, 157
Index Londonensis 206
International Conference on Genetics and Hybridisation (1906) 193
Mr G.F. Wilson's gardens, Wisley 160–1, 167, 317, 325
response to Amateur Gardeners' Society at Warley 299
Victoria Medal of Honour 14, 15–17, 18–19, 123, 129, 133–4, 230
Royal Institution 162, 165
Royal Microscopical Society 166
Royal Society 17, 166
Ruskin, John 112
Russell family 119, 156, 164, 212, 297
Russell, Henry 253–4

S

sabots, EW's 137, 146
Saint Thérèse of Lisieux 293
Salghetti-Drioli-Piacenza, Ursula and Guido 182, 184, 328
same-sex relationships, Victorian attitude to 109–10, 122
Sandow Curative Institute of Physical Culture 212
Sandow, Eugen 211–12
Sargent, Professor Charles Sprague 29, 170–2, 173–8, 180, 181–2, 194, 195, 200, 205, 207, 208, 210–11, 217, 218, 232, 241, 250, 251, 305, 309
Saturday Review 236–7
Sefton, Lady 111, 118, 126
Sexual Inversion (H. Ellis) 122
Shakespearean 'New Place' garden, Stratford-up-Avon 280–3, 325
Shakespeare Birthplace Trust 280, 300

Sharp, Cecil 193
Shenfield Lodge, Brentwood 251–2
Shenstone, James Chapman 317
shoplifting, EW arrested for 306–7
Silver Badge Soldiers 266–7
Sintenis, Paul 173
Sir James Dewar Lecturing on Liquid Hydrogen at the Royal Institution (H. Jamyn Brooks) 162
Sketch 268
smoking, cigarette 101, 118–19
Smyth, Ethel 114, 164, 203, 261
Société d'Acclimatation de France 238
Société d'Horticulture de France 311
Society for Psychical Research 40
Sotheby's 284, 318
South Africa 122
Southwark Bridge 221
spa treatments 45, 52, 56, 58, 61–4, 69, 211
Spetchley Park estate, Worcester 6, 8, 52–3, 55, 82, 130, 152, 272, 275–6, 282, 284, 288, 293, 296–7, 310, 317, 318, 320, 324
sports 37–8, 60, 104
sports days, Great and Little Warley 197, 209
Spring Grove, Isleworth 23–4
St Albans, Duchess of 238
St Aubyn family 153
St George's Chapel, Windsor 134
St John and St Elizabeth hospice, North London 293
St Paul Globe newspaper 192
Standard 258–9
Stapf, Otto 167, 290
Stearn, William T. 216, 320–1
suffragettes/women's suffrage 114, 164–5
Sweet Pea Society 160, 219
Sydenham, Robert 151

T

Tablet journal 81, 88
Tasker, Countess Helen 18, 23, 24, 26, 32, 35, 55–6
Tasker, Joseph 23
Tatler 268
tennis, lawn 37–8
Thatcher's Arms pub, Warley 212, 318
The Times 131, 192, 270, 272, 282, 315, 325
theatre and opera 36, 65, 91, 211
Thistleton-Dyer, Sir William 167, 172–3, 206
Thomas, Graham Stuart 321
Thorndon Park, Brentwood 150
Thory, C. A. 73
Tipping, Henry Avray 288, 299
Treaty of London 251
Tresserve, Willmott family villa in 19, 69, 72–7, 90–1, 104, 105–6, 116, 128, 156, 185, 208, 220, 242, 252, 328
    fire and redevelopment 198–201, 204–5, 207, 250
    gardens 77–9, 80, 87, 91, 92–3, 171, 187, 207
    sold to Lord Berkeley 284–5
Tremayne of Heligan, John 292–3, 297, 301
Truro Daffodil Show (1990) 158
Tufnell, Georgiana 'Gian' 105–7, 192–3
    correspondence with EW as Lady Mount Stephen 203–4, 211, 223–4, 227–9, 241, 242–3, 252–3, 312
    death and funeral 311–12
    and the Duchess of Teck 106, 115, 116, 126, 127, 129, 134
    EW's harpsichord 223–4, 227–9
    and Lord Mount Stephen 131–2, 134–5
    romantic correspondence with EW 107–19
Tweddle, Anne 98

'Two Modern Gardens' – *Saturday Review* feature 236–7
Tyrwhitt, Jaqueline 304

V

van Tubergen brothers 173
Vanderpant, Antoinette 315
Veitch, James 172–3, 176
Veitch Medal 328
Veitch nurseries 114–15, 173, 226
Veley, Lilian J. 169
Venables, Mary 164
Vernon House, Spring Grove 23–4, 30
Versailles Box-Planters 263, 272
Victoria & Albert Museum 284
Victoria Medal of Honour 14, 15–17, 18–19, 123, 129, 133–4, 230
Victoria, Princess 238
Victoria, Queen 13, 14, 15, 65–7, 72, 74, 91, 128–9
Vines, Vice President Professor 167
Viviand-Morel, J.V. 80
von Armin, Countess 193–4
Vyner, Nelly 239–40
Vyner, Robert 231, 239–40, 253

W

Wallace, Robert 271
walled garden, Warley Place 3, 88
Warley Farm, Brentwood 220, 265
    National Gardens Scheme 305
Warley Garden in Spring and Summer (E. Willmott) 213–14, 219, 236
Warley Garrison 33
Warley Lea, Brentwood 82–3, 141, 152, 220, 242, 251–2, 265, 272–4, 275
Warley Place and gardens, Brentwood 2–4, 211, 221, 282, 327–8
    abandonment of 317–18
    Alpine garden 3, 47–51, 68, 77, 78–9, 86, 89, 92, 235, 236, 302, 319, 325–6

INDEX

auctions arranged by Sotheby's 279, 284, 318
conservatory 3, 242
daffodils 2, 86, 96–7, 98, 112, 157, 328
demolition of 319–20
Essex Naturalists'/Wildlife Trust 322
EW commissions engraving of Willmott estate 152–3
EW inherits 151, 152
fern grotto 3, 49, 106, 112
gardening staff 51, 68, 92, 154–5, 209–10, 229–31, 241–2, 257, 300, 304
looting of plants 319
open days/village show and sports day 208–9
post-WWI training farm 267–8, 272–4
purchase and development of 32–4, 35
redecoration by Amédée Joubert & Sons 185
Rose and Robert's wedding 81, 82
rose garden 80, 171
visitor's book 132, 134, 148
walled garden 3, 88
Warley Place Volunteers 5
Warley village show and sports day 197, 209
Warwick, Countess of 266, 317
Warwick, Lady 283
Waterperry School of Horticulture 304
Watson, William 271
Webb, Sir Aston 271
wedding, Rose and Robert Berkeley's 81
Well Mead, Brentwood 88, 152, 220
Wellington, Duchess of 238
Wellington, Duke of 239
Whalley, Lady Harriet 66–7, 91, 93
'White Queen' *Narcissus* 98
The Wild Garden (W. Robinson) 35, 67

Wilde, Oscar 110, 122
Wilhelm II, Kaiser 249, 250–1
Wilks, Revd William 144–5, 151, 199, 212, 267, 276, 305
Williams, Canon 52
Williamson, Ella 157
Willmott (EW's sister), Ada 24–5, 30, 39, 42
Willmott (EW's mother), Ellen 22–3, 24, 28, 118
  death and burial 150
  gardening 29, 34–5
  health 34, 42, 45, 52, 130, 135, 136, 148–9
  Tresserve villa, Aix-les-Bains 75–6, 91
Willmott (EW's father), Frederick 22–4, 28
  buys EW a Jacob Kirkman harpsichord 27
  coaches, carriages and commuting 32, 36, 260
  death and burial 88, 150
  diaries 7–8, 36–7, 51, 52, 323
  family holidays 44–5, 47, 52, 54, 55, 72
  health 42, 45, 52, 55, 61
  land and investments 23–4, 36, 82–3, 87
  Maurice Berkeley and Rose 53–4, 82
  purchase and development of Warley Place 32–4, 35, 36, 47, 87
  Robert Valentine Berkeley and Rose 81, 82–3
  Tresserve villa, Aix-les-Bains 74, 75–6
  Warley social scene 37–8, 39–40
Willmott, Ellen Anne
  Aix-les-Bains spa resort 42, 47, 58–9, 61–5, 67–9, 91–2, 105–6, 158, 189, 202

371

(*see also below* Tresserve resort and villa)
Alpine Garden, Warley 3, 47–51, 68, 77, 78–9, 86, 89, 92, 235, 236, 302, 325–236
Amateur Gardeners' Society 298–300, 301
as an employer 155, 209–10, 229–31, 240, 241–2, 253, 257, 299–300, 304
Anne Hathaway's Cottage garden 300, 325
apprentices/protégées 304–5
approach to gardening 139–40
arrested for shoplifting 306
awarded Dean Hole Memorial Medal 301
awarded *Grande Medaille Geoffroy Saint-Hilaire* 238
awarded Peter Barr Memorial Vase 275
Bach Choir 231
birth and early years 24–5
budgie strangling story 323–4
butler and horse incident
car crash 219, 229
Casino Ancien Cercle 65, 91
Ceratostigma willmottianum 252
chauffer and Charron motor 187–9, 220, 221
Cornwall visit (1899) 153
created *Dame Patronesse* of *Société d'Horticulture de France* 311
daffodils 2, 4, 85, 89–90, 93, 94, 96–7, 98, 99, 117, 125, 151–2, 157, 158, 186–7, 255, 275, 309
death and burial of father 88, 150
death and burial of mother 150, 151
death and burial of sister 296–7
death, burial and memorial services 312, 314–15

death of sister, Ada 30
depression and loneliness 148–9, 150, 151, 152, 159, 162, 203, 257, 297
Diamond Jubilee Procession 129
dispute with neighbour, Count Lescher 155–6
distribution of derogatory leaflets 245–6
donation of *Herbarium Warleyense* 232
douche-massage and spa treatments 62–4, 69
'Ellen Willmott' *Narcissus* 97, 98, 125, 126, 144
family background 18, 22–4
family holidays 42, 44–5, 47, 52, 54, 55, 59, 72
financial difficulties 194–5, 200–2, 204–5, 208, 210–11, 219–22, 223–6, 227–30, 239, 241–2, 245–6, 248, 250, 252–3, 254–5, 260, 268, 276–7, 283–5, 290, 302
financial wealth 26, 35, 51, 55–6
First World War 251–2, 256, 257–8, 261–2
formal education 18, 25–7, 28–9
gardening school proposition 254–6
G.F. Wilson's gardens and the RHS 160–1
Hampton Court Palace gardens 269–72, 280, 300, 325
health 52, 56, 58, 59–64, 68, 74, 135, 148–9, 150, 151, 152, 154, 158–9, 211, 312
horticultural networking in Europe 160
houses Belgian refugees 251, 256
impact of sister's marriage 83, 87
inheritance from parents 151, 152–3, 154
interest in archaeology 309